"Arthur Just has written a jewel box of a memoir animating a personal pilgrimage told with lyricism and erudition that matches his passion for God, and not unlike that of C.S. Lewis's matchless memoir *Surprised by Joy*. Like Lewis, Just tenderly evokes a lifelong reach for transcendent definition beyond the material, wasteland-world. This memoir points the reader toward providence, deep faith, and a nourishing spiritual fulfillment defined in the context of a distinctly Lutheran worldview. Lewis took the title of his memoir from Wordsworth's famous verse, 'Surprised by joy—impatient as the wind.' Just rises to Wordsworth's joyous reach."

—Timothy S. Goeglein, Vice President, Government and External Relations, Focus on the Family

"Dr. Arthur A. Just's memoir is rich and multi-layered. Literature, hermeneutics, and theology are invitingly and compellingly imbedded in a personal journey that displays ecclesial and family events with candor and grace. His reflections are thoughtful and informed by insightful analysis. The reader will experience a life defined by the Eucharist; a life lived in and for the church; a life that views even tragedy in the light of Christ's suffering—*pro nobis*—'for us,' i.e., for our life and our salvation. May laity, seminarians, and pastors travel with Dr. Just, for that journey will place them with the Emmaus disciples as they receive Christ's gifts in his word and his meal—*Ever to Emmaus*."

—Dean O. Wenthe, President Emeritus, Concordia Theological Seminary

"Arthur Just, who has stood for almost fifty years in the very center of the revival of confessional Lutheranism, recounts how the Lord has made himself known to him in the Scriptures and in the Eucharist, in all sorts of circumstances and all sorts of people all over the world. The Lord opened his eyes, directed his thinking, and brought peace, repeatedly, consistently, and graciously, by word and sacrament. More than a memoir of a theologian, this is a song of praise."

—David H. Petersen, Redeemer Lutheran Church, Ft. Wayne, Indiana

"An Emmaus walk through the mind, heart, and life of Arthur A. Just Jr.—scholar, professor, missionary, liturgist, catechist, and pilgrim. This memoir weaves literary, biblical, and liturgical insight with sacramental theology and Christ-centered devotion. From Irving, Fitzgerald, and Hemingway to St. Luke's Gospel, from Ft. Wayne, Indiana to Mexico, Siberia, South America, Spain, and Africa, this book is more than one man's story—it is an invitation to pilgrimage."

—William M. Cwirla, Pastor Emeritus

Ever to Emmaus

Ever to Emmaus

A Theological Memoir

A. A. JUST JR.

Foreword by William C. Weinrich

WIPF & STOCK · Eugene, Oregon

EVER TO EMMAUS
A Theological Memoir

Wipf & Stock
An Imprint of Wipf and Stock Publishers
199 W. 8th Ave., Suite 3
Eugene, OR 97401

www.wipfandstock.com

PAPERBACK ISBN: 979-8-3852-7144-3
HARDCOVER ISBN: 979-8-3852-7145-0
EBOOK ISBN: 979-8-3852-7146-7

VERSION NUMBER 03/02/26

To Linda, who has walked alongside me all the way . . .

"And it came to pass that while he was reclining at table with them, he took the bread and blessed and broke it and gave it to them, and their eyes were opened and they recognized him; and he himself became invisible from them. And they said to one another, 'Was not our heart burning within us as he was speaking to us in the way, as he was opening to us the Scriptures?' . . . And they were expounding the things in the way and how he was known to them in the breaking of the bread."

(LUKE 24:31–32, 35—MY TRANSLATION)

Contents

Foreword

THE FOLLOWING IS A memoir. The word is taken from Justin Martyr's description of early Christian worship as he knew it. *Memoir* is Justin's term for the Gospel narratives, read as long as time permitted. Arthur Just adopts this term, intentionally, for his reflections on his life. So, the following is a gospel story, a story about the ongoing redemptive work of the Risen Savior. I think that is how one must read the following memoir. But, is that too bold a claim? Just does not make that claim, at least not explicitly. Yet, what he does claim is that his story arises from a real Gospel story, that of two disciples who meet the Risen Jesus on their way to the town of Emmaus.

The story goes like this: two disciples, one named Cleopas, the other unnamed, are walking to Emmaus. The Risen Jesus meets them, but "their eyes were held back so as not to recognize him" (Luke 24:16). The two were amazed that this Unknown seemed to know nothing of what had happened in Jerusalem "in these days." When they reported strange happenings, some women had found the tomb empty, and they wondered what it might mean. Jesus speaks: "Beginning from Moses and the prophets Jesus explained to them in all the Scriptures the things concerning him." When they arrived at Emmaus, the two disciples urged the Unknown Man "to abide with them." While reclining at table with them, the Unknown Man took bread, blessed it, broke it, and gave it to them. "And their eyes were opened and they recognized him" (Luke 24:31). Later, the two expounded to the gathered eleven what Jesus had said and "how he was known to them in the breaking of the bread" (Luke 24:13–35).

Now, in reading the following memoir, this story must be kept in mind. Just, in fact, insists upon it, for he refers to it throughout as he tells *his* story. It is, of course, possible to read the Emmaus account as pure account. A disciple named Cleopas and another were walking to Emmaus . . . who was that unnamed 'other'? Just refers to the account of Hegesippus (c. 180), who was steeped in the traditions of the early church of Jerusalem. Cleopas was the brother of Joseph, the father of Jesus, and so was Jesus' uncle. The other? Hegesippus does not say. But he does report that Cleopas had a son, Simeon, who was a well-respected, beloved bishop of Jerusalem. Best guess—that "other" was Simeon. That is the story told as history, ancient history.

But so told, it is no longer a memoir to be read in the liturgy of the church. For what is missing in the story as ancient story is precisely the reality of the Risen Christ who makes himself known in the breaking of the bread. And this is where *this* memoir, that is, Just's memoir begins and where it ends. "My beginning is my end," as Just himself asserts. Just's memoir reads his own life experiences as an experience on the way to Emmaus. That is, this memoir recounts how in many and various ways, the Risen Christ met him on the way of his sojourn and opened his eyes, led him to recognize the Risen Christ in the breaking of bread but also in the lives of those to whom he was sent.

And this is where Just's *memoir* becomes really interesting—or is it confusing? Just who *is* Arthur Just in his telling of his story? Is he a Cleopas who experienced his own dull eyes being opened to see? Just recounts the importance of two professors whose mentoring opened his eyes: his dissertation advisor, John F. McHugh of Durham, and Aidan Kavanaugh of Yale. To Just, these men were as Jesus, and to them, Arthur was as Cleopas. But along the way things turn. Arthur becomes as Jesus to others. He tells the story of his teaching at Concordia Theological Seminary, his efforts in the teaching of eager students just freed from Soviet tyranny, his remarkable pastoral enterprises in Spain, and, more recently, in the Dominican Republic. In these episodes there were hundreds of Cleopases! To them Arthur was as Jesus, opening their eyes to see the Risen Christ in the reading of the Scriptures and in the breaking of the bread. Indeed, among the more engaging chapters (in my view) are Arthur's erudite yet deeply evangelical pondering on the Gospel of Luke, and of Matthew, and of Paul's Letter to the Galatians, and, of all things, a very interesting and thought-provoking chapter on Mary. In all of these chapters, Arthur is as Jesus. For those who read these chapters, they are as Cleopas.

And what of Emmaus? Just where *is* that town, once so close to Jerusalem? We learn that Emmaus has other names—Middletown, Connecticut; Fort Wayne, Indiana; Madrid, Spain; Valencia, Spain; Mexico City; Novosibirsk, Siberia. In these places, and more, Arthur Just came to preach and to feed, just as did the Risen Jesus on that day when Cleopas and Simeon (!) met him on the road to Emmaus. In the following memoir, Arthur tells his story through the eyes of that story and *as a new, contemporary* version of that story. Those disciples of old said when Christ had left them, "Was not our heart burning [within us] as he was speaking to us in the way, as he was opening to us the Scriptures?" (Luke 24:32). Read the following story, so well told, and you will join those disciples in their delight, their joy, their recognition, and their passion.

Is Just's memoir a Gospel narrative? Too bold to say? Yes, bold to say, but, then, Christ is risen from the dead, and he meets us in preaching and the breaking of the bread!

A personal note: From time to time in the following, Arthur allows me to appear as a co-sojourner on the way to Emmaus. I remember those occasions well. But this, and I say this with deep gratitude: more often than not, Arthur was to me as Jesus, and I was to him as Cleopas. What a friend and colleague he has been! Gratitude!

William C. Weinrich, D.Theol.
Professor of Early Church History and Patristic Studies
Concordia Theological Seminary
Epiphany 2026

Acknowledgments

A MEMOIR IS AN acknowledgment of the many people who formed and shaped one, and a theological memoir is about those who were part of my formation as a pastor and a professor. You will find many of my mentors and colleagues named in this book. But I want to acknowledge a few of them again—and some who do not appear in this book.

In this theological memoir, there is no mention of the students who have been the most important part of my life as a professor. I thought about including a chapter on the joy of teaching at the seminary and how it is the best possible environment in which to teach. For those studying for the pastoral ministry and deaconess studies are committed to a holy task of serving the people of God as called pastors or consecrated deaconesses. Being with them in class is the highlight of the day, for they are attentive in class and always engage me in lively conversations about Christ and his church. I am so grateful for the many hours we've spent together poring over the Greek text, mining the depths of Scripture together, and all those insights we came upon in our studies. I always told them that I considered us colleagues in the ministry even though they were not yet ordained or consecrated, for we were all in the same task together of discovering how best to proclaim Christ to the people of God and bring them into communion with his flesh.

There have been two Graces during my pastoral ministry: Grace, Middletown at my beginning, and Grace, Naples at my end. The saints at Grace, Middletown taught me to be a pastor, and the saints at Grace, Naples confirmed for me that serving in the parish is the highest calling for a pastor.

Serving on a theological faculty has its joys and its challenges. So many of my colleagues could be acknowledged here, but I will limit it to those who have had the most influence on me and with whom I have worked most closely—and to whose friendship and support I am most grateful:

David Scaer, who gave me my theological foundation as a professor and a colleague.

William Weinrich who, with David, C. S. Mann, and Winthrop Brainerd, was part of an informal working group on the New Testament that led to my understanding of the New Testament as liturgical, catechetical, and pastoral, culminating in the Luke commentaries. I never walk away from a conversation with Bill where I don't learn something new. He agreed to write the foreword for this memoir, for which I am most grateful and honored.

Dean Wenthe, who, with Bill Weinrich, "saved" the seminary after Dean became president in 1996. Dean and I share the same theological commitments: he has been one of my greatest mentors and supporters, helping shepherd the Luke commentary through CPH as the general editor. Dean provided an environment at the seminary for the sacramental imagination to flourish and for our commitment to global theological education to blossom.

Lawrence Rast, who in taking over for Dean as president continued what he started and took it to a new level. It is a wonderful thing for one of your students to become your colleague and then your leader. Without Larry, our collaboration in theological education with OIM in Latin America would not have happened. He recognized immediately how vital this was for the mission of both the church and our seminary.

Charles Gieschen, who as academic dean and now provost has treated me as a cherished colleague and friend and allowed me to explore my desires to pursue global international during the final years of my tenure as a full-time faculty member. He almost never says no to me, and he supported a sabbatical in the spring of 2022 and 2023 for writing this memoir.

Richard Resch, my kantor at both the seminary and St. Paul's, my co-director at the Good Shepherd Institute, who, when I was dean of the chapel, was the rock upon which we built the liturgical life of our campus. He is the embodiment of what a pastoral professor should be, and his playing of the hymns every day in chapel and every Sunday at St. Paul's, singing in his choir with each of my three children, was spiritual therapy for our family.

Todd Peperkorn, dear friend and colleague, who was gracious enough to read this memoir and offer his encouragement towards publication.

There are so many of my friends in the ministry who have shared the joys and sorrows of the ministry. With David, Bill, Dean, Larry, Chuck, Richard, and Todd, they share with me this sacramental imagination. Again, too many to name, so to the ones who have walked most closely beside me during this journey:

Pastor Peter Ledic, my compadre, who ran alongside me on the soccer fields during our seminary days, who was a much-needed friend from Immanuel, Decatur, Indiana, during those dark days during the Babylonian captivity, providing a true "consolation of the brethren," and who shares my love for literature.

Pastor John Fiene, from the CTSFW class of 1980, who joined Peter and me on the soccer fields, who was my first theological interlocutor—especially on the identity of Luke's Theophilus—a true church planter who made possible my work in global theological education as pastor of Advent Lutheran Church by their generous support.

Pastor Scott Bruzek, who introduced me to the joys of teaching alongside him at Camp Arcadia, whose lectures always delight and provide such great pithy aphorisms—some of which are included in this memoir (e.g., "the baby Jesus," "lonely and unloved")—whose pastoral leadership at St. John's in Wheaton, Illinois, is the embodiment of what it means to be a pastor who presides as "strong, loving, and wise," and who also was a great support to my work in missions through St. John's.

Dr. John Bombaro, my new little brother, who was a dear colleague during my work in Eurasia when I was with OIM, and whose sacramental imagination now flourishes at St. James in Lafayette, Indiana. His creative spirit could launch a thousand missions if only he were allowed to set it free.

Keith Lingsch, who invited me to serve at Grace Lutheran Church in Naples, Florida, as a seasonal pastor from Advent to March. Working alongside Keith is one of the great delights of my ministry, and everyone at Grace can see that we complement one another and so enjoy our service together. After forty years of teaching, it is a gift to be preaching, celebrating the Eucharist, teaching Bible studies, and visiting the homebound. He has become the truest friend one can have in ministry.

To Aidan and John, to whom I dedicated *The Ongoing Feast*

To the editors at Wipf and Stock for graciously accepted this theological memoir for publication and for providing their support through the editorial process.

And finally, to my family:

To my sainted parents who instilled in me a love for Christ and his church.

To Jonathan, Karen, and Christopher, my siblings, who were with me during the early years of this wild adventure, especially in Mexico and Spain and Chatham.

To my children, Abigail, Nicholas, and Jacob, who grew up on a seminary campus, lived deeply in its theological life, love New Hampshire as much as I do, and remain faithful members of Christ's church.

To their spouses, Joshua, Haley, and Mica, who are the best son and daughters-in-law a father could ask for.

To my ten grandchildren, Emma, Clare, Rose, Anna, Zoe, Sophia, Magdalena, Avery, Henry, and Theodora, the joy of our lives.

And to Linda, to whom this memoir is dedicated, whose love and support made possible all the work I've done at the seminary and in the church, and whose love for international travel matches mine. She is the best companion along the way a man could ask for.

Abbreviations

AAL	Aid Association for Lutherans
ACCS	Ancient Christian Commentary on Scripture
AD	Anno Domini
ALC	American Lutheran Church
AP	Advanced Placement
BFMS	Board for Mission Services
BMS	Board for Mission Services
CPH	Concordia Publishing House
CTCR	The Commission on Theology and Church Relations
CTQ	*Concordia Theological Quarterly*
CTS	Concordia Theological Seminary
CTSFW	Concordia Theological Seminary Fort Wayne
CUI	Concordia University Irvine
DMin	Doctor of Ministry
DNA	Deoxyribonucleic Acid
DR	Dominican Republic
ELCA	Evangelical Lutheran Church of America
ESV	English Standard Version
FEDERE	Federación de Entidades Religiosas Evangélicas de España
FPH	Formación Pastoral para Hispanoamerica

GSI	Good Shepherd Institute of Pastoral Ministry and Sacred Music
HIV/AIDS	Human Immunodeficiency Virus/Acquired Immunodeficiency Syndrome
IELE	Iglesia Evangélica Luterana de España
ILC	International Lutheran Council
ILCW	Inter-Lutheran Commission of Worship
KGB	Komitet Gosudarstvennoy Bezopasnosti [Committee for State Security]
KJV	King James Version
LAC	Latin America and the Caribbean
LBW	*Lutheran Book of Worship*
LCA	Lutheran Church of America
LCMS	Lutheran Church–Missouri Synod
LSB	*Lutheran Service Book*
LW	*Lutheran Worship*
LXX	Septuagint
NFL	National Football League
NPR	National Public Radio
MA	Master of Arts
OIM	Office of International Missions
OSP	Old School Preppy
PocoMuse	Porter County Museum, Valparaiso, Indiana
PhD	Doctor of Philosophy
SMP	Specific Ministry Pastor
SMP Es/E	Specific Ministry Pastor—Español/English
STM	Master of Sacred Theology
TLH	*The Lutheran Hymnal*
UNESCO	United Nations Educational, Scientific and Cultural Organization
YDS	Yale Divinity School

Prologue

In my beginning is my end . . .[1]

The room was large and the sherry was dry. Books lined three sides of the room, all the way to the ceiling; on the fourth side, large windows overlooked the entrance to Ushaw College, the Roman Catholic school at the University of Durham in England. The rooms of the Rev. Canon John Francis McHugh smelled like old books. Sitting at the tables in the center of his study and living room (his only room, except a small bedroom and bathroom—but what a room), Fr. McHugh lifted the back of his hand to his nose and sniffed a pinch of snuff. A little of it settled on the front of his shirt. Since morning we had been working through the first hundred pages of my dissertation. It was time for a break.

"You write well, Arthur," he said as he leaned back in his chair. He was being kind. "But . . . this sounds more like a sermon. Your style is homiletical. No wonder. You've been writing more sermons than academic papers these past last five years. We need to make this sound like a PhD thesis."

Fr. McHugh, who insisted that I call him John, was old enough to be my father. We had met in May 1985 when I came to Durham to find out if he would agree to be my doctoral father. That I was at Durham was a miracle of sorts. Our son Nicholas was born in April, and the last thing on my mind was to pursue a doctorate. I had toyed with the idea of applying to the Notre Dame program in early Christian studies. But watching my colleagues Cameron MacKenzie and Dean Wenthe drive back and forth to South Bend for classes then take all kinds of exams,

1. This is a variation of the supposed last words of Mary, Queen of Scots. T. S. Eliot uses a variation of this in the first line of "East Coker," the second poem in his final opus, "The Four Quartets."

not to mention sweat through the thesis, made it an easy decision for me to decide not to enter the PhD at Notre Dame. I had suffered through enough rejections when I applied to college from Andover that I was not sure I wanted another rejection. My contract at Concordia Theological Seminary (CTSFW) to teach homiletics was for only three years, and I couldn't see doing this my whole life. So I wasn't that keen on a doctorate. I wanted no more classes, no more exams, especially after my Masters of Sacred Theology (STM) at Yale Divinity School (YDS). I was happy as a parish pastor, and I would be happy to return to the parish. I would give it three years and then take a call.

David Scaer, the academic dean, had other plans. He pushed and pushed me to apply to some program for a doctorate. During my first year of teaching at CTSFW, our neighbors were John and Bonnie Stephenson (and their little dachshund "Chemnitz"), who were in Fort Wayne for only one year. John had just received his doctorate from Durham; he knew they had a part-time PhD that only required a thesis and a final oral exam (*Viva*) and thought Durham would be a good place for me. "You write a book, Arthur, and they give you a doctorate." He suggested that I contact Durham with my topic and ask for Fr. McHugh as an advisor because of his interests in the New Testament and liturgics.

His advice turned out to be spot-on. Everything went as he had predicted. What he didn't mention was how much I would enjoy the seminars with the New Testament professors, as well as the stimulating conversations with the doctoral students. Although we didn't have required classes, these experiences were a significant part of my PhD studies. In many ways, I owe John Stephenson my academic career after taking the call to CTSFW in 1984. I was Fr. McHugh's last doctoral student, and he chose to work with me even though he was close to retirement, because he loved my topic—an investigation of Eucharist and eschatology in the Scriptures and the earliest eucharistic prayers. As he told me later, there was no debate by the Durham faculty about his becoming my doctoral father. They didn't see many sacramental theses cross their desks, and he was the logical choice. That I asked for him made it a done deal. He was delighted that his last thesis would be a topic near and dear to his heart.

As it was to mine. Yet during my MDiv studies at CTSFW, I wasn't even aware of the relationship between Eucharist and eschatology. It was through my classes in liturgics with Aidan Kavanagh at YDS for my STM that my eyes were opened. I had been encouraged to take his courses on baptismal and eucharistic liturgies by a local pastor who had just completed his STM at YDS. He said that Kavanagh would "rock my world," but I didn't realize how much. Standing before us in this large Georgian-Colonial classroom, in a course with the simple title "Baptismal Texts," was this tall, austere Benedictine monk with a perfectly round head, a shapely goatee, gray hair circling his head like a tonsure, and almost always in a black turtleneck. A Southern Baptist from Texas turned Benedictine, Aidan issued forth these sublime and sometimes hilarious lectures in a Southern accent. It took time to get used to. His expertise was in primary baptismal and eucharistic texts in all their glorious historical context, or what I would later call pastoral texts—early Christian catechetical, baptismal, and eucharistic texts. Here was the theology I was looking for—theology done through the pastoral acts.

Eucharist and eschatology were shot through the writings of the church fathers, particularly in the early Eucharistic prayers and mystagogical catecheses of the fourth century—and in the lectures of Aidan Kavanagh. Later I came to describe this as "heaven on earth" in the bodily presence of Jesus, or by the more esoteric term "inaugurated eschatology."[2] Kavanagh's classes taught me how all theology needed to be seen through the liturgy, that is, through Christ's presence here and now, the finite capable of the infinite. His book *On Liturgical Theology* showed me how theology is most embodied in the church's liturgical life—"primary" theology—the theology of "church's faith in motion" at the liturgy[3]—as opposed to "secondary" theology, the theology of academe, theology that reflects on primary theology. Fr. McHugh was right about my writing—I was used to writing primary theology, and now I had to adopt a different, more academic style.

Not everyone appreciates this distinction between primary and secondary theology,[4] but it is a corollary of *lex orandi, lex credendi*, the way

2. The Commission on Theology and Church Relations (CTCR) document on eschatology articulates the New Testament understanding of inaugurated eschatology that underlies the very nature of Christian worship: "The term inaugurated eschatology embraces everything that the Old and New Testament Scriptures teach concerning the believer's *present* possession and enjoyment of blessings which will be fully experienced whenever Christ comes again . . . Therefore, the Christian lives in the proverbial tension between the *now* and *not yet.* This tension underlies everything that Scriptures teach about eschatology. On the one hand, the end has arrived in Christ. The believer now receives the promised eschatological blessings through the Gospel and the Sacraments. On the other hand, the consummation is still a future reality. The Christian has *not yet* entered into the glories of heaven." Raabe, *End Times,* 17–19).

3. Kavanagh, *On Liturgical Theology*, 8.

4. For example, my colleague Kurt Marquart, a man of the liturgy, did not find these

we worship constitutes the way we believe. Such a perspective engages both the sacramental and missional imagination (yes, missional, for at the Eucharist, the church does the world as the world is to be done),[5] which reflects an eschatological view of Scripture as well as the "reality" of life lived in the church. Later in our curriculum review at CTSFW, we would embrace this notion of primary theology and describe this hermeneutic as teaching theology through the pastoral acts of baptism, preaching, and the Lord's Supper.

So how to begin my doctoral studies with Fr. McHugh? He asked about papers I had written at Yale, and the one most related to Eucharist and eschatology was the assignment given me by Professor Abraham Malherbe in his Lukan seminar. During my studies at YDS, I was a parish pastor at Grace Lutheran Church in Middletown, Connecticut, about a forty-five-minute drive over hill and dale to New Haven that I would make every Tuesday and Thursday in my little Volkswagen Bug. Often, I would go to class in a clerical collar, as I would make hospital calls on the way home. Dr. Malherbe, a devout Christian scholar from the Church of Christ in South Africa, knew that Lutherans were interested in the theology of the cross, and because I was one of the only pastors in the class and Lent was about to begin, he thought I should focus on the passion statements in Luke 24. His instruction to me was to read the passion language in Luke's final chapter as a Lutheran and a pastor, and to use it as a lens to read back into Luke's Gospel. When Fr. McHugh heard of this paper, he said, "Arthur!—Emmaus!—let's start there." So during my first year of doctoral studies, I expanded my twenty-five-page YDS paper into a hundred pages.

Fr. McHugh was a jolly man who knew much about everything. We were an odd pair. At thirty-two, I was tall and lanky and Fr. McHugh short and rotund. As one of my colleagues said when he met him during his visit to our seminary—he reminds me of Mr. Magoo! He was at the end of his teaching career, and I was at the beginning of mine. So, during tea or sherry, when we would take a break from our work together, he would often reflect on his teaching career at Ushaw College, the Roman Catholic college/seminary at the University of Durham in Northern England.

---

categories helpful.

5. A paraphrase of Kavanagh, *Elements of Rite*, 46: "What one witnesses in the liturgy is the world being done as the world's Creator and Redeemer wills the world to be done. The liturgy does the world and does it at its very center, for it is here that the world's malaise and its cure well up together, inextricably entwined."

Although he is not as well known as some scholars, his colleagues from Durham were such luminaries as C. K. Barrett and C. E. B. Cranfield. His colleagues at École Biblique in Jerusalem were Xavier Leon-Dufour, Roland de Vaux, and Pierre Benoit. He considered one of his dear friends Cardinal Ratzinger, later Pope Benedict XVI, with whom he served on the Pontifical Biblical Commission in the 1980s. Fr. McHugh would talk about the Commission, especially Ratzinger. He said he was the most intelligent person he ever met. I asked him once what language they spoke during their meetings. He laughed and pushed back his chair: "Arthur, what a great question. Members of the commission need to know five canonical languages: Italian, French, German, English, and Spanish. But when the Cardinal wants everyone to understand what he is saying he speaks to us in Latin!" He laughed again at the thought. I realized then, as I had throughout my life, that I was not the smartest guy in the room.

Although we never discussed his doctoral thesis, nor what became the driving principle of his own studies of the Scriptures and theology, it was not difficult to discern what shaped his theology from the company he kept. Like many classically trained British scholars, he knew a great deal about a great deal. Two of his interests outside of biblical studies were liturgical language and the interplay between the Reformation and the Counter-Reformation in the sixteenth century. He wrote an essay entitled "The Sacrifice of the Mass at the Council of Trent" that suggested that there were some at the council who were ready to adopt the Lutheran view.[6] Looking at the books he translated and the company he kept,[7] he came of age during the Nouvelle Théologie movement or Ressourcement, "returning to the sources" as it is sometimes called, which was a movement to restore a patristic biblical theology.

There was a memorable moment in the spring of 1986 when John and I had finished discussing those first hundred pages. I cited the penultimate chapter of Augustine's Confessions to support Luke 24:1 as a reference to the eschatological eighth day:

> In that eternal Sabbath you will rest in us, just as now you work in us. The rest that we shall enjoy will be yours, just as the work that we now do is your work done through us. But you, O Lord, are eternally at work and eternally at rest. It is not in time that

6. McHugh, "Sacrifice of the Mass."

7. Some of the scholars translated by McHugh were Roland DeVaux, Pierre Benoit, Xavier Leon-Dufour. McHugh was one of the scholars most responsible for the translation of *The Jerusalem Bible*.

> you see or in time that you move or in time that you rest: yet you make what we see in time; you make time itself and the repose which comes when time ceases.[8]

Fr. McHugh took a sip of sherry and said, "That's not a very good translation." And then he recited from memory, in Latin, the words of Augustine that I had cited in English. By that point, he and I had developed a familiar relationship, so I decided to banter with him. "I don't believe you know the Latin by heart." He pointed up into the corner of his library. "You'll find Augustine in Latin up there." I needed one of those sliding ladders to reach the book. I was tempted to race along the floor but thought better of it. I struggled to find the book and finally located it only after Fr. McHugh's prompting. My Latin was so poor I couldn't find the chapter. He took the book from me, placed his finger on chapter 37 and started reciting. He had it cold, word for word, as well as the chapters surrounding it. He had to memorize it in grammar school. I told him I knew the first lines of Chaucer's *Canterbury Tales* in Old English. He wasn't impressed. At that moment I fully realized that Fr. McHugh was playing in the major leagues and I was, at best, in Triple-A.

He laughed when he saw my amazement. "But Arthur, I have good news for you that I've been waiting to tell you until we finished reading your manuscript. I did a little research and found only a few monographs on Emmaus—one in English, one in German, and one in French.[9] How remarkable! There is room for another!"

We discussed how such an iconic and unique Lukan contribution to the Gospel narratives of Jesus should have received such little commentary. As we deliberated on where to go from Emmaus, it was Fr. McHugh who finally said, "Emmaus might be the theme of your thesis and the rest of your life." He was right. We never left Emmaus. I have never left Emmaus. It was then that he gave me this most sage advice. "Arthur, choose a topic for your doctoral work that you love, and that you can live off for your entire teaching career. Emmaus is a story that will serve you until you close your eyes in death. You will always be 'Ever to Emmaus.'" At the age of 32, that seemed like a fine idea. He was right about Emmaus.

8. Augustine, *Confessions*, 346.

9. Dillon, *From Eye-Witnesses to Ministers of the Word*; Wanke, *Emmauserzählung*; Guillaume, *Luc interprète des anciennes traditions*. As I was about to submit my thesis—another book on Emmaus—Wojcik's *The Road to Emmaus: Reading Luke's Gospel* appeared, but thankfully it was a gnostic reading and had very little in common with my thesis.

It became the story through which I read the rest of Luke's Gospel, as the evangelist himself suggests—"remember how he spoke to you while he was still in Galilee" (Luke 24:6) and "these are my words that I spoke to you while I was still with you" (Luke 24:44). It also became the programmatic biblical foundation for my teaching of the liturgy of the church as Word and Meal. Word and meal are also the foundation for the mission of the church. All these themes flow from the final verse of the Emmaus story: "And they were expounding the things on the way and how he was known to them in the breaking of the bread" (Luke 24:35—my translation).

My doctoral thesis was published in 1993 by Pueblo Publishing Company as *The Ongoing Feast: Table Fellowship and Eschatology at Emmaus*. It was Dean Wenthe who suggested I call it *The Ongoing Feast*. What was most gratifying in the reviews of my thesis were the comments by liturgiologists who affirmed that Luke 24:35 established the foundational structures of the liturgy as Word and Meal, liturgical structures that now and forever form the backbone of the historic liturgy.[10]

Fr. McHugh was so proud when he received his copy of *The Ongoing Feast*. We had done it. It was his as much as mine. He taught me to do exegesis and to write like an academic. How we enjoyed the discoveries we made along the way. How we enjoyed our conversations during tea and sherry. He prepared me well for my Viva, the oral exam at the end of the doctoral studies in England, especially for my internal examiner, James D. G. Dunn, who was supposed to be my supporter but who had made it very clear during my years at Durham that he did not like my thesis topic because it was literary and sacramental. Fr. McHugh used to be the dean during the days when his colleagues in the department were C. K. Barrett and C. E. B. Cranfield. He was very experienced in advising and reading doctoral theses. Jimmy, as Professor Dunn was called, had just become chairman of the department after the retirement of Barrett and Cranfield. Fr. McHugh was only a few years away from following them into retirement. During my years at Durham there were many American Pentecostal and Neo-Pentecostal students studying under Dunn because his doctoral thesis from Cambridge, "The Baptism in the Holy Spirit," was perceived as biblical evidence for Pentecostalism. Although I only spent a few weeks at Durham with Fr. McHugh every June, I did attend

10. My thesis on Luke led to me being offered the commentary on Luke by CPH, which ended up being the first two volumes published in the commentary series entitled *Concordia Commentary: A Theological Exposition on Sacred Scripture* (1996, 1997).

the PhD seminars and so became acquainted with Dunn's doctoral students. They were impressed with how much time I had with my doctoral father, especially as they were full-time students and I was the first part-time PhD student in the theology department (many would follow me in receiving their doctorates from Durham, including two of my colleagues at CTSFW—James Bushur and Jeffrey Pulse). The first crisis we faced with my Viva was that Fr. McHugh had just failed Jimmy's first doctoral student in his oral exam. Would it be payback time? Yet how would it look if the first two doctoral students failed during Dunn's chairmanship? So perhaps this was to my advantage.

I submitted my thesis on the Feast of St. Luke in 1989. I was so consumed in getting my thesis ready for the Viva that I was unaware of the date until that morning's chapel Eucharist, where I was the lector, and it dawned on me *in the lectern* that I had submitted on the feast day of my beloved St. Luke. The next four months were spent in intense preparation. I read everything Jimmy Dunn had written, as well as my other internal examiner, John Court, who had just published *The New Testament World* with his wife, Kathleen. Fr. McHugh chose John Court because he was sympathetic to my topic and was particular to narrative theology. He would later publish *Reading the New Testament*, which included an excellent chapter on narrative theology.[11]

As it turned out, I was over-prepared. The *Viva* was scheduled for the twenty-second of February at 4 p.m.[12] All I remember was how nervous I was beforehand, lying on my narrow bed at St. John's College, enveloped by the dampness of Durham. But during the Viva, I was cool and collected. John Court dispensed with his questions within the first half-hour. From then on, it was me and Jimmy Dunn. He went over the normal hour by twenty minutes, grilling me on every point that differed from his perspective on reading texts, which was less than sacramental. But I had read him carefully and knew where he was going with each line of inquiry. Finally, he said, "Arthur, you are like a chess player who is always a few moves ahead of me. You know me better than I know myself. Congratulations. Well done." They had no changes except some minor stylistic ones that I penciled in the official university copy at a desk

11. Court and Court, *New Testament World*; Court, *Reading the New Testament*.

12. It was the first thesis submitted from a computer, a "Fat Mac" from the University of Notre Dame that I was able to buy with Dean Wenthe as we started writing our doctoral theses in 1985. We learned to touch-type the Greek and the Hebrew. Fr. McHugh marveled at the technology, and I was able to help him obtain a similar set-up.

in the basement of the theology building. It was finished. They told me that from now on I could be called Dr. Just, which is what I am known by more than any other title.

Emmaus was my beginning, and now it is my end. As Fr. McHugh said, I am "ever to Emmaus." So now to revisit this marvelous story with fresh eyes, and other stories of my life, as we will be *Ever to Emmaus: A Theological Memoir.*

A Story of Pilgrimage

1

A Theological Memoir

My theme is memory, that winged host that soared about me one grey morning of war-time.

These memories, which are my life—for we possess nothing certainly except the past—were always with me. Like the pigeons of St. Mark's, they were everywhere, under my feet, singly, in pairs, in little honey-voiced congregations, nodding, strutting, winking, rolling the tender feathers of their necks, perching sometimes, if I stood still, on my shoulder; until, suddenly, the noon gun boomed and in a moment, with a flutter and sweep of wings, the pavement was bare and the whole sky above dark with a tumult of fowl. Thus it was that morning of wartime.[1]

"'My theme is memory,'" says Charles in *Brideshead Revisited*, the chapter entitled "A Twitch Upon the Thread." Memories are his life—always with him—like pigeons at St. Mark's square in Venice—such a vivid and trenchant comparison. But then, like a gun chasing the pigeons away, his memories become scattered in his brain. In this section of *Brideshead Revisited*, everyone gets twitched back into the boat. That's at the heart of his memories that take him back to the beginning—to Brideshead—to where

1. Waugh, *Brideshead Revisited*, 203.

he started the book. *Brideshead Revisited,* to be exact, with the memorable subtitle, *The Sacred and Profane Memories of Captain Charles Ryder.*

Memories. They are what *Brideshead Revisited* is about. Charles remembers Brideshead and all that it meant to him. He *revisits* it. Brideshead is the gun that creates the tumult. *Brideshead Revisited* is about Charles's memories of Brideshead, the place and all that happened to him there, especially his conversion and the conversion of others who, by the twitch upon the thread, were all hooked by God and reeled into the ark of Christendom.

Memories are tricky. Augustine claims he remembers events from his infancy, like the tenderness of nursing from the breast of his mother, Monica, and his lack of innocence as an infant as he greedily throws himself upon her.[2] My earliest memory goes back to when I was two years old in the backyard of our home in Lynn, Massachusetts, throwing a baseball with my father in the spring of 1955. It may have been when I was alone with him as my mother was in the hospital giving birth to my brother Jonathan. What sometimes brings that memory forth is the smell of newly cut grass in the spring. My memory is of an old two-family house, not unlike the ones my grandfather built as a carpenter in Providence, Rhode Island. Not only have I treasured that memory because it was with my father, but it was about baseball, one of my passions. Perhaps my grandson Henry will remember throwing a baseball with me in our yard in Fort Wayne or New Hampshire.

Some readers would like to hear more about my childhood and youth, and there will be glimpses of that throughout this memoir. Most of those memories are of interest only to me and those I love. But as a cradle Lutheran and a pastor/seminary professor for over forty years who has been exegeting texts most of his life, the memories that possess me now are the ones that come from my life lived in the cut and thrust of a rich pastoral and academic life. In collecting these memories, a theme has emerged that won't go away. If Emmaus is my beginning and now my end, what continues to return to me as central to my reflections of a life well lived are the themes of pilgrimage and conversion that have been at the center of my thinking, my preaching, and my teaching. In discussing a new curriculum for our seminary many years ago, we were asked to reflect on what we do in the classroom. My answer was very simple—I take them on a journey to conversion—even cradle Lutheran seminarians—a

2. Brown, *Augustine of Hippo*, 28–29.

pilgrimage to a way of seeing the world through a lens that might best be called a sacramental imagination.

This book began as a proposal to our academic dean, Charles Gieschen, as a theological memoir for my final sabbatical. After forty years, my full-time teaching career at Concordia Theological Seminary, Fort Wayne (CTSFW), was ending. My son Jacob, a partner in conversation about literature, especially poetry, first piqued my interest in the new and increasingly popular genre of memoir, something that I had never encountered in any meaningful way. His interest in memoir reflects the postmodern accent on identity that flows from narrative instead of propositional truth, particularly in his work at Porter County Museum in Valparaiso (PocoMuse for short), where he captures the stories people tell about their lives growing up in northwest Indiana. I often cite him in class: "We are the stories we tell ourselves about ourselves," his paraphrase of American anthropologist's Clifford Geertz's definition of culture: "Culture is simply the ensemble of stories we tell ourselves about ourselves."[3] This describes the Christian culture that culminates in the liturgy, where we gather around the words of Jesus that are "[an] ensemble of stories we tell about ourselves" as the family of God.

The first real memoir that I read in preparation for this book was by the poet Mary Karr, whose intersection of poetry and memoir also captured the attention of my son. She has many memoirs, but the one I read (listened to, in fact) was *Lit* because it tells the story of her conversion to Roman Catholicism. It's a rollicking tale, not for the faint of heart, but it is real and it is raw, revealing how Christianity has a power to overcome even the most formidable obstacles. Karr laments that she is known more for her memoirs than her poetry (and her troubled relationship with David Foster Wallace, the infamous novelist of *Infinite Jest*, who committed suicide as a victim of depression, and perhaps, from the darkness of our postmodern world). Her book *The Art of Memoir* helped me clarify what I was doing in this "memoir." Of the many memorable things she writes, this one sticks out most of all: "I once heard Don DeLillo quip that a fiction writer starts with meaning and then manufactures events to represent it; a memoirist starts with events, then derives meaning from them."[4] In this theological memoir I hope to derive meaning from certain events in my life that led me to think about theology the way I do.

3. Geertz, *Interpretation of Culture*, 448, 452.

4. Karr, *Art of Memoir*, xvi.

For Mary Karr the most important aspect of the memoir is the voice, that authentic persona that sounds like who you really are. No posing, no pretense. As she says, "Each great memoir lives or dies based 100 percent on voice. It's the delivery system for the author's experience—the big bandwidth cable that carries in lustrous clarity every pixel of someone's inner and outer experiences. Each voice is cleverly fashioned to highlight a writer's individual talent or way of viewing the world."[5] She gave me courage to find my voice, and it has taken me awhile to discover it, if in fact I have. I'll let the reader decide.

As helpful as Mary Karr is about the genre of memoir, what I am attempting here is not a memoir in the traditional sense. I am not a memoirist, nor do I pretend to be, for as my doctoral father said, I write sermons, commentaries, theological essays, and theological books. But the story of my theological development cannot be told apart from the way that story unfolded through the people who shaped me and the experiences I had with them. The classic advice to novelists and memoirists is "show, don't tell," and though I may do more showing than telling in some of my sermons, theology professors generally do more telling than showing. What was most important to me about Mary Karr was that she is a convert with a deep Eucharistic piety that sets her apart from most memoirists.[6] The genius of her memoirs is that her conversion rings true

5. Karr, *Art of Memoir*, 35.

6. As a sample of Karr's candor, here is what she says about the Eucharist in an interview from *Image*, Vol. 56, 2007:

> Image: You've written about how the experience of reading poetry also creates a type of communion. How are poetry and liturgy different and the same? How do they inform each other, for you?
>
> MK: . . . The eucharist changes you—I don't experience it this way every time, but that's the ideal. It heals you. It doesn't just keep you alive.
>
> I feel that in taking the eucharist a lot of my anger at my mother was simply healed. A lot of my anger at myself was simply healed, because I had already been forgiven, and that is so large. The Ignatian exercises brought on a real dark night of the soul for me. As part of the exercises, you pray to know the nature of your own sinfulness. Let me tell you, that was the darkest time, the most dangerous time. I had moved my mother, who was then seventy-five years old, to a new house closer to my sister. I went to help her unpack. She was dislocated and confused, really upset, crying, and she was raging at me as she had raged when I was younger, calling me names. I went off at her and shouted her down . . . I just went off at her. That's the nature of my sinfulness. Through grace I had been mostly relieved of my anger and disappointment in

because it's unexpected. As you read her advice on how to write a memoir, you can see that she followed her own counsel. When she tells how she became a Roman Catholic, it's a surprise, but when you follow her closely, you realize that it's not as much a surprise as it seems. It makes perfect sense. Like the apostle Paul, she entered the kingdom through suffering.

At the time I suggested to Dean Gieschen a memoir for my sabbatical project, my colleague and mentor, David Scaer, to whom I owe my theological foundation, published his much-anticipated memoir *Surviving the Storms*. Much of his memoir covered my life at CTSFW as a student (1976 to 1980) and professor (1984 to the present). I was amazed at his recall and the notetaking he had done during his life. As much as I enjoyed the personal details and the political intrigue, I found his story more riveting when he reflected theologically about the contours of his tenure as a "doctor of the church," even how he had changed over the years in his thinking, as each new decade brought new theological challenges he addressed with his most incisive theological mind.

His memoir led me to Carl E. Braaten's memoir *Because of Christ: Memoirs of a Lutheran Theologian* (he was a fellow venerable Lutheran theologian of David Scaer). That then led to the memoir of the famous Lutheran homiletician Richard Lischer's *Open Secrets: A Memoir of Faith and Discovery*. And to be completely ecumenical, and because he was a friend and colleague of my doctoral father, I read Benedict XVI's *Last Testament*, what he claims is his final book, and then his earlier memoir about his life as Cardinal Ratzinger in his *Milestones: Memoirs: 1927–1977*. This, of course, led me to Augustine's *Confessions*.

So now, because of my son and Mary Karr, I am drawn to memoirs because they are embodied memories transformed into story with

---

her. She didn't have anything I needed anymore, and I could be close to her and love her as she was without wanting her to be a different way, and there was a lot of peace between us. She's a complicated person, a difficult person, but things were easier with her the last ten years of her life.

That's what the eucharist changed for me: that was not how I talked to my mother anymore. That is not how I talk to my child. Occasionally I talk to a cabdriver that way. This year I've had a lot of medical issues, lots of doctors and procedures. It's been scary. But at no point in all of this did I shout at anyone, not even myself, for not being able to climb up the stairs, for being too tired. When I was tired, I lay down, and that's what the eucharist does for me. Lying down is not my natural stance.

interpretation. What all these memoirs have in common is that they are *Christian* memoirs. The memoirs of those who do not confess the Christian faith are often melancholy, since for them death is the end. They try to be hopeful, even triumphant, but in the end, there is only death and nothing more. Not so for those who die in Christ. Memoir is the story of how eternity broke into their lives, how their story was lived out by faith in things unseen and unknown. Although it would be difficult to convince those who know not Christ that Christians are the only humans who are truly alive, it's true. The power of Christ's resurrected life is what carries them along through suffering and joy. His fleshly presence in them, though hidden to the world, is real and lively, making their lives, and their memoirs, memorable. And what is most remarkable about Christian memoirs is that they are often *stories of conversion!*

So, what kind of memoir is this?

Some claim that Augustine's *Confessions* was the first Christian memoir. If so, it set the pattern of how Christian memoirs differ from other memoirs. For a Christian, life goes on after death, and the life remembered is a life shot through with the presence of Christ in mercy. Augustine's *Confessions* tells a conversion story of his journey from unbelief to faith. His recorded memories describe how he was snatched out of the present evil age into a life of grace through the voice of a child singing in a garden. Augustine's *Confessions* is a compelling story of his journey from darkness into light into a new life now lived as pastor and bishop of Hippo through a series of "conversions"—from hedonism to philosophy/ Wisdom, then to Manichaeism, and finally to the Church Catholic. Augustine's conversions are so compelling that they set the standard for all Christian memoirs.

So, my proposal to Dean Gieschen was for another kind of memoir, in the spirit of my CTSFW colleague, but more a theological memoir, that is, a story of how I came to think as I do at the end of a long career of teaching theology at a Lutheran seminary. The events I want to describe are the ones that led to the evolution of my theological perspective. Like many people, especially during these changing times from the middle of the twentieth century into the twenty-first, I've changed the way I think theologically. Since seminary and graduate school, my thinking has deepened and broadened rather than undergone radical changes. But there were a series of conversions that led me now to reflect on my identity as a Lutheran pastor and professor at the end of his teaching career. My "conversions" are much less dramatic than Augustine's. I began my life with an innocent Lutheran piety that sustained me through prep school, but then in college dabbled with a mild form of secular humanism, only to turn to a dead orthodoxy during my seminary years at CTSFW. Now, after my graduate studies and my teaching career, I consider myself an "evangelical Catholic." So, this "memoir" reflects on how I have changed in the way I think and do theology.[7]

As I thought through how I was going to do this, and the reading that I gravitated to in preparing for this memoir, I realized the story of my theological pilgrimage was a conversion story of sorts, not from unbelief to faith but from one way of viewing theology to another or, better said, from learning a way of interpretation that opens up the Scriptures to its deeper christological meaning. This opening up of Scriptures is what Jesus did for the two disciples on their pilgrimage to Emmaus. This way of interpretation is what some of us call "the *blick*," a view or panorama of theology that sees out over all of Scripture from a particular place. That particular place, that *blick*, is a view of the Scriptures that interprets them through the lens of a sacramental imagination, through "inaugurated eschatology," or what has been embodied in my teaching and writing as "heaven on earth," "the eighth day," the "now, not yet"—or in the words of the Easter proclamation: "This is the feast of victory for our God, for the Lamb who was slain *has begun his reign*, alleluia!"[8]

The *blick* happened to me during my years as a pastor in Connecticut through my preaching and pastoral care and through my studies at YDS, especially with Aidan Kavanagh. As much as I value my studies at CTSFW, especially the warm relationships with the professors and my fellow students, and immersion in the biblical languages, there was, so to speak, very little eschatology in the curriculum and the teaching. It was rather flat-footed, a straight-up dead orthodoxy with the exception of a few professors like David Scaer, James Voelz, and William Weinrich

7. See Brown, *Augustine of Hippo*, 9, who in the preface offers these opening words about how Augustine was defined by the changes in his life: "I have tried in this book to convey something of the course and quality of Augustine's life. Not only did Augustine live in an age of rapid and dramatic change; he himself was constantly changing. The historian . . . can also seize some of the more elusive changes in the man himself: he will be constantly reminded, often by a stray detail—nothing more, perhaps, than by a turn of phrase used in addressing a friend—of the long, inner journeys of Augustine."

8. Grime and Vieker, *Lutheran Service Book*, 155.

(I had the Old Testament introductory course with Dean Wenthe in the fall and then he took a call—he was not a professor during the rest of my time as a student). As a result, I took as many courses from Scaer, Voelz, and Weinrich as I could. Yet still, if you were to ask me if liturgical or eucharistic eschatology formed me from their classes, I wouldn't be able to answer in the affirmative. To be fair, I did not have ears to hear it if they were teaching theology through a sacramental lens. What I learned from Aidan, and did not comprehend at the seminary, is that liturgy is primary theology and that the Eucharist is more than the forgiveness of sins—that there is a larger reality that many of us did not know or understand. What I learned from Aidan I immediately applied in my pastoral care, especially for those who were grieving the loss of a loved one. The experience I had with the death of a young confirmand from an evil cancer I have spoken about and written about since I arrived at the seminary in 1984. The *blick* is the most significant hermeneutic for exegesis, preaching, and pastoral care. But in 1984, when I returned to CTSFW to teach, although I had the *blick*, I did not know it. What I knew is that something had shifted in my theology from my parish experience and studies at YDS.

In 1985, in my second year of teaching at CTSFW, I moved from a small dark study in the tunnel between Wyneken and Loehe Halls to Jerome Hall, to a room with a view of Kramer Chapel. A magnificent study to which I was unworthy as a junior faculty member, but I was thrilled to be in the center of the faculty with such a spacious, comfortable, and bright place to work. It was in this study, and in my studies at two and seven Tyndale on the CTSFW campus and my barn in New Hampshire, that I wrote my PhD thesis and later the CPH commentary on Luke's Gospel. Jerome Hall was a lively meeting place for professors in those days where we would gossip about this and that but more often about some theological issue. At some point during that year Voelz, Weinrich, Wenthe, and I were in a passionate discussion about biblical theology. Although I was a colleague, I was not an equal. Throughout my life, perhaps because of my experience at Andover, I was always quite aware that there were others who had greater firepower than I did. These three men, along with David Scaer, had shaped me into the theologian I was at CTSFW, but like them, I had gone away and sat at the feet of non-Lutherans, non-Missouri Synod Lutherans—Voelz at Cambridge with C. F. D. Moule, Weinrich at Basel with Bo Reicke, and Wenthe at Princeton, and then at Notre Dame with Eugene Ulrich. I would engage in the conversation with my colleagues but rarely would lead the conversation. That day I talked about what I had learned at YDS from Aidan, especially about liturgy as primary theology, and the work I was doing on the Emmaus story for my first submission to Fr. McHugh. There was a pause in the conversation, and in typical Voelzian fashion, he turned to Wenthe and Weinrich and said, "Hey guys, Just has the *blick*." That simple statement opened a world of conversation about what was the essence of the faith we confessed. What we reflected on that day is how each of us came to the *blick* from a different perspective—Voelz from the New Testament, Wenthe from the Old, Weinrich from Patristics, and for me from the liturgy and Luke's Gospel. From that moment on, the *blick* was our secret gnosis, and as we critiqued and evaluated others, the final test was—"does he (or she) have the *blick*."

To have the *blick* is to see things clearly in the Scripture. It derives from a high christology and high sacramentology, affirming that the finite is capable of the infinite, that sees all of time collapsed in the person of Jesus—past, present, and future—because he is the eternal one in the flesh. The *blick* is most clearly embodied in the liturgy, in both preaching and Eucharist, in burning hearts from the teaching on the road and opened eyes in the breaking of the bread. Only at the Eucharist, where true certainty comes to the believer, are the eyes opened, for the Eucharist is, more than anything else, the embodiment of the *blick*. These two parts of Emmaus—Word and Meal—are the means for mission, another accent of Luke 24, and central to how, from the beginning, the apostles and the early Christians brought people to the faith—through the *blick*. The Emmaus story itself is a story of conversion.

So as this theological memoir began to take shape in my mind, it evolved from chapters of my "greatest hits" to a book that used moments in my life that changed or redirected the trajectory of my theology and my teaching. They are not "conversions" in the normally marked meaning of the word, but they were moments when the *blick* was manifested in a new and fresh way. These turning points in my life will be my way of telling my theological story, which is the story of my life. One thing I learned early on after ordination is that I do not have an office; I have a study—the life of the mind is crucial to my identity as a pastor more than any meeting I've ever attended—that I don't have a job, I have a vocation—that my vocation and my life are inseparable—and it all centers in the Eucharist.[9]

9. See the Flannery O'Connor citation in chapter five: "Novel Theology—The Catholicity of the Biblical Narrative."

That is why, in many ways, it all goes back to Emmaus and flows from Luke's marvelous memoir of two disciples walking home from Jerusalem at the end of the first Easter Day. Opened eyes in the breaking of bread is the climax of Luke's Gospel, his "memoir" of Jesus after consulting many sources (Luke 1:1–4).[10] But even more it is also the moment of "conversion" for the Emmaus disciples who went from standing still, sad-faced, gloomy (that wonderful Greek word σκυθρωποί!), to having their eyes opened—the first time in Luke's Gospel where a human being recognized Jesus as the crucified and risen Christ. *Ever to Emmaus: A Theological Memoir* seems like a fitting title for my story because we are always on pilgrimage to Emmaus for hearts to burn and eyes to be opened in the breaking of the bread. Opened eyes in the breaking of the bread is the greatest moment of conversion in Luke's Gospel, and the moment of my own theological conversion and the heart of my teaching that converts students to the sacramental imagination.

Here from Emmaus I derived the themes of my teaching and my work in global theological education—biblical theology reflected in Jesus' christological opening of the Scriptures on pilgrimage to Emmaus; conversion and Eucharist through the opened eyes of the Emmaus disciples in the breaking of the bread; and mission as these disciples return to Jerusalem to tell the full story of Jesus' death and resurrection. The following citations affirm these themes, one by an Arminian (Grant Osborne), who gives us the wonderful slogan "the word and the bread . . . the means to mission," and one by a Roman Catholic (Richard Dillon), who speaks of Luke's *mission enterprise* and the *missiological consequence*:

> *The word and the bread are the means to mission.* Luke wants to show that the presence of the Lord in teaching and eucharistic fellowship empowers the church for participation in Jesus' mission to the lost (cf. Luke 19:10). Verse 32 [24:32] graphically illustrates this point; the disciples' hearts "burned within" them when Jesus "opened the Scriptures" in the recognition experience. Mission is the result of this recognition as the disciples rush back to Jerusalem to tell the Eleven about the Risen Christ . . . The result of recognition is mission; both are linked with the

10. Justin Martyr, *First Apology*, 66, not only calls the Gospels "memoirs" but connects them to the Eucharist: "For the apostles, in the memoirs composed by them, which are called Gospels, have thus delivered unto us what was enjoined upon them; that Jesus took bread, and when He had given thanks, said, 'This do ye in remembrance of Me. . .'" See chapter seven: "Returning to Emmaus—The Gospels as Kerygmatic Narratives."

> resurrection and Jerusalem as the starting point for the church's outreach.[11]
>
> As risen Lord, present in word and sacrament, he shows himself the *goal and meaning of all the scriptures*, and he imparts to his followers that ministry of the word which continues to unlock the secret otherwise hidden away in the sacred pages. *His voice* is what continues to be heard in that ministry of the word (thus [Dt 18:15, 18] can be invoked by his witnesses, Acts 3,22–23), for it is only *in personal encounter with him*, and from that perspective, that the whole mystery of God's plan of salvation is opened to the eye of faith.—That is, in the final analysis, the teaching of the Emmaus story.[12]

Luke's Emmaus journey as pilgrimage is a major theme in my teaching and in my life. Jesus shows us the way through his own pilgrimage to suffering. We follow him on the way—our *camino*—to the new Jerusalem by baptism and faith, a pilgrimage of suffering with and through him. Both Jesus' pilgrimage and ours have been captured in my teaching in the Gospel narratives, especially Luke's accent on Jesus' destiny in Jerusalem (9:51, the turning point in Luke's Gospel where Jesus turns his face to go to Jerusalem), and in my liturgical teaching, where the Gospel pilgrimage is recapitulated at every Sunday Eucharist. But also in my life, where walking all five hundred miles of the Camino in 2008 with my son Jacob from San Jean Pied de Port in France to Santiago de Compostela in western Spain was a life-changing experience.

At the end of a pilgrimage, we are not where we started, both physically and spiritually. Things happen along the way that change us. Looking back, we remember where we came from, how we arrived where we are now, and how we are somehow a different person than the one who began the journey. Sometimes at the end of pilgrimage, we look back at our journey and reflect on where we started and where we are now as a personal recollection of embodied memories transformed into story with interpretation. This book will be the story of how I arrived where I am today *theologically and spiritually* and what I have learned along the way about the faith my children and my grandchildren will inherit.

One more thing. The church I inherited from my parents is not the same church I now serve. That is stating the obvious. What is not so obvious is why. What has changed in over sixty years? One explanation is that

11. Osborne, *Resurrection Narratives*, 124–25 (emphasis mine).

12. Dillon, *From Eye-Witnesses*, 155 (emphasis Dillon).

I was raised in a modernist church and my children and grandchildren are now living in a postmodern world. Is there a such a thing as a post-modern church? Perhaps. This book will argue that a postmodern church will look like a premodern church, and that means that "tradition" must be either reinvented or restored as a way forward for the generation of my children and grandchildren—and that the *blick* may be "the key of knowledge" Jesus spoke about to the Pharisees in his tirade against them in Luke (11:52). What every generation must do is hand down this key so that they might be *Ever to Emmaus*.

2

A Just Conversion

The Road to Sounion

Each and everyone of us has a story to tell about our lives. The story of my family would begin with my grandmother, Concordia,[1] who was the daughter of a pastor, the Reverend Henry Schaeffer. He served as pastor of St. Paul Lutheran Church in Providence, Rhode Island, where my parents were baptized, confirmed, and married. I was baptized at St. Paul's by Pastor Karl Graesser on the nineteenth of July 1953, forty-three days after I was born in Salem, Massachusetts. My earliest memories of church are from the sanctuary where my great-grandfather served, wood and stone and the smell of old hymnals. It was a numinous space. Every time I visit there is a flood of good memories, even though it was the place for the funerals of my grandparents, my mother, and other members of our family.

When I was ordained in 1980, my grandmother Concordia gave me a little box with a ring and a little note. It was a gold wedding band that my great-grandfather was given on the day of his ordination, after his graduation from the seminary in St. Louis in 1878, the year the LCMS Synod celebrated its thirtieth anniversary. At that time, to be ordained was to be married to the church. This ring was 102 years old, and as I write, it is now 147 years old. Ever since my ordination I wear it on my

1. You read that right—she was named Concordia. So was her daughter, whom we called Aunt Connie. Although we are East Coast Lutherans, we are LCMS blue bloods—we have relatives who came over on the boat with C. F. W. Walther and Martin Stephan.

right hand. As I like to say, holding up my left hand—married to Linda—and then my right hand—married to the church.

Before my grandmother passed away at the age of ninety-five, she told her grandchildren and great-grandchildren the story of our family. She was living in Florida by then, and we sat around the living room and recorded her words.[2] The smell of my grandmother, what I came to know as a parish pastor as the smell of all grandmothers, permeated the air. My wife, Linda, claims that it is the smell of Palmolive soap. What struck us was that the story of her family and the story of the church were inseparable. She couldn't imagine telling her story without telling the story of Lutheranism as she experienced it from the late nineteenth century. Perhaps some of you have similar experiences with your family. It made me wonder how I would tell the story of my family to my grandchildren, or how my children would tell it to theirs. Since the age of twenty-three, my life has been defined by Lutheranism. As my children grew up on the seminary campus, their stories may be like mine—stories of how they were shaped by living within a theological community that lived and breathed Lutheranism. Even now, two of my grandchildren attend St. Paul's Lutheran Church in Fort Wayne where their great-grandfather, grandmother, and father went to school. They are fourth generation students at the oldest parochial school in Indiana.

What is true of my family is not true of most. We know how unique we are, for better or for worse. Things are so different from the time of my grandmother—and even from my own children's—upbringing. The world has changed so much and makes no sense anymore. Its so complicated now. As one person said, it seems as if the world has lost its story.[3]

My original intention was not to include a personal chapter about my own journey to the holy ministry and where I am today at the end of a theological career. Yet the more I read about the memoirs of Christians, the more I was reminded of my own story and how it could not be separated from the life of the church. Mary Karr's insightful book about writing memoirs, *The Art of Memoir*, was an encouragement to write about my own pilgrimage. Writing about myself is not easy, and most of my life I have avoided this. As a young pastor I almost never referred to myself or my experiences in my homilies. I think that was a mistake. I do more of

2. Sadly, those tapes were destroyed by a hurricane that flooded their home.

3. Jenson, "How the World Lost Its Story," 19–24.

that now. In the classroom I tell pastoral war stories, but they were more about my experiences than my thoughts about those pastoral events.

The Lutheran roots of my family go back to the nineteenth century in the Missouri Synod. My grandfather Just is from Cottbus, just south of Berlin, in what is now Saxony, Germany, and my maternal grandparents are Germans from Romania. They called themselves Transylvanian Lutheran Saxons. So, I am 100 percent Saxon and 100 percent Lutheran, and from a family of many pastors.

Many years ago, someone suggested that I read Penelope Fitzgerald's novel *The Blue Flower* without telling me why. Some have called her final novel a masterpiece, and in 2012 *The Observer* described it as one of the "ten best historical novels." It takes place in Thuringia and Saxony (Jena, Leipzig, and Wittenberg), where both Linda and I have family roots. What was shocking was the discovery that one of her chapters was entitled "The Just Family."[4] So if Penelope Fitzgerald could write about the Just family, so could I, especially on how it led to my "conversion" to become a Lutheran pastor. So before entering the theological part of this memoir, first a word about my own journey to the holy ministry, which is, as I suggested, a conversion story of sorts. The genre of memoir demands it, so here goes.

A Cradle Lutheran from the East Coast

In so many ways, even before going to seminary in 1976, my identity was centered in being a cradle Lutheran from the East Coast, which has always made me suspect in the LCMS. It was one of the reasons why, during the tensions in the 1980s when the President of Synod was reluctant to give prior approval to prospective faculty candidates at CTSFW, I snuck through the process even though I was a recent graduate of CTSFW. At the time I was pastor of Grace Lutheran Church in Middletown, Connecticut, a recent STM graduate of Yale Divinity School (YDS), with a New England pedigree. I did not fit the profile of prospective faculty members that Dr. Robert Preus was calling to the seminary in the early 1980s. I was not his first choice, but I received a last-minute call in June of 1984 to teach homiletics, something I was not trained for, as my studies at YDS were in New Testament, with a minor in liturgy. But David Scaer, the academic dean at that time, was seeking a more exegetical approach

4. Fitzgerald, *Blue Flower*, 47–50.

to homiletics and they liked the sermons I submitted to them as part of the vetting process—and, frankly, they were desperate for a homiletics professor, as the venerable Dr. Henry Eggold had died in 1982, and they had not replaced him. My call to teach preaching was only a bridge until they found someone with true homiletical credentials.

In late June of 1984, after much deliberation, I decided to turn it down. I was exhausted from my STM studies at YDS, and I wanted to devote my full-time energies to Grace, Middletown. We loved our little church on the edge of town, with the wild Connecticut countryside falling off behind it all the way to Long Island Sound. Middletown was a small city on the Connecticut River, amid a revival, especially in the downtown, and we felt very much at home in our parsonage. Most of all, as an exegete with a growing interest in liturgics, I was not convinced that I was qualified to teach homiletics. I was a preacher but knew very little about the art of preaching beyond what I learned at the seminary. At thirty-one years old, with only four years of pastoral experience, I was younger than the average age of the seminarians at that time. I felt too young to go to the seminary to teach. Life was good at Grace, Middletown, and I wanted to continue to be a parish pastor.

But things had not always been good at Grace. It was a conflicted parish when I was installed on the twenty-ninth of June 1980. It had suffered during the synodical controversies in the 1970s, had lost almost half its membership to other congregations, and what was left was a faithful remnant of older, founding families of the church going back to the beginning of the twentieth century. They had chased out the pastor before me, and the New England District was reluctant to allow them to call another pastor. They had been vacant for almost two years, but perhaps a candidate from the seminary might be what one official described as a "sacrificial lamb." Both my cousins were pastors in the New England District, and one of them in a position of leadership. He called me after I received the call to Grace and said, "You're going to the church with the 'dragon lady.'" I soon learned who she was, a victim of all the adversity this little congregation on Randolph Road in Middletown had experienced in the past ten years. I soon realized that what this congregation needed was healing, to understand themselves as a community, a family. The more I heard, the more I was unsure whether I knew how to help them heal their wounds.

But I dug in. Before leaving the seminary for ordination and installation, I set up with congregational leadership what turned out to be a lively Vacation Bible School. From the first week, I started calling on every family member in the church. I went to their homes at their invitation, sat at their kitchen table or in their living room and listened to their stories, heard their woes if they were willing to share them, and told them that I was here at Grace, Middletown, to be their pastor and that I hoped they would continue to come to worship or return again if they had been away.

During the two-year vacancy, no one had died in the congregation—they were waiting for a pastor—and that first summer there were a number of funerals. I would visit the homebound and then a few weeks later they would die. Members would tease me that perhaps I should stop visiting people because I was the kiss of death. Our local hospital, Middlesex Memorial Hospital, was close to the church, and I went there every day to discover if there were members in the hospital who had forgotten to tell me. Families had lost the habit of calling the church office when their loved ones were hospitalized. The hospital kept a file of index cards of people, and I would flip through it to see if they identified as Lutheran and then check it alongside the membership book of Grace to see if they belonged to our church (there were three Lutheran churches in Middletown). Within a few months the oral tradition among the members was that this young pastor was making an effort to get to know them.

It was wonderful work. Preaching, teaching, visiting. Getting a handle on who was a member and what they needed—hearing their stories—becoming known as their pastor. I will never know if this is what bound us together, for on the eleventh of September, almost three months after my installation, we learned of the tragic murder of Linda's sister Barbara in as horrible a circumstance as you could imagine. The saints at Middletown embraced us in our suffering. They came to believe that through our own suffering, we could identify with their sufferings. They took care of us, especially Linda. They loved us back into as much of a normal reality as we were capable of at that time. When our daughter, Abigail Barbara, was born almost a year later, she was their child as much as ours. Everyone wanted to hold her, for in her we saw the resurrection of Linda's sister. Her birth healed the congregation as much as it healed us. She was the first baptism in almost three years. We became a family. From then on, there was a change in the congregation. We had frequent potlucks, built a pavilion behind the church for picnics—*with beer!*—and enjoyed being together as the family of God.

The one thing they did not teach me at the seminary in the 1970s was how much people suffer. This I learned quickly as a parish pastor in Middletown, Connecticut. It was only after Linda and I suffered that great loss of her sister that I began to understand the meaning of suffering. It was only through dealing with people in suffering, especially in ministering to them when their bodies were wracked with pain and sickness, and at the moment of their death, that I came to understand that the greatest pastoral care we can give people in suffering is to make them aware that Christ is present for them *bodily* in the liturgy, even a liturgy done in a hospital room or at a deathbed. What I came to understand is how the "angels and archangels and the whole company of heaven" proclaim that we are part of a larger community, a heavenly one, and that in Christ, heaven is on earth, and in our holy communion we are joined with our loved ones who are in Christ. Here the hermeneutic of "inaugurated eschatology," the *blick*, reaches its pastoral goal. I'm not sure whether the saints at Grace, Middletown fully captured what I was preaching to them and saying to them in their moments of suffering, but I think that some of it got through. What bound us together as a family was suffering and making meaning out of suffering in Christ.

After the first year of parish work the elders gave me permission to study for another degree. In my second year at Grace, I began studies at Wesleyan University in an MA program of religious studies. Wesleyan was in Middletown, less than two miles from where we lived. In an intimate wood-paneled room with a large seminar table, Ron Cameron, a student of Helmut Koester at Harvard (making him a third-generation Bultmanian) led us through the Gospels and the epistles of Paul. In the fall semester, I learned how to do higher criticism in a course entitled "The Other Gospels: Non-Canonical Gospel Literature." There were only two of us in the course; the other student was David Frankfurter, now a renowned professor of religious studies at Boston University. Ron had us write form or source critical papers for each non-canonical Gospel by comparing them to the four canonical Gospels (intertexuality). We would present our papers in class and discuss them in detail in connection with the texts we were studying. Here is where I learned the language of higher criticism by doing it. In a strange way, it gave me unique insights into the meaning of the Gospels. Ron published a book by the name of the course,[5] and David and I are acknowledged in the foreword. In the

5. Cameron, *Other Gospels*.

spring, we were together again with Ron in a course entitled "Paul and His Opponents," where we did a mirror-reading of Paul's major letters to try and reconstruct the theology of his opponents. Again, this was a remarkable way to take a deep dive into what Paul was about in his epistles.

The year after Wesleyan, I applied these courses to an STM at YDS. The two years of studying at Yale while serving as pastor at Grace were the most stimulating and exhausting years of my life. The STM at Yale was the most formative degree of my academic career, because it gave me my focus and my direction, as I discussed in the first chapter about the Emmaus story. Yale was much more conservative than Ron Cameron's courses at Wesleyan. It took me by surprise. Kavanagh took me by surprise. One of the most memorable moments, however, was in Brevard Child's "History of Hermeneutics" course. He was one of the giants at Yale and in the Society of Biblical Literature. A pious, soft-spoken man, he began the course by saying, "Higher criticism is dead. And that's a good thing. It's faith-destroying and it doesn't promote congregational life." He was, with Kavanagh, part of the project of Carl Braaten and Robert Jenson entitled *Reclaiming the Bible for the Church.*[6] Child's essay was entitled "On Reclaiming the Bible for Christian Theology." In the 1980s, the faculty at Yale was still interested in how the church was the place for theological reflection; perhaps not as far as we did in 1990s at CTSFW with our mantra "Theology is Done through the Pastoral Acts," but that language would have resonated at Yale during my student days.

Almost immediately after finishing my degree, I received the call from the seminary to teach homiletics. Unbeknownst to me, the leadership of Grace had met to talk about my call without informing me, and they called a meeting to discuss it. I remember telling Linda that this would be a perfect occasion for me to announce that I was returning the call to the seminary. The president of the congregation began the meeting by telling me that the council had met, and they wanted me to know that, even though they loved us and wanted us to stay, they thought it would be best for the church at large for me to take the call because I was destined to be a professor. I was flabbergasted. I told them that I was about to announce that I was staying at Grace, but they told me to go home and discuss it with Linda. When I got home, I told her, "You won't believe what just happened." Even though Fort Wayne is where Linda grew up, we both loved life in Connecticut and especially at Grace, and

6. Braaten and Jensen, *Reclaiming the Bible for the Church*

my parents were only sixty miles away. It had been a long time since I lived this close to them. It was a hard decision. But it seemed as if CTSFW was my destiny, and so, after much prayer and conversation, we were off to Fort Wayne for what turned out to be the rest of my career.

The Journey to CTSFW as a student from 1976 to 1980

Although I experienced imposter syndrome as a young professor at CTSFW for a couple of years, especially due to my lack of formal education in homiletics, I found that in teaching homiletics you could teach everything that mattered—exegesis, sermon preparation, systematic theology, pastoral theology, even history. Grading sermons was somewhat arduous, but it was also one of the best ways for students to learn how to improve their preaching, and I devoted a great amount of time to giving feedback on sermons. When I started work on a doctorate in Luke in 1985, the academic dean added Luke's Gospel to my teaching schedule. It was wonderful for the next four years to be teaching Luke while writing a thesis on Luke 24.

But teaching homiletics was not in my sights when I entered the seminary in 1976 as an East Coast Lutheran whose first experience of the Midwest was arriving at the Fort Wayne Airport on a hot September day. A taxi took me to Dorm G on the campus of the newly moved Concordia Theological Seminary. The taxi driver could tell I was in culture shock. *It was very hot.* Even the strong wind didn't feel refreshing. You could see the heat rise from the pavement. Everything was brown and dry. Little did I realize as we drove through the city for my first time that Fort Wayne was called "Fort Rain, Windiana." I was greeted at the dorm by a distant cousin, Ricky Schuller, someone I did not know very well. The whole experience was surreal. By 1976 I considered myself a world traveler, as I've been on my own since I was 15 years old, having lived in Mexico City from 1966 to 1974, traveling back and forth from prep school outside Boston to Mexico City by myself, often going standby, negotiating the Byzantine customs at the Mexico City airport with contraband that my mother asked me to bring. My trip to Fort Wayne came via Spain, where my parents lived, and Chatham, Massachusetts, on Cape Cod, where we maintained a summer home. I had been accepted at the seminary in St. Louis, even at Seminex, but my cousins, after first encouraging me to go to Seminex and then to St. Louis, left the decision in my hands. The reason I chose Fort Wayne over St. Louis was that it was a shorter drive from Cape Cod.

After graduating from college in 1975, I decided to take what is now known as a gap year between college and a career. I worked on the Cape until November, saving as much money as I could. Since my parents lived in northern Spain (in a little town called Algorta outside Bilbao), I decided to travel around Europe with two college friends in a bright yellow Volkswagen Camper Van, later joined in Paris by my brother Jonathan. We spent Christmas in Austria learning how to ski in Saalbach, and then at the beginning of January, the three college amigos headed south to Madrid, where we traveled throughout southern Spain up the coast, through Barcelona and Andorra to the French Riviera, Italy, Greece, Macedonia, Yugoslavia, Austria, Germany, France, the Netherlands, England, Scotland, and then back to northern Spain through France—18,000 miles in seven months. That's why, after all that travel, Fort Wayne was more of a culture shock for me than going to Mexico or Spain or waking up in a parking lot on the coast of Yugoslavia, where we had stopped late one evening because it was abandoned, only to find ourselves surrounded by a market of Yugoslavian peasants who looked at us as if we had disembarked from a spaceship from Mars. In my hubris as a world traveler, I considered myself a preppy snob, a sophisticate finding himself at CTSFW among a bunch of mostly Midwestern seminarians.

The trip through Europe with my buddies changed my life. It's where I finally allowed to surface what I had been running away from all through college. Francis Thompson's "The Hound of Heaven" had finally caught up to me. It was my first conversion. Although now my story must be told from the perspective of Lutheranism, as we began our travels through Europe in 1976, my story had little to do with the Lutheran church or my Lutheran roots and very little to do with the pursuit of my future vocation as a pastor. Yet this trip through Europe is where I discovered my pastoral destiny, something the family had hoped for, especially my grandmother and father, as our family was a family of pastors—great-grandfather, great-uncles, uncle, cousins, etc. From a young age, it was almost expected that I would go into the ministry. Even the vocational tests in a psychology course at my secular college, Union College in Schenectady, New York, indicated that pastor ranked at the top of the list of possible vocations. But at the end of my college career, my studies at both Andover and Union seemed to be calling me to another kind of life.

Like many who came out of the sixties and seventies, I was caught up in the existential search for the meaning of life. It was all we talked about in college. I entered the fray as an innocent—a good kid from a pious Lutheran family who was set apart by my father's decision in 1966 to move his family from Pelham Manor, New York, where he worked in the Manhattan headquarters for General Electric, to Mexico City to serve as the manager of finance. Both my mother's parents had died, as well as my father's father, so they felt somewhat freed from their familial ties in the United States. My only remaining grandmother, Concordia, was in good health and living with her daughter near us in Pelham. The only difficulty for my family was leaving Village Lutheran Church in Bronxville, New York, where we had become very active members. My parents loved the urbane, sophisticated feel of this congregation, and Pastor Howard Holter was perfect for our family at that time. The President of the Atlantic District, Karl Graesser, who baptized me, was a member. At Village I had my first year of confirmation, sang in the choir, served as an acolyte and crossbearer. At the time I didn't realize that Village Lutheran was considered "high church," but here I learned to cross myself at the invocation, pax domini, and benediction. The liturgy was simple, elegant, and unfussy. It was assumed that this kind of liturgy is what one did when we gathered as church. At thirteen, I was on the trajectory to follow in the footsteps of my two cousins and go to Concordia College, Bronxville, and then on to the seminary at St. Louis. I was an Eastern, high-church Lutheran bound to become a pastor, even though I didn't know it at the time.

Mexico City

My father, a quiet and reserved man, possessed a lively intelligence that he kept hidden most of time. He was Phi Beta Kappa in his junior year at Yale in physics, a select group at that time, a man who should have become a PhD in physics and taught at a major university. Instead, he went to Wharton Business School. He spent his entire thirty-seven year career with General Electric. It was my mother who urged my father to become a businessman instead of an academic. I still marvel at his decision to move us to Mexico in 1966, something everyone thought was risky at best, foolhardy in the extreme. At that time, Mexico was considered an exotic and strange land where not many people vacationed, let alone lived and worked. But we left New York for the defining adventure of our young family. I was the oldest of four children at thirteen, followed by Jonathan (eleven), Karen (seven), and Christopher (five). On our way to our new home in the city of Mexico, we first headed west to Jefferson City, Missouri, and California to visit relatives, (and Disneyland!), our first taste of real travel.

In 1966, as we arrived in Mexico City, we all noticed a sign that said its population was 8,000,000. Today it is 22,000,000. For the eight years we lived in Mexico the peso was eight cents, the pollution was minimal, and the rainy season in the summer could be set by your watch. At 7,350 feet, the temperatures in Mexico City were very temperate, averaging in the seventies all year round. It was the kind of weather most of us dream about. We lived in one of the toniest barrios in the city, Lomas de Chapultepec at Montes Escandinavos 209, right off the principal street in Mexico City, Paseo de la Reforma, a street that stretched from our neighborhood to the *Angel de Independencia* by the María Isabel Hotel in the center of town, and beyond that to the Zócalo and the cathedral, which was the heart of the city. Paseo de la Reforma was designed in the nineteenth century to be a model of the Champs-Elysées in Paris, and it was worthy of this comparison. We would regularly take a cab for one peso from our house to downtown Mexico City without any fear and with the blessing of our parents.

For us, the eight years in Mexico City were a kind of paradise, for we were caught up in the joyful, colorful, and festive character of the Mexicans and their way of life. It felt like an ongoing party. But it was also because of our church life at Iglesia Luterana del Buen Pastor, where I was confirmed in 1967. We were a joint mission church between the LCMS and the American Lutheran Church (ALC), so they would rotate pastors from one synod to another. Most of the members were Americans like us, from multinational companies like my father—General Electric, General Motors, Ford, 3-M, International Harvester, etc., even people from the Rockefeller Foundation—with some long-time residents of Mexico City among its membership. There were very few Mexican members, as most services were in English. Many of the children of these families became our friends, went to school with us, forming a tight community of Lutheran expatriates in a foreign land. Our social life was rich and full. We looked forward to going to church as a part of this vital community of Lutherans who were bound together by a common faith and a common experience of being strangers in a strange land.

My first year in Mexico City, we enrolled at a very fine school within walking distance of our house. Escuela Sierra Nevada on Avenida Sierra Madre, or "Crocker's," after its founder, Maude Crocker, was a wonderful way to transition into a new culture. The studies were rigorous; most of our fellow students were Americans who were also learning a new language and a new culture. Mr. Ritter, my eighth-grade teacher, was tall, dapper, laconic, with a very dry sense of humor. He pushed us hard, and I found myself not only enjoying it but wanting more. I found delight in the challenges of this completely new world. Everyone in the family adapted well, especially my younger sister and brother. Within six months they were fluent in Spanish. My mother especially thrived. She was an outgoing and hospitable woman, and Mexico allowed her to take it to a new level. My father provided new experiences for us from the many opportunities for travel in Mexico. He was a planner, and we simply followed. I learned from him the value of seeking ways to enhance life's value by careful travel planning. We even experienced our first earthquakes, where time seemed to suspend itself. One time in the old classrooms at Crocker's, with its metal desks and chairs, we were taking a test, and the next minute we were all crammed together against a wall as an earthquake shook our classroom so much that it pushed us to one side of the room.

Phillips Academy, Andover, Massachusetts

Ninth grade at the American High School was a noticeable drop in educational standards compared to Crocker's. As many of my father's colleagues were sending their children to the United States for high school, I applied to several New England prep schools. One of my vivid memories is turning the corner on Montes Escandinavos after school and seeing my mother and brothers and sister waving a letter of acceptance to Phillips Academy, Andover, Massachusetts, the school I had set my heart on.

The decision to go to Andover in the fall of 1968 at age fifteen as a Lower Middle (at Andover the order was Junior, Lower and Upper Middle, Senior) set the trajectory for the rest of my academic life. It was a singular, life-shaping experience—all boys, all academics, all sports. I quickly learned that I was not the smartest kid in the room but that I could keep up through hard work and I had good instincts. My father insisted that I take Classical Greek in case I wanted to be a pastor or a doctor. That I remember the names of my three professors shows how memorable they were and how much those classes shaped me—Carl Krumpe, Vincent Pascucci, and the infamous Alston Hurd Chase, chairman of the Classics department, translator of the *Iliad*, and co-author of the famous Chase and Phillips grammar, *A New Introduction to Greek*, along with his colleague Henry Phillips from our rival prep school, Phillips Academy in Exeter, New Hampshire. These professors drilled the Greek paradigms into my head. We soon became capable of reading portions of Xenophon's *Anabisis* and Homer's *Iliad* and *Odyssey.* One of my few regrets was not continuing with Greek in college, but because of the rigor of my Andover classes, I adapted quickly to Koine Greek as a first-year seminarian in 1976 with the inimitable Dr. Waldemar Degner. Little did I know that my Greek studies at Andover would lead to a career in teaching the New Testament in Greek at CTSFW, one of the many decisions by my father that changed the trajectory of my life.

At Andover we studied hard, played hard, and watched the world come undone during the Vietnam War and the protests we saw both near and far. The Students for a Democratic Society (SDS) from Harvard came to our campus, recruiting us. In 2021, at the height of the pandemic, to mark our fiftieth reunion from Andover, two of our classmates, both professional filmmakers, made a documentary of our class. In the interviews conducted over Zoom, we came to realize how much Vietnam shaped our Andover class of 1971, the only freshman college class during the Vietnam war without the benefit of a deferment, making everyone in our class eligible for the draft. During our freshman year in college, from 1971–72, there was a great deal of anxiety, especially those with a low draft number. Mine was 87, and because we lived in Mexico at the time, I was in draft board 100 in Washington, DC. As I came to learn, it was more likely for me to be picked from that draft board than the son of a congressman or senator. During the spring of 1972 the draft numbers were published in the local newspaper—50, 55, 60, 65, 70, 75. And then it stopped. I was twelve clicks away from being drafted. The anxiety over Vietnam, and whether I was going to be drafted, caused a pall over me during my freshman year.

My memories of college are more complex because of Vietnam and the draft. At Andover I was trying to survive in a highly competitive world and compete with very talented classmates both academically and athletically. Yet despite the pressure of competition, we enjoyed the simplicity of a structured life during adolescence that focused all our energy on studies and sports and gave us a particular kind of joy. I never worked as hard as I did at Andover, but I was happy, loved my classes, made great friends, and found great satisfaction in succeeding in a demanding and exacting environment. A great camaraderie existed among us as we competed in the classroom and on the athletic fields. Andover gave me a great deal of confidence. Sadly, I did not stay in touch with my classmates as I should have. On of the virtues of the pandemic because of the documentary, I reconnected with my classmates by Zoom that showed that the fun-loving Andover spirit was alive and well. This proved true when in June 2022, we gathered at Andover for our fifty plus one reunion. It was a blast connecting with old friends and making new ones. It was Linda's first experience of Andover (we had only visited briefly before), and she was surprised how "normal" everyone was. As she said, she expected to see the great leaders of industry, and instead it was a gathering of artists and musicians and literary folk. She enjoyed the reunion almost as much as I did.

Yet the end of my time at Andover was a great disappointment. In our senior year, there was this unspoken yet palpable competition among many to get into an Ivy League school. My earnest desire was to follow in my father's footsteps and go to Yale. But my SAT scores were not as high as most of my classmates, so I was not accepted at Yale or Brown and ironically was only accepted at St. Olaf in Northfield, Minnesota, and Union College in Schenectady, New York, where I lived for seven years from ages two to nine and where my father went for his first year of college before enlisting in the army during World War II (I chose Union over St. Olaf because it was in the East). All my close friends were accepted at Yale, so that added to my sadness. I felt a certain shame not measuring up to these guys I loved and respected. I wanted to continue my studies in college alongside them. It took me years to come to terms with this, and it affected my time at college, especially at the beginning, and blunted some of the confidence I had gained at Andover. There was, many years later, a certain vindication in my STM studies at Yale Divinity School. I believe that part of my success at YDS was because I had found my love—exegesis, theology, and now liturgy!

During our Andover days, weekly chapel was required, as was attendance at some Sunday service, whether at the campus chapel or the denomination of your choice. I regularly attended Faith Lutheran Church in Andover, the last mission congregation of Augustana Lutheran Church, founded in 1962 by the Lutheran Church of America. The church met for her first years at Peabody House at Phillips Academy, and the church building was completed in 1967, my first year at Andover. I was warmly welcomed every Sunday by Pastor Hartland Gifford and the members of Faith Lutheran. Throughout my Andover years, my weekly attendance at a Lutheran church kept me grounded in the Lutheran faith, even though it was not a Missouri Synod Lutheran church, which, at the time, made no difference to me.

One vivid memory of the consequences of going to a Lutheran church instead of attending the chapel at Andover was that our services were in the morning and the chapel services for the students were in the late afternoon, at least during the winter months. On the twelfth of January 1969, at the third Super Bowl, I was one of the only students able to watch the New York Jets upset the Baltimore Colts 16–7. A few students gathered at the Andover Inn, one of the only televisions on campus, to watch that memorable win by Joe Namath and the underdog Jets. It is perhaps one of the reasons I am such an avid football fan. I remember rooting for them and the New York Giants when we lived in Pelham Manor. My father was more a Giants fan than a Jets fan, but they were a new, exciting team, and it was hard not be caught up in the glamour and swagger of Joe Namath. With my father, though, I was partial to the Giants. (The other memorable sporting event I remember from Andover was the upset of the Mets over the Orioles in 1969—we attended Mets games when we lived in Pelham Manor from 1962 to 1966, during their first two years of existence at the Polo Grounds, when Casey Stengel was their manager.)

One of my earliest memories was getting my hair cut by my father in the kitchen in our house on Sutherland Drive in Scotia, New York, while watching what some people now call the greatest game ever played, the 1958 NFL championship between the New York Giants and the Baltimore Colts, an overtime win by the Colts. I still remember the names of many of the players—Frank Gifford, Johnny Unitas, Rosey Brown, Sam Huff, Raymond Berry, Gino Marchetti, and the inimitable Andy Robustelli. I had forgotten that for the Giants, Vince Lombardi was the offensive coordinator and Tom Landry the defensive one, two coaches who in 1966 and 1967 met for the final NFL championships, both won by the Packers. We had moved to Mexico City for those years, and the only NFL team we could watch were the Cowboys, so we began to root for them. Our love for the Cowboys was sealed when Calvin Hill joined the team in 1969 after a memorable career at Yale with Brian Dowling and the infamous undefeated 1968 team that tied Harvard 29–29 in "The Game," the final game of the season for both teams. When Jerry Jones became the owner and fired Tom Landry, that ended our love affair with the Cowboys. We returned to rooting for the Giants, especially as two Andover classmates, Bill Belichick and Ernie Adams, became coaches under Bill Parcels and went on to win two Super Bowls. Ever since Adams and Belichick have been with the New England Patriots, they have been my team. It was agony to watch the two Super Bowls when the Giants and Patriots met. A bittersweet result, no matter which team won.

Another reason I loved the Giants was because Y. A. Tittle, the Giants quarterback from 1961 to 1964, lived in Pelham Manor, and his son was in my class at Prospect Hill Elementary School. One day, Y. A. Tittle picked up his son from a touch football game we were having in the fields of Prospect Hill, and he came out onto the field and started throwing passes to all the kids. The stuff of legends.

Union College, Schenectady, New York

The reason my recollections of college were more complex than Andover was because everything I believed as a Lutheran was tested during these years. I'm certainly not alone in this experience. Union was a small liberal arts college, second-tier when compared to the top small Eastern schools like Amherst, Williams, Wesleyan, and Middlebury, but an excellent school nonetheless, founded in 1795, the second chartered school in New York after Colombia University (it was, however, not as old as Andover, which was founded in 1778).

Union was a pre-med and engineering machine. I joined the pre-med program unprepared for the intensity of the program, in which I had little interest and less facility. The pre-med success of Union attracted many Jewish students, especially from Long Island. My roommate for the first two years was Roy Rubinfeld from East Rockaway, Long Island, a pre-med student who helped me through my science courses. He devoured them with glee, whereas I quickly found out that I was more attracted to the humanities. Roy went on to be Ronald Reagan's eye surgeon.

At Andover I took American History with Frederick Allis, which felt like all the American history I would ever need. He was a delightful teacher, perhaps my favorite during my Andover days, and his course was pure pleasure. He made me love history. At the time he was the head of the AP evaluators in American History. He gave us great advice on how to score well on the AP exams: "Gentleman, write a killer first and last paragraph. Sometimes that's all I read. And conclude by saying, 'Thus we see that.'" This American History course with Fritz Allis is one of the reasons I switched majors in my sophomore year at Union to history. What motivated me was Stephen Berk, the dynamic teacher of courses in Russian and European history. When those courses ran out, I became a joint major in History and English and French literature, for I loved interpreting texts. Two of my good friends were philosophy majors, and so I also dabbled in philosophy but soon realized that I was not an abstract thinker. The interpretation of novels gave me particular joy, and I learned how to do literary criticism.

In the early seventies, great music accompanied the unrest of the Vietnam War. Together we discovered artists like Bob Dylan, Neil Young, Leonard Cohen, and Joni Mitchell. We studied hard, argued endlessly about the meaning of life, and enjoyed being in college. We thought of ourselves as existentialists. Philosophy, psychology, and literature courses were the fodder for our discussion. I once tried to talk to a Jewish friend about what I believed as a Christian. It was, of course, after we had a couple of beers and I had the courage to suggest that the Christian faith had something to offer our philosophical ramblings about the meaning of life. He turned to me and said, "Arthur, if you ever talk to me about Jesus again, I will cease to be your friend." I was shocked by his vehement response. Sad to say, I never did talk to him again about what I believed as a Christian, for I realized in that moment I did not have the knowledge or the language to talk to him about what I believed. That haunted me during the rest of my college days. I didn't know what I believed, and the Christianity I knew was no match for Wittgenstein or Heidegger or Kant. But I didn't pursue enriching my Christian faith. I buried it. I didn't want to think about it. I valued my friendships—and our conversations—more than exploring what I believed as a Christian.

This led to confusion and the tension I was feeling in my life between my experiences in college and what I experienced on Sunday mornings at Zion Lutheran Church, the church we attended when our family lived in Schenectady between 1955 and 1962. Pastor Robert Albohm was a formidable pastoral presence who enchanted me in my childhood and now haunted me in college. Zion was a short walk from the campus, and most Sundays, I made my way to that beautiful sanctuary, gazing at the reredos of the triumphant risen Christ and the cowering Roman soldiers wondering if this was the way, if this was the truth. There was such cognitive dissonance between what I was thinking, learning, and discussing during the week, and what I heard from Pastor Albohm and experienced at the Eucharist at Zion among good, faithful Missouri Synod Lutherans, including Marilyn Fleming, my first-grade teacher and a dear friend of our family. If there was one thing that kept me steady and faithful during my college years it was the effort of dragging myself out of bed on Sunday mornings and worshipping with the Missouri Synod saints at Zion. As I always say to students, going to church is a good thing.

The Decision to Go to the Seminary

Upon graduation from college, I had no sense of what I wanted to do with the rest of my life. Law school was a possibility, but the thought of studying law left me cold. As much as I admired my father's career as a businessman, it did not appeal to me as a career. I wanted to stay in the humanities, but I wasn't sure if I was up to a MA or PhD. Although we didn't use the term at that time, I was burned-out and without any direction. Although I don't suffer from depression and think of myself as an optimistic person, I felt lost and depressed. My father sensed all of this, especially my indecision about a career after college, so he suggested a tour around Europe. How prescient my father was in how this would help me clarify what I wanted to do with my life and led to my decision to become a pastor. But as we embarked on our travels, this was not clear to me.

What did happen from the beginning of our travels in Spain with my two friends from college, both of whom suffered from the same malaise I was experiencing, was that I kept running into Christians everywhere we went in Spain, France, and Italy. Later, I came to learn they were Pentecostals, of whom I had no idea who they were or what they believed. The more we talked about Christianity, the more I realized that I was not one of them. I was confused. What did I believe? What I was hearing did not conform to my very marginal Small Catechism theology. Again, I was thrown back to my conversation with my Jewish friend and my inadequacy to articulate what I believed. I began having conversations with my two traveling companions, Rick Leveille and Bruce Sostek, about religion and about what we believed. Rick was a lapsed Roman Catholic, and Bruce was a practicing Jew. We hadn't talked much about our religious backgrounds, but now we were. I wanted to know more about Christianity, but I had no theological books with me. When we arrived in Rome, I found a bookstore with theological books in English and bought Paul Tillich's *The History of Christian Thought* and Francis Schaeffer's *The God Who Is There*. I knew nothing of Tillich and very little of Schaeffer. All I knew of him was that he had the same last name as my pastor great-grandfather, and what I learned from my sister Karen, who was attending Aiglon, a high school in Chesières-Villars in Switzerland, just up the road from L'Abri, where Schaeffer had founded a community that both engaged the world and also retreated from it. Later in our journeys we would visit my sister and go to L'Abri.

I devoured these two books, but they led to more questions, as I had no center, nothing to really compare them to, because *I still didn't know quite what we believed and what I believed*. All I had was the experience of the faith, but I had not internalized it. I did not know the Scriptures or even the Small Catechism, except what I had memorized in Sunday School and confirmation classes. I had no texts on which to stand and no biblical memory and therefore, no real language to articulate the faith. "Memory is essential for Christian thinking, and like all memory it is particular and privileges certain moments and even in the Christian past, certain books and ideas, certain terms, and most of all certain persons. It begins with what has been received."[7]

So, I was searching in a fog, while at the same time enjoying my travels with my two friends, talking about the things we talked about in college—books, movies, music, ideas—and now religion. We met lots of great people, ate great food, drank great beer, and learned about great wine. We had extraordinary experiences, but underlying all the fun was this lingering malaise, and increasingly I was torn up by an intense desire to figure out what I believed. When we arrived in Athens, Bruce decided to fly to Israel to pursue his Jewish roots, so Rick and I, while killing time until Bruce returned, headed south to Sounion, at the very most southern tip of the Attic peninsula, where we parked our VW Camper next to the Poseidon Temple. At that time, you could drive right up to the temple. We popped the top of our camper and stayed there a couple of days.

It was there, overlooking the Aegean Sea, that I decided to go to the seminary. I really don't know why it was at that moment that I made that decision. Maybe it was the stunning beauty of the place and my own angst and agitation over my theological uncertainties. Perhaps it was the loneliness I felt on top of that lonely cliff jutting into the sea where

7. Wilcken, *Spirit of Early Christian Thought*, 174.

Poseidon's temple had presided over the fate of many. I wasn't sure that I wanted to be a pastor, but in my convoluted logic at that time, I figured the best place for me to figure out what I believed was at one of our Lutheran seminaries.

In the fall of 2021, Linda and I led a tour to Greece with my compadres Scott Bruzek and Peter Ledic. We had a charming and learned guide with the delightful name of Kaliope. On our arrival in Athens, torrential rains closed the Acropolis because of mudslides. So, our guide decided to save the Acropolis for the last day of the trip after a very early flight to Athens from Turkey after visiting both Istanbul and Ephesus. That morning Kaliope met a group of sleep-deprived travelers who were in desperate need of a nap. In her Grecian wisdom, she took us on a tour to an unknown place. As we were heading south, I asked her where we were going. "To Sounion, of course," she replied. What a delightful surprise! This would be my first visit to this life-changing place after forty-four years. It was just as I remembered it from that moment when I decided to go to the seminary. Kaliope confirmed that it was possible to have parked alongside the great Poseidon temple in 1976, even though it is now a protected national park with no access by car.

It set me to thinking about that tour of Europe with my college friends and my own process of "conversion" to my calling as a pastor. Those Andover and Union years, although fundamental to my formation as a human being, veiled me in a fog, in a search for identity and meaning. Something was lifted off me at Sounion in the spring of 1977 as I overlooked the beauty of the sun on the Aegean waters. I had a sense of direction I didn't have before making the decision to go to the seminary. Besides getting married to Linda in 1978, this moment at Sounion was the most important decision I'd ever made in my life. Reflecting on it now, the words of the prodigal come back to me: "And he came to his senses" (Luke 15:17), or more literally, "He came to himself." Was this myself, this desire to figure out my theology, my faith, to find a new way through learning about God and the meaning of life through theology instead of philosophers, novelists, and songwriters? Until now my brief life was a deliberation within myself about who I am, where I come from, where I am going. During those formative years at Andover and Union I was looking for my identity as a "psychological man" through "expressive individualism,"[8] and what I was really looking for was an identity

8. See Trueman, *Rise and Triumph of the Modern Self*, 43–49. The term "psychological man" is from Rieff, *Triumph of the Therapeutic*, 3, and "expressive individualism"

formed through a community of faith. I was looking inward when in fact, I should have been looking outward. This only began to make sense to me much later, during my studies with Aidan Kavanagh on the liturgy, and later on, in reading Jerome Neyrey's book on *The Social World of Luke-Acts*, when I came to realize that we live in an individualistic society and not a dyadic one.[9] It was in the liturgy of the body of Christ, the church, especially at the Eucharist, where I came to know who I am and found my home. In my final years, what I want most in life is to be near the sources of my identity: Linda, the Eucharist, my children and grandchildren, my church, and CTSFW, the place that has nurtured and sustained me for over forty years.

I have often wondered about this inner dialogue we have within ourselves that sometimes causes us to "come to our senses," to come to who we really are. It happens often when I am writing, having no clue as to where I am headed, but then this dialogue takes over and clarity comes and a direction presents itself. Often, after an unpleasant situation with someone, I wonder, "What was I thinking?"—"What were they thinking?"—"What inner dialogue are we each having that creates this tension, and what is the way out?" Perhaps this is why I read so many novels—to hear that dialogue, for novelists and memoirists try to capture this inner conversation. Like in Ian McEwan's novel *Saturday*, where he

---

and the "culture of authenticity" are from Taylor, *Secular Age*.

9. Neyrey and Malina, *Social World of Luke-Acts*, 72–73:

> Individualism was and still is a way of being a person totally alien to the scenarios of the first-century Mediterranean world . . . The personal, individualistic, self-centered focus typical of contemporary American experience was simply not of concern to first-century Mediterraneans. Given their cultural experience, such self-concerned individualism would appear quite boring and inconsequential. For group survival would be dysfunctional . . . To understand the persons who populate the pages of the New Testament, then, it is important *not* to consider them as individualistic. They did not seek a personal, individualistic savior or anything else of personal, individualistic sort. If those people were not individualistic, what or how were they?
>
> We submit that what characterized first-century Mediterranean people was not individualistic, but "dyadic" or group-oriented personality. For people of that time and place, the basic more elementary unit of social analysis is not the individual person but the dyad, a person in relation with and connected to at least one other social unit, in particular, the family.

captures what's going on in the protagonist's head during a real awful Saturday.[10]

While working on this memoir, I read Robert Wilcken's *The Spirit of Early Christian Thought: Seeking the Face of God* for a course on Diakonia at Luther Academy in Riga, Latvia, as part of the Livonian project. In the chapter "Seek His Face Always," Wilcken notes Augustine's citation of Psalm 105:4: "Let us set out on the street of love together making for Him of whom it is said, 'Seek his face always.'" It was so important a citation for Wilcken that he made it the subtitle for his book. Wilcken cites Tertullian about his "acute analysis of the term *word*, *logos* in Greek, *ratio* or *sermo* in Latin." What he said next made me stop reading for a moment: "There is a sense, he says, in which reason in a human being can be understood to have its own existence." Wilcken's interpretation of this is worth noting in full:

> Tertullian's point is subtle. As human beings we think of ourselves as a single self, with our own individual consciousness, and we look at the world from the perspective of a unique subject. Yet, reasoning is always dialectical, it involves questioning, saying yes and then saying no, a back and forth in the mind as words, ideas, and concepts challenge, criticize, or confirm each other. Such silent dialogue takes place within the mind; no word is spoken. In thinking, one becomes aware of an other within oneself which, paradoxically, is oneself. This other, of course, takes many forms depending on the topic and purpose of the deliberations, whether one is thinking alone or is in discussion with someone else. Yet the other is always present in the form of a question, an alternative, a doubt, a contrary proposal, or a complementary thought. The very term *deliberation* suggests that thinking is a kind of conversation that goes on within the self.

This clarified for me what goes on in us—body and soul—during our lives. This internal conversation and deliberation is what caused me to "come to my senses" at my Sounion "conversion" and in the conversations I had within myself during my Andover and Union days, and especially during those seven months traveling through Europe. This, I believe, is what happens to everyone who goes through a conversion experience. Luke even uses this language of inner dialogue in the annunciation, as the angel Gabriel appears to Mary and with the greeting

10. McEwan, *Saturday*.

"rejoice," addresses her as the Daughter of Zion and the new Israel: "And Mary was troubled at this word and dialogues [within herself] what sort of greeting this might be" (1:29—"διαλογίζομαι, I consider, ponder, reason, argue, debate").[11] If such a dialogue went on in Mary, think of what Paul experienced when he was blinded by the light. For three days he was in Damascus before Ananias laid hands on him and his eyes were opened and he was baptized. Or Augustine's long deliberation that led to his conversion by the voice of child in a garden to "take up and read." Or in the sublime and inscrutable poetry of T. S. Eliot, especially in his poem "Ash Wednesday." One wonders how, in the process of evangelization, we could be more intentional in directing the inner conversation of those who are bit by the Gospel and are seeking His face always.

If this is all that Wilcken had to offer, it would be enough. But there is more. He compares these two voices in our head with "what takes place in God":

> Because human thinking involves a back and forth within the mind, it is plausible, argues Tertullian, to speak of a kind of second person within us. Tertullian is not interested in establishing a truth about human psychology, though he wrote a large book dealing with the human soul, but in drawing an analogy between the human mind and God's nature. Human beings were made in the "image and likeness of God." If one can speak of a "partner in conversation" in the human mind, an "associate" if you will, "how much more completely . . . does this take place in God, whose image and similitude you are said to be. Even while silent one has in himself reason, and in reason word . . . So I have been able with good reason to conclude that even before the world came into being God was not alone, for he always had in himself Reason, and with Reason Word, who came to be beside himself by activity within himself." God does not live in solitude.[12]

Now I see how coming to my senses at Sounion was not simply an act of the Holy Spirit, moving within my inner dialogues to direct me on a new but unknown path, but also an embrace of my creation by God as a human being in the "image and likeness of God." I was using "Reason Word" to take me on the adventure of a lifetime.

11. Goodrich and Lukaszewski, *Reader's Greek New Testament*.

12. Wilcken, *Spirit of Early Christian Thought*, 98–100. Wilcken cites Tertullian's *Against Praxeas*, 5, 7, and 11.

When we returned to Athens that spring of 1976, I called my father and told him the news. His only reply was, "It's about time. If you go to the seminary, I'll pay for it." To this day, one of the great surprises in my life is that I stuck with this decision through my travels in Europe, through that summer working on the Cape, and enrolled at CTSFW in the fall of 1976.

3

The Camino

My Theme is Pilgrimage

"All the way to heaven is heaven, because Jesus said, 'I am the way.'"

"Every step of the way to heaven is heaven."

St. Catherine of Siena[1]

"*Se hace camino al andar.*"

"The way is made by walking."

Antonio Machado, Spanish poet[2]

"A pilgrimage is a journey undertaken in light of a story . . .

to situate oneself within God's story . . .

to be touched—even transformed or converted—

by salvation history, God's metanarrative."

Arthur Paul Boers, *The Way Is Made By Walking*[3]

1. As cited by Martin, *Last Things*, 39.
2. Machado, *Border of a Dream*, 192.
3. Boers, *Way Is Made By Walking*, 180.

My Theme Is Pilgrimage

Even before my son Jake and I set forth on our pilgrimage to Santiago de Compostela in June of 2008, when Jake was nineteen and I was fifty-five, pilgrimage was my theme. For we are all looking for home, prodigals wandering in the wilderness of sin, looking for our Father's house. Like the Emmaus disciples, we journey towards home only to return to Jerusalem. For us, home—Jerusalem—is the Eucharist. So we are always on pilgrimage—to Eden restored, to paradise regained, from the Jordan to Jerusalem, from font to table. This longing is so deep, so human, that Christians throughout the ages have felt compelled to pilgrimage, walking from their homes to Jerusalem, to Rome, to Santiago, to Canterbury.

Home is where Christ is with his saints, and as Christ is present at font, pulpit, and table, the liturgy is where his saints come home to God in him. Even so, that did not stop the baptized from wandering across the world in search of home, especially to sacred spaces built over the tombs of the saints. Rome, of course, is Peter's city, her first bishop and pope, a natural destination for pilgrimage to his tomb under the altar of St. Peter's in Vatican City. If the tomb is empty, as in the Church of the Holy Sepulcher in Jerusalem, so much the better.

The patron saint of Lutherans is Paul, and Wittenberg is our pilgrimage destination, not because Paul is buried there but because the tomb of his greatest disciple is found in the Castle Church. After spending a sabbatical in the Old Latin School in Wittenberg, Linda and I have fallen in love with Luther's town. Since justification by grace through faith is the doctrine upon which the church stands and falls, we honor Luther, the re-discoverer of this central doctrine of the church. Paul's tomb is also an object of pilgrimage as he too is buried in Rome, first interred with Peter in the catacombs, and then transferred to St. Paul Outside the Walls. He is also the patron saint of London, where St. Paul's Cathedral holds the tombs of Lord Nelson and the Duke of Wellington, who are not Lutherans.

And then there is James, the other son of Zebedee, the first of the twelve to be martyred when Herod Agrippa I was tetrarch of Judea, Galilee, and Samaria. James was martyred in Jerusalem during Passover:

> About that time Herod the king laid violent hands on some who belonged to the church. He killed James the brother of John with the sword, and when he saw that it pleased the Jews, he

> proceeded to arrest Peter also. This was during the days of Unleavened Bread. (Acts 12:1–3)

This little episode, often overlooked, changed the entire life of the church. Tradition tells us that St. James the elder, the son of Zebedee, the first martyred apostle, is buried in the cathedral in Santiago de Compostela, a long way from Jerusalem, his burial the story of legend that is worthy of our consideration, for legends have consequences.

The pilgrimage to Santiago de Compostela is one of the three greatest pilgrimages in Christendom, alongside Jerusalem and Rome, dating back to the AD 812. The Camino, as it is now called, was declared in 1987 a "Cultural Route of the Council of Europe" and in 1998, declared a UNESCO World Heritage site. Today it is clogged with tourists who walk it for all the wrong reasons. But *peregrinos*, which is Spanish for "pilgrims," have walked to Santiago de Compostela on the western coast of Spain to visit the tomb of St. James the Elder, martyr and a member of the inner circle of Jesus' disciples, along with Peter and the evangelist John, his brother. Some pilgrims start in France or Germany, although the traditional place to begin is San Jean Pie de Port, eight hundred kilometers from Santiago, which is about 500 miles. Medieval pilgrimages to Santiago were said to swell to hundreds of thousands.[4] The pilgrimage to Santiago de Compostela clearly captured the imagination of the medieval church for all the right reasons, and for all the wrong reasons.

One of the most poignant memories of my life was standing on the sloping lawn of Abbot House at Phillips Academy in Andover, Massachusetts, Cochran Chapel looming in the distance, watching my parents drive away to Logan Airport in Boston to head home to Mexico City. It was the fall of 1968; I was fifteen years old and about to enter the fray of a rigorous and all-consuming life of a high-powered prep school in New England. What I experienced in that moment of parting from my parents was one of the most heartbreaking feelings of homesickness I've ever felt and one of the most deeply felt feelings I remember. Tears just burst from my eyes, and I sobbed uncontrollably as I watched them drive away. I would not see them until Christmas. I wasn't sure I could make it until then. Homesickness defined my life for the next few years, even though I adjusted to Andover and came to love it—even the travel from school to home in Mexico City. But I loved my family more, and I loved our home in Mexico, and I missed my parents and my brothers and sister and the

4. See Sumption, *Age of Pilgrimage*, 162–63, 237–38, 248, 252–53.

life we had created for ourselves there. And there was also a girlfriend I left behind. Back then we wrote airmail letters, and I wrote many, almost every day. How I looked forward to the mid-morning break when we checked our mailboxes in George Washington Hall to see if there was any mail from home.

Home. Our family has had many houses, but if someone asks me where I'm from, where's my home, I hesitate. Although I was born in Massachusetts, I only lived there for two years, unlike my parents who could say they were born and raised in Rhode Island, where they attended the same confirmations class, courted, and married in the Ocean State—at St. Paul's where my great-grandfather was once the pastor in Providence. My father left for college, then the war, and my parents' first year of marriage was in New Haven, Connecticut, for my father's final year at Yale. But their children really had no city, no place to call home. We grew up in so many places—Swampscott, Massachusetts; Schenectady and Pelham Manor, New York; Mexico City; Algorta, Spain. My schooling was in the Northeast (and Mexico City)—prep school in Andover, Massachusetts and college in Schenectady, New York.

That's one of the reasons why, during our years in Mexico and Spain, my father bought a house in Chatham, Massachusetts, as a home base in the summer when we would visit the States. He knew we were without roots and wanted to make the summer house on Cape Cod our home. For a while it was. Some of my fondest adolescent and college memories were working on the Cape in the summers—first in West Yarmouth the summer my father bought the home in Chatham. That summer, when I was eighteen, I stayed with the Hill family, falling in love with their daughter Chrissie (unrequited), working at a fruit and produce business, wrecking their truck because the brakes didn't work, spending an afternoon in the Hyannis Jail until Jeanne Hill bailed me out, and then later in Chatham washing dishes at The Captain's Table, waiting on tables at The Squire, or selling men's clothes at Mark, Fore, and Strike (Mark for shooting, Fore for golfing, and Strike for fishing). The Cape became our home away from home in the summer, for we had to work through high school and college, and trips to Mexico and Spain were only for Christmas. One of my father's great regrets was selling the Cape House, but they had settled in Wilton, Connecticut, at that point and he didn't want to carry two homes as he moved towards retirement. For similar reasons, we bought a home in New Hampshire in 1985 for summers, to create a home that we owned and could call our own, since we lived in seminary housing for twenty-seven years. My children (and now my grandchildren) are fiercely passionate about New Hampshire and the house there. They identify with New Hampshire as home as much as they do Fort Wayne (although the seminary campus has special meaning for them as the place where they came of age).

So where is my home? When people ask me where I'm from, the best I can do is not a city or a state—I say I'm from New England.

That is why I was always haunted by the reference in Luke's Gospel where Jesus said: "Foxes have holes, and birds of the air have nests, but the Son of Man has nowhere to lay his head" (Luke 9:58). When I started working on my thesis and teaching Luke's Gospel, I learned from Joseph Fitzmyer's Anchor Bible Commentary on Luke that this was part of "the Lucan Geographical Perspective," or what I called in my commentary "the Journey"[5]—to Jerusalem—to Jesus' death. The Gospel begins and ends in the temple in Jerusalem—at the beginning in the Holy Place with Zechariah and Gabriel (Luke 1:5–25) and at the end with the disciples returning to the temple with great joy, praising God (Luke 24:53). Jesus may have been born in Bethlehem, raised in Nazareth, and settled in Capernaum for his three-year ministry, but he was defined by his wandering, always in motion, moving from place to place—Galilee, Samaria, and then the final journey to Jerusalem—nowhere to lay his head—no home except his Father's house in Jerusalem. He was a pilgrim always on pilgrimage. That's why the question of Cleopas to Jesus during the Emmaus journey could be translated, "Are you the only pilgrim in Jerusalem who does not know what has happened in her during these days?" (Luke 24:18).

Jerusalem. Even before I knew of Luke's preoccupation with Jerusalem, I was taken up by the Holy City for my STM studies. In a class entitled "Anthropology of Ritual Behavior," I became more acutely aware of the theological significance of sacred place and sacred space because of divine presence. How the story of the Bible is one of pilgrimage to a sacramental land, whether it be Egypt or Canaan or Zion. Place is sacred and creates identity as home. Why do Jacob and Joseph want their bones taken back to Canaan for burial? Because Canaan is their home (Gen 50:12–13; Josh 24:32).[6] Jerusalem as sacred place goes back to Abraham and Melchizedek, King of Righteousness, King of Salem—Jerusalem, the king's valley, the city of peace. Perhaps Jerusalem has captured my

5. See Just, *Concordia Commentary: Luke 1:1–9:50*.

6. We want to be buried in New Hampshire in the cemetery next to our summer home where we have so many pleasant memories of family.

imagination because I was born in Salem, Massachusetts, and early on learned that my Salem was the Antichrist to Jerusalem. Perhaps this is why I yearned for the Jerusalem of Abraham, David, Solomon, and Jesus. I've been to Jerusalem four times, once for an archaeological dig in 2000, and then leading tours in 2012, 2019, and 2023. Jerusalem always feels like home, a city I could easily live in. The Jerusalem Cross defines my life—the central cross for Jesus' death in Jerusalem—the four crosses for the four Gospels and the four corners of the earth—Gospels and mission—that about sums up my life as a pastor and a professor.

When Aidan Kavanagh had us read Cyril of Jerusalem's mystagogical catechesis during my STM studies, I was completely captivated. Here was a fourth-century bishop in the city of Jesus' death and resurrection, inheriting holy spaces for which he must create holy liturgies for the holy days. Jerusalem as the holy city becomes the icon of his identity as pastor and bishop. In his writings and his life, it all comes together—Scripture, liturgy, and pastoral care—all defined by a holy place. For as we read Cyril the mystagogue, we must always bear in mind that we are not hearing the sophisticated and detailed argument of a theologian addressing his peers, but rather we are eavesdropping on the intimate conversation of a bishop, in his most pastoral role, describing to a very select group of initiates the great mystery they have just experienced. So, on Easter Monday he explains the mysteries to the newly baptized as they gather around the tomb, leaning against the screen that guards the tomb as he interprets for them what happened on the night of their baptism. Not just any tomb but the tomb of Jesus in Jerusalem that lies thirty-five meters from Golgotha, the place of his crucifixion. Holy place, holy space. Writing my STM thesis on Cyril's third mystagogical catechesis on the Holy Chrism, the intense biblical and christological character of baptism was clear. Imagine how those newly washed Christians heard Cyril's mystagogical catecheses in Jerusalem, in the Church of Holy Sepulcher, at the place where Christ rose from the dead. It captured my imagination:

> "Having been *baptized into Christ*, and *put on Christ*, ye have been made conformable to the Son of God; for God having *predestined us to the adoption of sons*, made us *share the fashion of Christ's glorious body*. Being therefore made *partakers of Christ*, ye are properly called Christs, and of you God said, *Touch not My Christs*, or anointed."[7]

7. Cyril, *Mystagogical Catechesis III*, On the Holy Chrism, 63. Italics are the citations from the Scripture, showing how biblical Cyril was in his catecheses. My STM

Then there is Emmaus. *Ever to* Emmaus—ever on a journey that begins and ends in the same place. Sitting in that book-lined study at Ushaw College in Durham, Fr. McHugh exclaimed, "Why Arthur, Emmaus is a circular journey, that when travel is involved, you often end up where you start!" We debated with each other about the identity of the site of Emmaus. A stadion is 607 feet or 192 meters, making the distance roughly seven miles, or about a two-hour walk. There is no archaeological evidence of a place seven miles from Jerusalem. But there is evidence of a place three and a half miles away. The possible solution is that the sixty stadia represent the round-trip distance, requiring about one hour each way. In any event, the Emmaus meal took place near, but well outside, the boundaries of Jerusalem. The prodigal leaves home only to return—so with the infancy narrative, Luke's Gospel, and Emmaus. All begin and end in Jerusalem. Home.

Many people have commented over the years on how much I have traveled and continued to travel, as my full-time pastoral career ended with my work in global theological education. Travel has been my life since age fifteen, when my parents left me standing alone on the lawn of Abbot House in Andover bawling my eyes out but planting in me at that young age a wanderlust that still persists. During the pandemic, when we were all grounded for over a year, I found myself enjoying being at home, working from home, not traveling. Perhaps because we travel so much, when we are "at home" in Fort Wayne or New Hampshire, we are loathe to go anywhere. We just want to be "home." As "retirement" is now upon us (or modified service, as we call it at CTSFW—teaching only when I want, which for now is the spring quarter), unlike many people, I am not yearning to travel but to stay home. And most importantly, staying close to my church, to home, to the Eucharist, to the new Jerusalem.

Perhaps there was a time when I would have resonated with the notion that "the journey is life." Years ago, the journey was enjoyable, but not anymore, especially during Covid. But for me, it was never the journey but the destination that mattered. Family in Mexico City or Spain, our home in New Hampshire, and during all those journeys to places to teach, whether it be Siberia or Kenya or Spain or the Dominican Republic or Romania or Taiwan or Wittenberg, it was the work that we were doing

---

thesis was precisely on Cyril's use of Scripture, namely, "An Analysis of Cyril of Jerusalem's Use of Scripture in the Third Mystagogical Catechesis on the Holy Chrism." The biblical citations above are from Gal 3:27; Eph 1:5; Phil 3:21; Heb 3:14; and Ps 105:15. This thesis was published in John Kleinig's festschrift.

and the people we were serving that were the reasons for the journey—the handing down of the faith, the preaching and celebrating Eucharist with people who shared a common confession, in their homes, in hotel rooms, wherever we could gather. Sure, I loved seeing the sights, but that was always a "reward" for the time and effort of traveling to these places, in the words of my son Nicholas, to deliver the goods.

If you read carefully the travel narrative in Luke's Gospel (Luke 9:51–19:28),[8] as Jesus turns his face to Jerusalem and to his "lifting up" (Luke 9:51), there is a definite change in the character of the story Luke tells. Throughout two and half years during his Galilean ministry (Luke 4:14–9:50) Jesus is the peripatetic missionary, traveling from city to city, proclaiming the kingdom of God and healing. Luke carefully marks the time and place where Jesus is. He is active and spirited in his movements from here to there, always returning home to Capernaum, to the synagogue there, strategically located on the Way of the Sea. Capernaum was the perfect stopping point on the journey, so that Jesus had maximum opportunity to deliver the goods to people traveling from Damascus down the Jordan River to the west, to the Mediterranean, either to Caesarea Maritima or Ptolemais, or to the east, to the Decapolis, the ten gentile cities east of the Jordan.

But as soon as he sets his face to go to Jerusalem, the action slows down; a ninety-mile journey that should take five or six days takes him six months. We're eight chapters into the travel narrative, and Jesus is still on the border between Samaria and Galilee. Time references are few and place references even fewer. Jesus' destiny may be in Jerusalem, but he is taking his time making his way there. Perhaps he's tired. Perhaps he's weighed down by absorbing into his flesh all our sicknesses and diseases, all our sins. Maybe he's exhausted from fighting off the demons he releases from people who are possessed. There is no spring in his step. It's more of a slog. But arrive he does, in triumph and sadness, people praising him with hosannas and Jesus weeping for the holy city that will soon put him to death. "Would that you, even you, had known on this day the things that make for peace" (Luke 19:42). Jerusalem, the city of peace, will witness the most violent moment in the history of the world at the crucifixion of Jesus.

For Jesus, the journey was not life, but his life was a journey to a place—a holy place—Jerusalem—to sanctify with his blood both

8. See Just, *Concordia Commentary: Luke 9:51–24:53*.

Jerusalem and the entire creation. Jesus journeyed because of his destiny and the destination he had to reach—the atonement of the world's sins on a tree outside Jerusalem.

From San-Jean-Pied-de-Port to Santiago de Compostela in 2008

For thirty years I wanted to take the pilgrimage to Santiago, going back to my first acquaintance with the Camino del Norte during our years of living in Algorta, Vizcaya, Spain, a little village north of Bilbao in the heart of the Basque Country, from 1974 to 1978. Guernica was only twenty-five miles from our home. It is the town Picasso made famous in his painting of the horrors of the Nazi bombs Franco allowed to be rained down on this town that was the soul of Basque identity. The Camino del Norte ran through Bilbao, and we would run into it now and then in our travels around the province of Vizcaya, especially when it went by some of the beaches we would visit, in particular near Santander and the Altamira caves near Santillana Del Mar (which closed to the public forever soon after we were privileged to visit them). Later, when I served the Lutheran Church of Spain for the LCMS in 2002, our base of operations was in Pola de Siero near Oviedo in Asturias, where the Camino Norte ran just north of us and we would crisscross the Camino on our way to the spectacular city of Gijon. So, I was familiar with the Camino from my two extended times in Spain and had heard so much about it from the Spaniards we knew.

If you are a Spaniard, your patron saint is Santiago, and once in your lifetime you must walk at least part of the Camino to get your Compostela, a medieval indulgence that now has become a tourist token. I have two of them, so I have my bases covered just in case salvation is not by grace alone but by works of the law.

Jake and I planned to walk the entire Camino from San Jean-Pied-de-Port in southern France to Santiago de Compostela in western Spain in June and July of 2008, about five hundred miles or eight hundred kilometers (I used the abbreviation "K" for kilometers, but we found out that no one else does). The goal was to reach Santiago on the twenty-fourth of July for the Feast of Saint James on the next day. Jake was finishing high school that spring, and we talked about walking it after my trip to Kenya in June, rendezvousing in London. Jake was preoccupied with his final winter and spring of high school. In the spirit of my father, I took it upon myself to plan our itinerary. I also prepared my fifty-five-year-old body for the rigors of walking five hundred miles in twenty-six days.

The itinerary I set for us was ambitious—an average of thirty kilometers per day (about twenty miles, although there were a few days where we walked closer to thirty miles). We had to keep this pace to reach Santiago on the day before the feast. I even selected certain places that we might stop. When our Camino was over, we both noted that we stuck quite close to the schedule I had plotted out from the comfort of my home on the seminary campus in Fort Wayne. There were some excellent resources to read, wonderful maps and guides. What makes the Camino possible is that there are registered *albergues* or *refugios* along the way, like inns or hostels, that pilgrims are allowed to stay in for a nominal fee (about five to seven euros a night). But you must have a pilgrim passport, like the one we obtained on the first day in San Jean-Pied-de-Port. One could stay in any pilgrim *refugio* registered with the Camino. At every *refugio*, or even along the day's walk, you would get a stamp in your passport that would track your progress. When you arrived at the office in Santiago that gave out the *Compostelas*, they would scrutinize your passport to make sure that you had the right stamps. My passport from 2008 is framed in my study at home.

Our camino to the Camino began in Biarritz, France. where we caught a train to San-Jean-Pied-de-Port. I had a slight acquaintance of Biarritz from living in Bilbao. My mother took frequent trips there with her French friend Noel. The train was an old rickety one, and Jake and I spent a thoughtful hour looking at one another with wide eyes as we traveled through the soft mountains where Hemingway would come fishing. Our first real hike was from the train station to the place where we would obtain our Camino passports. It felt like a hallow moment. The elderly French ladies in this ancient building who issued our pilgrim passports made it feel that way. Assisting pilgrims was their vocation. We were setting out on a life-changing journey, and they lent this simple moment a solemnity that I was unprepared for. We found our *refugio* with bunk beds crammed in a room that could sleep twelve. We took our first leap of faith to "trust the baby Jesus," as my good friend Scott Bruzek likes to say, leaving our backpack by the beds we had marked as ours. Jake always took the upper bunk because of his ability to negotiate the ascent without a struggle. Jake was not yet a red wine drinker, but that evening he had his first taste of good local French wine. I decided early on that we would eat our breakfast on the way, carry our lunch, and eat a *menu del día* every night. Food was our biggest expense, but neither one of us wanted to cook in the *refugios*, even though we did share meals along the way with people we met who invited us to eat with them.

The next morning, on the twenty-eighth of June, we awoke to the rustling of *mochilas* (backpacks) as the pilgrims began preparing for the first leg of the Camino, considered by many to be the most difficult—seventeen miles up the Pyrenees and then five miles down into Roncesvalles in Spain. The day was cool and very humid, with fog and clouds accompanying us along the way. It was mystical on many levels—the mountains, the wispy clouds surrounding us, coming and going, sometimes revealing spectacular scenery—and because I was running a fever, I was blowing snot in every direction from catching an "African" cold in Kenya. Yet we did it, I did it, and though it tested me, it wasn't as bad as I thought it would be, and my legs and my breathing on the hills were up to the challenge. Jake was like a mountain goat, climbing up rocks when we would stop for a rest. We reached the point of descent where the road broke in two, one by way of a paved road, longer and more gradual, the other a shorter, straighter shot down along a rocky mountain path. It was a perfect place for a late lunch, feasting on the bread, sausage, cheese, and wine we had bought in France. Many people passing us commented on what an ideal spot we had chosen. We decided to head down on the mountain road, shorter but steeper, and this was the most difficult part of the day, especially for my knees and thighs.

Roncesvalles is famous in both legend and history for the death of Roland and the defeat of Charlemagne by a ragtag group of Basque tribes. The *refugio* here was magical, a long stone building with bunks and racks for boots. It was how you pictured the place pilgrims would stay. We headed to a bar early to get a good seat for the European Football Championship between Spain and Germany. We decided to eat tapas and drink beer. Jake got a seat near the television, and I found a seat at the bar next to an older gent, who was sipping on a reddish-brown drink on ice. Towards the end of the game, I asked him what it was. "*Pacharán*," he replied. It is what Europeans call a digestive, often made of fruit or strong wine. *Pacharán* came from the sloe fruits (sloe gin) of a blackthorn shrub where the berries are soaked in anisette with coffee beans and a cinnamon stick. It was delicious. He called it a *chupito*, one of the many after-dinner digestives from Spain we have come to love in our family (I also love the national drink of Romania, *palinca*, another digestive made from fruits like plums, which is an acquired taste for most). Later, on the

Camino, when we entered Galicia, we learned to drink *Orujo de Hierbas*, a type of aguardiente, a "burning water" but with a sweetness that is addictive. It has become a favorite in our family, especially for my daughter-in-law Mica. With my newly discovered *Pacharán* I celebrated Spain's 1–0 victory over Germany and toasted Fernando Torres who scored the winning goal.

Leaving Roncesvalles early the next morning, a sign indicated that Santiago was eight hundred kilometers away. We pushed hard those first few days, perhaps a mistake, especially the day after going over the Pyrenees. By the fourth day I woke up depressed and said to myself, "Do I really want to do this for twenty-two more days?" But we soon learned what the Spaniards meant when they talked about the "*milagro de la noche*" (miracle of the night), and every morning we were fresh and ready to go. It didn't hurt that on this fifth day, about an hour into our walk and very early in the morning, we came upon a bodega with a spigot where you could get as much wine as you could drink and carry away. Even though it was early, we indulged and filled up our *bota*, a leather wineskin for carrying wine. It was called Fuente de Vino, fountain of wine, and it rejuvenated our spirits at a most critical moment for me on the Camino. Spain is a great country.

At nineteen, Jake of course experienced no physical issues—not even a blister—in hiking shoes he never broke in. My stretching helped me, especially at the beginning, and my training paid off. The Camino was a real physical test for me and even for Jake. We traveled fast, faster than most. It was necessary for us to reach Santiago for the feast of Saint James. For me, this was non-negotiable. But it meant that we would pass people and sometimes never see them again, even though we reunited with many of them in Santiago because we spent a few extra days in this special city after arriving on the twenty-fourth of July. Neither of us had experienced tiredness the way we did at the end of a long day. But our rigor at the beginning paid off because it put us in great shape. Even though we still tired at the close of the day, our legs were able to push on to the end, and we never experienced the sheer exhaustion of those first few days. We could go hard and fast at times. My speed on the flat parts became notorious, so that later on, Javier and Paco, the two Spaniards who joined us for the final push to Santiago, gave me two nicknames—*Fatiga*, which has the same meaning in Spanish as it does in English but dripping with irony because they commented to Jake, "*¿Cuándo se cansará tu viejo*?" (when will your old man tire out?). The other nickname was *Locomotoro*, less ironic, for they said I was like a train going downhill with a mission. But those names only applied on the flats and downhill. When we hit even a gentle slope, and especially on the stiff climbs, Jake would take off like the nineteen-year-old soccer player he was, and I would slowly, very slowly plod up the hill. But I never stopped, and after the initial shock, when I thought my lungs were going to burst, my body's motor stopped revving and would adjust, and I just kept on, sometimes for as long as an hour or more, trudging up the hill. Often, when I'd get to the top, Jake would be sitting there with some Spaniards, laughing and smoking a cigarette, causing my sore lungs to involuntarily spasm at the thought. And there were times, at the end of a very long day, we could see our destination in the distance and yet know that we were still five or six kilometers away, which at that time in our day was about an hour and half more of walking.

At one point, in O Cebreiro, where the final part of the Camino officially begins, Jake and I noted something about our feet that we were both experiencing. For the first twenty kilometers or so, our feet were fine, but then for the last part of the day, the bottoms of our feet would be sore and painful, burning, like our nerves were on fire. These were not blisters (Jake had none; I had only a few), but it was as if the soles of our feet had become raw. We'd switch to our Chaco sandals, which seemed to help a little. When I got back to the States, the bottoms of my feet were numb for months. When I asked my doctor about it, his reply was simple: "What do you expect when you walk five hundred miles in twenty-six days carrying thirty pounds?" My hips were never the same after the Camino, finally leading to a hip replacement in the fall of 2025.

Jake is more given to simplicity than I am, so he fell very quickly into the easy rhythm of our days, although he did come to learn some things from me along the way. We always left before sunrise, in the cool of the day, after my time of stretching. We would walk for two or three hours until the cafes opened, and we could stop for what became the most satisfying meal of the day—*cafe con leche* and a Spanish *tortilla* made of egg, potatoes, and onions with really good bread. We could knock out twelve-plus kilometers by breakfast, which was almost half a day's walk. As we walked, we would sometimes pray Matins together. Often, we walked in silence—Jake is not a talker in the morning. I also took advantage of these quiet hours to pray—it was the perfect venue to let your mind go into all the things that overwhelm you. Later, on the Camino, I would tell Jake the story of our family, as many stories as I could remember. This pricked his interest, and he began to pepper me with questions. Now as a curator at Porter County Museum in Valpariso, Indiana, Jake cherishes these personal narratives that lay out the history of a place. Perhaps these family stories laid the foundation for what became a part of his vocation.

What makes the Camino so special are the people you meet along the way. The Camino is an international event, especially for Europeans. In 2008, the Camino was still unknown to most Americans, so we met only a handful of our fellow countrymen as we walked. Martin Sheen's movie *The Way* was still two years away. More than anything, this movie led Americans to walk the Camino. Most of the people we encountered were either Spaniards or Europeans. Many we would see when we were walking and then strike up conversations with them in our *refugios*, during the evenings, after dinner, in the bars and cafes of the town we were in. There was an instantaneous bond between all of us. We were in this together. This was an adventure of a lifetime. So the major topic of conversation was always the Camino itself—where did you start (we always received looks of admiration when they learned we started in France and went over the Pyrenees on our first day); how are holding up physically; what is your pace; and then the most important question of all, what everyone wanted to talk about—why are you walking the Camino?

What fascinated me were the reasons people gave, as varied as the people themselves—escaping a bad marriage, needing a break from a career, recovering from a divorce, grieving over the loss of a spouse, a honeymoon! Some were in it for the adventure, the physical test, but they were rare. Most of the people we talked to were lost—lonely and unloved (another Bruzek expression)—and they were searching for something they hoped they would find on the Camino. Most of these folks would resonate with the notion that "the journey is life." Sadly, the destination—Santiago de Compostela—was only a secondary consideration.

What surprised me most was to find so many of them had no idea about the history or religious significance of the Camino. How many blank stares I received when they asked me why I was walking the Camino. My answer was always "to celebrate the Feast of Saint James on the twenty-fifth of July, his saint's day." Many didn't even know who Saint James was, or that the word "Santiago" was for Saint James, San Iago. This always offered me an opportunity to tell them the biblical story in simple terms—about the big three, Peter and the sons of Zebedee, James and John, how James traveled to Spain to preach the Gospel and is credited with bringing Christianity to Spain along with Paul, who followed him after his three missionary journeys were over. This, of course, raised all kinds of questions. Many knew nothing of this. And when I told them about the martyrdom of James in Acts 12, and how Spaniards must have traveled to the Holy Land to take his bones and bury them in Santiago, they were flabbergasted. Then I would tell them how the Camino for me was about the destination as much as the journey. About the *botafumeiro* they would swing with incense, going back to the medieval pilgrims who smelled so bad they needed something to cover up the smell. How much I was looking forward to the Pilgrim's Mass when we would arrive on the twenty-fourth of July, and then the Mass for St. James on the next day. That the Eucharist was the center of world made new in Jesus, and that is why it is the center of my life, but that, sadly, in this place of apostolic presence, I could not partake because my church was not in fellowship with the Roman Catholic Church in Spain.

Almost everyone was sincerely interested in the story of why Jake and I were walking the Camino, and that included the story of St. James and the mystery of the Eucharist. I learned on the Camino that if you tell your story with passion and conviction, they will listen to even the most arcane details if they are part of the story, and that people are interested in hearing what the Bible has to say. I tried to tell them how the life of a saint like James the Elder, son of Zebedee, is more about Jesus than it is about that saint, or better said, how Christ is present in that saint. The Gospel reading for the feast of St. James is Mark 10, an ideal passage to talk to others about the true, full humanity of Jesus and his death as a ransom for many. That Jesus is the truest pilgrim of all, coming from another place, a heavenly one, journeying into our world through the womb of the Virgin Mary, taking on our flesh, wandering here and there, healing the sick, forgiving sin, casting out demons, raising the dead, having no place to lay his head. He becomes flesh to make pilgrimage to Jerusalem for us, to fulfill his destiny and ours. His humanity was defined not by honor and glory but by shame and suffering. He who knew no sin becomes sin for us, becomes our servant, coming into this world not to be served but to serve and give his life as a ransom for many.

How many were puzzled when I told them that the true, fully human Jesus drinks a cup of God's wrath against sin so that we might drink the cup of his blood in the Eucharist, that is now a cup of forgiveness and life. The true, fully human Jesus is baptized in blood, cleansing the world from its sin and shame. Baptism in blood brings Jesus shame but gives us honor. James's martyrdom is a baptism in his own blood, as Peter and Paul later experienced in Rome, as millions of Christians have over the last centuries. The reason why the saints make pilgrimage to Jerusalem and Rome and Santiago is to remember the sacrifice of Jesus and his apostles, to recall what it means to serve as Christ served, to recall that in eating his body and drinking his blood, we participate in his pilgrimage, in his faithful walk to death.

The Camino reminded me how unchurched the world is, how little they know about Christianity, how little my fellow pilgrims knew about the origin of the Camino.

But how many pilgrims over the centuries have resonated to Jesus' death for his neighbor as the source of our love for our neighbor? In a world that is increasingly hostile to Christianity, our greatest witness will be how we embody the faith in love and mercy. What we do in loving our neighbor may be the greatest testimony to who we are and what we believe about life and love.

There are pilgrims who make pilgrimage to Santiago de Compostela in faith, following faithful Jesus, to honor faithful James, who drank Jesus' cup and was baptized with Jesus' baptism. This was even true of the two Spaniards who accompanied us during the last ten days of our pilgrimage. Javier and Paco, perhaps not the most devout of Spanish Catholics, were visibly moved when we arrived in the square of the cathedral in Santiago de Compostela. They walked the Camino to attend Mass at the Feast of St. James, to hear the Gospel from Mark 10, to watch the *botafumeiro* cense the crowds. They were true pilgrims, *peregrinos*, and they knew taking such a pilgrimage reminded them that all of life itself is a journey from birth to death. For John Bunyon, it was called *Pilgrim's Progress: From This World to That Which Is to Come. Pilgrim's Progress* is an arid journey, across wastelands, desolate and lonely, like our journey in this world across the wasteland of a brokenness of our own making, like parts of the camino from St. Jean Pied-de-Port to Santiago de Compostela.

For us, life is a pilgrim's progress from baptism to death, which is the entrance into eternity. In the waters of holy baptism, we get death over with as we die and are buried with Christ, reborn to new life in Christ that never ends. In baptism we put on Christ, entering a life of drinking his cup and being baptized with his baptism. Baptism enters us into a life of pilgrimage.

So, as we journey to our destination of full communion with Christ in heaven, we live under the cross, where we are continually living in Christ. Our pilgrimage is always to the font, to the hearing of Jesus' living voice, to a table where we feed upon his holy food to sustain us on our trek. Our pilgrimage climaxes in our physical death, which is an entrance to full communion with Christ in his heavenly home. The goal of the journey is to live in Christ's presence forever and to feast at his table for eternity. The Christian pilgrimage is accompanied by angels and archangels and all the company of heaven as we journey with them in Christ.

The *botafumeiro* is swinging today in Santiago de Compostela, a foretaste of that time when, as Luther's great hymn says, the smoke of incense swirls around the throne. To that heavenly feast we are now invited, for our pilgrimage ends at the eucharistic feast, where James and Peter and Paul will gird their loins and serve us, because their Lord came not to be served but to serve and give his life as a ransom for many.

The following is an excerpt from my journal on a day that marked a turning point in our Camino.

Notes from the Camino Journal, Sixth of July 2008, Eighth Day of Camino

Today was the first time I wondered if we could go as far as we had hoped. Then, as we were leaving Redecilla del Camino before dawn, we heard that there was no *refugio* in San Juan de Ortega, our destination for the day.

I needed to stretch even longer this morning before leaving, especially with my new thigh problem from going downhill into Santo Domingo de la Calzada. I never thought I would be thankful for plantar fasciitis, but the therapy I needed before we left for Camino caused me to stretch everyday. It saved me from more leg issues. Yesterday's walk included a severe hill going up into Cirueña, where I pushed harder than I should have. Then on the descent into Santo Domingo, so steep and long, my thigh muscles went into spasm and began to hurt with a vengeance. I hardly made it. Jake was waiting lunch by a fountain in the square. A little ibuprofen and some *tinto*, an elastic brace and some stretching made it possible to go on. I had my doubts. And now, the day after, the thigh muscles are still tight and need stretching too, along with everything else. Fortunately, that evening in the *refugio*, I ran into a physical therapist, who gave me an exercise to stretch my thighs. *¡Que suerte!*

There was a young French boy in front of us setting a brisk pace, so Jake and I took off right behind him and knocked off twelve kilometers to Belorado without incident. One of the blessings was the weather, as it was overcast, misty, even a slight drizzle. I covered my backpack and wore my windbreaker, for it was that cool. Good thing it wasn't as hot as yesterday because the way would be uphill most of the day, although the first twelve kilometers were gradual.

Finding no place open for breakfast, we made a quick meal of cheese and bread and took off for Villafranca Montes de Oca. Again, it was a gradual grade, and we made our way quickly, arriving by 11:30 a.m. That's twenty-four kilometers in five hours. Not bad. We feasted in the misty rain on our normal fare, including a little *tinto*, and then at noon took off for San Juan de Ortega.

Having looked at the topographical map, I was a little spooked by the elevation, for the first part looked like a stiff climb. Jake was nonplussed. Fortified by lunch, we made our way without incident. There were many on the road, but after the first two kilometers, Jake took off to get us a spot in the *refugio* at San Juan de Ortega, about another twelve-kilometer walk. He was fresh and young and feeling strong.

Yesterday, as we were traversing this long, rolling plain with wheat fields spread out in every direction and pockets of poppies dotting the cream-colored countryside, Jake commented that for one month during the Camino we would experience all reality from the perspective of our feet, that is, at the pace we could walk. How this changes your perception of reality—everything is slowed down, with no iPods or cell phones, the only sound our feet on the path, the swish of our backpacks, and the sound of other *peregrinos* we pass along the way. Sometimes it's only us, the wind and the natural world around us. I had to think about that, but it became a defining aspect of our walking. We had to slow down. Life had to slow down for us. If there was one thing I learned from the Camino, it was this important lesson. Although I haven't lived by it, I frequently recall that for over a month, we saw the world from the pace of our walking. Our entire life was centered on the road we walked. Our home was our backpack, and we became hypersensitive to our bodies.

There are moments on the Camino when I hit a rhythm, and it all seems to work. This is how I felt today. As I liked to ask Jake, "Are you feeling the love of the Camino?" The walk was beautiful, through woods with stunning arrangements of purple flowers in small fields, interlaced with what looked like upside-down parachutes of white lace, or large white buttercups. It was almost unreal. You had to look twice to fully appreciate the delicacy of such natural flower arrangements. This part of the Camino is completely unpopulated, so the only people on this wooded walk were *peregrinos*. All day long I felt strong, and especially on the last twelve kilometers, when I passed many *peregrinos*. Today was the first time on the Camino that I felt strong coming into my destination for the night.

At one point, though, it appeared as if we had outpaced everyone again. There was no one else to pass—Jake was up ahead, and I had a good six kilometers to go. At this time of day in my walk, and with the elevation, this would take me over an hour. So, I found myself walking all alone in these uninhabited woods, seeing *peregrinos* resting alongside the road in the trees, probably because it was a slow but stiff climb. I took out the prayer chaplet with a cross that I had brought along for my prayers and started rubbing its smooth surface, drifting off in mindless reflection. Although I may not have realized it when we charted this adventure, I was walking the Camino for moments like this, to think and ponder things, and to pray. There is something peaceful about walking with a dozen kilos on your back, sweating and striving for eight hours a day, with a goal in mind but with so much time in between to yourself, to your own imaginings. I have spent more time in solitude on this Camino than at any point in my life, I think, even though Jake and I walk together much of the time.

My mind kept drifting to things of the church, and how to realize my dream of returning here to Spain as a Lutheran missionary, as a professor of the gospels and Paul, and to teach them a true biblical theology of Mary. Although I love what I do, I am forever searching for something more, and I prayed about this restlessness. At one point, I started thinking about how to incorporate my love for novels into my teaching, especially having just reread *A Prayer for Owen Meany* for the umpteenth time, about how the biblical narrative is the one great narrative that explains all, and that a book like *A Prayer for Owen Meany* and other novels prove this. Isn't that what fiction is all about: the search for *the* story that makes sense of the world? In Fitzgerald's "great American novel," Gatsby is looking for the fulfillment of that dream at the end of a dock on Long Island. And Charles finds it, not in the magnificence of Brideshead but in the Catholic faith, at a deathbed, after many years rejecting, even ridiculing the faith of Sebastian and Julia. Many of the great books I read in my English classes at Andover and Union all had the same theme. Humankind, says Augustine, will never be at peace until it finds God: "Thou hast created us for Thyself, and our heart is not quiet until it rests in Thee."[9] How I can relate to that, and yet how trite and cliché that sounds to many in our world. But it's true, especially in our fragmented world, among all these dysfunctional families. Wouldn't it be great to find some way to give them that peace of knowing that there is a larger narrative of which they are a part. That we're not just a random combination of DNA or that we are disposable, even when we become inconvenient to our parents or too old to function as our children would like. Again, I affirmed my determination to return home and read Augustine's *Confessions* again.

How simple this day was, I thought. Wake up early, eat a little something, drink lots of water, stretch, and then walk to a small town in the mountains of northern Spain. And meditate and think as God's creation is opened before us in the mountains outside Burgos.

I also thought of all the pilgrims who had traveled this lonely stretch of the Camino in the Montes de Oca, sometimes afraid for their lives. This stretch was known for its bandits when San Juan de Ortega came back here in these dangerous mountains to establish a shelter for pilgrims to Santiago, after his own pilgrimage to the Holy Land and his miraculous escape from a storm at sea. The ancients were right about pilgrimage—it clears the mind. There was such conflict in my soul after visiting Kenya again with the deaconesses, seeing all the suffering and death from HIV/AIDS, and then the turmoil and tension of these first days of the Camino, whether I was up to the itinerary we had set for ourselves, me with that terrible "African" cold from all those AIDS orphans blowing snot all over me on our last day at the orphanage in the slums of Kibera in Nairobi. But Jake and I survived the climb over the Pyrenees on that first day from San-Jean-Pied-de-Port to Roncesvalles and the brutal pace we set for ourselves those first few days. That early pace toughened us up, putting us in great shape, and now the Camino was embracing us, in all its simplicity, with its peace and serenity, feelings I hadn't felt for years. I wanted to pray to God to show me the way, as silly as that sounds. What better place than on the way of St. James.

Lost in these reveries, I was shocked when I arrived in San Juan de Ortega so quickly. Jake had been there awhile, and there was a *refugio* for pilgrims, and he had secured us a prime place. The *refugio* was next to the monastery and church. There was not much else in this village. As you

9. Augustine, *Confessions* 1.1:1.

entered it, there was an expensive *hostal* on the left (fifty euros a night for two), and then a little further on the right, the church, monastery, and the *refugio.* The man who stamped my pilgrim passport and registered me into the *refugio* apologized for not having dinner for us, but it was Sunday and he had responsibilities for the Pilgrim Mass at six p.m. I was surprised that there would be a Mass in the evening, so I decided to go. Jake begged off the Mass but would meet me for dinner. He was going to nap instead. After showering and washing clothes, I spent an hour drinking a beer and writing in my journal, for today seemed to be a turning point in my physical test, and those final twelve kilometers in the woods had left me in a state of peace and quietness.

I was surprised how cool it was in the shade in these Montes de Oca, and that even in the sun it was quite comfortable. I decided to spend time in the church before service. As I said, there wasn't much to this town: the church and monastery and *refugio* were about all there was to this lonely stop on the Camino. They were all in one long building, in an L-shape, so that as you faced the church, the *refugio* and monastery were on your left, with a small tavern for tapas and drinks at the very end of the longer side of the L. Separating that building from a grouping of trees on your right was a courtyard, with benches to sit in the shade or the sun. No pavement here, just dirt roads and paths that had been trod upon by centuries of pilgrims. One could see how this would have been an oasis for *peregrinos* when San Juan de Ortega created this refuge in the woods in the eleventh century.

San Juan de Ortega was also known as a master architect, and his small church in this isolated town was a testament to his powers. I was anxious to see the capital that portrayed the annunciation. During the spring and fall equinoxes, the sun on one of the columns of the church would light up the Virgin Mary. After our day of quiet walking, it was comforting to hear the prayers of the saints for all of us who were on pilgrimage. Although I could not join them at the Eucharist, I could join them in the prayers of others.

In many of these old churches, it is dark at six p.m., even in July. But not this one. It is light and airy, even though the center of the church is dominated by a tomb surrounded by a stone shelter. As I entered the church I was overcome by the smell of incense, and I had to find a place to sit down. The incense was so visceral that I was flooded with memories of all those churches I had visited in Mexico and Spain, and the sad memories of how many Lutherans rejected incense as "Roman Catholic."

It is the smell of Christ, the smell of the mysteries by which we have communion with his flesh. I don't know how long I sat there, praying with words and that even more intense sort of prayer, the Spirit praying through me as all these memories passed through my mind.

Then I heard a rustle of movement and realized that others had come into the church and seated themselves around me. I stood as they stood, and then, hearing the invocation, I involuntarily made the sign of the cross. It had been a while since I had heard the liturgy in Spanish, but a second round of emotion swept through me as I listened to those familiar words, words that comforted me. It was as if I had returned to the place I was meant to be, in a stone church with incense and the simple cadences of the historic liturgy, alongside fellow believers who were gathered on this beautiful, cool July evening to be blessed as *peregrinos* on the way to Santiago de Compostela.

The images in my head did not stop, my mind could not be turned off as the liturgy had its way with me. The elderly Spanish woman beside me in her mantilla was clearly devout. She prayed prayers that were from her heart. Entering a church like this, after a long strenuous walk, I was experiencing holiness. The priest at this small church was an older man, bent over, his vestments too big for his slight frame. But he had a kindly face, and when he spoke, his strong voice belied his humble appearance.

The priest's homily was for us, for *peregrinos* who were on pilgrimage to Santiago de Compostela. He told us that our pilgrimage and its physical and emotional suffering was just a reminder of the greatest pilgrimage in the human story, Jesus' journey to his suffering and death. Ever in motion toward his goal, Jesus reveals to us that all of life is a journey, that we are always making pilgrimage from birth to death, and for a Catholic, from rebirth in baptism to resurrection and eternal life in the new Jerusalem. I thought to myself, that's what I teach, that's what I believe. He told us that San Juan de Ortega understood that at this point in the Camino, many pilgrims were ready to give up, for there were still over five hundred kilometers to walk to Santiago, the destination of our pilgrimage. For those of us who started in San-Jean-Pied-de-Port, we were not yet a third of the way there. The temptation was to stop at Burgos and leave the Camino there. Or, in the words of Jesus, maybe we wanted to take our hands off the plow and look back to our old lives, to where we were before Camino. And if we did, said the priest, we would not complete the Camino. Is this what we wanted?

On Camino, he said, we are like Jesus, ever journeying, nothing but what we carry on our backs, no place to lay our head. Yes, you have a nice *refugio* here in our monastery, but it is not your home, for tomorrow you will be in *Burgos* or *Hontanas* or *Hornillos del Camino*. But not home. The pilgrimage is your home. Your sore, dusty feet are your home, for they carry you to that next stage of the journey, that next stop along the way to Santiago. Your backpack is your home, your fellow *peregrinos* are your family, your home is the journey itself—the Camino. Pilgrimage is what we are all about, what the Bible is all about, always moving, always journeying to our destination, to that place with Christ and all the saints—the heavenly Jerusalem. Only those who keep their hands on the plow, who don't wander this way or that, who don't look back at where they came from, only those are the ones who are fit for the kingdom of God.

It was breathtaking to hear the Spanish priest expound the mystery of suffering! He concluded by reminding us that both Jesus and *peregrinos* on the Camino have a destination to reach—Jesus to Jerusalem and *peregrinos* to Santiago—one in the Holy Land, the other in northwestern Spain. How different they appear. But he asked, is there really that much difference? In Jerusalem, Jesus was being obedient to his Father's will, to travel the road set before him, a road that necessitated suffering, real suffering, and death by crucifixion. In Jerusalem, Jesus was coming home to his destiny, and in coming home, he was bringing us and all of humanity with him, restoring to us what he had created us to be—a body and soul cleansed by its union with him. Jesus' sacrifice on the cross—where God's wrath against sin killed him—was his way of coming home and bringing us with him. I remember he repeated that thought, because he wanted us to remember how important the cross was as the place we come home to God in Christ. Then, he added, the cross is where we are set free to love as God has loved us.

But then the priest said something I will never forget, for it was what we had experienced in talking to people about why they were walking the Camino. As a priest in this parish for twenty-five years, he had seen countless pilgrims walking the Camino for all kinds of reasons. But he believed, deep down, that we were all walking this road for one reason and one reason alone—we were searching for our home, and perhaps, perhaps, on these paths we would find it in Christ, and that when we arrived in Santiago, we might know where our true home was.

Saint James, our Santiago, found his home in persecution and death at the hands of Herod Agrippa. The priest said that only through suffering does one enter the kingdom, as all the apostles and early church martyrs attested to with their deaths. As we now continue our journey tomorrow, we are not to take our hands off the plow and look back. For Jesus does not require our hearts to be pure to follow him along the way—Jesus does not even want to know why we are searching for our home, just that we are—Jesus does not care that we tried to make a home of our own without him—Jesus does not even care that we follow him because we are tired of our sins, discouraged that they have not brought happiness, that they have not brought us peace. Jesus, he said, will welcome us home as his pilgrim children no matter what, no matter how broken we are, no matter how dark our lives have become, no matter how convoluted our reasons are for coming home to him. He wants us to know that home is where he is and that he is here, in this humble church on the Camino. Jesus' home is at this table of body broken, blood poured out. Here is where you can now lay down your head, in the bosom of Jesus, the greatest *peregrino* who ever lived.[10]

I watched the other pilgrims with their hands outstretched to receive Christ's body and blood and come home. Watching them take and eat, I thought of the peace the Eucharist gives me and how that peace was now on their lips and in their mouths. I wondered how many pilgrims had received the body and blood of Christ in this place. How many saints in the world entered this eternal communion with Christ and his saints on this day alone through his ongoing feast? How I marveled at the obedience of the saints in this humble Spanish church, as I often do in my own church of St. Paul's—saints going forward in a reverent line of worshipers to receive the gift of Christ's flesh in their mouths, to eat the very flesh of the Son of God. How hungry I was for the body and blood—for Jesus. That was the hardest thing about the Camino—a fast from the Eucharist—and that when we celebrated the feast of Saint James in Santiago on the twenty-fifth of July, we would have to watch others commune. Did all these pilgrims know that in this liturgy the story of God's love is played out in every place where Eucharist is celebrated? Here is the story the world is looking for whether they know it or not, a love story told with such simplicity, with its rhythmic sounds, its clean movement, its

10. The priest at San Juan de Ortega preached a fine sermon to the peregrinos about what it means to walk on a journey to a destination like Santiago as Jesus walked to Jerusalem. I have taken literary liberties with his brief homily, which happened to be on Luke 9 and the Samaritans, to capture why my son Jake and I walked the Camino. Some of this paragraph was inspired by Nouwen, *Return of the Prodigal*, 106–9.

assurance, its confidence, its inevitability—a story of our coming home to God in Christ.

The priest invited all the *peregrinos* forward for a blessing at the end of the Mass. I felt awkward and out of place as I looked around and saw fellow pilgrims from our *refugio* come to be blessed by the priest. As he made the sign of the cross, he looked at me and smiled, as if he knew I was a seminary professor and was taking it all in. I noticed that the man who checked us in at the *refugio* was vested and served as an attendant at the altar. He too looked at me and smiled. We had spoken briefly at check-in; he was the one who told me about the Mass, and I had told him I was a professor of New Testament and liturgy.

After such an experience, I was famished. I felt at peace, even joyful, almost giddy. I had experienced something special and wanted to tell Jake all about it. The restaurant at the expensive *hostal* was serving a great *menu del día* at nine euros with a bottle of wine, *fabada*, a soup of beans and ham from Asturias, and *morcilla*, a Burgos sausage filled with rice that came with *ensalada mixta* that I had come to treasure as something fresh and cold. All my favorite things. A feast!

4

Novel Theology

The Catholicity of the Biblical Narrative

The first novel that captured my imagination was F. Scott Fitzgerald's *This Side of Paradise*. There was something about his prose, the use of language, the sheer delight in reading such an accomplished writer. It was my first year at Andover when we were all discovering how to be clever and literate in our speaking and writing. English literature courses were the pride of Andover, and we were all reading the same books as we also wrote essays and short stories and poems. Andover was an Ivy League factory, Fitzgerald was writing about Princeton, my best friend and roommate was destined to be a Tiger (he eventually went to Yale), and Fitzgerald was what we all aspired to be—a novelist.

The novels kept coming in and out of our classes, and although I'm a slow reader, I consumed them as fast as I could. I was learning the landscape, that is, learning the various schools of American and British literature. There were, of course, Fitzgerald and Hemingway, but also Forster, Melville, and Conrad. T. S. Eliot's *The Love Song of J. Alfred Prufrock* and *The Wasteland* were required reading, and I still use *Modern Poetry* for my reference to 20th-century poems, as well as my father's copy of *Four Quartets*, which he used at Yale in the late 1940s, published in the United States in 1943. As I started this memoir, I was going to include a chapter on T. S. Eliot, for I had come upon a book by Russell Kirk entitled *Eliot and His Age* that outlined how important Eliot's conversion to high Anglicanism was for his life as a poet and how Christianity shaped the trajectory of his poems from *The Wasteland* (Inferno) to *Ash Wednesday* (Purgatorio) to *Four Quartets* (Paradiso). I wrote a chapter on Eliot but decided it didn't really fit this theological memoir, so I published it in *Concordia Theological Quarterly* (CTQ) as "T. S. Eliot—Pilgrim in the Wasteland."[1]

As I mentioned earlier, I was a History-English major at Union College. My thesis was on Wallace Stevens's poetry, with special attention on his hermeneutic of the imagination as the new god, as he played his blue guitar and created reality. Stevens's poetry was difficult, but his story was compelling—a Hartford insurance agent by day and poet by night, a seemingly quiet and reserved man, yet he punched out Hemingway in a bar in Key West. I still return to *The Necessary Angels: Essays on Reality and the Imagination* to remind myself where I came from and where I am now.

One of the more compelling courses at Union was "The Bible as Literature" taught by Hans Joachim Freund, a true Renaissance man whose passionate lectures about the Scriptures were peppered with great paintings that often illustrated his interpretation of the biblical narrative better than any written commentary. It was from Professor Freund that I first became interested in the intersection of art and the Bible, something that still fascinates me. His class also made me think of Scripture in a new way, as literature, beautiful literature, and I still cite him as describing the story of Jesus' birth in Luke 2 and the twenty-third psalm in the King James as the finest examples of English prose.

Two things stuck with me through my studies of English literature at prep school and college—how does the biblical narrative figure in great English novels? It was Professor Freund in another class, on the great novels of the twentieth century, who first alerted me to the underlying "Christian" character of many of the novels I loved. As he would say, it is impossible to engage our Western cultural heritage without knowing something about the Bible. At one point he remarked that his course on the Bible as literature should be the first required course for all English majors, since you could not understand great literature in the Western tradition without knowing the stories of the Bible. It was through him, and others, that I became sensitive to the christological character of many of the novels we were reading. This is something I attempted at the seminary in the history course "The Church Since 1650" with Dr. Heino Kadai, in a paper on the Christology of Fyodor Dostoevsky's *The Brothers Karamasov*.

1. Just, "T. S. Eliot," 254–70.

This paper has been lost to the ages, but I remember how much I enjoyed bringing together my interests in both theology and literature.

Our real obsession in prep school: something, it seems, almost everyone aspired to was that absurd notion that one day one of us would write the next great American novel, even though I was self-aware enough then to know it wouldn't be me. What I wanted to do, especially after seminary, was to write a "Christian" novel. This led me to Flannery O'Connor and other great Catholic novelists like Graham Greene, Evelyn Waugh, J. R. R. Tolkien, and C. S. Lewis, among others. Although these novels were very fulfilling, I also discovered other authors who embraced "Christian" themes that often surprised and always delighted me. One was *Dracula* by Bram Stoker in the new Ignatius Critical Editions by series editor Joseph Pearce. As my maternal grandparents are Transylvanian Lutheran Saxons from Romania, I finally read this iconic book that took place near where my grandparents were born. Little did I realize how eucharistic *Dracula* is, and what protects them from evil are the holy things of the Lord's Supper. Joseph Pearce became my northern star in this fascination, with both Christian themes in literature and the stories of conversion captured in his book *Literary Converts*.[2] He made me realize how the twentieth century was filled with converts to Catholicism from the literary world, among them the aforementioned along with Oscar Wilde, Malcom Muggeridge, Edith Sitwell, Siegfried Sassoon, Hilaire Belloc, G. K. Chesterton, Dorothy Sayers and more. During the late nineteenth and early twentieth centuries the Christian faith and the biblical narrative defined these authors through a lively commitment to a deeply eucharistic piety.[3] The oft-quoted statement by Flannery O'Connor captures this piety when, at a dinner party with Mary McCarthy, who was raised Catholic but left the church and whom O'Connor describes as "a Big Intellectual," as the conversation turned to the Eucharist, the host remarked that now as a lapsed Catholic, "she thought of it as a symbol

2. Stoker, *Dracula*; Pearce, *Literary Converts*. Pearce serves as general editor of Ignatius Critical Editions. These critical editions of the classics highlight the Christian themes of books that are part of the literary canon. This edition of *Dracula* by Bram Stoker is edited by Eleanor Bourg Nicholson (2012) whose footnotes are a book unto themselves. I was shocked that not only did Stoker get the geography right, but it was the eucharistic hosts that were crucial to warding off the Satanic evil of Dracula. It is a sacramental novel.

3. Although Dana Gioia, in his essay *The Catholic Writer Today*, laments that this community of Catholic writers has disappeared and the literary world is the poorer because of their absence, unlike the middle of the twentieth century, especially in the post-war period from 1945 to the death of Flannery O'Connor in 1964.

and implied that it was a pretty good one." O'Connor writes that she replied, "in a very shaky voice, 'Well, if it's a symbol, to hell with it.' That was all the defense I was capable of but I realize now that this is all I will ever be able to say about it, outside a story, *except that it is the center of existence for me; all the rest of life is expendable*."[4] These words of Flannery O'Connor have always resonated with me as the Eucharist is central to my existence, especially as my mortality becomes more palpable, for all else *is* expendable.

It was during our Camino in 2008, as a way of passing the many hours of walking, that I conceived in my head the structure and characters of a novel. At the end of the day, after a shower and a nap, I wrote down in a journal the thoughts I had about a novel I wanted to write during the seven to eight hours of walking. The novel was to be about a conversion, a Christian coming-of-age story that would be structured around the three parts of the rite of passage—separation, transition, and incorporation. And it would be a love story as well, two older adults, Santiago Lucas Domingo and Tabitha Watch Hill, who meet and fall in love on the Camino to Santiago de Compostela on the day that Luke has a spiritual catharsis in the liturgy in the church at San Juan de Ortega (see my chapter on the Camino). Luke is an English literature teacher at Classical High School in Providence, Rhode Island, and comes from a pious Lutheran family. His uncle, Pastor James McCue, is a retired Lutheran pastor. Tabitha is a conservator who is applying to the Prado in Madrid to restore El Grecos for the quatercentenary of his death in 2014. She does not have a strong Christian background. They both enter the Lutheran catechumenate at St. Mary's church in Providence, Rhode Island, after the Camino for Tabitha's confirmation as a Lutheran and Luke's reaffirmation of faith.

Although Luke and Tabitha are madly in love, Tabitha is recovering from addictions and becomes obsessed with the Carmelites by reading Teresa of Avila and St. John of the Cross. She finds herself becoming so caught up in the catechesis of the Lutheran pastors, including Luke's uncle, that she contemplates joining the Carmelites, either in Boston or in Concord, New Hampshire.

Two parallel narratives are interwoven in this romantic novel: the romance of Luke and Tabitha, focusing on her dilemma as to whether she should marry Luke or Jesus, in the tradition of Thérèse of Lisieux, and Luke's search for the great metanarrative through the novels he teaches

4. O'Connor, *Habit of Being*, 124–25.

in his honors English class at Classical. Luke's struggle is told through transcripts from his classroom with twelve lively and spiritually engaged students. The novels discussed in class are *A Prayer for Owen Meany*, *Brideshead Revisited*, *The Great Gatsby*, and *Old School* (*A Room with a View* and *For Whom the Bell Tolls* are featured in a context outside the class). These discussions highlight how the biblical metanarrative is fundamental to these novels.

This romance between Luke and Tabitha is told during Holy Week and the Easter season of 2004 with some flashbacks. Tabitha visits the Carmelites in Boston and Concord. They persuade her to marry Luke, and all is well until Luke tragically dies in a pedestrian accident. Tabitha connects with his students in their grief over Luke's death. They were to be married on Pentecost, and Tabitha decides after church that day to drive to Concord and join the Carmelites. This would leave open the possibility for a follow-up novel on Tabitha in Toledo, Spain, as restorer/nun of El Greco paintings and the travails of her life there.

Although this novel will never see the light of day, for I could not find the voice or the plot to make it work, the process of writing it was one of the most satisfying experiences in my writing career.[5] What I discovered in writing it, and the way I conceived of incorporating the six books into the novel, was that there are popular, classic, even best-selling novels with deep Christian themes. In my novel, four of these novels were discussed in an English Honors class with twelve capable students, six boys and six girls, who engaged in a lively discussion of the books. One of my few regrets in my teaching is that I never offered an elective theology and literature that I would have entitled "Novel Theology," a course that would have used novels like these in a seminar that explored Christian themes and the foundational character of the biblical narrative. The closest I've come is a lecture in our final Theologia course on the Lord's Supper in the spring of the Sem IV year entitled "The Sacramental Imagination: The Lord's Supper as an Optic of Life," where I discuss theology and literature.

So instead of a course, I offer two chapters in this theological memoir that demonstrates the Catholicity of the biblical narrative. My

5. In the summer of 2024, I attended a Writer's Workshop with the Community of Writers in Olympic Park, California, on writing fiction to prepare for the writing of a historical novel on Barnabas and Paul. It was intense, and I learned so much about writing fiction that I would feel a little more confident to revive this novel knowing what I now have learned. I attended the workshop through the intercession of my dear friend, Michael Carlisle, a literary agent in New York City, who has been connected to the Community of Writers for decades through his parents.

original intention was to have just one chapter on all three novels, but there was too much to say, and one of the novels offered me a chance to include some comments on Luke's Gospel, so I've divided this into "Novel Theology—The Catholicity of the Biblical Narrative" and "*Old School*—Hemingway and the Prodigal." The chapter "Novel Theology" will include *The Great Gatsby* by F. Scott Fitzgerald and *A Prayer for Owen Meany* by John Irving. The reason I chose them will be self-evident, but to put it in a rather prosaic way, these two books represent the Lutheran distinction between law and gospel that is, no matter what anyone might say, fundamental to the biblical narrative.[6] The second chapter, on *Old School* by Tobias Wolff, has become inextricably intertwined with my own identity because it's about prep school in the 1960s, about honor and shame, and about Ernest Hemingway, who was revered by us at Andover. But most importantly, this short novel cannot be understood apart from the parable of the prodigal son, a lodestar in my teaching. Perhaps these chapters on these three novels will inspire readers to take up these books to discover their Christian themes.

The Great Gatsby

Many people believe *The Great Gatsby*[7] is the greatest American novel of the 20th century. Fitzgerald knew that he had written a masterpiece. He told his editor, Maxwell Perkins, "I want to write something new—something extraordinary and beautiful and simple and intricately patterned." T. S. Eliot said of it, "In fact, it seems to me the first step American fiction has taken since Henry James."[8] But the critics didn't review it well, even though they thought it well crafted. Most considered it light fiction. Fitzgerald believed that everyone misunderstood what he was trying to say: "Of all the reviews, even the most enthusiastic, not one had the slightest idea what the book was about." In his lifetime, it didn't sell well, and he died not knowing that it would become the classic of classics.

It is a classic because it's about the great American dream—the Green Light—a failed dream, however, but still available to everyone,

6. To be fair, the critique is against a wooden and false use of the distinction of law and gospel, especially superimposing it on the biblical text that misinterprets the intent of the author.

7. Fitzgerald, *Great Gatsby*.

8. FABER AND GWYER LTD. Publishers 24 Russell Square, London, W.C.1. 31st December, 1925 F. Scott Fitzgerald, Esqre., % Charles Scribners & Sons, New York City.

starting with those Dutch sailors who first saw "a fresh, green breast of the new world," from that lyrical conclusion to the novel. It was a sad dream too, because there's no one honorable or admirable in this book. Even Nick, the narrator, fails on both accounts and is, perhaps, the most tragic figure in the whole book. It's even hard to love Gatsby, whom some critics see as a Christ figure because the novel ends with Gatsby stretching out his arms and his hands like Christ on the cross. There are even some who see Gatsby, carrying his air mattress to the pool, as a parallel to Jesus' *Via Dolorosa*, for both are carrying "the instruments of their death."

What is Fitzgerald trying to say? *The Great Gatsby* could be described as a kind of metanarrative of the reality Fitzgerald sees in the Jazz Age (1920s—between the two World Wars). The gospel, according to Gatsby, is the American dream, a dream focused on materialism and wealth. America as the land of opportunity, where anyone can pull themselves up by their bootstraps, where anyone can be Horatio Alger. In some ways, it's all about the pursuit of greatness. Gatsby is the *great* hero who, by embarking on his *great* voyage from Minnesota around the world to West Egg, Long Island, with the *great* goal of reclaiming Daisy as his own, undergoes the *great* dangers of bootlegging and gambling and Tom Buchanan's *great* carelessness.

The greatness of *The Great Gatsby* is defined by this great carelessness, portrayed as a journey from Long Island to Manhattan where one must go through the Valley of the Ashes—a violent and murderous passage—a tragic one—the heart of Gatsby's failed dream. Fitzgerald is replacing the grand, universal narrative that he grew up with as a Roman Catholic—the narrative of a Messiah born in Bethlehem under the humblest conditions—with another Messiah, James Gatz from humble North Dakota, whose smaller, local narrative about the virtues of the West versus the carelessness of the East helps explain the material world of the Jazz Age. Gatsby is Gatz *reinvented* as the quintessential American entrepreneur, "a 'son-of-god' who is about his Father's business . . ."

> The truth was that Jay Gatsby, of West Egg, Long Island, sprang from his Platonic conception of himself. He was a son of God—a phrase which, if it means anything, means just that—and he must be about His Father's Business, the service of a vast, vulgar and meretricious beauty. So he invented just the sort of Jay Gatsby that a seventeen-year-old boy would be likely to invent, and to this conception he was faithful to the end.[9]

9. Fitzgerald, *Great Gatsby*, 104.

One of the reasons we read novels is to see our humanity revealed to us by men and women who are astute observers of human nature. Up until recently, these observations were grounded in a Judeo-Christian morality. This is true of *The Great Gatsby.* In reading Fitzgerald, you know that he knows the Bible. Today, however, our postmodern and post-Christian world has lost its connection to the biblical story, the story of our faith. As Robert Jenson puts it, "The world has lost its story."[10] Questions about where we come from, where we are going, and how we are to live along the way used to be addressed by the culture through the "realistic narrative" of the Bible that made sense to the world as it shaped its story. It wasn't too long ago that even those who were not very religious would have to tell the story of world in a way that was inseparable from the biblical narrative as told by God, the "universal storyteller."[11] In fact, one would not be considered an educated person, read good literature, converse with others unless one was knowledgeable of the Bible. But this is not true anymore. The world no longer knows the story and therefore does not order its life according to the themes of that story. In previous generations, the church assumed a rudimentary understanding of the contents of the Scriptures by the culture, and they ordered their mission with the knowledge that the world shaped its story according to the realistic narrative of Scripture.

Unless you know the biblical story, you cannot understand how Gatsby is "a son of God . . . about His Father's Business." Fitzgerald clearly knew the final story in Luke's infancy narrative, how it announces through the twelve-year-old Jesus his destiny, that His Father's Business was bloody sacrifices in a temple, which points to the temple of Jesus' body offered up on the cross. That's why Jesus can say the temple is His Father's House, a place of sacrifice, and the business of that house is a bloody one. So also, Fitzgerald announces Gatsby's destiny—he will be sacrificed upon the cross of carelessness that comes from devoting himself to all those "glittering things" (see below). If Jesus' cross is a cross of expiation, Gatsby's cross (the mattress) runs afoul the mystery of love gone all wrong because its metanarrative was the failed American materialistic dream. Fitzgerald could only write about Gatsby as "a son of God . . . about His Father's Business" if he knew the Bible and grew up in the church.

10. Jenson, "How the World Lost Its Story," 19–24.

11. Jenson, "How the World Lost Its Story," 21.

Most commentators of *The Great Gatsby* do not consider seriously enough that Fitzgerald was a Roman Catholic living in a Calvinist world. Saul Bellow, however, understood this in his novel, *Humboldt's Gift*:

> "If Scott Fitzgerald had been a Protestant," said Humboldt, "Success wouldn't have damaged him so much. Look at Rockefeller Senior, he knew how to handle Success, he simply said that God had given him all his dough. Of course that was stewardship. That was Calvinism."[12]

James Gatz of North Dakota "sprang from his Platonic conception of himself." Platonism is anti-Catholic because it is anti-matter, anti-stuff, now dressed up in the new clothes of Calvinism and rationalism and modernism. The world, the body, the flesh doesn't really matter. Some Protestants even go so far as to bifurcate body and soul—the body bad, the soul good (to cite my dear colleague Larry Rast). What matters is a twisted cosmology that yearns and looks for a greater reality in the transcendent. Daisy—the house and the parties—was Gatsby's transcendence. Lovely until you get shot in your own swimming pool. But what nags at us in reading *The Great Gatsby* is that Fitzgerald understood, perhaps subconsciously, that the worldview he grew up with was antithetical to Princeton's Presbyterian roots, where he came of age as a writer and an adult.

The irony is that Fitzgerald's Gatsby is not a good Catholic but a good Protestant, a Lutheran to be exact, who believes in the Protestant work ethic, the great end and real business of living.[13] Humboldt didn't go far enough. Gatsby's the good Calvinist, which is why success didn't really damage him. What damaged him was his dream. Jay Gatsby is James Gatz's imperfect copy of an eternal, heavenly, transcendent person who was in love with Daisy in Louisville during the war years, a young girl he took for himself in an almost violent way—"ravenously and unscrupulously" is the way Fitzgerald puts it—"took her because he had no real right to touch her hand."[14] The whole thing is a sham, a rationalistic

12. Bellow, *Humboldt's Gift*, 17.

13. This phrase comes from the 1778 Constitution of Phillips Academy in Andover, Massachusetts. The founder, Samuel Phillips Jr., set out "to lay the foundation of a public free School or Academy for the purpose of instructing Youth, not only in English and Latin Grammar, Writing, Arithmetic, and those Sciences, wherein they are commonly taught; but more especially to learn them *the Great End and Real Business of Living*" (italics mine). The first time I read Gatsby, I was at Andover.

14. Fitzgerald, *Great Gatsby*, 156.

construction so that Gatsby might be a god to the great American dream, to the great end and real business of living.

What stunned Gatsby was that his dream wasn't materialism—it was love. He was shocked that he fell in love with Daisy, the perfect Platonic person for his perfect Platonic image of himself. His problem, though, was that he fell in love *with a real person, flesh and blood*, and she with him. Listen to the honestly of this paragraph.

> "I can't describe to you how surprised I was to find out I love her, old sport. I even hoped for a while that she'd throw me over, but she didn't, because she was in love with me too. She thought I knew a lot because I knew different things from her . . . Well, there I was, way off my ambitions, getting deeper in love every minute, and all of a sudden I didn't care. What was the use of doing great things if I could have a better time telling her what I was going to do?"[15]

Gatsby may appear shallow with the pretense of the house, the clothes, the yellow car, and those shirts(!!!), but in the end it was all about love. The problem is that Daisy was not worth the dream or the pilgrimage to that dream. Yes, *The Great Gatsby* is a pilgrimage book. And it's Catholic too. Although I just called Gatsby a good Protestant, he's also a good Lutheran, or better, an evangelical Catholic. He falls in love with *the mystery* of Daisy. Nick knows it—"there was a ripe mystery about it"—for Gatsby "had committed himself to the following of a grail."[16]

There was much soul-searching among the literati after the first World War. It seemed during the "roaring twenties" as if "the world had lost its story." During World War I, you had French and German Christians hunkered down for ten months in 1916 killing each other, estimates running from a half a million to a million casualties. No wonder T. S. Eliot felt compelled to publish *The Wasteland* (1922). Fitzgerald may have been influenced by this great poem. *The Great Gatsby* was written in 1925. Its themes were part of the conversation in the 1920s. What Fitzgerald writes about is a moral wasteland—a wasteland where carelessness is the operating procedure for life. Which is why between the two places in this novel where people travel—West/East Egg and New York City—is a valley of ashes, like Eliot's valley of dry bones—a wasteland—an image Eliot borrowed from Ezekiel and Fitzgerald may have borrowed from Eliot.

15. Fitzgerald, *Great Gatsby*, 157.

16. Fitzgerald, *Great Gatsby*, 155–56.

What happens in the valley of ashes between the sordid characters is the embodiment of the moral wasteland. Death occurs in the valley of ashes.

Eliot published his poem *The Hollow Men* the same year *Gatsby* came out, so Fitzgerald couldn't have read it. But *The Hollow Men* captures Dante's portrayal of the entrance into hell in *Inferno, Canto III*, and Fitzgerald, like Eliot, was influenced by Dante. In Dante's *Purgatorio*, Beatrice's eyes represent the spiritual reality that Dante longs for but also dreads. He ascends into paradise by fixing himself on Beatrice's eyes. Not many have compared Gatsby's obsession with Daisy with Dante's obsession with Beatrice. Dante sees Beatrice once, when she's eight and he's nine, and not again for nine more years, and these were both passing encounters. She marries someone else, dies young, he marries someone else, and after Beatrice's death, writes this incredible prose/poem about her called "La Vita Nuova" (The New Life), which is about his love for her. And she is of course the character in Dante's *Divine Comedy* that guides him through the afterlife, a sort of embodiment of spiritual love. It's such a wonderful love story. But what does Eliot say in *The Hollow Men*—the "Eyes I dare not meet in dreams/In death's dream kingdom." These must be Beatrice's eyes.

After the death scene in the valley of ashes George Wilson, the husband of Myrtle—the woman who dies after Daisy hits her with a car (she was the mistress of Daisy's husband Tom)—George is asked in his grief what appear to be a random series of questions:

> "Have you got a church you go to sometimes, George? Maybe even if you haven't been there for a long time? Maybe I could call up the church and get a priest to come over and he could talk to you, see?"
>
> "Don't belong to any."
>
> "You ought to have a church, George, for times like this. You must have gone to church once. Didn't you get married in a church? Listen, George, listen to me. Didn't you get married in a church?"
>
> "That was a long time ago."[17]

Fitzgerald repeats "church" six times and wonders if George should call a priest. This is a natural request for a good Catholic. But Wilson has no church, and if Fitzgerald had even a remnant of Catholicism left in him, he would know that the Roman Catholic Church teaches that

17. Fitzgerald, *Great Gatsby*, 165.

there is no salvation outside the church. Not having a church is like not having a God. But there was a God for Fitzgerald in his youth, and even a couple of priests who were very important to Fitzgerald growing up. He had a cousin, Thomas Delihunt, a Jesuit, with whom he was very close. He went to a Catholic prep school, the Newman School in Hackensack, New Jersey, which is probably why he's so well read—because it was a great school. There was a priest there too, Father Sigourney Fay, who had such a huge influence over Fitzgerald that he dedicated his first novel to him, the novel that brought him fame, *This Side of Paradise*. Father Fay was urbane and witty, a society priest, and the model for Monsignor Thayer Darcy in *This Side of Paradise*, who was a significant influence for Amory Blaine, the protagonist in the novel. Blaine had a moment when he wanted out, wanted to flee to Mexico, to escape, or—to cite Fitzgerald—to be "delivered from right and wrong and from the hound of heaven." Fitzgerald published *This Side of Paradise* in 1920, and Fay died in 1919. Friends say that Fitzgerald was devastated by Fay's death. That he had lost his best friend. But it wasn't his death that led Fitzgerald to declare he was no longer Catholic. Fitzgerald had already declared his self-excommunication the year before, in 1918, saying that it was his "last year as a Catholic." That's quite an admission to make, that at the age of twenty-two, one was leaving the church.

There is a short story entitled "Absolution" that Fitzgerald wrote as a prelude to *The Great Gatsby*. It is one of the saddest stories I've ever read. We read it in our "Theologia: Lord's Supper" class, and students are stunned by the theological acumen of Fitzgerald and the despair it represents. It recalls what Augustine said about God as "the tremendous lover":

> Heaven and earth and all that is in the universe cries out to me
> from all directions,
> that I, O God, must love you.[18]

Perhaps Fitzgerald heard this cry when he wrote "Absolution" and *The Great Gatsby*. From the citation above from *This Side of Paradise*, Fitzgerald knew Thompson's poem. But a good Lutheran, even a good Catholic, knows you can't love God unless you know that God loves you. We long for God's love so that we can, in return, love him. To love him is to love ourselves and then our neighbor as ourselves. It's at the heart

18. Scott, "God, the Hound of Heaven," 39.

of Jesus' teaching. Yet, at the end of his poem, Thompson has this plea of God to us:

> Whom wilt thou find to love ignoble thee,
> Save Me, save only Me?[19]

One wonders if Fitzgerald was asking that very question when he wrote *The Great Gatsby.* He knew Gatsby's dream was the wrong one. Fitzgerald knew it when he wrote "Absolution" in June of 1923. I had not read this short story until recently, and it is the key, the lens through which to read *The Great Gatsby.* Fitzgerald suggests this to his editor Maxwell Perkins: "As you know it was to have been the prologue of the novel but it interfered with the neatness of the plan."[20] Rudolph Miller from "Absolution" is a foretaste of James Gatz, who becomes Jay Gatsby. And this short story has a priest. The opening line of "Absolution" says it all:

> There was once a priest with cold, watery eyes, who, in the still of the night, wept cold tears. He wept because the afternoons were warm and long, and he was *unable to attain a complete mystical union with our Lord.*[21]

His watery eyes are a theme right out of *The Great Gatsby.* But what startles here is "*a complete mystical union with our Lord.*" Not with God but with our Lord, who is Jesus. The whole story is about making confession and taking holy communion with a soul cleansed and worthy to receive the body and blood of Christ. Fitzgerald knows his Catholicism. How else could he write a line like this one about Rudolph Miller—"or else to tempt the thunderbolts by receiving the Body and Blood of Christ with sacrilege upon his soul"—as Rudolph contemplates a beating from his father for not going to communion. Rudolph's inner thoughts are about what it means to sin and make confession. And despite feeling unworthy, Rudolph takes communion:

> The bell rang sharply, and the priest turned from the altar with the white Host held above the chalice:
> "*Corpus Domini nostri Jesu Christi custodiat animam mean in vitam aeternam.*"[22]

19. Thompson, *Hound of Heaven,* stanza 6, lines 9–10.
20. Kuehl and Bryer, *Dear Scott/Dear Max,* 72.
21. Fitzgerald, "Absolution," 259 (emphasis Fitzgerald).
22. Fitzgerald, "Absolution," 268.

So, the priest comes to Rudolph with the host and says, "May the Body of our Lord Jesus Christ preserve my soul to life everlasting." What Fitzgerald now says about Rudolph receiving the body of Christ says it all about Fitzgerald's struggle with the hound of heaven:

> Rudolph opened his mouth. He felt the sticky wax taste of the wafer on his tongue. He remained motionless for what seemed an interminable period of time, his head still raised, the wafer undissolved in his mouth. Then again he started at the pressure of his father's elbow, and saw that the people were falling away from the altar like leaves and turning with blind downcast eyes to their pews, alone with God.
>
> Rudolph was alone with himself, drenched with perspiration and deep in mortal sin. As he walked back to his pew the sharp taps of his cloven hoofs were loud upon the floor, and he knew that it was a dark poison he carried in his heart.[23]

Everyone else is alone with God, but Rudolph is alone with himself, unworthy of the holiness stuck to the roof of his mouth. He's unclean, walking back from receiving holiness filled with Satan's dark poison. He has committed blasphemy. Rudolph is Fitzgerald—Fitzgerald is Rudolph. But the holocaust is not complete. Rudolph has enough faith to go back to Father Adolphus Schwartz, his priest with cold, watery eyes to confess his sin and receive absolution for the dark poison in his heart. But it wasn't going to happen. Fr. Schwartz is of the devil too, 'the beads of his rosary were crawling and squirming like snakes upon the green felt of his table top.' His absolution to Rudolph is this—the theme of *The Great Gatsby*:

> "When a lot of people get together in the best places things go glimmering."[24]

Glimmering! Then he says:

> "The thing is to have a lot of people in the center of the world, wherever that happens to be. Then"—his watery eyes widened knowingly—"things go glimmering."[25]

Glimmering again! As Rudolph says, "This man is crazy." Fr. Schwartz keeps repeating this thing about things going glimmering. That's his absolution for Rudolph. He's pointing Rudolph to West Egg, to

23. Fitzgerald, "Absolution," 269.

24. Fitzgerald, "Absolution," 270.

25. Fitzgerald, "Absolution," 270.

that glimmering mansion with glimmering people in one of those glimmering parties Gatsby would throw to impress Daisy. Rudolph gets it. He understands what this all means:

> All this talking seemed particularly strange and awful to Rudolph, because this man was a priest. He sat there, half terrified, his beautiful eyes open wide and starring at Father Schwartz. But underneath his terror he felt that his own inner convictions were confirmed. There was something ineffably gorgeous somewhere that had nothing to do with God.[26]

That "something ineffably gorgeous somewhere that had nothing to do with God" is *The Great Gatsby.* That's Gatsby's shattered dream, shattered in a godless place, a valley of ashes, Doctor T. J. Eckleberg looking out with unseeing eyes. "Absolution" started with Father Schwartz looking for a mystical union with his Lord and ends with him crying "Oh, my God!", and with Fitzgerald's beatific vision, his view from this side of paradise:

> Outside the window the blue scirocco trembled over the wheat, and girls with yellow hair walked sensuously along the roads that bounded the fields, calling innocent, exciting things to the young men who were working in the lines between the grain. Legs were shaped under starch-less gingham, and rims of the necks of dresses were warm and damp. For five hours now hot fertile life had burned in the afternoon. It would be night in three hours, and all along the land there would be these blonde Northern girls and the tall young men from the farms lying out beside the wheat, under the moon.[27]

F. Scott Fitzgerald knew that hound of heaven was after him. He knew the truth of the Scriptures and his Catholicism, even though he may not have believed it. If only he, and his characters Father Schwartz and Rudolph and Gatsby, heeded these words from "The Hound of Heaven." God is calling all of them to come home.

> All which thy child's mistake
> Fancies as lost, I have stored for thee at home:
> Rise, clasp My hand, and come![28]

26. Fitzgerald, "Absolution," 271.
27. Fitzgerald, "Absolution," 272.
28. Thompson, *Hound of Heaven*, stanza 6, lines 14–16.

So, does Fitzgerald come home? Can we say of Fitzgerald what he said of Gatsby—"Blessed are the dead that the rain falls on?" Fitzgerald ends "Absolution" in the Midwest in the wheat fields, under the moon. *The Great Gatsby* ends in the East, on the shores of Long Island, under the same moon as in "Absolution." Perhaps these final words of *The Great Gatsby* by Nick Carroway describe Fitzgerald's attempt to escape from the hound of heaven—"borne back ceaselessly into the past."

> Most of the big shore places were closed now and there were hardly any lights except the shadowy, moving glow of a ferry-boat across the Sound. And as a moon rose higher the inessential houses began to melt away until gradually I became aware of the old island here that flowered once for Dutch sailor's eyes—a fresh, green breast of the new world. Its vanished trees, the trees that had made way for Gatsby's house, had once pandered in whispers to the last and greatest of all human dreams; for a transitory enchanted moment man must have held his breath in the presence of this continent, compelled into an aesthetic contemplation he neither understood nor desired, face to face for the last time in history with something commensurate to his capacity for wonder.
>
> And as I sat there, brooding on the old unknown world, I thought of Gatsby's wonder when he first picked out the green light at the end of Daisy's dock. He had come a long way to this blue lawn and his dream must have seemed so close that he could hardly fail to grasp it. He did not know that it was already behind him, somewhere back in that vast obscurity beyond the city, where the dark fields of the republic rolled on under the night.
>
> Gatsby believed in the green light, the orgiastic future that year by year recedes before us. It eluded us then, but that's no matter—tomorrow we will run faster, stretch out our arms farther. . . . And one fine morning—
>
> So we beat on, boats against the current, borne back ceaselessly into the past.[29]

A Prayer for Owen Meany

In some ways my interest in novel theology all began with *A Prayer for Owen Meany* (henceforth referred to as *Owen Meany*) by John Irving.[30]

29. Fitzgerald, *Great Gatsby*, 189.
30. Irving, *Prayer for Owen Meany*.

Irving came to fame with his novel *The World According to Garp,* which I've never read. However, his *Hotel New Hampshire* caught my attention because Irving was a New Hampshire boy, born in Exeter, and a graduate of Phillips Exeter ten years before I graduated from its rival, Phillips Andover in Massachusetts.[31] But it was *A Prayer for Owen Meany,* published in 1989, the year my son Jake was born, that captured my imagination. My dear friend Peter Ledic was the one who introduced me to this book while he served as pastor of Immanuel Lutheran Church in Decatur, Indiana. It was shocking to read such a deeply "Christian" novel from John Irving. This novel became a rite of passage in our family when you became a teenager. What I discovered in Irving was the joy of uncovering Christian themes in his novel. As someone who has come to love the apostle Paul through his epistle to the Galatians, I will focus on the Pauline typology in *Owen Meany.* And I'll let you hear Irving's voice by citing large sections of his novel.

John Irving tells an outrageous story, as he does in most of his books. *Owen Meany* is a little over the top. Yet it's a story that you can follow and become involved in. Irving always has a plot, and he ties it up very neatly at the end with an extraordinarily moving conclusion. And there is always, in his own words, *information.* He's not a wordsmith like he accuses many contemporary writers of being. But I love the way he uses language. As he says of himself, he follows in the tradition of nineteenth-century writers—Dickens, Hardy, Tolstoy, Hawthorne, Melville—great writers not obsessed with "originality of language" but with "the larger, plainer things . . . the story, the characters, the laughter, and the tears." Irving likes to compare himself to Dickens. Irving's comparison of himself to Dickens explains a lot about *Owen Meany.* Listen to what he says:

> George Bernard Shaw, who admitted to getting most of his satiric methods from Dickens, said that the thing to do is to find one true thing and exaggerate it, with levity, until it's obvious. I know it is not very postmodernist to be obvious, but politically one has to become more and more that way.[32]

The "one true thing" that Irving offers us in *Owen Meany* is faith—and the miracles that produce faith as they are embodied in the character

31. Phillips Academy in Andover, Massachusetts, was founded in 1778 by Samuel Phillips. Three years later in 1781 his uncle, Dr. John Phillips, founded Phillips Academy in Exeter, New Hampshire. They have been fierce rivals ever since.

32. Irving, *Paris Review,* 1986. See also Plimpton, *Writers at Work,* 425.

of Owen Meany. And then Irving exaggerates it. In this way, he is no modernist but either premodern or postmodern. He wants us to believe in the supernatural—that faith exists and miracles do happen. His book is about faith in faith. It's about the faith of Johnny, Owen Meany's best friend and the narrator of the book. The book begins and ends with faith. Here's the beginning:

> I am doomed to remember a boy with a wrecked voice—not because of his voice, or because he was the smallest person I never knew, or even because he was the instrument of my mother's death, but because he is the reason I believe in God; I am a Christian because of Owen Meany.[33]

In the conclusion, Johnny refers to that prayer Owen Meany prayed over the grave of Johnny's mother, Tabitha: INTO PARADISE MAY THE ANGELS LEAD YOU.[34] (When Owen speaks, Irving puts his speech in CAPITAL LETTERS!) Tabitha, beloved by Owen, died at his hands when she was hit by his foul ball in a baseball game. Johnny, who struggled with doubt, comes to believe in the resurrection and speaks these same words over Owen's grave. That's the prayer for Owen Meany: INTO PARADISE MAY THE ANGELS LEAD YOU. That's the prayer we should pray for everyone: INTO PARADISE MAY THE ANGELS LEAD YOU. Owen believed that with his whole heart. That's why Owen wasn't afraid. He believed INTO PARADISE MAY THE ANGELS LEAD YOU. It's "the one true thing"—faith and miracles—with paradise as the end of faith's pilgrimage—the final miracle. Here's the conclusion to *Owen Meany:*

> There's a prayer I say most often for Owen. It's one of the little prayers he said for my mother, the night Hester and I found him in the cemetery—where he'd brought the flashlight, because he knew how my mother hated the darkness.
>
> "INTO PARADISE MAY THE ANGELS LEAD YOU," he'd said over my mother's grave; and so I say that one for him—I know it was one of his favorites.
>
> I am always saying prayers for Owen Meany.
>
> And I often try to imagine how I might have answered Mary Beth Baird, when she spoke to me—at Owen's burial. If I could have spoken, if I hadn't lost my voice—what would I have said to her, how could I have answered her? Poor Mary Beth Baird? I left her standing in the cemetery without an answer.

33. Irving, *Prayer for Owen Meany*, 13.

34. Irving, *Prayer for Owen Meany*, 131.

> "Do you remember how we used to lift him up?" she'd asked me. "He was so easy to lift up!" Mary Beth had said to me. "He was so light—he weighed nothing at all! How could he have been so light?" the former Virgin Mother had asked me.
>
> I could have told her that it was only our illusion that Owen Meany weighed "nothing at all." We were only children—we are only children—I could have told her. What did we ever know about Owen Meany? What did we truly know? We had the impression that everything was a game—we thought we made everything up as we went along. When we were children, we had the impression that almost everything was just for fun—no harm intended, no damage done.
>
> When we held Owen Meany above our heads, when we passed him back and forth—so effortlessly—we believed that Owen weighed nothing at all. We did not realize that there were forces beyond our play. Now I know they were the forces that contributed to our illusion of Owen's weightlessness; they were the forces we didn't have the faith to feel, they were the forces we failed to believe in—and they were also lifting up Owen Meany, taking him out of our hands.
>
> O God—please give him back! I shall keep asking You.[35]

What makes Irving so readable are his characters, and the character of Owen Meany sets this book apart. He is an antihero, small and strange looking, not a great physical presence but outspoken, confident, and very clear on who he is. Perhaps this is why so many people love this book, why Irving is a bestseller. Phil Jackson, former coach of Michael Jordan's Chicago Bulls and then coach of the Los Angeles Lakers, had some of his players read *Owen Meany.* He sees this book as worth reading for professional basketball players. *Owen Meany's* appeal is its accent on identity and destiny and faith. Many of us want to identify with Owen Meany because he knows his identity. His friend Johnny is afraid because he doesn't know who he is. Johnny needs Owen to show him the way. Owen is not afraid because *he believes in the resurrection of the body*. This book is all about the resurrection and the body and the resurrection of the body.

Owen is not afraid because he knows about the end of his life, an end he sees written on a tombstone in *The Christmas Carol*, a play that occurs in the middle of the novel, with Owen as the baby Jesus (one of the most outrageous chapters in the book—where Mary Beth Baird plays the

35. Irving, *Prayer for Owen Meany*, 542–43.

Virgin Mary). Owen records this as the last entry in his diary: "TODAY'S THE DAY! '. . . HE THAT BELIEVETH IN ME, THOUGH HE WERE DEAD, YET SHALL HE LIVE; AND WHOSOEVER LIVETH AND BELIEVETH IN ME SHALL NEVER DIE.'"[36]

This emphasis on the resurrection of the body comes from St. Paul whom Owen resembles. Both St. Paul and Owen are described as "chosen instruments"[37]—in fact, it is what sets Owen apart because he knows he was chosen for something miraculous, but he and the reader don't find out his destiny until the last pages of the book. St. Paul is described as "untimely born," Owen as "born too soon."[38] Throughout *Owen Meany*, Irving portrays him as a "freak"—his voice, his size, his weight, his enormous head. This could also be said of Paul. The expression "untimely born" used of St. Paul describes a child from miscarriage or abortion, unformed, undeveloped, repulsive, "a monster," "horrible thing."[39] In 2 Corinthians Paul's opponents mocked his physical appearance, saying he was some sort of a freak—he himself uses the word "fool"—and that is certainly what his opponents say of him, especially his rhetoric, and, one could conclude, his voice. In 2 Corinthians 10, Paul says, "For they say, 'His letters are weighty and strong, but his bodily presence is weak, and his speech of no account.'" Paul doesn't dispute this, and most agree that up against his opponent's rhetorical skills, these so-called superlativea-postles, Paul was no match. He goes on to call himself a "fool for Christ" and that "I am speaking as a fool," boasting in his weakness, in his suffering. In fact, the *Acts of Paul and Thecla*, a much later document than anything written in the New Testament, describes Paul as "a man small of stature, with a bald head and crooked legs, in a good state of body, with

36. Irving, *Prayer for Owen Meany*, 534.

37. Acts 9:15–16: "Go, for he is a chosen instrument of mine to carry my name before the Gentiles and kings, and the children of Israel. For I will show him how much he must suffer for the sake of my name."

38. First Corinthians 15:8, the chapter on the resurrection: "Last of all, as to one untimely born, he appeared also to me." See Irving, *Prayer for Owen Meany*, 14–15, who describes Owen like this: "[Owen] was the color of a gravestone; light was both absorbed and reflected by his skin, as with a pearl, so that he appeared translucent at times—especially at his temples, where his blue veins showed through his skin (as though, in addition to his extraordinary size, there were other evidence that *he was born too soon.*) His vocal cords had not been developed fully, or else his voice had been injured by the rock dust of the family's business."

39. Bauer, *Greek-English Lexicon*, 275.

eyebrows meeting and nose somewhat hooked, full of friendliness; for now he appeared like a man, and now he had the face of an angel."[40]

In the ancient world this description of Paul is that of a *hero.* Paul's physical appearance would make him to be a hero in that time and place. Owen Meany is like Paul—a hero and a martyr who give up their lives. John Irving begins *Owen Meany* with a citation from Leon Bloy's book *The Pilgrim of the Absolute*, which says: "Any Christian who is not a hero is a pig." Irving has been accused of being too obvious, but the clincher on the St. Paul/Owen comparison is that Owen's real name is Paul. Like Paul, Owen has visions, and in one of them he sees his name, his *real* name, on the grave—Paul O. Meany Jr.—and in Owen's words, "IT SAID THE WHOLE THING." Johnny gets it when he says, "Of course, he needed a saint's name, like St. Paul; if there is a St. Owen, I've never heard of him."[41]

Throughout *Owen Meany* there is a sense of foreboding, as Owen becomes increasingly aware that he was chosen for a purpose, an angel sent from God, with a destiny of great importance. Johnny, in reflecting on this, confirms that Irving wants us to understand Owen as the apostle Paul, and he sums up why this book is about faith, identity, and destiny:

> That was when I first began to think about certain events or specific things being "important' and having "special purpose." Until then, the notion that anything had a designated, much less a special purpose would have been cuckoo to me. I was not what was commonly called a believer then, and I am a believer now; I believe in God, and I believe in the "special purpose" of certain events or specific things. I observe all holy days, which only the most old-fashioned Anglicans call red-letter days. It was a red-letter day, fairly recently, when I had reason to think of Owen Meany—it was January 25, 1987, when the lesson proper for the conversion of St. Paul reminded me of Owen. The Lord says to Jeremiah,
>
> Before I formed you in the womb
>   I knew you,
> and before you were born
>   I consecrated you;
> I appointed you a prophet to the
>   nations.

40. *Acts of Paul and Thecla*, 3:2.

41. Irving, *Prayer for Owen Meany*, 368–69.

> But Jeremiah says he doesn't know how to speak; he's "only a youth," Jeremiah says. Then the Lord straightens him out about that; the Lord says,
>
> Do not say, "I am only a youth";
> for to all to whom I send you
>   you shall go,
> and whatever I command you
>   you shall speak.
> Be not afraid of them,
> for I am with you to deliver you,
>   says the Lord.
>
> Then the Lord touches Jeremiah's mouth, and says,
>
> Behold, I have put my words
>   in your mouth.
> See, I have set you this day over
>   nations and over kingdoms,
> to pluck up and to break down,
> to destroy and to overthrow,
> to build and to plant.
>
> It is on red-letter days, especially, that I think about Owen; sometimes I think about him too intensely, and that's usually when I skip a Sunday service, or two—and I try not to pick up my prayer book for a while. I suppose the conversion of St. Paul has a special effect on a convert like me.
>
> And how can I *not* think of Owen—when I read Paul's letter to the Galatians, that part where Paul says, "And I was still not known by sight to the church of Christ in Judea; they only heard it said, 'He who once persecuted us is now preaching the faith he once tried to destroy.' And they glorified God because of me.'[42] How well I know that feeling! I trust in God because of Owen Meany.[43]

A Prayer for Owen Meany ends with Owen's great act of heroism in saving the lives of Asian children and the nuns who accompany them. His courage saves them but leads to his death. But before he dies, Owen sees the fulfillment of his destiny, the goal of a tradition and its ritual he had followed for his short but meaningful life. It is a moment of pure ecstasy as he makes his "rite of passage" from life through death into paradise.

42. Irving may not have realized that Paul sees his calling and his birth in line with the prophets, like Isaiah and Jeremiah, where he says in Gal 1, "But when he who had set me apart before I was born, and who called me by his grace."

43. Irving, *Prayer for Owen Meany*, 83–84.

"I'M AWFULLY COLD, SISTER—CAN'T YOU DO SOMETHING?" as he lay dying in the arms of one of the nuns. "Then whatever had troubled him passed over him completely, and he smiled again—he looked at us all with his old, infuriating smile"[44]—the smile of the beatific vision, of angels leading him into paradise. As Johnny lifted him up to save the children so now is Owen's final lifting up into his own salvation. Owen's final mystical experience—his final *Catholic* moment as the angels carry him into paradise—makes one think of Jesus' words to the thief on the cross, "Today, you will be with me in paradise."

It was disconcerting, though, that Owen seems to have a moment of uncertainty, after he had just comforted that poor nun with "WHOSOEVER LIVETH AND BELIEVETH IN ME SHALL NEVER DIE."[45] He seems stricken to Johnny, "something deeper and darker than pain crossed his face," and then the cold, as if the devil was coming for him. But then the smile, the beatific smile of certainty, the final truth appears before his eyes, and he has joy at the freedom he is about to enter. This is Owen's rite of passage into paradise. At Owen's funeral, Johnny is reminded of the note in the *Book of Common Prayer*, in connection with "An Order for Burial." He calls this note sensible. It is more than sensible. It's what Owen believed with his whole heart and what we too should believe.

> The liturgy for the dead is an Easter liturgy . . . It finds all its meaning in the resurrection. Because Jesus was raised from the dead, we, too, shall be raised. The liturgy, therefore, is characterized by joy . . . This joy, however, does not make human grief unchristian . . .[46]

Owen is the noble hero, but he is more. That's what Irving wants us to remember—"that Owen Meany had been a miracle, too." He believed *with understanding* that he was part of this greater story, that his destiny was in God's hands, even though he didn't know all the particulars. His whole life was for that one moment where he would save the children. Like Leon Bloy, he came home to Rome, albeit more dramatically, in the arms of a nun. But like Leon Bloy, who led Jacques Maritain and George Rouault back to Roman Catholic church, Owen helped Johnny come back, maybe not all the way to Rome but to Canterbury, which, for Owen, was better than the Congregationalists. Leon Bloy was right—Owen was

44. Irving, *Prayer for Owen Meany*, 541.

45. Irving, *Prayer for Owen Meany*, 541.

46. Irving, *Prayer for Owen Meany*, 497.

a Christian—and he was a hero. Owen's "Catholic" pilgrimage ended in the arms of a nun who held him as he was carried by the angels into paradise. How will Johnny's pilgrimage end? How will yours end? How will mine? I now understand that it's about God's search for me—my pilgrimage began and ended in Wittenberg, for which I am most grateful because Lutheranism will always be my home.

But there are a couple things that still haunt me about this book. Johnny learned from Owen that this much is true—miracles matter, the body matters, and that faith has consequences. There are not many heroes like Owen, for whom that passage from Mark at his funeral *does not* apply: "I believe; help my unbelief." But I believe Mark 9:24 applies to most of us. It applied to Johnny and to Johnny's father, Rev. Merrill, a chronic doubter, who presided at Owen's funeral and who discovered faith through Owen.

> When he finished reading this passage, Pastor Merrill lifted his face to us and cried out, "I believe; help my unbelief!" Owen Meany helped *my* "unbelief" . . . "Compared to Owen Meany, I am an amateur—in my faith," Mr. Merrill said. "Owen was not just a hero to the United States Army—he was *my* hero" . . . "He was *our* hero—over and over again, he was our hero; he was *always* our hero. And we will always miss him," the Rev. Merrill said.[47]

Owen Meany is *my* hero too, which is why I still cherish this book. But I can identify with Rev. Merrill and Johnny because I am like them—oh God, "I believe; help my unbelief!" I think we all need an Owen—to take care of our bodies, to help us embrace the suffering. I have hope for Johnny, because he now realizes that "there were forces beyond our play . . . forces we didn't have faith to feel . . . forces we failed to believe in—and they were lifting up Owen Meany, taking him out of our hands." Johnny now believes in those forces, and I think most of us want to believe in them too.

"O God—please give him back! I shall keep asking You."

47. Irving, *Prayer for Owen Meany*, 499.

5

Old School

Hemingway and the Prodigal

As a pastor and seminary professor, my taste in fiction shifted. Although I would occasionally return to the canon—Hemingway, Fitzgerald, James, Conrad, etc.—I began to seek out Christian writers and novelists. That's how I discovered Tobias Wolff and his novel *Old School.* It was through an article in 2005 in Commonweal by Paul Contino that I discovered both Wolff and *Old School.* Contino was a professor at Valparaiso University when Wolff published *Old School* (2003).[1] It's also how I discovered the eucharistic stories of Andre Dubus. Contino's article is entitled "This Writer's Life: Irony and Faith in the Work of Tobias Wolff."

The first two paragraphs showed why I needed to read Tobias Wolff:

> "I can't live without it." Tobias Wolff was talking to me about irony . . . Like any morally serious person, Wolff knows that irony has its risks: "Irony [can be] a way of not talking about the unspeakable . . . It can be used to deflect or even to deny what is difficult, painful, dangerous—that is, consequential" . . . As a Catholic, [Wolff] recognizes the myriad ways that irony can unsettle our imagined autonomy and sharpen an awareness that we need and are needed by others. Indeed, as the gospel narratives demonstrate, the Christian faith itself is made vital by an ironic story: the savior comes as a helpless infant, dies as an

1. Paul Contino taught at Christ College, Valparaiso, when my daughter Abigail was a student there.

> executed slave, and rises in glory on the third day. It is this kind of rich irony that Wolff's writing suggests: *the stories we tell, the narratives of our lives, are upended to make room for what we call God's story.*[2]

Wolff's claim is that the stories of our lives are upended by God's story, especially through the Gospel narratives. That's what preaching on the Gospels should do—upend our lives by helping us understand that the Gospel story is our story. Irony has also interested me, especially when applied to the Scriptures. Many believe it's impious to think of the Scriptures as "ironical," but in some ways, if Contino and Wolff are right, the Gospel story of Jesus' suffering, death, and resurrection is an ironic one. In my work on the Emmaus story, it certainly could be said that the unveiling of the passion and resurrection facts to the Emmaus disciples (or, even better, what Richard Dillon calls "the messianic passion-mystery") is deeply ironical.[3] The passion-mystery is both ironic and incomprehensible until it is reversed by the divine intervention of the risen Christ and only then, when he opens their eyes in the breaking of the bread.[4] Irony and mystery seem to go together, and without them the Scriptures would not be such a sublime narrative but just another dogmatic textbook. Ironical stories seduce you into the contemplating the mystery of our humanity in new and fresh ways, and this is especially true of the Scriptures where we are confronted with the mystery of our humanity in the divine flesh of Jesus.

The other reason I was intrigued by *Old School* was because it was semi-autobiographical, from Wolff's prep school days at The Hill School outside of Philadelphia, from 1960–61. Seven years later, in 1968, I would start my prep school career at Andover, so his description of prep school in the 1960s brought back memories of these most formative years of my life, especially the significance of the honor code and what I later would describe in my teaching as "honor and shame." Andover was all about

2. Contino, "This Writer's Life," 1.

3. Dillon, *From Eye-Witnesses*, 132.

4. Again, Dillon, *From Eye-Witnesses*, 19–20 (emphasis Dillon): "If the whole tomb experience is now to become a contrasting episode to the risen Lord's own instilling of the Easter faith (24:25ff.), then the painstaking establishment of all the *bruta facta* ["bare facts"] of the experience will serve only as the foil *ex parte hominis* ["on the part of man"] to the risen One's activity! . . . The *fact* of the empty tomb begets *perplexity* and requires the *interpreting word* of the angels. Here we encounter the first of three combinations of *unintelligible facts* versus *elucidating word* which will constitute the controlling pattern of this chapter's design (vv. 2–3 *vs.* 5–7; 19–24 *vs.* 25–27; 36–43 *vs.* 44–49)."

honor and shame. These categories first came to my attention through Jerome Neyrey and Bruce Malina's book *The Social World of Luke–Acts.* They define honor as "the positive value of a person in his or her own eyes plus the positive appreciation of that person in the eyes of his or her own social group."[5]

Teenagers live in an honor and shame culture, as they are discovering who they are and therefore care deeply about what others think about them. What resonated with me about *Old School* was how Wolff captured how important honor and shame were for us in prep school. If I had any doubts about whether I would like this book, Wolff's first three paragraphs clinched it.

> Robert Frost made his visit in November of 1960, just a week after the general election. It tells you something about our school that the prospect of his arrival cooked up more interest than the contest between Nixon and Kennedy, which for most of us was no contest at all. Nixon was a straight arrow and a scold. If he'd been one of us, we would have glued his shoes to the floor. Kennedy, though—here was a warrior, an ironist, terse and unhysterical. He had his clothes under control. His wife was a fox. And he read and wrote books, one of which, *Why England Slept*, was required reading in my honors history seminar. We recognized Kennedy; we could still see in him the boy who would have been a favorite here, roguish and literate, with that almost formal insouciance that both enacted and discounted the fact of his class.
>
> But we wouldn't have admitted that class played any part in our liking for Kennedy. Ours was not a snobbish school, or so it believed, and we made this as true as we could. Everyone did chores. Scholarship students could declare themselves or not, as they wished; the school itself gave no sign. It was understood that some of the boys might get a leg up from their famous names or great wealth, but if privilege immediately gave them a place, the rest of us liked to think it was a perilous place. You could never advance in it; you could only try not to lose it by talking too much about the debutante parties you went to or the Jaguar you earned by turning sixteen. And meanwhile, absent other distinctions, you were steadily giving ground to a system of honors that valued nothing you hadn't done yourself.

5. Neyrey and Malina, *Social World of Luke–Acts*, 25–26.

> That was the idea, so deeply held it was never spoken; you breathed it in with the smell of floor wax and wool and boys living close together in overheated rooms.[6]

At the time, most novels I was listening to on tape, back in the old days of the Sony Walkman. I came about listening to books by accident. I had been a jogger for years, but my osteopath told me to stop running all together and start walking because of the structure of my back and a bulging disk I struggled with now and then from my days as a student playing soccer at CTSFW. I remember his admonition well: "Human beings were created to walk; they should only run when they're scared and being chased."[7] But as a type A, running was fast and efficient, and walking took more time and was boring. Listening to books on tape was Linda's suggestion. Like many teachers, I was a bad listener at first, and I found it difficult to concentrate without rewinding the tape repeatedly as my mind wandered. But after a few months I became an avid listener and could walk for an hour or more without a pause to rewind. What I found was that listening to books was even better than reading them, and I used my own experience in my teaching in liturgics about reading and listening to the text, encouraging students to teach their people how to listen to the Word of God and their sermons.

That there is a great difference between hearing a book and reading sounds obvious, but the differences are subtle. Listening to a book is much more visceral because hearing is more intense and stimulates the imagination more than reading. There is something about the heard word that goes deeper, is fuller, more real. It's a voice in the ear, and the words are formed in the mind by a voice that is distinct and has a real presence about it. The voice interprets the words by the way the words are read—inflections, pauses, etc. The eye is more passive, the ear more active. The ear engages more than the eye. There is more embodiment when the word is heard. You cannot help but feel more involved in the reading when you listen to the book instead of reading it, especially by expert readers who are artists, and therefore interpreters. Their voices become familiar, tied to the text—the voice of the author himself. A marvelous example of this was listening to Ann Patchett's *Tom Lake* as read by Meryl Streep. After such a sublime experience of her embodiment of

6. Wolff, *Old School*, 3–4.

7. Bailey, *Poet and Peasant*, 181, notes that when the father in the parable of the prodigal son girds his loins so that he can run to his son, this was insane act, for in the ancient world, "great men never run in public."

the protagonist in her reading, I can't imagine that the actual reading of the novel could possibly measure up to hearing it from her. This would have been true of the hearing of Scripture in church until the Gutenberg press. For most people, until the time of the Reformation, Scripture was heard with the ears, not read with the eyes.

Words are embodied in voices in the person reading the text to you. Otherwise, they are just words on a page. You must hear poetry. It must enter your ears. Jesus said it all the time to his disciples, telling them, literally, to "stick my words in your ears." What he is saying to them is "hear this embodied word with your whole being." It's why many are somewhat adamant about not printing out the lessons in bulletins but forcing people to "hear the Word" as Jesus commands—"He who has ears, let him hear."

The narrator of *Old School* hears this embodied word when Robert Frost reads his own poems to the boys:

> His awkwardness took nothing from his poems. It removed them from the page and put them back in the voice, a speculative, sometimes cunning, sometimes faltering voice. In print, under his great name, they had the look of inevitability; in his voice you caught the hesitation and perplexity behind them, the sound of a man brooding them into being.[8]

Brooding them into being—now that's great writing. Here's another difference I discovered between listening to a book and reading it. When you're listening, you can't go back and reread, see the words, ponder them. Sure, you can rewind the tape and re-listen, but it's not the same. You can't study them when you're listening. It's like jumping into a river—the text keeps flowing and you must flow with it. You get carried away by the hearing. That sometimes happens with reading, that you get swept along and lose yourself in the flow. Also, when you're reading a book with your eyes, you know that you're coming to end of the book. I always look to see how many pages in the book, so I'm anticipating the end as I count down the pages—ten to go, five to go. You know that this book is going to end soon. You become involved in the ending because you know it's near. There are virtues to that too—an involved reader, a reader conscious of how and when the author is going to bring his or her story to an end. But that's not the case when you're listening to a book. You don't know when you're near the end. You might have a sense that you're close, but you can't see it, you can't fully anticipate it. You're captive to the heard word.

8. Wolff, *Old School*, 50.

If you read any of the reviews of *Old School*, commentators note Tobias Wolff's propensity for changing the scene or the characters in many of his stories. That's true of *Old School*. Who's Arch Makepeace? Yeah, we've seen him here and there in the narrative, a beloved English professor, the Hemingway guy, but he's a minor character, and then all of sudden at the end, he's the main thing. The last chapter, "Master," is about Arch. I know I was confused when I was listening. I thought something was wrong with my tape. I popped it out and looked, couldn't really tell, and popped it back in. Here we've been immersed in the life of this student who wants to be a great writer and is searching for his identity after recently discovering his Jewish roots, and then all of a sudden, it's about Arch Makepeace, his marriages, his sister, his life taking center-stage.

So, here's my point. My first encounter with *Old School* was listening to the book. Only later, in preparation for my never to be published novel did I sit down and read it. In my first experience with *Old School*, I was not prepared for the ending as I was listening. I had no idea that the book was coming to a close. I was not ready for Arch—the former dean, the great professor of English literature—returning to his old prep school through the blue haze of smoke at the first fall faculty meeting, having left in shame from allowing the community to think he had a friendship with Ernest Hemingway. I was not prepared for someone shouting to him—"Ecce homo"—Arch—who had accepted the provision of return to the prep school under the stony gaze of the headmaster, now seeing that very headmaster run to greet him. I must confess; I had to stop walking when I realized I had reached the end of *Old School*. I was so shocked, so stunned by the ending, I couldn't walk anymore. Couldn't stop the tears when I realized that I had just heard the final paragraphs of *Old School*.

> Arch heard them well before he got to the house. They were in the headmaster's garden. Of course—they always gathered for drinks there before getting down to business. It sounded as if they'd been drinking, their voices loud, hilarious. A blue haze of smoke hung over the garden. As he came in under the rose-covered trellis someone yelled Arch! Ecce homo! and every head turned.
>
> Arch stopped and looked down the garden to where the headmaster stood by the drinks table with another master. The headmaster said, Late for his own funeral! and everyone laughed, then he put his glass down and came toward Arch with both hands outstretched. Though the headmaster was the younger man, and much shorter, and though Arch was lame

> and had white hairs coming out of his ears and white stubble all over his face, he felt no more than a boy again—but a very well-versed boy who couldn't help thinking of the scene described by these old words, surely the most beautiful words ever written or said: His father, when he saw him coming, ran to meet him.[9]

Those *are* the most beautiful words ever written, and I knew exactly where they came from (but how many readers today could identify the source—in my Andover book club, no one picked up on this). I was completely undone by the ending. *These are my favorite words in Luke's Gospel*—the father standing on the veranda of his estate every day, looking down the road that leads to the house, hoping to see his prodigal son coming home, waiting for that moment when he would run and embrace his son and welcome him home. The entire trajectory of *Old School* narrowed down to this one verse from the parable of the prodigal son: "And while he was still afar off, his father saw him and had compassion, and running, fell on his neck and kissed him" (Luke 15:20—my translation). By ending his novel with these words—"surely the most beautiful words ever written"—Wolff shows that he not only knows the Gospels but also understands them, perhaps better than most. He incorporates one of the most important verses in Luke's Gospel in a most sublime and meaningful way *as the climax of his novel.* He captures not only the essence of what he is trying to say in his novel but what Luke is trying to say in the parable of the prodigal son. It may be one of the greatest endings of a book. Stunning. It comes upon us so completely unexpected and yet so right, the only way this novel could end, the moment when the prodigal, and Arch, are overwhelmed by grace.

So why is this ending so poignant? It brings to a climax this story about identity, self-consciousness, the stories we tell about ourselves, honor and shame, the centrality of literature and poetry, suffering and forgiveness. The unnamed narrator is an outsider, not one of the privileged Easterners, but from the West Coast, and most importantly, though raised a Roman Catholic, discovers while he is at prep school that he has Jewish roots (a great irony of *Old School* is that, in a book about identity, the narrator has no name—so I'll call him "Old School Preppy," or OSP for short). He carefully cultivates his identity, a cool and capable editor of the student literary magazine, and although not from money, carries himself as if he was one of the elites, which he is in the literary world

9. Wolff, *Old School*, 195. For some unknown reason, Wolff never puts quotation marks in the dialogue of his characters.

of this prep school that values literature above everything else. But it's a facade and he knows it.

At the center of the story is the visit of a literary figure every quarter and the writing competition that gifts the winner with a private audience with the poet or writer. In the fall it's Robert Frost, the winter Ayn Rand, and the spring Ernest Hemingway, who is a reappearing presence throughout the book because of his supposed relationship with Arch Makepeace, the beloved dean and professor of English. Of course, our OSP desperately wants to win the audience with Hemingway because he's more a storyteller than a poet, and as Mr. Ramsey said (one of the young professors), "One can imagine a world without essays . . . Stories, though—one could not live in a world without stories."[10]

But this young aspiring storyteller has writer's block until he reads a story by Susan Friedman in *Cantiamo*, the journal of Miss Cobb's, a girl's prep school. For the first time in his young life, her story describes the OSP's true identity and tells the story of his life. So, he plagiarizes the whole story with some minor name changes because it tells the story he now wants to tell about himself. Through this story he understands for the first time who he is. He doesn't even think he is plagiarizing, for this isn't Susan's story, it's *his* story—it told the truth about himself, revealing to himself and to everyone who read this story, the revelation of his true identity where the "dross of self-consciousness transformed into the gold of self-knowledge."[11] Here is how he rationalizes his plagiarism:

> *Everything's okay.* That was the last line in the story, this story where nothing was okay. I went back to the beginning and read it again, slowly this time, feeling all the while as if my inmost vault had been smashed open and looted and every hidden thing spread out across the pages. From the very first sentence I was looking myself right in the face.
>
> It went beyond the obvious parallels. Where I really recognized myself was in the momentary, undramatic details of Ruth's life and habits of thought . . .
>
> The whole thing came straight from the truthful diary I'd never kept . . . Every moment of it was true.
>
> How do you begin to write truly? I went back to that first sentence. I hope nobody saw me pick up the cigarette butt off the sidewalk . . . It made me cringe. This was not how I would

10. Wolff, *Old School*, 131.

11. Wolff, *Old School*, 132.

> ever want to be seen, though in my own cigarette-craving I had done that very thing, and more than once . . .
>
> I had stopped going to confession right after my mother died. Even as a young boy, I'd performed it grudgingly and with no payoff I was ever aware of. But in writing those words I felt at least an intuition of gracious release. To strip yourself of pretense is to overthrow a hard master, the fear of giving yourself away, and in that one sentence I gave myself away beyond all recall. Now there was nothing to do but go on.
>
> Word by word I gave it all away. I changed Ruth's first name to mine, in order to place myself unmistakably in the frame of these acts and designs, but kept Levine, because it made unmistakable what my own last name did not. I changed the city to Seattle, Caroline to James, and brought other particulars into line. I didn't have a lot of adjusting to do. These thoughts were my thoughts, this life my own . . .
>
> I finished the story just before the bell rang for breakfast. I read it through and fixed a few typos, but otherwise it needed no correction. It was done. Anyone who read this story would know who I was.[12]

The story is so raw that, in the words of Arch Makepeace, "It was hard to tell the truth like that."[13] Mr. Ramsey is even more lyrical with our OSP about why his story was so good:

> Without stories one would hardly know what world one was in. But I'm not saying this very well. Mr. Ramsey stared out over the garden. It has to do with self-consciousness, he said. Though I'm no believer, I find it interesting that self-consciousness is associated with the Fall. Nakedness and shame. Knowledge of ourselves as a thing apart, and bound to die. Exile. We speak of self-consciousness as a burden or a problem, and so it is—the problem being how to use it to bring ourselves out of exile. Whereas our tendency is to love ourselves in the distance, wouldn't you say? . . .
>
> Lost in the distance, Mr. Ramsey said again. It's a wonder we're not all barking. And of course we would be if we hadn't any way to use self-consciousness against itself, or rather against its worst inclinations—morbidity, narcissism, paranoia, grandiosity, that lot. We have somehow to turn a profit on it. Which is, I must say, exactly what that story of yours does. "Summer Dance." A marvelous story! Pure magic. No—no—not magic.

12. Wolff, *Old School*, 125–27.
13. Wolff, *Old School*, 186.

> Alchemy. The dross of self-consciousness transformed into the gold of self-knowledge. Enough. I see I'm embarrassing you. But I had to tell you, for my own sake if not yours, what a superior piece of writing that is.[14]

Old School is about as self-conscious a book as I've ever read. Subtle, but as aware of itself as one can be. The OSP comes to self-knowledge through the worst kind of suffering for a prep school adolescent, for he understands what this unnamed school is all about. He was a poser and often felt his nakedness and shame. But by claiming that girl's story for his own, he was cleansed and clothed in what he felt was his true self. Ironically, the shamelessness of this self-conscious plagiarized story was his way of bringing himself out of exile and getting the absolution he did not feel after going to confession. Only in this story did he discover the truth about himself and establish his own identity. This is what the writing of Tobias Wolff is all about. His memoirs, *This Boy's Life* and *Pharaoh's Army*, are his attempts to bring himself out of exile. Tobias Wolff is this OSP, as well as Arch and the prodigal. It about him and it's about us. What the OSP felt in reading Susan Friedman's story, we feel in reading *Old School*. We're all naked and ashamed, in exile from ourselves, searching for that story that explains all, that metanarrative that postmodernism insists does not exist. Some of us are more self-conscious than others, that is, some of us know we're naked and ashamed. Some of us spend a lifetime discovering that reality. Only a few have the courage "to tell the truth like that."

Of course, it comes out that this story was not the author's, and he is kicked out of school. From my own experience at Andover, plagiarism or cheating was the worst sin, almost unforgivable, for it violated the sacred honor code. You were better off getting caught drinking or smoking or having a girl in your room than plagiarizing or cheating on a test. The one who dismisses him for his grievous act is the dean, Arch Makepeace. In dismissing the OSP, Arch is undone by his own shame at allowing the false narrative that he was a dear friend of Hemingway to thrive. So, he resigns from the school and leaves to live with his sister, for he sees his own plagiarized life as a sin against the school and the students he loved. It was a holy place, this prep school, and he was unclean. Both he and the OSP are prodigals who must leave their home because of their shame.

Both the OSP and Arch need their honor restored, and such honor comes from without, from the community. The OSP is restored by

14. Wolff, *Old School*, 132.

becoming a great writer who is invited back by Mr. Ramsey, now the headmaster, as a visiting author to sit at the same table as Robert Frost, Ayn Rand, and Ernest Hemingway. The prodigal comes home.

But how about Arch Makepeace? Wolff's remarkable ending is the restoration of his honor. But Arch's shame is more complicated. He was a master and should have known better. He couldn't take his own hypocrisy, which he believed shamed the school he loved. He felt he lost his honor because of that shame. So Arch kicks himself out and then hits rock bottom and comes to his senses. He's overwhelmed by what he misses about teaching, about being with the boys at *Old School.* He missed the honor of living in community, and he hated the shame he brought on that community he loved. You see, Arch thought that he had sinned against the community because he couldn't take to heart his own teaching. His sense of honor, his honor code, was killing him. As Ramsey said to the OSP about the honor code when he was invited back, "You did get the bum's rush. Cursed to the tenth generation. We do things differently now."[15] With such an honor code, there was no forgiveness, no redemption. But he felt he had nowhere to go. He had hit rock bottom.

> He missed the tumult in the hallways between classes, and how the boys parted to make a path for him. He missed their noise and their woolly smell and their deep silence in chapel. He missed their good manners. He missed bucking them up when they got homesick or discouraged and surprising them with his forbearance when they ran aground—hadn't they figured him out yet, after all these years! He missed how the boys went crazy in the first snowfall, and broke into song at any excuse, and forgot themselves in the excitement of finding something interesting in a poem, especially if Arch hadn't seen it. He missed all of that, and knowing the people around him, and being known. He missed a certain shy glance in which he saw respect and warmth and even some wonder. Arch wanted that back, as much as the rest. He wanted it all back.[16]

That last line is a killer—"He wanted it all back." Arch writes the headmaster that he's willing to come back "on whatever terms were possible."[17] He'll take the remedial classes, a room in the village. Or in the words of the prodigal son, "Make me as a hired worker." And so, he comes

15. Wolff, *Old School*, 174.
16. Wolff, *Old School*, 192.
17. Wolff, *Old School*, 193.

back, and Wolff surprises and stuns us with that final scene of restoration and redemption that ends with "the most beautiful words ever written."

But how about Hemingway? If *Old School* ends with the sublime Gospel of Luke 15, it is curious that Ernest Hemingway, a late convert to Roman Catholicism who struggled with his faith his whole life, becomes the means for Wolff to offer us a theology of suffering. The OSP begins his journey to self-knowledge through understanding Hemingway's woundedness. He is startled by Ayn Rand's criticism of Hemingway. At first, he was completely besotted by her vision of life, but when she went after Hemingway, whom he both revered and lovingly mocked,[18] he began to realize that she failed to grasp the brokenness of "human reality":

> Her ridicule of Hemingway brought this home to me. Not immediately, of course. My first reaction was shock—at her unfairness not only to the writer but to a character for whom I had a great liking. Wretched eunuch, she'd called Jake Barnes, as if the fact of such a wound, of woundedness itself, made him merely pathetic. I knew Jake pretty well, having read *The Sun Also Rises* twice the previous summer. He'd gotten about the worst break I could then imagine, but he wasn't wretched. He took pleasure in how Paris came to life in the morning. Pleasure in food and drink and travel, in watching men face dangerous animals, in fishing, in friendship. Jake lingered on these things. He watched the life around him with interest. You could sometimes feel the pulse of hopeless longing, but you could not say that Jake was wretched. It was wrong, and it was mean.
>
> It had become a fashion at school to draw lines between certain writers, as if to like one meant you couldn't like the other. So far I'd avoided the practice. I liked most of what I chose to read and saw no point in reducing my pleasures by half. Ayn Rand jolted me into taking sides. She made me feel the difference between a writer who despised woundedness and one for whom it was a bedrock of life.[19]

In the 1970s both Hemingway and Jake Barnes from *The Sun Also Rises* became iconic for me because our family lived in Bilbao, Spain,

18. See Wolff, *Old School*, 14, for their mocking of Hemingway. It's priceless: "Anyway, I myself was in debt to Hemingway—up to my ears. So was Bill. We even talked like Hemingway characters, though in travesty, as if to deny our discipleship: That is your bed, and it is a good bed, and you must make it and you must make it well. Or: Today is the day of meatloaf. The meatloaf is swell. It is swell but when it is gone the not-having meatloaf will be tragic and the meatloaf man will not come anymore."

19. Wolff, *Old School*, 94.

which is near Pamplona and the famous running of the bulls. We became engrossed in bullfighting, and Hemingway, along with James Michener's *Iberia*, which became our guide to Spain. John Fulton, the American bullfighter who considered Hemingway a friend, became a famous painter in Seville, and we bought his prints. His one painting hung on the wall of my room in G-4 at CTSFW when I was a student. The British and American expatriates in *The Sun Also Rises* gathered in Pamplona because they were walking part of the Camino of Santiago de Compostela (in late June of 2008, my son Jake and I walked through Pamplona on the Camino). So, at my urging, because of my love for Hemingway and *The Sun Also Rises*, I persuaded our entire family to attend the Feast of San Fermín and the running of bulls in 1975, the year I graduated from college.

We had heard that it was a raucous affair, as Spaniards have a particular way of celebrating these kinds of feasts, but San Fermín is insane, even by Spanish standards. Our entire family spent three days swept up in a crowd that partied for almost a week without much sleep. On the first day of the running of the bulls, all of us agreed to reunite in a place to watch this spectacle after a night of reverie. We all showed up, except my brother Jonathan, who was nowhere to be found. My parents didn't give it much thought, for Jon always beat to his own drummer. But we kids all knew what he was up to.[20] My mother, who was a worrier at heart, started screaming when she saw her son's blond head running out in front the bulls (everyone else was screaming so no one made her any mind). Knowing Jon as I did, I could see he knew what he was doing. He had great instincts. Thankfully he made it to the bullring without harm. He may have survived the bulls but not a tongue-lashing from our mother.

The oral tradition at the unnamed prep school in *Old School* was that Arch Makepeace was the basis for Bill Gorton, one of the characters in Hemingway's novel. Both my boys know that I agreed to naming them Nicholas and Jacob (Linda always picked the names and I had veto power) because of Nick Carroway in *The Great Gatsby* and Jake Barnes in *The Sun Also Rises*. When they were older I told them that if all else failed they could open a bar called "Nick and Jake's" and hang pictures of the novels of Hemingway and Fitzgerald on the walls.

Jake Barnes. Like the OSP, Ayn Rand's blasphemous defaming of Jake Barnes hit home with me too. He was played by Tyrone Power in the movie, with Ava Gardner as Lady Brett Ashley—perfect casting.

20. The birth order is me (1953), then Jonathan (1955), and then three years later Karen (1958) and Christopher (1960). We're all boomers.

At Andover, Jake Barnes personified that cool demeanor in the face of enormous suffering. We all agreed that he had about the "worst break" a guy could have—a wound that's at the heart of our male identity. Wolff's description of how Jake Barnes found ways to enjoy life after such a devastating injury made me revisit the book. He was right—Jake Barnes found a noble way through the suffering, and the way he handled his injury showed that Hemingway gets woundedness. The OSP is right—Ayn Rand made us take sides, and I'm with the OSP: "She made me feel the difference between a writer who despised woundedness and one for whom it was a bedrock fact of life."

Woundedness as a "bedrock fact of life" might be one way of thinking about original sin and its consequences. For Lutherans, how we handle our own woundedness in Christ is at the heart of a theology of suffering, which I wrote in the margin of *Old School* when he called woundedness "the bedrock of life." What Ayn Rand forces the OSP to do is revisit Hemingway's collection of short stories *In Our Time*. I must confess I'm more given to novels than to short stories, and I hadn't read *In Our Time* since Andover. I enthusiastically revisited *The Sun Also Rises* but reluctantly returned to *In Our Time*. But I didn't know then what I know now—that the title of this book comes from a prayer in *The Book of Common Prayer*: "Give peace in our time, O Lord." In rereading *In Our Time*, I also saw what the OSP found in Hemingway's stories and novels—that all his protagonists are wounded and that this "woundedness" was the bedrock of Hemingway's fiction. It made me wonder if this was related to his conversion to Roman Catholicism—that he saw in Christ's suffering and the suffering of his body the church, the bedrock of all woundedness. Nick Adams from *In Our Time* struggles with loss, grief, alienation, and separation. He suffers. The title of this book of short stories is spot on—in suffering all we can pray for is "peace *in our time*." Both the OSP and I were as surprised as anyone at the woundedness of Hemingway's characters. Here's how that OSP expresses this woundedness in Hemingway's *In Our Time*:

> All these wounds and scars . . . I'd never linked them up before, but when I did they began to seem the most visible symptoms of a general condition that included the Swede's despair, Francis Macomb's humiliation, Krebs' inability to feel . . .
>
> I already admired Hemingway above all other writers, but the truth was that I'd been drawn to him mostly by his life—that is, by the legend of his life—and by a set of ideas about his work

> that spilled over from the legend. I'd gone in looking for images of toughness, self-sufficiency, freedom from the hobbles of family and class and conventional work, so that's what I'd found. Now I was reading a different writer. Hard things happened in these stories, but the people weren't hard. They felt the blows. Some of them gave up and some came back for more, but coming back wasn't easy . . .
>
> How had I missed that? Reading the story now, I saw everything through the shimmer of Nick's fragility.[21]

"The shimmer of Nick's fragility." I too had read Hemingway through the lens of his life as the consummate man among men—ambulance driver, fisherman and hunter, boxer, a bullfighting aficionado, a hard-drinking womanizer. But when you change your perspective, read him through a different lens, you find that underneath all the macho-posturing there was fragility—woundedness. Here's some great pastoral advice for how a pastor should view his people who struggle with sin even though they are in Christ and Christ is in them—"Hard things happen in these stories, but the people weren't hard. They felt the blows. Some of them gave up and some came back for more, but coming back wasn't easy . . ." The circumstances of life can overwhelm the saints in our congregations, but with good pastoral care, good preaching, our people will come back to Christ by a pastor who connects their sufferings to the sufferings of Christ, especially through the Eucharist, so that they may say with Paul, "For to me to live is Christ, and to die is gain" (Phil 1:21).

A. O. Scott titles his review of *Old School* "Famous Writers School." He notes that "the book is about nothing if not the making of a writer—though it is also, just as plainly, about a writer's failure."[22] What writers reveal in their writing is themselves. The OSP shows us that in Hemingway's Nick Adams stories he is showing us himself—that maybe this macho image of Hemingway we've come to embrace wasn't the real Hemingway. I know I was fooled. The real Hemingway was like the people who inhabited his stories. The OSP says it better than I can:

> We had been taught not to confuse the writer with the work, but I couldn't separate my picture of Nick from my picture of Hemingway. And I had a sense that I wasn't really supposed to, that a certain confusion of author and character was intended. But the man who lived in these stories was not the steely

21. Wolff, *Old School*, 95–96.
22. Scott, "Famous Writers School.".

> warrior-genius whose image had so fogged my first impressions. He was in most respects an unremarkable, even banal man who got things wrong and suffered from nervousness and fear, fear even of the workings of his own mind, and who sometimes didn't know how to behave. I hated the way he dumped Marjorie in "The End of Something." Telling a girl whose love you'd taken advantage of that it wasn't *fun* anymore? I judged him for that, thinking how much better I would've handled it.
>
> I judged him, but I also understood that he'd allowed me to, and this was chastening. Knowing that readers like me would see him in Nick, he had given us a vision of spiritual muddle and exhaustion almost embarrassing in its intimacy. The truth of these stories didn't come as a set of theories. You felt them on the back of your neck.[23]

Reading that made the back of my neck tingle. Here is that modern/postmodern divide. Truth as a set of theories or truth that you feel on the back of your neck. *Aldente*, as Aidan Kavanagh would say about good liturgy. A little raw, a little undercooked. One of the dangers of confessional Lutheranism, especially when propositional truths infect our liturgies and preaching, is that it is overcooked. The hymns we sing, the sermons we hear, and the liturgies that contain them should somehow comprehend the sufferings we bring to church so that there are moments when we feel them "on the back of our neck."

So how can we not *love* Hemingway if he is indeed that wounded, broken, nervous, fearful man of his stories. He's real and he lets us know he's real, and it makes his public image so much richer. He had guts all right, courage to go on the front lines of a war, to face many dangers, but his greatest act of courage was to reveal himself to us in his stories. The OSP said it best—"to let himself be seen as he was." Identity. The OSP only sees who he really is from his plagiarized story because he sees who Hemingway really was from his stories. Hemingway is the OSP's first step towards seeing his true identity:

> It wasn't exactly true that I'd told no expository lies. Most of my stories had been meant to seem autobiographical, and thus to give a false picture of my family and my life at home—of who I was. I'd allowed myself to do this by thinking that, after all, they were just stories. But they weren't really stories, not like "Big Two-Hearted River" was a story, or "Soldier's Home." It struck me that Hemingway's willingness to let himself be seen as he

23. Wolff, *Old School*, 96–97.

> was, in uncertainty or meanness or fear, even empty of feeling, somehow gave the charge of truth to everything else. My stories were designed to make me appear as I was not. They were props in an act. I couldn't read any of them without thrusting the pages away in mortification.[24]

That's why our OSP had to plagiarize that story, for in all his other stories he was an Old School Poser. But this plagiarized story was the story of his life, and he claimed it as such: "Anyone who read this story would know who I was." There was absolution in his plagiarism, because for the first time he was telling the truth about himself. Talk about irony. Here he's stealing a story he didn't write, and it's the most truthful moment of his life. Arch—the truth-seeker in his teaching and his writing—nailed it: "It was hard to tell the truth like that." But that's what the OSP did—told the truth about himself, like Hemingway, like Wolff.

The truth at the center of both *Old School* and Hemingway's characters is redemptive suffering. Like the OSP, we are able to see that we're all wounded and that to be human is to be weak and vulnerable. There is another character in Hemingway's novels, Robert Jordan in *For Whom the Bell Tolls*, who may embody better than all his characters this woundedness. Again, at Andover, in Kemper Auditorium, where fifty-plus years later our class of 1971 would screen the documentary of our class, I watched Gary Cooper as Robert Jordan in *For Whom the Bell Tolls* and had my first adolescent crush—the incandescent Ingrid Bergman as Maria. What a story! What a movie! At that time, we were living in Mexico, so the Spanish connection was not there. But later, when we moved to Spain and we first visited Franco's tomb in *Valle de los Caidos* (the Valley of the Fallen), a monumental site in the Guadarrama mountains and the setting for Hemingway's novel during the Spanish Civil War, I took up Hemingway's novel for the first time and found that I liked it even more than *The Sun Also Rises*. It was only later, however, in writing my never-to-be published novel, that I saw Hemingway's chiastic structure, and more importantly, the theme of redemptive suffering.

Hemingway wanted everyone to see the truth of the Spanish Civil War, the truth of war itself. That's why he wrote *For Whom the Bell Tolls*. In a speech by Hemingway to the American League of Authors in New York City, Carnegie Hall on the fourth of June 1937, before the publication of

24. Wolff, *Old School*, 109–10.

For Whom the Bell Tolls, he offers a clear statement of his philosophy of life and why he writes:

> A writer's problem does not change. He himself changes, but his problem remains the same. It is always how to write truly and having found what is true, to project it in such a way that it becomes part of the experience of the person who reads it.[25]

Such a statement could not be said of many postmodern novelists. Hemingway believed in truth, and he communicated it in *For Whom the Bell Tolls* through a very careful structure that is concentric, like the famous chiasms from Luke's Gospel. Hemingway offers us a frame, an *inclusio*, beginning and ending with Jordan and the pine trees. In the novel, Robert Jordan alerts us to look at reality like a merry-go-round, like the rotation of the planets revolving around the sun or like a wheel with spokes and a hub. Critics compare Hemingway's structure to the bullring, moving towards the center, where the dance with death takes place between matador and bull. At the end of *For Whom the Bell Tolls*, the dance with death is the bridge to Segovia that Jordan is determined to blow up. The bridge itself is symbolic, separating the two sides, sky and river, and the conflicted Spanish couple: Pilar, the courageous mystic, and her husband, Pablo, the ruthless, cowardly realist. The bridge is the center circle, that liminal place between heaven—*la gloria*, mystery, and love—and earth—war, suffering, and death.

Everything points to the bridge. We usually build bridges, but here they're blowing one up. The title of the book comes from the metaphysical poet John Donne, who meditates on his suffering and pain while recovering from a near-fatal illness. It begins with "No man is an island" and ends with "For whom the bell tolls, it tolls for thee." We usually build bridges to islands. We need connectedness, union, communion. But Jordan thinks the whole future of mankind may depend on blowing up that bridge, even though he also knows it might be futile. But he's going to do it because it's his destiny, it's his bull to fight, his final mystery, and he's in the center of the bullring—he's got his sword—and he's going in for the kill.[26]

25. American League of Authors in New York City, Carnegie Hall, June 4, 1937.

26. The entire romance of Robert and Maria in this novel is compressed into three days, through which they experience their own suffering, death, and resurrection. No one will ever know if Hemingway intended to connect these three days to Jesus' three days of suffering, death, and resurrection, but it is provocative.

The first martyr on the bridge is called Anselmo. He hated killing. In the novel, he's the good Catholic, or one who wanted to be a good Catholic. Jordan loves him. Hemingway loves him. He's the Christian in the bunch. That's what Jordan calls him, something rare in Catholic countries. A strange remark, but Anselmo is the true Catholic. Hemingway devotes a whole chapter to Anselmo, showing us his Christianity, or at least, how much he hates the war and the killing. For example, he talks about how there must be this great penance, and if there is no religion after the war, at least there must be what he calls a "civic penance . . . That all may be cleansed from the killing or else we will never have a true and human basis for living . . . There must be a penance of some kind for the cleansing of us all."[27] Anselmo is lonely. Prayer is what helped him in his loneliness in the old days. He misses that. What he wants is cleansing, atonement. Perhaps Hemingway called him Anselmo because of St. Anselm, bishop of Canterbury (around the year 1000). He was Augustinian in his theology, which meant that he wrestled with the relationship between faith and reason. Faith always preceded reason, but reason describes what faith believes. He's known for lots of things, like the ontological argument for the existence of God, but for our purposes, for Hemingway, it's his theory of atonement that matters.

Anselm was interested in how sin is atoned for, what theologians call expiation, and sometimes his theory of atonement is called the satisfaction theory of atonement. He believed that sin was like a debt that needed to be paid, a matter of justice, that is, the one for whom the debt is owed needs for that debt to be satisfied. If sin is a debt to God, the only one who can satisfy that debt, pay it off, is Jesus, God and man, who was sinless, who owed no debt, so that by his sacrificial death he could pay off our debt. Jesus atones for sin by suffering and dying. Here is how God gets justice—what Paul called "justification," and which for Lutherans is the doctrine upon with the church stands or falls. Anselm's theory was important in the formulations of the atonement during the Protestant Reformation. What Anselm was trying to do was explain the mystery of the atonement. I think Hemingway knew it well, demonstrated in this reflection by Anselmo about killing and about the Spanish ethos:

> It must really be a great sin, he thought. Because certainly it is the one thing we have no right to do even though, as I know, it is necessary. But in Spain it is done too lightly and often without

27. Hemingway, *For Whom the Bell Tolls*, 196.

> true necessity and there is much quick injustice which, afterward, can never be repaired. I wish I did not think about it so much, he thought. I wish there were a penance for it that one could commence now because it is the only thing that I have done in all my life that makes me feel badly when I am alone. All the other things are forgiven or one had a chance to atone for them by kindness or in some decent way. But I think this of the killing must be a very great sin and I would like to fix it up. Later on there may be certain days that one can work for the state or something that one can do that will remove it. It will probably be something that one pays as in the days of the Church, he thought, and smiled. The Church was well organized for sin. That pleased him and he was smiling in the dark when Robert Jordan came up to him. He came silently and the old man did not see him until he was there.[28]

Anselmo desired the church, needed the church. He died with a sort of peace, a calmness. As he said, he was not happy, but he was also not lonely or afraid. He even thought to himself, "If I die on this morning now, it is all right." He was at peace with the need to atone for the killing he did at the bridge. There was even a sense of oneness Anselmo felt as he was about to blow the bridge. Hemingway put it this way:

> He was one with the wire in his hand and one with the bridge, and one with the charges the *Inglés* had placed. He was one with the *Inglés* still working under the bridge and he was one with all of the battle and with the Republic.[29]

Robert Jordan is portrayed by Hemingway as a man living between modernism and postmodernism. Jordan is a scientist and now a blower-up of bridges. He still believes in man's rational capacity to overcome the problems of this world. He believes in the Republic, in social progress, even in Communism to a certain degree, but in every case he's not naive, he knows the downside, he's not an idealist. But he still operates as if war will solve Spain's problems, that blowing up the bridge will be that one rational act upon which the whole future will turn. But Robert is conflicted about it all. He wants to believe in mystery, but something holds him back. Like Hemingway, he's bought into the modern metanarrative, yet both know that there is this undiscovered country of *la gloria*, this undiscovered country of El Greco and San Juan de la Cruz and Solomon's

28. Hemingway, *For Whom the Bell Tolls*, 197–98.
29. Hemingway, *For Whom the Bell Tolls*, 443.

Song of Songs.[30] There is a mystical union that gives meaning to suffering and he wants it bad. He wants to believe in the one grand metanarrative that Anselmo has, even though he hasn't been to church in years.

Hemingway asks us to recall an old spiritual, "Roll Jordan Roll," and the protagonist named Jordan remembers how they shouted that at football games when he was carrying the ball. He remembers it as he is under the bridge, about to blow it up. If the bridge is central to this book, so also is the name Jordan and the River Jordan. He looks down and sees the creek below that is no bigger than the Jordan River in the Holy Land. He says to himself, "As Jordan goes so go the Israelites."[31] We are crossing the Jordan here, from the wilderness of science into the promised land of mystery. If science blows up the bridge, we can't cross the River Jordan because we've destroyed this man-made bridge. Instead, we must walk on water, on the stones to be exact, like Joshua and the Israelites. We have to have faith in the mystery, in the great narrative of them all, the biblical one, the one filled with mysteries, the metanarrative you have to have faith to believe in, the one that was not created by the powers of a rational mind, or by the powers of a scientific method, but by the power of an indestructible life, as the book of Hebrews puts it. You can't "prove mysteries." They just are. The biblical narrative doesn't need legitimization, it just is. You don't "prove" this narrative, you proclaim it.

Jordan's knows he's going to die. But is he going to enter the mysteries? Yet he's already there, through Maria, through the earth moving, through *la gloria*. He's there in Pilar, in his oneness with Anselmo, oneness with his family of Spaniards fighting for a just cause, this family who has shared this journey with him. He entered the mysteries during these three days leading up to the blowing up the bridge, and these three days have set him free. That's why he can say, "I'm all right now however she goes." And he is all right. He's made the move. The bridge is blown. He's crossed the Jordan. No matter what happens, he's entered the mysteries, embraced the grand narrative, even lived it.

30. Hemingway, *For Whom the Bell Tolls*, 380, references El Greco and San Juan de la Cruz in speaking about the mystery of *la gloria*: "But his mind, that was his best companion, was thinking La Gloria. She said La Gloria. It has nothing to do with glory nor La Gloire that the French write and speak about. It is the thing that is in the Cante Hondo and in the Saetas. It is in Greco and in San Juan del la Cruz, of course, and in the others. I am no mystic, but to deny it is as ignorant as though you denied the telephone or that the earth revolves around the sun or that there are other planets than this."

31. Hemingway, *For Whom the Bell Tolls*, 438.

Robert Jordan is Joshua, the Old Testament Jesus, crossing the boundary between the wilderness and the promised land, between life and death. But Joshua needs the rocks to cross, he needs a miracle. Robert Jordan is like Jesus, like all of us, in that he must suffer and die to enter the mysteries. Only then will he discover that undiscovered country, that place where mystery is full and it is clear.

Crossing the Jordan, entering the mysteries. It happens through suffering. Suffering, and making meaning out of suffering—that is the great mystery of life. For it's in suffering that we find the truth about ourselves. No truth to be found in the *Übermensch*. But there is truth in Nick's fragility. Truth among those who felt the blows. That's real. That's life. It's how you interpret the blows and how you handle them that is what ultimately matters. Some give up and some come back for more—and those who embrace the truth of suffering, embrace its mystery, and cross the Jordan, even here, right here, in this life, looking to the one who suffered on behalf of all—they're the ones who make meaning out of suffering. To cross the Jordan is to be forsaken, and only then enter paradise. That's what I learned from Hemingway's stories—that hard things happen but that the people aren't hard. They're as fragile and vulnerable as Hemingway was—as vulnerable as old Nick and Jake and Robert and Henry and Krebs—as vulnerable as each and every one of us.

Jesus and Mary

6

Returning to Emmaus

The Gospels as Kerygmatic Memoirs

EMMAUS WAS MY BEGINNING, my middle, and now my end. How could it not be if our life is lived out at the ongoing feast that is itself a participation in what Emmaus is and points to? Those two disciples walking from Jerusalem to Emmaus and back again are the quintessential pilgrims who in their journey recapitulate the narrative Luke writes.[1] Emmaus captures the entire paschal mystery, and the two Emmaus disciples embody the confusion, denial, and conversion of everyone who struggles with the mystery of Christ's incarnation and passion, and how in the Eucharist we proclaim his death until he comes.

Most Lutherans will at one time or another cite Paul's words from Romans 10:17: "So faith comes from hearing, and hearing through the word of Christ." Those two Emmaus pilgrims are the first post-Paschal converts because they had communion with the flesh of the resurrected Christ in their ears, as he spoke to them on the way, burning their hearts, and opening their eyes in the breaking of the bread. Faith came to them

1. Just, *Ongoing Feast*, 30n14: "This observation was first brought to my attention by my thesis supervisor, Dr. J. McHugh, who suggested the 'circular journey' or 'ring structure' for the Emmaus meal. He pointed out in correspondence that 'when travel is involved, you often end up where you start. E.g. the Infancy Gospel begins, and ends, in Jerusalem, indeed in the Temple; the entire Gospel begins, and ends, in Jerusalem, and in the Temple. Paul, on his journeys, gets back to his starting point (except his final journey, but cf. Ac 1:8). So also Emmaus: the pair go back to Jerusalem."

through hearing the Word of Christ in both his teaching on the road and in the breaking of the bread.

Before Easter, Mary is the first convert at the annunciation when, after the moment of conception, she issues her fiat, "Let it be to me according to your word." It was the Word that she believed—the word of the angel Gabriel who catechized her as a messenger from heaven. The thief on the cross inherits paradise *today*, converted at the moment of atonement as he heard and saw the "Word made flesh" die before his eyes. Jesus catechized him through his words on the cross, especially the Psalms about the suffering, righteous one. At the end of the Easter Day the Emmaus disciples complete Luke's kerygmatic conversions as Jesus broke open the Scriptures for them and opened their eyes in the breaking of the bread. What separates Mary and the thief on the cross from the Emmaus disciples is that Mary and the thief were not converted by the means for mission—Word and Meal. Theirs was a conversion from personal experience of an angel, or of Jesus himself.

Interpreting Texts

It was at Andover and then at Union that I discovered how much I loved interpreting stories—or, as many prefer, narratives, for some people think of story as something that is not true, like fiction. My life has been centered in interpreting texts—at prep school and college, reading novels and some poetry and trying to find meaning in them—and then at seminary, interpreting in Greek the greatest narratives ever written—Matthew, Mark, Luke, and John—the four canonical Gospels. The reason I decided to write this book as a "memoir" is because Justin Martyr called the Gospels "memoirs" in the context of describing the worship of early Christians on Sunday, the eighth, eschatological day:

> And on the day called Sunday, all who live in cities or in the country gather together to one place, and *the memoirs of the apostles* or the writings of the prophets are read, as long as time permits; then, when the reader has ceased, the president verbally instructs, and exhorts to the imitation of these good things.

Justin Martyr testifies that the memoirs of the apostles preceded the celebration of the Eucharist:

> *For the apostles, in the memoirs composed by them, which are called Gospels*, have thus delivered unto us what was enjoined upon

> them; that Jesus took bread, and when He had given thanks, said, "This do ye in remembrance of Me, this is My body;" and that, after the same manner, having taken the cup and given thanks, He said, "This is My blood;" and gave it to them alone.

This certainly sounds like Emmaus—the memoirs of the apostles and the breaking of the bread—the means for mission—the means for conversion. Before you can receive the Eucharist, you must first hear and inwardly digest the narrative—the memoirs of the apostles which are now called Gospels—and then be washed at the font:

> And this food is called among us Εὐχαριστία [the Eucharist], of which no one is allowed to partake but the man who believes that the things which we teach are true, and who has been washed with the washing that is for the remission of sins, and unto regeneration, and who is so living as Christ has enjoined.[2]

In his church, Justin Martyr read the memoirs of the apostles continuously, as was the custom in the early church, as they did not yet have a canon as we now have.[3] A continuous reading of the Gospels was also how the Gospel writers intended their Gospels to be heard—as a narrative that was created by the evangelists to be read and preached in the liturgy. They would read for "as long as time permits," perhaps an hour or more, and then they would preach on the narrative for another hour, the pastor instructing and exhorting the saints to imitate what they heard from Jesus in the Gospels. This reading of Scripture—the Liturgy of the Word—came to be known as the Liturgy of the Catechumens. The Gospels were written for the church to be used by the church in her liturgy to catechize the unbaptized and nurture the baptized in their eucharistic life, creating for them, through preaching, "a hunger and thirst for righteousness."[4]

That Luke calls his Gospel a narrative in his prologue (1:1) shows that his memoir is a literary work subject to literary analysis. He also tells Theophilus that he is composing a systematic narrative, literally a narrative "in order." This systematic order is more than a chronological or historical order—it is a kerygmatic one, that is, Luke orders his Gospel so that it could be preached. Justin Martyr and the early fathers surely captured this, and it was only later that the church abandoned a continuous reading and preaching on the Gospel that has now been reclaimed in the

2. Justin Martyr, *First Apology*, 66.
3. See Just, *Heaven on Earth*, 202–4.
4. See Just, *Concordia Commentary: Luke 1:1–9:50*, 4–7.

three-year lectionary.[5] Luke's kerygmatic order is to present an historical narrative that is filled with theological significance. He unfolds the life and ministry of Jesus in such a way that the hearer of the Gospel may enter the story of Jesus and make it their own.

As a literary work, Luke is fond of themes. For example, he uses cloth bands that wrap the body of Jesus at the moment of the incarnation—"Ye shall find the babe wrapped in swaddling clothes, lying in a manger" (Luke 2:12 KJV); at the moment of atonement—"And he took it down, and wrapped it in linen, and laid it in a sepulcher that was hewn in stone, wherein never man before was laid" (Luke 23:53 KJV); and at the moment of resurrection—"Then arose Peter, and ran unto the sepulcher; and stooping down, he beheld the linen clothes laid by themselves, and departed, wondering in himself at that which was come to pass" (Luke 24:12 KJV). In this way, Jesus' body wrapped in cloth bands is a sign of the incarnation, the atonement, and the resurrection—the kerygma of the church.

Luke also uses moments of conversion to mark the same kerygma—the incarnation through Mary, the atonement through the thief on the cross, and the resurrection through the Emmaus disciples. But the conversation of the Emmaus disciples with Jesus on the road—his teaching—becomes paradigmatic for the catechesis which takes place before every conversion that happens in Christendom after that climactic moment of the breaking of the bread at Emmaus.

Teaching Luke in the 1980s and 1990s

Beginning in 1986, when it became clear that my thesis would be on Luke's Gospel, our academic dean, David Scaer, thought it would be helpful if I took over teaching the Luke class. It was also when I began to teach liturgy, as the worship wars were beginning and Dr. Scaer was sending me out into the church to talk about the liturgy, since I minored in liturgical studies at Yale Divinity School. Teaching Luke and the liturgy are the delights of my teaching career. However, during CTSFW's "Babylonian captivity" from 1989 to 1996, I was forbidden to teach Luke's Gospel.[6]

5. See Wilkinson, John. *Egeria's Travels to the Holy Land*, 253–77, on "The Old Armenian Lectionary."

6. The Babylonian captivity is our way of referring to the time between the presidencies of Robert Preus and Dean Wenthe (1989–96), when there was an effort to close CTSFW and many of us were persecuted and threatened with dismissal. For a detailed description of these years, see Weinrich, "Concordia Theological Seminary 1985–2010."

Ironically, this was when I was writing the commentary on Luke. The first volume was published in 1996, the same year that Dean Wenthe became the president of CTSFW, and the second volume in the following year. So, most of the commentary was written when I was not allowed to teach the Gospel I had come to know and love. Why? Because it was alleged that I taught that the breaking of the bread at Emmaus was the Eucharist.

My "punishment" of not teaching Luke while I was writing the commentary for Concordia Publishing House (CPH) made me acutely aware that there were forces beyond my control who were vehemently opposed to even suggesting that Emmaus was the Eucharist. What this group lacked was a "sacramental imagination."[7] When I began teaching Luke, knowing how virulent this group was—and we have scars to show for it—I was very careful to never say in class that the breaking of the bread was the first Eucharist, even though I certainly believed that it was. I knew the consequences. I was careful to say that it was an act of table fellowship where Jesus was teaching and eating at the table and that what set it apart from other acts of table fellowship was that Christ was present *at this meal* in his resurrected/glorified presence.

I also made clear that it was not a coincidence that Luke was the only the evangelist who framed the three days of passion and resurrection with meals. He begins the three days with the Last Supper in Luke 22, where he institutes the Eucharist after sundown on the Day of Preparation (Friday for Jesus and Thursday for us), and he ends the three days with the Emmaus meal in Luke 24 at the end of that first Easter Day, as the day was ending. At this meal, *for the first time in the Gospel*, Jesus is recognized by a human being as the crucified and resurrected Lord *in the breaking of the bread*. The same constellation of language is used at the feeding of the five thousand, the Last Supper, and Emmaus—the language of table fellowship. But I never said in class that Emmaus was the Eucharist.

7. See Weigel, *Letters to a Young Catholic*, 86, 92, 99: "The bedrock Catholic conviction [is] that *stuff counts* . . . [G. K Chesterton] was an ardent defender of the sacramental imagination—the core Catholic conviction that God saves and sanctifies the world through the materials of the world. . . . the sacramental imagination [is] the experience of the extraordinary through the ordinary . . . The sacramental imagination suggests another set of chapter headings [for the history of the world]: Creation, Fall, Promise, Prophecy, Incarnation, Redemption, Sanctification, The Kingdom . . . Salvation history is the human story, read in its true depth and against an appropriately ample horizon. Thus the romance of orthodoxy—getting the story of salvation history straight as His-story—is the romance of the world. And the adventure of orthodoxy is the greatest of human adventures."

Many students, however, drew their own conclusions, and for most it was painfully obvious that Luke framed the Triduum with eucharistic meals, beginning with the institution of the Eucharist on Good Friday and concluding with the first post-resurrection Eucharist on Easter Sunday. More than one student asked why the evangelist, who was so careful in the way he shaped his narrative, would begin the three-day Paschal mystery with a eucharistic meal and not end it with one? My careful response was an informed shrug.

If you read carefully *The Ongoing Feast*, my doctoral thesis, you will also see that I never call Emmaus the Eucharist. In writing my thesis, my advisor, Dr. John F. McHugh, insisted that we handle this matter with great care, that is, that I should never use the words "Eucharist" or "Lord's Supper" in connection with Emmaus, since my internal examiner, James D. G. Dunn, a minister in the Church of Scotland and the Methodist Church of Great Britain, would have found this to be objectionable. Like some of my colleagues, he too lacked a sacramental imagination. Dr. McHugh catechized me on how to be careful not to refer to Emmaus as the Eucharist.

During the presidency of Robert Preus, we had protection to use our sacramental imagination in our teaching if we were careful. But as soon as he was deposed in 1989 and the new administration took over, we hunkered down and became even more judicious in the way we spoke about all things sacramental. When I was asked point-blank by the academic dean what I believed, I told him that I believed Emmaus was the Eucharist, for the very exegetical reasons listed above, but that I never said that in class, that I let the students make that determination based on our careful exegesis, which is what I thought I was supposed to do as a professor of biblical studies. He, of course, rehearsed for me all the arguments that someone like Jimmy Dunn would have given for Emmaus not being the Eucharist—"no wine" being the most popular reason it couldn't be the Lord's Supper. In my oral exam with Dunn, he asked me that very question. I responded that the table fellowship at Emmaus is described by Luke as reclining at table for a festive meal and that such meals always included wine. It was unthinkable, inhospitable, not to have wine. Jimmy Dunn was nonplussed, in its British meaning (bewildered), and not in the common American understanding (unimpressed). As a good academic, he *was* impressed by the argument that the Lukan Paschal mystery was framed by the Eucharist.

Those who argue against understanding Emmaus as the first Christian Eucharist resort to systematic arguments. For example, that the

Roman Catholics use Emmaus to argue for communion in one kind (see footnote below from the *Lutheran Confessions*) and that the Zwinglians use Emmaus to deny the bodily presence of Christ in the Supper. Many systematicians even cite Luther and Bugenhagen in support of their less-than-exegetical interpretation of Emmaus. When I cited the Lutheran Confessions in support of the exegetical freedom to interpret Emmaus as referring to the Lord's Supper, the academic dean was nonplussed in the American sense (unimpressed).[8] Exegetes and systematicians who argue against Emmaus as the Eucharist don't appreciate how this sublime narrative fits in Luke's overall plan, that is, they don't understand what Luke is doing from his prologue to the Emmaus story. Systematic arguments, especially in polemics, even from the Lutheran fathers of the sixteenth century, always seem to trump exegetical arguments.

To be charitable, none of those who argue against Emmaus as the Lord's Supper have studied Emmaus—or Luke—as I have. But their passion for dismissing Emmaus as the Eucharist belies a deeper concern, and thus the reason for this personal diversion into internecine seminary matters from CTSFW's Babylonian captivity (although I have to confess, it is a little cathartic to write about this after all these years—I am beginning to understand why memoirs are so alluring to people, both the authors and the readers—thank you, Mary Karr!).

The reason it is important to understand Emmaus as the first post-resurrection Eucharist is that *the eyes of the Emmaus disciples are opened in the breaking of the bread*![9] They are not opened in Jesus' teaching on the road that gave them burning hearts but did not open their eyes. As I have said countless times, Luke 24:31—"and their eyes were opened and they recognized him; and he himself became invisible from them"—is the

8. McCain, *Concordia*, 320–21, where in the Apology to the Augsburg Confession, Emmaus is referenced in Article XXIII in connection with "Both Kinds in the Lord's Supper": "First, they imagine at the Church's beginning, it was customary at some places to give out only one part of the Sacrament. However, they are not able to produce any ancient example for this. They quote the passages mentioning bread, as Luke 24:35, where it is written that the disciples recognized Christ in the breaking of bread. They quote also other passages (Acts 2:42, 46; 20:7) about the breaking of bread. *Although we do not object if some interpret these passages as referring to the Sacrament*, it does not make sense that only one part of the Sacrament was given. According to the ordinary usage of language, naming one part also means the other" (emphasis mine).

9. The breaking of the bread was the first designation for the Lord's Supper or the Eucharist; another reason Emmaus is eucharistic. See Dufour, *Sharing the Eucharistic Bread*, 15: "The only two names given to the Eucharist in the New Testament are 'the breaking of the bread' and 'the Lord's Supper.'"

climax of Luke's Gospel, for it is the first time a human being recognizes Jesus as the crucified and risen Lord. In this chiastic verse, Jesus is in the center.[10] And *this is the moment of conversion for the Emmaus disciples.* But it is climactic only because hearts first burn with the opening up of Scriptures (and later, among gentiles, bodies are washed). Emmaus teaches us that Word (teaching on the road) and Sacrament (the breaking of the bread) must go together. In that order. The teaching prepares for the opening of the eyes. Word prepares for Sacrament. It was the way of table fellowship in the ancient world.[11] For this reason, in the church's liturgical rite, the main structures of Word and Sacrament have endured since Jesus sat at table with the Emmaus disciples. Here is another reason why it is important to see Emmaus as the Eucharist. The final verse of the Emmaus story sets the foundation for the liturgy and her structures: "And they were expounding the things on the way [Word] and how he was known to them in the breaking of the bread [Sacrament]" (Luke 24:35—my translation).

When the disciples celebrate the Lord's Supper with Jesus at Emmaus, they are eating and drinking again with him in his kingdom, for his kingdom has come in his death and resurrection. The apostle Peter knew how important it was to see that Jesus engaged in eucharistic table fellowship after his resurrection, for he says in his sermon to Cornelius in Acts 10 how the witnesses of his resurrected body "ate and drank with him after he rose from the dead" (Acts 10:41). I do alert students to the many reasons why some argue that it is not the Lord's Supper. But most see the genius of Luke's literary craftsmanship and even more, his theological purpose—that Jesus is teaching his disciples that he will be present for them in a new way, which is why he becomes invisible to them at the Emmaus meal. He will come to them from now on through the memoirs of the apostles, which will incorporate them into the narrative of Jesus' life, and then he will open their eyes in the breaking of the bread.

Writing the Commentary on Luke

While the new leadership at CTSFW from 1989 to 1996 was trying to wipe out a sacramental imagination on our faculty (I always said that

10. See Just, *Concordia Commentary: Luke 9:51–24:53*, 1016–19.

11. See the excursus "Jesus' Table Fellowhsip" in Just, *Concordia Commentary: Luke 1:1–9:50*, 231–41.

what threatened them was "too much Christ" in our teaching), CPH had the wisdom and foresight to start a commentary series with Jonathan Grothe, Dean Wenthe, and Christopher Mitchell as the leaders of this most significant contribution to the church's life. Our specific instructions were to read the Gospels as Lutherans, through the ecumenical creeds and the Lutheran Confessions, and to especially read it as an ecclesial and liturgical document, that is, to use our sacramental imagination, even though they didn't use those words. Here is how they put it in the editor's preface that begins every commentary in this series:

> A fourth conviction is that, even as the God of the Gospel came into this world in Jesus Christ (the Word Incarnate), the scriptural Gospel has been given to and through the people of God, for the benefit of all humanity. God did not intend his Scriptures to have a life separated from the church. He gave them through servants of his choosing: prophets, sages, evangelists, and apostles. He gave them to the church and through the church, to be cherished in the church for admonition and comfort and to be used by the church for proclamation and catechesis. The living context of Scripture is ever the church, where the Lord's ministry of preaching, baptizing, forgiving sins, teaching, and celebrating the Lord's Supper continues. Aware of the way in which the incarnation of the Son of God has as a consequence the close union of Scripture and church, of Word and Sacraments, this commentary series features expositions that are *ecclesiological* and *sacramental*.[12]

Although Thomas Oden did not issue the same directive to me in compiling the wisdom of the church fathers for the Lukan volume on *Ancient Christian Commentary on Scripture* (ACCS), what he and the editors wanted at InterVarsity—to cite the general introduction of all the commentaries—was "the most noteworthy remarks of key consensual exegetes of the early Christian centuries."[13] A little later in the introduction, Oden fleshes this out:

> Selections focus more on the attempt to identify consensual strains of exegesis than sheer speculative brilliance or erratic innovation. The thought or interpretation can emerge out of individual creativity, but it must not be inconsistent with what the apostolic tradition teaches and what the church believes. What

12. Just, *Concordia Commentary: Luke 1:1–9:50*, xii. Ironically, the Lukan commentary was written during our Babylonian captivity

13. Just, ACCS, xi.

> the consensual tradition trusts least is individualistic innovation that has not yet subtly learned what the worshiping community already knows.[14]

I was fortunate that my major editor was Joel Elowsky, my colleague from St. Louis who together with Tom Oden had published the Mark volume, the first edition of the ACCS. Joel would go on to publish the two volumes on John. The ACCS certainly had more Reformed authors than Lutheran or Catholic ones, so sacramental interpretations were lacking in many of the commentaries even though the church fathers read the Scriptures ecclesially, liturgically, and sacramentally.[15] I scoured the fathers for sacramental readings, and Joel supported every one of them. A discerning reader of the ACCS will notice that my choice of readings reflects the sacramental imagination of the church fathers.

When the ACCS was published in 2003, I was exhausted from writing Luke commentaries, which began with my sabbatical in 1993–94, when I prepared my doctoral thesis for publication as *The Ongoing Feast*.[16] But Dean Wenthe knew I needed a project, so he encouraged me to write a hermeneutics, especially in light of my experience in interpreting a Gospel. This appealed to me because of my extensive experience in interpreting texts ecclesially, liturgically, and sacramentally. But I have never found hermeneutics to be an interesting topic, and I did not want to spend an inordinate amount of time reading the secondary literature on hermeneutics, which is often more philosophical than theological: I learned in college that I am not given to philosophy. I am more a practitioner than one who reflects on the practice, or as I like to say, some people like to write and talk about how to interpret a text—I just like to interpret them. Using liturgical categories, I am more given to primary theology (liturgy, preaching, catechesis) than secondary theology (reflections on theology like hermeneutics). And in many ways, the editor's preface cited above said it better than I could.

This lack of interest in reflecting on the hermeneutical task was not my own bias. When we created "the new curriculum," we decided not to have a hermeneutics course but teach hermeneutics by doing it and showing the students how to interpret texts implicitly and not explicitly,

14. Just, ACCS, xii.

15. See Just, ACCS, 382, for Augustine on Emmaus as the Eucharist: "And no one should doubt that his being recognized in the breaking of bread is the sacrament, which brings us together in recognizing him."

16. It was Dean Wenthe who gave me this title.

like the course I took at the seminary, "Principles of Biblical Interpretation" (PBI). Back then, the exegetical department wanted to give us rules of interpretation, and as I came to learn from Jesus in the Emmaus story, there is only one rule:

> And he himself said to them, "O foolish and slow in heart to believe in all the things that the prophets spoke! Was it not necessary for the Christ to suffer these things and enter into his glory? And after beginning from Moses and from *all the prophets*, he explained to them in *all the Scriptures* the things concerning himself. (Luke 24:25–27—my translation)

All the prophets in *all* the Scriptures—the things concerning himself—the passion and resurrection facts—not some of the Scriptures—not a golden messianic thread—but *all* the Scriptures are christological and speak about Jesus's death and resurrection. Sometimes that's hard to see, but it's true, and it's there for those who have eyes to see and ears to hear—for those who have a sacramental imagination!

The Key of Knowledge—Luke 24:25–27 and 11:52

This christological and sacramental hermeneutic gives one entrance into the certainty of faith which comes only through the Gospel memoirs that preach Jesus into the ears of catechumens and believers. This hermeneutic is what Jesus calls "the key of knowledge" (Luke 11:52), where he chastises the Pharisees for not seeing with eyes to see: "Woe to you lawyers, because you took away *the key of knowledge*; you yourselves did not enter in, and those entering in you prevented" (my translation). Harsh words. This key of knowledge opens up Scripture and imparts the kind of knowledge the Emmaus disciples received when Jesus opened their minds to understand the Scriptures about "the things concerning himself," and they "knew" him in the breaking of the bread. In Luke 11, Jesus says that this christological key was the responsibility of those who held offices (such as lawyers, who were biblical scholars) to disseminate a proper messianic knowledge to the people. However, they abused their office by not using the key—not imparting the knowledge of salvation to the people nor even believing it themselves. The disciples must wield the "key of knowledge" in accord with Christ's words, or else they will fall under the same condemnation as the lawyers.

These lawyers—and the rest of the scribes and Pharisees and "this generation" (11:50)—will participate in the rejection of God's spokesmen by rejecting God's final prophet, Jesus, for they are "slow in heart to believe in all the things that the prophets spoke." For the lawyers and scribes, this is the ultimate offense, since they are the official interpreters of the Scriptures, possessing the "key of knowledge," but they abuse their "office of the keys." They possess the key that gives access to faith as it is proclaimed by the prophets in their words and lives. This "key" is the Messiah proclaimed in the Old Testament Scriptures, which only comes from a sacramental imagination. In interpreting Scriptures, this is the only hermeneutic that is necessary.

The Certainty of Knowing Jesus by Faith

But we are getting ahead of ourselves. If Emmaus is Luke's end, we must go to his beginning, his prologue, unique among the Gospel writers, where he sets in motion the themes that will climax at Emmaus. Luke's prologue is crucial to understanding Emmaus as the Eucharist, the climax of the Gospel, and the moment of conversion, when eyes are opened in the breaking of the bread.

What is crucial to Luke is to understand his Gospel as catechesis for catechumens like Theophilus, the person to whom he dedicates his Gospel. Luke uses the word for catechesis in the final verse of his prologue: "in order that you come to recognize completely (ἐπιγνῷς—a derivative of the verb "to know") the certainty of the words through which you have been catechized (κατηχήθης)" (Luke 1:4—my translation). The "words" Luke writes that catechize catechumens he calls a "narrative." Luke is writing a story about Jesus based on other narratives such as Matthew's Gospel. As we have noted, Luke uses the word "narrative" in the first verse of his Gospel: "Since many have endeavored to reproduce a narrative (διήγησιν) concerning the events that have come to fulfillment among us . . ." (Luke 1:1—my translation).

This narrative contains the words Luke uses to catechize Theophilus about "events," the things that happened in history which Luke now records. A narrative about events is the story that Luke tells about Jesus—what Justin Martyr calls "memoirs." The meaning and content of "words" as "narrative" is the Gospel that Luke writes to catechize his catechumens about the events of Jesus life and ministry. These events were witnessed by the twelve, the women, the seventy, and the faithful remnant, with the final climactic event of the great conversion of the Emmaus disciples. Words and Events—these two go together as the two "structures" that form the foundation for apostolic liturgy that has been handed down to us today—teaching and healing—Word and Meal—the structures of the liturgy and the means for mission.

In my beginning is my end—the liturgical structures are foretold in the prologue (Luke 1:1–4) and reach their climax at Emmaus (Luke 24:35). Together, words as narrative form the core of what becomes know as "the liturgy of the catechumens" by the early church fathers. For this reason, Luke ends his prologue with the goal he has in mind for his Gospel—*certainty* in the words as narrative that comes only when eyes are opened in the breaking of the bread. Catechesis in the catechumenate precedes baptism, and the climax of a full conversion is the Lord's Supper, which comes immediately following washing at the font, for after you are reborn, the church feeds you holy food.

There is another word in the final verse of Luke's prologue that connects it with the conversion of the Emmaus disciples—the word for recognition or knowing—translated above as "recognize completely." Luke writes his narrative so that catechumens like Theophilus might come to recognize in full (ἐπιγνῷς) that Jesus is the crucified and risen Messiah. But how will Theophilus come to recognize completely that the words through which he has been catechized are certain? That recognition is the recognition of faith's certainty. This recognition that Jesus is the crucified and risen Christ first happens for a human being by sight and by faith at Emmaus, where Luke uses the same word for recognition in describing what the Emmaus disciples experienced when their eyes were opened "in the breaking of the bread"—"and their eyes were opened and they recognized him (ἐπέγνωσαν)" (Luke 24:31).

"Recognize" is one of Luke's many synonyms for faith and its certainty in the reliability of Christian catechesis. Perhaps we should return to the translation of "knowing" because it captures best the character of this recognition. It is not a knowledge that is noetic or that comes through the senses. The Emmaus disciples do more than simply see Jesus for who he is and understand more fully the words he had spoken to them during his ministry about his death and resurrection. This "knowing" is the knowing of Genesis in the communion Adam has with Eve as husband and wife. The Emmaus disciples now "know" Jesus because they participated in his body and blood, his flesh, and by that knowing they had communion with him. The Emmaus disciples may have "known" the historical facts about Jesus' passion and resurrection (Luke 24:18–24), but they did not understand the meaning of those facts (24:25), nor had they experienced that sacramental oneness that comes from participation in the very flesh of Christ. They did not know what Paul knew when he wrote the Corinthians about what it means to "know" Jesus in the breaking of the bread:

> The cup of blessing that we bless, is it not a communion/participation/fellowship (κοινωνία) in the blood of Christ? The bread that we break, is it not a communion/participation/fellowship in the body of Christ? (1 Cor 10:16—my translation)

The goal of Jesus' catechesis—and of the Emmaus narrative—is for the hearer "to believe in all the things that the prophets spoke" (24:25). At the beginning of the story in 24:16, the disciples' eyes were kept by God (theological passive) from perceiving Jesus; at the end of the story, the veil was taken away by God. Faith's certainty (1:4) came only when Christ interpreted the passion and resurrection facts and revealed himself in the breaking of the bread by incorporating them into his own flesh. *This is why it must be the Eucharist at Emmaus for this recognition is a communion with his flesh.*

These events, these "passion and resurrection facts" as they are described by Jesus in Luke 24, are now given to the Emmaus disciples in "the breaking of the bread," in body broken and blood poured out. To reiterate, one of the ironies and truths of the Emmaus story is that Jesus' catechesis on the road created burning hearts, but his words failed to open their eyes. It was only "in the breaking of the bread" that their eyes were opened and they "knew" him by their incorporation into his crucified and risen flesh.

So when Theophilus (whom we will describe below as a gentile convert—a godfearer like Luke?—to the Christian faith) attended the first Eucharist, in which Luke's Gospel was read and preached upon—he came to the table with a burning heart, knowing and believing that he had heard the living voice of Jesus in Luke's Gospel narrative and that this teaching prepared him to "know" the risen Christ "in the breaking of the bread" in a way not unlike the union of husband and wife, where the two become one flesh. "This mystery is profound, and I am saying that it refers to Christ and the church" (Eph 5:32).

In this, Theophilus and all believers who follow him can be certain that Word and Event, Word and Miracle, Word and Meal, are the source of faith's certainty and the means for mission.

Luke and Theophilus—Gentile Converts?

So how did the evangelist Luke come to such a profound understanding of the Gospel? He was certainly a convert—but from what? Hellenistic Judaism? Paganism? His knowledge of the Old Testament, of Jerusalem and the temple, was so profound, he must have been either a Hellenistic Jew or a gentile god-fearer. Recently someone suggested that he could have been a priest,[17] which would account for his intimate knowledge of the liturgical rites of Judaism and would mean that he was a priest in the way Barnabas was, a Levite from Cyprus, not a Palestinian Jew but a Hellenistic one. This is an intriguing suggestion, as it would mean that over half of the New Testament would have been written by a Pharisee (Paul) and a priest (Luke). However, as attractive as this might be, it seems unlikely.

Scholars seem to be split between whether Luke was a Hellenistic Jew or a gentile/godfearer. Even the assessment of Eusebius—that Luke was a native of Antioch, Syria—would not indicate his religious origins, for the city and the church in Antioch were a mixture of Jews and gentiles.[18] But whether you choose Semitic origins or gentile ones, like everyone in the first century, Jew and gentile alike, Luke was a convert, and he may have

17. Strelan, *Luke the Priest*. Ambrose might be cited to support Strelan's thesis. See Just, ACCS, 1–2: "And the Evangelist, writing in historical mode, makes his beginning in narrative form: 'There was,' he says, 'in the days of Herod, the King of Judea, a certain priest named Zachariah,' and continues the story with a full and orderly description. Hence, those who think that the four living creatures described in the Apocalypse are to be understood as the four books of the Gospel wish this book to be represented by the calf; for the calf is the priestly victim. This Gospel is represented fittingly by the calf, because it begins with priests and ends with the Calf Who, having taken upon Himself the sins of all, was sacrificed for the life of the whole world. He was a Priestly Calf. He is both Calf and Priest. He is the Priest, because He is our Propitiator. We have Him as an Advocate with the Father. He is the Calf, because He redeemed us with His Own Blood."

18. See Just, ACCS, 2, from Eusebius on Luke: "Luke, who was by race an Antiochian and by profession a physician. He long had been a companion of Paul and had more than a casual acquaintance with the rest of the apostles. He left for us, in two inspired books, examples of the art of healing souls that he obtained from them. These books are, namely: 1) the Gospel . . . 2) The Acts of the Apostles, which he composed not from hearsay evidence but as evidenced before his own eyes. They say that Paul was actually accustomed to quote the Gospel according to St. Luke. When writing about some Gospel as his own, he used to say, 'According to my Gospel.'"

been responsible for the conversions of many gentiles in Macedonia and Achaia, if there is any truth to the tradition that he was the pastor of the church in Philippi.[19] And what he learned from his own conversion, he reflected in the way in which he shaped his Gospel.

So, this is what we may be able to say about the evangelist.

He was a physician and a companion of Paul. As Eusebius suggested, Luke and Acts are "examples of the art of healing souls" (see footnote), and Luke's Gospel has more miracles of healing than the other Gospels. The "we sections" of Acts suggest that he not only traveled with Paul but was a good friend of Paul's going back perhaps to when Paul came to Antioch in AD 42, if Luke was in fact a resident there at that time (sanctified speculation). Luke could have been among the first converts in Antioch or perhaps came to believe in Jesus after Barnabas came to Antioch from Jerusalem. Antioch would have been a good place to become a physician, and he may have been Paul's physician after his first missionary journey when he suffered a stoning and was left half-dead along the side of the road outside Lystra. In all likelihood, Luke would have known and perhaps been close friends with both Barnabas and Paul. If Paul died in AD 65, that means Paul and Luke were friends for over twenty years. Since Paul was in Jerusalem for most of his adult life attending the Gamaliel school for Pharisees, and Barnabas was in Jerusalem for many years, perhaps as a priest, they would have both participated in the temple rites and would have an intimate knowledge of them, especially an understanding of their significance in connection to the holiness and purity codes. If Paul and Barnabas were friends of Luke's for twenty years, they had a great deal of time to catechize Luke on the temple rites and other Jewish matters that are shot through Luke's Gospel. If this is true, Paul and Barnabas were Luke's catechists. And there's every reason to believe that Luke may have spent some time in Jerusalem himself.

In October of 2001, I became even more convinced that Luke was from Antioch through a report on NPR and an article in the *New York Times* entitled "'Body of St. Luke' Gains Credibility."[20] It supported Eusebius's claims that Luke was from Antioch, as well as the Eastern tradition that claims Luke died in Thebes, Greece. Both reports indicated that some of Luke's remains were translated to his tomb in Thebes, which had

19. See my essay "Luke's Canonical Criterion," 259–60, where I argue that Paul was a pastor in Philippi. Parts of that essay are adapted in this chapter.

20. Wade, "'Body of St. Luke'"; All Things Considered, "Saint Luke." https://www.npr.org/2001/10/16/1131534/saint-luke

been awaiting his relics for centuries. Like many relics, Luke's traveled from place to place, particularly from Constantinople to the Basilica of St. Justina in Padua, Italy (she is an early fourth-century martyr). The skull of St. Luke is claimed by St. Vitus Cathedral in Prague, Czech Republic, where many of us were present at a Mass for the Feast of St. Luke in 2022 during a theological conference.

These reports from the *New York Times* and NPR piqued my interest, although I did not pay too much attention to them. However, in February 2002, Linda and I led our first Nawas seminary tour to Greece and Turkey. Our guide Fay, a PhD in archaeology from the University of Minnesota and a faithful member of the Greek Orthodox Church, was also devoted to the evangelist St. Luke. At that time, the CPH commentary was not even five years old, and I was working on the ACCS commentary on Luke, so the third Gospel was very much a part of my working life. As our trip started, Fay and I had lively conversations about Luke and Paul and the role Greece played in the New Testament. She not only confirmed the story I heard on NPR and read in the *New York Times*, she was also completely convinced that on the seventeenth of September 2000, a rib from Luke's skeleton, the one closest to his heart, was now in Thebes, given by the bishop of Padua to Metropolitan Hieronymos as an ecumenical gesture of reconciliation between East and West. Now one relic from St. Luke found a home in the same ancient sepulcher, which tradition claims is the first resting place of the evangelist. Even though Thebes was not on our itinerary, it was on the way to Delphi from Athens, and after taking a survey of the bus, everyone agreed that we must stop to visit the tomb of the evangelist St. Luke.

For many on that tour, Thebes and St. Luke's sepulcher became one of the highlights of our trip. Thebes is not a tourist town like other places in Greece, so our driver, off his regular route, found himself in downtown Thebes with a bus too large for its narrow streets. But his expertise in maneuvering around tight corners provided great entertainment for both the people on our bus and the residents of this sleepy town. The Church of Agios Loukas is located outside the town in an unassuming setting, small and quaint. All forty of us piled out of the bus to be greeted by a young priest with perfect English who charmed us with the story of how Luke's rib made its way to this isolated spot. Again, his story conformed to what we had heard from several different sources. After photos with him next to the sepulcher of St. Luke, many happy LCMS pilgrims to

Greece and Turkey hopped back on the bus to make their way to the great pagan shrine of Delphi.

In piecing together what we know of Luke, Paul, and Barnabas, it makes perfect sense that this Syrian from Antioch, who was pastor in Macedonia, would be buried in Thebes, Greece, where he and Paul made their mark as pastors and missionaries to the gentiles.

The Gospel of Luke for Jewish Christians Evangelizing Gentiles

There is no doubt that Luke is a Gospel written for gentiles during the third phase of evangelization in the ancient church, right after the Pauline missionary journeys had come to end. But a subtle distinction should be made. Gentiles would have a difficult time understanding Luke's Gospel unless they had an interpreter. How could they understand the significance of beginning and ending the Gospel in the temple without knowing the significance of God's holiness in the temple?[21] How could they understand the significance of the shift of the locale of God's presence from the temple to the womb of the virgin Mary? Or the synagogue liturgy in Luke 4 and the Passover Seder in Luke 22? (Luke has the only evidence of a synagogue liturgy in the New Testament and the most detailed structure of the Passover among the Gospels.) Or how could they understand his eighth-day theology without knowing the significance of the Sabbath? To understand Jesus, one needs to understand his Jewishness, and how could a gentile know this without catechesis from someone who did? Luke's Gospel would be incomprehensible to them in its detailed descriptions of what it meant to be a Jew, especially a worshiping Jew. For this reason, I have always maintained that Luke is writing a Gospel for Jewish Christians who are evangelizing and catechizing God-fearers and pagan gentiles. One of those God-fearers and/or pagan gentiles is Theophilus.

Some people find it troubling to claim that Scripture needs an interpreter and is not self-evident (perspicacious in its narrowest meaning). Although the response to the CPH commentary on Luke was overwhelming positive, the few negative comments I received centered on the claim that Luke did not write to gentiles directly, because it would be hard for them to understand the Jewishness of Jesus, but that Luke wrote to Jewish Christians who would interpret Luke for gentiles in their pre-baptismal

21. Luke 1:5–25, with Zechariah in the Holy Place offering the atonement sacrifices. Luke 24:53: "And they were through all time in the temple, blessing God." (my translation)

catechesis. In retrospect, I wish I had included a brief paragraph that supported the claim that Scripture needs an interpreter by referring to the scene in Acts 8 between Philip and the Ethiopian eunuch.

The conversion of the Ethiopian eunuch is often used as an example that you do not need to catechize before baptism. But what is this eunuch reading when Philip meets him on the road? It's the prophet Isaiah, specifically, Isa 53, one of the most profound statements in the Old Testament on the passion of the Christ. The Ethiopian eunuch must have had some knowledge of the Old Testament, but like many of the Jews in the first century, although they knew the Old Testament Scriptures, they did not know the full messianic significance of what they were reading. They did not have "the key of knowledge." Philip seems to understand this and asks him, "Do you understand what you are reading?" (Acts 8:30). The Ethiopian eunuch's response supports my contention that Luke's Gospel to gentiles needs Jewish Christian interpreters. He says to Philip, "How can I, unless someone guides me?" (Acts 8:31). Although the Ethiopian eunuch chose wisely in reading Isa 53, he did not understand its meaning, especially its messianic meaning concerned suffering, which is why he asks Philip, "About whom, I ask you, does the prophet say this, about himself or about someone else?" (Acts 8:34). Philip then delivers the goods: "Then [he] opened his mouth, and beginning with this Scripture he told him the good news about Jesus." (Acts 8:35). Because he knew the Scriptures, there was no need to prevent him from being baptized, like all the Jewish converts who compose the large numbers of converts in the first part of Acts of the Apostles—even at Pentecost—for he was given "the key of knowledge" by Philip.

The Ethiopian eunuch becomes paradigmatic for all converts to the Christian faith in the first century, including Luke and Theophilus. Even Jews need an interpreter, which is why Paul goes from synagogue to synagogue opening up the Scriptures to them. N. T. Wright, in his *Paul: A Biography*, suggests that Paul followed a formula in his preaching in the synagogue like the one in Corinth:

> "We must assume that he rehearses yet again the familiar narrative: Abraham, Exodus, David, exile, hope. The focus is likewise the same: scripture speaks of a Messiah who dies and rises again, and this Messiah is Jesus . . . He summarizes this even more sharply: 'When I came to you . . . ,' he says, 'I decided to know

> nothing in my dealings with you except Jesus the Messiah, especially his crucifixion.'"[22]

Such an outline may have been how Philip told the good news of Jesus to the Ethiopian eunuch, who clearly was a God-fearer who knew the Old Testament Scriptures. Both Philip and Paul are interpreters for both Jews and gentiles.

Theophilus as a Philippian Catechumen

But if Luke was a catechumen and a gentile convert, so also was Theophilus—perhaps a catechumen in the church in Philippi—a wealthy man who offered to serve as a literary patron of Luke's Gospel during that celebration of the Pascha of AD 58, when Paul came through Philippi and the "we section" of Acts begins again. Perhaps the "most excellent Theophilus" to whom Luke dedicates both the Gospel and Acts was a wealthy catechumen in Phillipi.

Could this Theophilus be like many gentiles who were yearning for a Gospel to be written for them? Assuming Matthean priority, could Theophilus, a gentile, have been listening to Luke preach on Matthew for seven years and now be willing to serve as a literary patron, a financial one, for a Gospel in his own "language," so to speak, a Gospel for him, a gentile, a Roman citizen, so that he could hear the Jesus story from an Hellenistic point of view? Matthew's Gospel was reliable and certain, but Theophilus desired a Gospel for him and people like him, one that is Pauline, written now at the end of Paul's missionary journeys, written for the churches Paul had founded among the gentiles in both Asia Minor and Europe. Could Luke's Gospel now be used in the conversion of the gentiles and the gentile mission by Jewish Christian pastors and catechists for evangelizing and catechizing them?

The danger of a "new" Gospel is that it would be measured against the "certainty" of Matthew's Gospel, with all its Jewish and Jerusalem gravity. Could Luke measure up? Could Theophilus and the gentiles in Philippi be "certain" that Luke's Gospel could serve as catechesis for gentiles as Matthew's Gospel had served as catechesis for Jews, and then

22. Wright, *Paul*, 212–13. See also 118–21 for Wright's more extensive description of what this first looked like in Paul's sermon in the synagogue of Antioch Pisidia during his first missionary journey. Wright, *Paul*, 119, notes that Paul "was announcing *the fulfillment of the long-range divine plan*" (emphasis Wright).

later bring certainty for gentiles like Theophilus? Would Jerusalem approve? Perhaps this is the reason Luke refers to Cleopas by name as one of the Emmaus disciples. Tradition affirms that Cleopas is Joseph's brother, Jesus' uncle, and the other unnamed disciple is Simeon, Cleopas's son, Jesus' cousin, the second bishop of Jerusalem. Simeon would have been presiding over Jerusalem when Luke's Gospel began circulating in the churches. As the Gospel of Paul, Luke's Gospel may not have been as well received in Jerusalem as it was in other places. But what better way to receive approbation that to have the bishop of Jerusalem give his episcopal imprimatur as one of the Emmaus disciples, a level of "certainty" that would not go unnoticed by the Jerusalem church.

So, could the Jesus story be told from another point of view, a Hellenistic one, and from a Pauline perspective? The purpose of Luke's prologue to his Gospel, addressed to "most excellent Theophilus," is to affirm that his Gospel was as reliable as Matthew's and that the oral and written traditions that Luke used to compile his Gospel were as faithful and true to the Gospel story as Matthew's. Could the prologue's final word—"certainty," "reliability," "truth"—reach its goal for Theophilus only when he reads in Luke 24 that the eyes of the Emmaus disciples were opened in the breaking of bread, and only then did they recognize him *because certainty finally comes at the Eucharist*?

Theophilus is a real person, *not* some archetypal "lover of God," even though such a designation was made by Origen and later by Ambrose who used Origen's commentary on Luke for his own commentary.[23] Theophilus is Luke's literary patron, a God-fearer, who has been catechized by Jewish materials (Matthew) but who may now be encouraging Luke to write a gospel for the catechesis of gentiles by Jewish Christians. Like Luke, he is interested in the conversion of his own people. Living in the historical context of the first century, he is a gentile seeking certainty in a gentile way from Luke and Paul.

23. Just, ACCS, 4, from Origen: "Someone might think that Luke addressed the Gospel to a specific man named Theophilus. But, if you are the sort of people God can love, then all of you who hear us speaking are 'Theophiluses,' and the Gospel is addressed to you. Anyone who is a Theophilus is both 'excellent' and 'very strong.' This is what the Greek word Θεόφιλυς [Theophilus] actually means." Or Ambrose, "Exposition of the Gospel of Luke," "So the Gospel was written to Theophilos, i.e., to him whom God loves. If you love God, it was written to you. If it was written to you . . ."

The Two Audiences of the Gospel

In the prologue that is dedicated to Theophilus, Luke is telling him another important "key of knowledge" for interpreting his Gospel—how the eyewitnesses *from the beginning* became ministers of the Word and delivered the narrative of Jesus's suffering, death, and resurrection to Theophilus and others like him. *Eyewitnesses* and *ministers of the Word* are the two intended audiences addressed by the evangelist in his Gospel, both of which taken together constitute the *first-century audience.*

The first of these two audiences—the eyewitnesses—include the twelve apostles, the seventy(-two), the crowds/people, and the religious establishment, that is, those people who were present for the historical events described in the Gospel. For example, the first audience would be Mary at the annunciation, or the leper when he was cleansed by Jesus in Luke 5, or the widow and her son at Nain and the crowds who saw Jesus perform that great miracle. The first audience historically participates in the very life of Jesus himself, even though during his earthly life they never fully understand what was happening. *The first audience never fully understands the gospel until the end of the story.* They fail to comprehend that Jesus must go to Jerusalem, give up his life in an atoning sacrifice to release the world from its bondage, rise on the third day, and ascend on the fortieth day. To use the language of Luke, they didn't know about his departure (9:31) or his lifting up (9:51)—his movement from heaven to earth and back to heaven.[24] Not only did the first audience fail to understand what was happening, they rejected Jesus when he spoke about himself in the passion predictions about how he must go the way of suffering and death. The eyewitness disciples become increasingly confused and cannot comprehend what he must do (Luke 9:22, 44–45; 17:25; 18:31–34). *This first audience does not understand God's plan of salvation in Jesus until after the resurrection and Pentecost!*

The second audience is the community of believers who received Luke's Gospel, which would include the twelve and the seventy-(two) who are now *ministers of the Word.* But it is also composed of catechumens like Theophilus, who are either preparing for baptism or are already baptized and communing with Christ in the Eucharist. These are liturgical Christians who are living in a eucharistic community. They receive and use Luke's Gospel in the context of liturgy as part of the Liturgy of the Word, along with readings from the Old Testament and other New

24. Just, *Concordia Commentary: Luke 1:1–9:50*, 22.

Testament documents. The difference between the first and second audiences is that Luke's eucharistic community of catechumens *knows the end of the story*—they know that Christ has gone to the cross, risen, ascended, and that after Pentecost, he is continually present in the church through his Spirit in the liturgy of the church. Jesus' presence in both his human and divine natures is just as real in his church as it was in his earthly ministry. It is a *real presence* in body as well as in spirit. It comes through the proclamation of the Word and the administration of the Lord's Supper.

Luke's audience can now hear the historical events of Luke's Gospel with ears that hear. As a gentile from Antioch, catechized by Matthew's Gospel through the teaching of Paul and Barnabas, Luke himself would have understood the benefits of a Gospel written for him to be used by Jewish Christians like Paul and Barnabas to catechize him, a gentile or godfearer, in the way of Jesus. How much more would a Macedonian Greek like Theophilus, living far from the eastern Mediterranean cities of Antioch and Jerusalem, living in Philippi, a gentile city, appreciate and treasure such a Gospel? As a pastor in Philippi, Luke knew that the saints in his church would hear the Gospel not unlike the Emmaus disciples heard it. The "teaching on the road" occurred in the Liturgy of the Word (catechesis) and "the breaking of the bread" in the Liturgy of the Lord's Supper. For unbaptized catechumens, the Liturgy of the Word explained what would happen when they entered this eucharistic community of the baptized. For baptized catechumens, the Liturgy of the Word illumined and strengthened their baptismal union with Christ and prepared them for his coming in the Lord's Supper and at the parousia. *It cannot be overemphasized that those who receive Luke's Gospel hear, in light of the passion and resurrection facts, Pentecost and Christ's ongoing presence in the church.*

As an example of how the different audiences interpret the words of Jesus, let's take the controversial passages in John 6. Throughout my career, John 6 has been a lightning rod among Lutherans, as to whether the words of Jesus are to be taken as eucharistic or not. Although I understood the arguments on both sides, there always seemed a much simpler explanation than what was being offered. It was only when I began to look at John 6 from the hermeneutical perspective of the two audiences that I began to see how there may be a way forward for both sides.

For the first audience, the disciples of Jesus and all who were present when he first spoke the words recorded in John 6, they would have been incomprehensible, let alone understood by them as eucharistic. What could Jesus possibly have meant when he said, "I am the living bread that came down from heaven. If anyone eats of this bread, he will live forever. And the bread that I will give for the life of the world is my flesh" (John 6:51)? Or even these more perplexing words: "Truly, truly, I say to you, unless you eat the flesh of the Son of Man and drink his blood, you have no life in you. Whoever feeds on my flesh and drinks my blood has eternal life, and I will raise him up on the last day. For my flesh is true food, and my blood is true drink. Whoever feeds on my flesh and drinks my blood abides in me, and I in him." (John 6:53–56). John shows us that this first audience is struggling to make meaning out of these words of Jesus: "When many of his disciples heard it, they said, 'This is a hard saying; who can listen to it?'" (John 6:60). We must agree. This is a hard saying. At this point in his ministry, it would be almost impossible to understand what Jesus means that his flesh is bread and that unless we eat the flesh of the Son of Man and drink his blood, there is no life in us.

Jesus knew they were perplexed by his words and points them to the future, when he will ascend to his Father, when they will be able to understand "the words that I have spoken to you [that they] are spirit and life" (John 6:63) because his Spirit, the Holy Spirit, will have come upon them at Pentecost to enlighten them to understand the full eucharistic meaning of his words *because they now know the end of the story*.

And there is also this. The second audience looks back at the words of John 6 from a table where they are eating his flesh and drinking his blood. They now understand what he was saying to them when those words seemed incomprehensible. The one intended sense of those words in John 6 is that Jesus was talking about how he would feed them with his body and blood in the ongoing eucharistic life of the church after Pentecost, even though they did not understand that is what he meant when he first spoke those words.

Like the Synoptic Gospels, John's Gospel is a book of the church, written for the church, to be used by the church in its proclamation of the Gospel to the unbaptized and the baptized in its celebration of the Eucharist. This eucharistic community now reads the words of Jesus in John 6 as they now stand at font, pulpit, and altar where Christ is present in his flesh. Thus, the context in which Scripture is received and understood is *liturgical*, that is, a church that worships Christ, who is present in the reading and preaching of the Word and the receiving of the Sacraments. This sacramental reading as the second eucharistic audience is also part of the "key of knowledge" that opens up the Scriptures to its true christological meaning.

7

A Lukan (and Lutheran) Theology of Mary

THE VIRGIN MARY FIRST captured my attention in Mexico City when we visited *Insigne y Nacional Basílica de Santa María de Guadalupe*. For a thirteen-year-old Lutheran boy, this was an eye-opener. Watching the young and old crawl on bloody knees up the steps of the *basílica* to pay homage to one of the most famous apparitions of the Virgin in the world impressed upon me that there was something about Mary that caused these people such veneration and devotion. These acts of raw piety were both stunning and disturbing because it seemed more like worship than devotion. In subsequent years, especially with my work in Latin America, the Caribbean, and Spain, I came to understand how the blessed Virgin overshadowed Jesus.

When Pastor Ted Krey, the regional director of Latin America, the Caribbean, and Spain, asked me to represent him in Spain for ten weeks in 2012, I told him that when speaking to the Spaniards about Mary, I would hold her with the utmost respect and honor. He wholeheartedly supported me, confessing that when he started his missionary work in Venezuela, he wished he had spoken more positively of her. We both agreed that someone should write a biblical (and Lutheran) theology of Mary, and for these past fourteen years I've threatened to do so. This theological memoir is my attempt to reflect on why Lutherans need to hold Mary in the highest regard.

When I reentered Spain's deeply Marian culture in 2002, almost every Spanish church represented both Jesus and Mary in statuary and other forms of art, but Mary often seemed to take precedence over Jesus. Devotion to Mary is deeply embedded in Spanish culture, going back to time of the New Testament, when St. James, the elder son of Zebedee, visited Spain and, as legend holds, received an apparition of Mary on the banks of the Ebro River in Zaragoza on the second of January in AD 40. This was four years before James's death in Jerusalem as the first martyr among the twelve apostles of Jesus (and before Mary's dormition and assumption, according to Roman Catholic tradition). Spaniards make pilgrimage to the *Catedral-Basílica de Nuestra Señora del Pilar* in Zaragoza on the twelfth of October, Columbus Day, El Día de la Hispanidad (The Day of Hispanic Identity). Zaragoza is now the center of Spain's Spanish identity and its Marian piety.

So, Spaniards consider their Marian piety apostolic. It is also tied to the reality of human suffering and Mary's role in comforting those who suffer. This is so perfectly illustrated by the *La Virgen de los Desamparados*, patroness of the city of Valencia, whose image is housed in her *basílica*, which stands next to the cathedral but draws more people daily for worship and devotion. This Virgin, dedicated to the those who are broken, downtrodden, and forsaken, demonstrates Mary's appeal for all those suffering from loneliness and despair. Her image leans forward a little as if she is reaching out for us, holding a lily in one hand and the baby Jesus grasping a cross in the other hand, a posture so endearing to the *Valencianos* that they call her the *Geperudeta* (hunchback) of Valencia. This Valencian Virgin captures why Mary is so revered among Spaniards and Latin Americans: she is our mother, the mother many never had, who cares for us with a heart of compassion and love. Her Son, by comparison, is often seen as a stern taskmaster and lawgiver who is inaccessible because of his great suffering.

This Valencian Mary is beloved because she is *La Virgen de los Desamparados*, the one who comforts and consoles the forsaken and the desolate. As early as the fifteenth century, she inspired the building of a hospital for the mentally ill and the insane, which then led to the building of a *basílica* to house her image (on the site of a Roman temple).

Such devotion to the Virgin Mary is typical of much of Spain and Latin America because she inspires people in a way that Jesus does not.

She is their mother, the mother of the church, and everyone needs a mother. But some expressions of devotion, like the one we witnessed in Valencia, can be unnerving for Lutherans. The move from devotion to worship is sometimes imperceptible as Mary becomes the focus of our redemption instead of Jesus.[1] Many expressions of Marian piety are hard to defend and go beyond the biblical evidence. This example from Valencia shows how important Mary is to so many people in Christendom—that to ignore her importance hinders our evangelization of those who hold her with such honor.

So, what does the Bible say about Mary, or more specifically, what does Luke have to say about Mary (I will make brief references to John 2 and Rev 12)? My focus will be on four things: Mary as the New Israel, the Temple, and the Ark of the Covenant; Mary's Hermeneutic of Humility—Breaking What Is Whole and Making Whole What is Broken; the Memoirs of Mary as She Ponders the Meaning of Jesus' Birth and Suffering; and Mary as the New Eve and Mother of the Family of God.

In discussing these four points, I will also consider beliefs about Mary which some churches hold that are not *explicitly* in the Bible, as to whether they are defendable and worthy of our attention.

What Does Luke Say About Mary as the New Israel, the Temple, and the Ark of the Covenant?

It was my doctoral father, John McHugh, who first introduced me to a biblical theology of Mary with his monumental book *The Mother of Jesus in the New Testament*.[2] His influence on my interpretation of the infancy narratives in the CPH Luke commentary is clearly apparent where I

1. I always commented that you never see Mary on a cross, and then I did. Jesus on one side and Mary on the other, a graphic expression that Mary is a co-redeemer. It was shocking to say the least. In October 2025, however, the Vatican, with Pope Leo XIV's approval, said that the church is not to refer to Mary as the "co-redeemer" of the world. This is clearly a positive move for the Roman Catholic view of Mary.

2. McHugh, *Mother of Jesus*. There are three other books I consulted in writing this chapter and highly recommend them, one from a Protestant and the other two from Roman Catholics: Scot McKnight, *The Real Mary*; Scott Hahn, *Hail, Holy Queen*; and Brant Pitre, *Jesus and the Jewish Roots of Mary*. I also highly recommend "Do Whatever He Tells You: The Blessed Virgin Mary in the Christian Faith and Life"—A Statement of Evangelical and Catholics Together—November 2008.

attempt to show *from the text* how Mary is portrayed as the new Israel, the temple, and the ark of the covenant. This is the place to begin.[3]

Everything that needs to be said about Mary could be discerned from the first two chapters of Luke, and in truth, from the annunciation. The evangelist shapes his story of the infancy of John the Baptist and Jesus by paralleling these last two great figures in salvation history yet showing that Jesus is the greater one. The old covenant is giving way to the new. John is great before the Lord, but Jesus is Great. As they begin their ministries, John is the forerunner who prepares Israel for the incandescent holiness Jesus brings as the Holy One of God. The baptism of Jesus is the breaking point for Luke between old and new, but in Luke 3:20 we find John locked up in prison before the baptism of Jesus (3:21–22), where John goes unnamed. This indicates that his ministry of preparation is over; the Messiah has arrived to begin his work of redemption. John retreats, as he says in John's Gospel: "He must increase, but I must decrease" (John 3:30).

Matthias Grünewald's painting of the crucifixion of Jesus on the Isenheim altarpiece captures John's role: standing on the left of Jesus, John points to him, a lamb at his feet, and you can almost hear him saying, "Behold, the Lamb of God, who takes away the sin of the world!" (John 1:29). John's role is to point to Jesus, and then he fades away by dying a martyr's death.

Mary plays a similar role to John the Baptist. Matthias Grünewald's crucifixion places her on the right of Jesus, the place of honor, weeping because the prophecy is coming true—the sword is piercing her soul. She is on the right because she is greater than John. Even though John, the greatest of the all the prophets (Luke 7:28), prepared the way, Mary is indispensable to our salvation. Without her, there would be no incarnation. Without her, Jesus would not have flesh and blood. But as soon as she gives birth to the Savior, like John, she also must say, "Jesus must increase, but I must decrease." Mary does appear again—in the visitation and the Magnificat, her programmatic hymn (Luke 1:39–56); at the birth of Jesus (Matt 1:18–25; Luke 2:1–20); in the temple in Jerusalem at Jesus' presentation and when he returns at twelve years old to teach (Luke 2:21–40; 41–52); at the wedding of Cana (John 2:1–12); during Jesus' ministry (Mark 3:31–35; 6:1–6; Luke 11:27–28); at the cross (Mark 15:40–41; John

3. Readers will recognize parts of the Lukan commentary woven throughout these pages. For a fully exposition of some of the points, see Just, *Concordia Commentary: Luke 1:1–9:50* and *Concordia Commentary: Luke 9:51–24:53*.

19:25–27); at Pentecost (Acts 1:12–14); in Gal 4:4, where Jesus is said to be born of a woman; and in Rev 12, as the woman clothed with the sun.[4]

These are not insignificant appearances, but they emphasize that Mary's role has changed. At Cana, the fourth commandment is reversed, and she learns to be obedient to her son; during Jesus' ministry, she realizes that Jesus is forging a new family, of which she may be its first and most important mother (see the kinship laws and Pentecost below); and at the cross, she suffers alongside Jesus, the sword piercing her soul and all of Israel. But what strikes us about Mary here is her complete normality—the real Mary is a worried mother, a searching mother, and a suffering one.[5]

But a Lukan theology of Mary begins and ends in Nazareth at the annunciation (Luke 1:26–38). It is one of four uniquely Lukan passages that define his Gospel and set the tone for his theological themes (the other three are: 4:16–30, release from bondage in the sermon in Nazareth; 15:11–32, mercy and joy in the prodigal son; and 24:13–35, Word and Meal, the foundational liturgical structures and the means for mission in the Emmaus story). The theme Luke announces in the annunciation is that there is now a shift in the locale of God's holy presence—from Israel with its temple and ark to the womb of the Virgin Mary, who now is Israel reduced to one upon whom the glory cloud, the *Shekinah* of God's presence, now rests. Mary the woman is the one who gave Jesus his blood and his human DNA.[6] How could we not honor Mary and show her our greatest devotion—not only is she the mother of our Lord, as Elizabeth calls her (Luke 1:43), but the mother of God, the *Theotokos*, as the council of Ephesus affirmed in AD 431. At the annunciation, Mary, like the temple and the ark, is now the dwelling place of God on earth—not because of who she is but by the grace God has gifted her.

4. Even the great Protestant scholar Ben Witherington III acknowledges the woman in Rev 12 is Mary, as cited by Pitre, *Jesus and the Jewish Roots of Mary*, 32: "I would suggest . . . that this figure [the 'woman' of Revelation 12] is both *the literal mother of the male child Jesus,* and also *the female image of the people of God.*"

5. McKnight, *Real Mary*, 106, notes that there are "217 verses in the New Testament in which Mary plays a part."

6. Hahn, *Hail*, 95–96, cites these poignant words from John Henry Newman: "It was no heavenly body which the Eternal Son assumed . . . No, He imbibed, He sucked up her blood and her substance into His Divine Person. He became man from her and received her lineaments and her features as the appearance and character under which He should manifest Himself to the world. He was known, doubtless, by His likeness to her, to be her Son."

Mary as the New Israel

The angel's first words to Mary are these: "Rejoice, favored woman, the Lord is with you" (Luke 1:28—my translation). The ESV has "greetings" instead of "rejoice," which it is, but it is so much more. This Greek word (Χαῖρε) is addressed to the "Daughter of Zion" twice in the LXX: in Zeph 3:14 and Zech 9:9, suggesting that Mary is now to rejoice (Luke 1:46–56) because the Savior has come to her—the Lord is with her—the Lord will soon be in her womb. As the daughter of Zion, the angel is addressing Mary as "the New Israel."

John McHugh captures the full meaning of this:

> [Zephaniah] envisages the day of salvation as already begun and calls upon the Daughter of Zion to rejoice with all her heart, not to fear, because the Lord is with her, as her king and saviour. This is exactly the message of the angel in Luke 1:28–33: Luke envisages the two Annunciations as the dawning of the day of salvation (Luke 1:77–79), and Gabriel therefore tells Mary to rejoice, not to fear, because the Lord is with her, and because she will bear within her womb a son who will be the king of Israel and its saviour.[7]

Mary is a "favored woman" (κεχαριτωμένη—"full of grace"—the passive is theological: she has been shown unmerited grace *by God*). "Mary is a vessel to receive, not a fountain to dispense."[8] The idea of merit is incompatible with the character of divine grace (cf. Rom 4:4, 14) and human total depravity (cf. Rom 3:9–20). If worthiness is asserted, grace vanishes, and the Gospel is replaced with Law. The Venerable Bede, drawing on Ambrose, correctly traced "grace" back to its source, which is Christ, not Mary: "Well is she called 'full of grace,' for she has received the grace . . . of conceiving and bringing to birth the very author of grace."[9]

Grace is always a gift and never something earned or merited. This is true because, like all of us, Mary was born with original sin and remained a sinner her whole life. The immaculate conception, although

7. McHugh, *Mother of Jesus*, 41–42. McHugh, 38–39, also notes, "The imperative form Χαῖρε, far from being a conventional greeting, always refers to the joy attendant on the deliverance of Israel; wherever it occurs, it is a translation of a Hebrew verb meaning 'Rejoice greatly!' (or 'shout' for joy)."

8. Lenski, *Interpretation of Luke's Gospel*, 62.

9. Translation by McHugh, *Mother of Jesus*, 48, citing Bede, *In Lucam*, I, 28: *Corpus Christianorum: Series Latina* 120, p. 31, and Ambrose, *In Lucam*, II, 9: *Corpus Christianorum: Series Latina* 14, Pars IV, p. 34.

noble in its attempt to preserve Mary's womb as a holy place to receive the Son of God, cannot be demonstrated by appealing to her being "full of grace." In fact, Mary's response to the angel seems to imply that she is a sinner, which is why Gabriel comforts Mary with words of absolution for one who is afraid to stand in the presence of this holy theophany because of her sin: "Do not fear, Mary, for you have found favor with God" (1:30). This is the second time Gabriel has given absolution to a sinner. He declared the same thing to Zech (1:13). Gabriel acknowledges this absolution by reiterating, for the second time, that Mary "has found favor with God" to be both forgiven of her sins and set apart as the Mother of God. Mary is not to be alarmed or afraid of her unworthiness. What now comes to her by the Holy Spirit is pure grace, pure gift, even though she is a sinner.[10]

The Lord is with Mary (1:28) in two senses. He will come upon her and overshadow her, and the presence of the Lord will be in her womb. As Eve contained in her womb all humanity that was doomed to sin, now Mary contains in her womb the new Adam who will father a new humanity by his grace (Rom 5:12–21). Thus, the angel says "rejoice," for Israel—humanity—is now to be reborn through the Son in Mary's womb. The Lord is with Mary—he is with his church.

Mary as the Temple and the Ark of the Covenant

Addressed as "the daughter of Zion," Mary "was deeply troubled at the word and pondered what sort of greeting this might be" (1:29). So, in the next five verses, the angel helps her troubled and sinful heart. First he announces that she will conceive: "And behold, you are going to conceive in your womb and bear a son"—the annunciation!—and then he catechizes her as to the identity of this child by means of names or titles—Jesus, the

10. See Luke 5:1–11 and the great catch of fish, where Peter, after falling on his face and proclaiming, "Depart from me, for I am a sinful man, O Lord," Jesus pronounces absolution on him by saying "Be not afraid." Luther captures this in this sermon on Luke 5 in *Sermons*, Vol. 4, 162: "Not only does Christ give comfort to poor, terror-stricken Peter by the kindly words in which he declares and offers to him his grace and absolution, but he goes on to strengthen this comfort by the great promise that he will give him something far beyond anything he has hitherto received from him . . . 'From henceforth,' Christ says, 'thou shalt catch men.' That Peter is not to be alarmed on account of his unworthiness and sins is, in itself, an abundant comfort and grace. However, he is not only to have the forgiveness of his sins but is also to know that God intends to accomplish still greater things through him by making him a help and comfort to others."

one who save his people from their sins (Matt 1:21)—Great—Son of the Most High—eternal King over the throne of his father David and the house of Jacob.

On hearing this, Mary gains her composure and asks the biological question. Like Zechariah, Mary knows she is hearing from the angel Gabriel something beyond her ken. It will take a miracle surpassing all that God has done before. But unlike Zechariah, her wondering is not laced with skepticism. She poses a simple and honest question: "How will this be, since a man I know not?" (1:34—my translation—this is the knowing of Genesis in the communion Adam has with Eve as husband and wife—see my discussion in the previous chapter on ἐπιγνῷς/ἐπέγνωσαν in Luke 1:4 and 24:31). Scriptures never portray Mary as somber, meek, or mild, like many of the countless paintings do, as well as many of our Christmas hymns. Mary is fiery and feisty and full of passion. What is being asked of her is extraordinary, unparalleled. Her conceiving in her womb cannot happen as other conceptions do. It must be miraculous.

Gabriel's response to Mary's probing question about how she will conceive is the very moment when she conceives. The Word of the angel is a performative Word that creates what it says, like the performative Word in Genesis, when God created the cosmos by speaking into nothingness and bringing into being the creation. So the angel declares to Mary these words that create what they say—the child in her womb is holy, the Son of God:

> The Holy Spirit will come upon you (Πνεῦμα ἅγιον ἐπελεύσεται),
> and the power of the Most High will overshadow you (δύναμις ὑψίστου ἐπισκιάσει);
> for that reason the child to be born will be holy (τὸ γεννώμενον ἅγιον);
> he will be called Son of God (κληθήσεται υἱὸς θεοῦ) (1:34–35; my translation)

This same Spirit that comes upon Mary is the one that hovered over the waters and brought forth creation (Gen 1:2). During the exodus Yahweh's presence, his *shekinah*, overshadowed Israel in the pillar of cloud and fire (Exod 13:21–22; 14:19–31); it stood at the entrance to the tabernacle when Yahweh spoke with Moses (Exod 33:9–10); it overshadowed ([LXX]) the tabernacle as the glory of Yahweh filled it (Exod 40:35); it descended on Jesus at his baptism (3:22); it overshadowed him at his transfiguration (9:34, where ἐπεσκίαζεν is also used); and it will be promised to the disciples by Jesus just before his ascension when they are "clothed with power from on high" (24:49). As the Holy Spirit comes upon Mary, she conceives Jesus as holy, the Son of God. This is the moment of the incarnation of our Lord (1:35).

Like Mary, Luther also asked the biological question. How did Mary conceive by the Holy Spirit? He offers a quintessentially Lutheran answer—Mary conceived when the Word came into her ear. *She conceived through the power of God's Word.*[11] Similarly, the Word of the Gospel begets faith in the heart of the hearer: "So faith comes from hearing, and hearing through the word of Christ" (Rom 10:17). This corresponds to Mary's conversion—she is the first catechumen, since catechumens were called hearers of the Word.[12]

Mary receives two more titles or designations from Gabriel for this child that has now taken residence in her womb—that which is begotten in you is "holy"—the Holy One—so her womb is like the holy of holies in which dwells the ark of the covenant.[13] And if the first name given to this child was Jesus—the Savior—the last name is "Son of God." As "Son of God" and "holy," Jesus is set apart by God to cleanse Israel—and all humanity—from sin and to inherit for them the kingdom promised by the Father.

The coming of the Holy Spirit upon Mary may remind the hearer of the descent of the Spirit on Jesus at his baptism and the gift of the Holy Spirit in holy baptism. When the power of the Most High overshadows her, God becomes incarnate—becomes flesh—becomes part of Mary's flesh. That may call to the mind of some Christians the reception of the

11. Luther, "Sacrament of the Body and Blood of Christ," compares the conception of Jesus through the word spoken to Mary with the real presence of Christ's body in the Supper, effected through the Words of Institution.

12. Some enterprising Greek student might observe that the verbs are in the future tense—the Holy Spirit *will* come upon you (ἐπελεύσεται); the power of the Most High *will* overshadow you (ἐπισκιάσει)—so the conception could not happen at this moment when Gabriel speaks but points to a future event. But future tense in Greek (like in English, Spanish, and German) is the most intense and emphatic present tense. As an example, when my boys were little and misbehaved, I would say to them: "you will go to your room." They did not say to one another—"Pops used the future tense; we have all the time in the world." They knew that this was an emphatic "now!"

13. Hahn, *Hail*, 60–61, is particularly poignant on this point: "Whatever made the ark holy made Mary even holier. If the first ark contained the Word of God in stone, Mary's body contained the Word of God enfleshed. If the first ark contained miraculous bread from heaven, Mary's body contained the very Bread of Life that conquers death forever. If the first ark contained the rod of the long-ago ancestral priest, Mary's body contained the divine person of the eternal priest, Jesus Christ."

body and blood of Christ into the believer's body in holy communion. If so, then the annunciation is a first glimpse of the pattern of incorporation into the church that will be followed throughout Luke–Acts: catechesis, baptism, and Lord's Supper—the pattern continued by the post-apostolic church. Mary prefigures this as she receives catechesis from the angel (1:31b–33), the Holy Spirit comes upon her (1:35a), and she receives the flesh of Christ (1:35b).

But how about Mary as the ark of the covenant? If she is Israel, the temple, and the holy of holies, she is a temporary and portable vessel housing the immanent presence of the true God. Mary now fulfills the purpose of the ark of the covenant. My doctoral father first suggested to me an interesting series of parallels between Mary's journey to the hill country of Judah and the movement of the ark of the covenant to the same locale on its way to Jerusalem:

> The two stories open with the statement that David and Mary "arose and made a journey" (2 Sam 6:2; Luke 1:39) up into the hill country, into the land of Judah. On arrival, both the Ark and Mary are greeted with "shouts" of joy (2 Sam 6:12, 15; Luke 1:42, 44). The verb used for Elizabeth's greeting in Luke 1:42, (ἀνεφώνησεν) is, in the Septuagint, used only in connection with liturgical ceremonies centred round the Ark; it is best translated as "intoned." The Ark, on its way to Jerusalem, was taken into the house of Obededom, and became a source of blessing for his house (2 Sam 6:10–12); Mary's entry into the house of Elizabeth is also seen as a source of blessing for the house (Luke 1:41, 43–4). David, in terror at the untouchable holiness of the Ark, cried out: "How shall the Ark of the Lord come to me?" (2 Sam 6:9); Elizabeth, in awe before the mother of her Lord, says, "Why should this happen to me, that the mother of my Lord should come to me?" (Luke 1:43). Finally, we read that "the Ark of the Lord remained in the house of Obededom three months" (2 Sam 6:11), and that Mary stayed with Elizabeth "about three months" (Luke 1:56).[14]

Long before *Raiders of the Lord Ark*, the whereabouts of the ark have fascinated people. What happened to the ark that was missing for six centuries, since 587 BC? There is a tradition that Jeremiah, before the temple was destroyed, took the ark to Mount Nebo, where he hid it in a cave. This story is confirmed by 2 Macc 5:2–8:

14. McHugh, *Mother of Jesus*, 62.

> Jeremiah came and found a cave, and he brought there *the tent and the ark and the altar of incense*, and he sealed up the entrance. Some of those who followed him came up to mark the way but could not find it. When Jeremiah learned of it, he rebuked them and declared: 'The place shall be unknown until God gather His people together again and show His mercy. And then the Lord will disclose these things, and the glory of the Lord and the cloud will appear.'

Mount Nebo is where Moses looked out over the promised land, a land he would never enter because he broke faith with God at the waters of Meribah. In April 2023, as one of the leaders of ninety-eight pilgrims to the Holy Land, we visited Mount Nebo. Our learned guide told us this story of Moses, but then he said this remarkable thing: "Moses did finally enter the promised land in the transfiguration of our Lord, where he and Elijah appeared on the mountain with Jesus and Peter, James, and John." How true. Could not the same be said of the ark of the covenant? It never returned to the promised land, to its rightful place in the temple's holy of holies, lost forever. But in the annunciation, the ark of the covenant has returned to Israel in the womb of the Virgin Mary. Mary's womb is the restoration of the ark to Israel.[15]

From the annunciation in Luke 1:26–38, Mary is to be honored, even venerated, for at the conception of Jesus, her womb was considered by the evangelist to be the New Israel, the temple, and the ark of the covenant.[16]

15. This insight comes from both Hahn, *Hail*, 51–53, and Pitre, *Jesus and the Jewish Roots of Mary*, 51–54: "The Holy of Holies, which was supposed to house the Ark of the Covenant, was empty. Nevertheless . . . there was a Jewish tradition that the location of the lost Ark would one day be revealed." Both Hahn and Pitre support this argument from Rev 12. Pitre, *Jesus and the Jewish Roots of Mary*, 60–63, for example, suggests that "both the Ark and the woman appear to be in the heavenly Temple . . . the heavenly Ark is being associated with the heavenly woman . . . For John, the woman and the Ark are dual symbols for the same person." Although this argument is appealing, it is based on the Assumption of Mary, which has its own problems (see below).

16. See Just, ACCS, 19, where Mary as Israel, temple, and ark became embedded in the liturgy and piety of the ancient church, as is reflected in this hymn to Mary by Theophanes, a hymnographer and bishop of Nicaea from AD 842–845, in his Canon of Annunciation:

> The angel: Rejoice, lady; rejoice, most pure virgin! Rejoice, God-containing vessel! Rejoice, candlestick of the light, the restoration of Adam and the deliverance of Eve! Rejoice, holy mountain, shining sanctuary! Rejoice, bridal chamber of immortality!
> Theotokos: The descent of the Holy Spirit has purified my soul; it has sanctified my body; it has made me a temple containing God, a divinely adorned tabernacle, a living sanctuary and the pure mother of life.

Yet after giving birth to Jesus, like John the Baptist, Mary decreased as she pointed to her Son, who was now the Holy One of God in the flesh.

Mary's Hermeneutic of Humility—Breaking What Is Whole and Making Whole What is Broken[17]

If the annunciation establishes the identity of Jesus as the Holy One, the Son of God, and his mother Mary as the *Theotokos*, the Mother of God, Mary's Magnificat sets the agenda. "The Magnificat is like an aria in opera; the action almost stops so that the situation may be savored more deeply."[18] What we savor is how Mary now announces the themes of Jesus' ministry and the themes of Luke's Gospel. Luther was devoted to the Magnificat and wrote a treatise on it that surprises many Lutherans because his Marian piety affirms the perpetual virginity of Mary and her sinlessness.[19] What Luther does capture is the essence of Mary's song through his "hermeneutic of humility," which is the hermeneutic of both Mary and Jesus.

In response from the praise of Elizabeth, Mary declares "that all the glory is due to God: this is the theme of the Magnificat."[20] In good Hebraic synonymous parallelism, Mary sings that her soul magnifies the Lord and her Spirit rejoices in God her Savior. Beginning with the highest of doxologies Mary teaches us the reason we were created—to praise God. Mary's song announces the great themes of Luke's Gospel in her hymn, which praises God for his mighty acts of salvation. Dare we say that Mary is telling us that theology is doxology, that theology must

---

> The angel: I see you as a lamp with many lights; a bridal chamber made by God! Spotless maiden, as an ark of gold, receive now the gift of the law, who through you has been pleased to deliver humankind's corrupted nature!

17. This expression comes from Luther, "Magnificat," 299: "God is the kind of Lord who does nothing but exalt those of low degree and put down the mighty from their thrones, in short, *to break what is whole and make whole what is broken*" (emphasis mine).

18. Tannehill, *Narrative Unity I*, 31.

19. See my essay "My Soul Magnifies the Lord," 37–53 where I cite Luther, "Magnificat," 323: "She does not want you to come to her, but through her to God"; 327: "Mary also freely ascribes all to God's grace, not to her merit. For though she was without sin, yet that grace was far too great for her to deserve it in any way"; 329: "We ought to call upon her, that for her sake God may grant and do what we request. Thus also all other saints are to be invoked, so that the work may be every way God's alone."

20. McHugh, *Mother of Jesus*, 73.

sing?[21] The Lord is magnified because the births of Jesus and John are interpreted as acts of mercy. Perhaps this is what Luther means when he describes the threefold purpose of the Magnificat:

> Just as a book title indicates what is the contents of the book, so this word "magnifies" is used by Mary to indicate what her hymn of praise is to be about, namely, the great works and deeds of God, for the strengthening of our faith, for the comforting of all those of low degree, and for the terrifying of all the mighty ones of earth. We are to let the hymn serve this threefold purpose; *for she sang it not for herself alone but for us all, to sing it after her.*[22]

Luther understands that in Luke's Gospel, Mary personifies Israel; she is the first catechumen, she is the church, for he makes this astounding observation: "How many came in contact with her, talked, and ate and drank with her, who perhaps despised her and counted her but a common, poor, and simple village maiden, and who, had they known, would have fled from her in terror?"[23] As the New Israel, Mary sings a hymn that praises God precisely because the child in her womb is the greatest demonstration of God's "hermeneutic of humility."

This is Luke's theme of the great reversal, where God *breaks what is whole and makes whole what is broken.* The infancy narrative proclaims the full ramification of the incarnation for the cosmos and how the Christ child and his messianic program make all things new in all *humbleness and poverty and suffering.* Mary, the mother of God, the personification of Israel, and the personification of the church, announces that Jesus comes to scatter the arrogant in the imagination of their hearts, to pull down the mighty from their thrones, to exalt those of low degree, to fill the hungry with good things, to send the rich away empty.[24] To see these acts of reversal as expressions of God's *mercy* is at the heart of Luther's

21. Franzmann, *Ha! Ha! Among the Trumpets*, 92.

22. Luther, "Magnificat," 306 (emphasis mine).

23. Luther, "Magnificat," 329, as cited by McKnight, *Real Mary*, 14.

24. McKnight, *Real Mary*, 104–5, makes this insightful observation about the parallels between the Magnificat and the Epistle of James: "One could easily extend these observations to the similarities between Mary's Magnificat, her own Magna Carta, and the themes of another son, James. Sometime read the Magnificat quickly and then read the letter of James quickly. . . . [when James writes] 'Humble yourselves before the Lord, and he will lift you up,' he's introducing pure Magnificat. This is probably the message he heard at home his entire life."

commentary on the *Magnificat*, for, as he says, "How can one know God better than in the works in which He is most Himself?"[25]

Luther's interpretation of the Magnificat is christological, as it is centered in how God enters our cosmos in order to bring us back into communion with him through the fleshly, bodily presence of Christ in a grand act of reversal on the cross, and then, in the cruciform lives of those who daily take up that cross and follow him—starting with Mary. Our way back to God is "in Christ" (ἐν Χριστῷ), in humility, through his body, a body conceived in the Mother of God who, in bearing the child in her womb, is Israel, temple, and ark. What other reason does she have to magnify the Lord, to rejoice in God her Savior? As Luther said, "She sang it not for herself alone but for us all, to sing it after her," which is what we do as church when we gather to praise God in evening prayer.

The Memoirs of Mary as She Ponders the Meaning of Jesus' Birth and Suffering

Mary's Magnificat is the only canticle or narrative we have from her, but she is certainly part of the Gospel tradition, and the Lukan infancy narrative is mostly her memoir. At the end of Luke's birth narrative, he notes, almost in passing, that "Mary treasured all these things (τὰ ῥήματα), pondering them in her heart" (Luke 2:19). "These things" (please note the Greek word that will be fleshed out below) are the words that the shepherds rehearsed for Mary concerning the appearance of the angels and the content of the angels' message. In essence, what Mary treasured in her heart was that the baby Jesus, wrapped in swaddling clothes and lying in a manger, was the God-given sign of the Christ, whose birth signals glory in heaven and peace on earth. Although it is possible that Mary did not fully understand this at the time, in view of her faithful response to the angel who had visited her, it is likely that she received these words with joy and perceived their meaning.

Mary remembers. It's a great Lukan theme. Jesus tells the disciples, "Do this in remembrance of me" at the Last Supper; the angel tells the women at the tomb to remember the passion prediction in Galilee; and the women remembered his words and reported them to the eleven who considered them "utter nonsense." It is fair to say that if Mary had not treasured these things and remembered all that happened to her—the

25. Luther, "Magnificat," 332.

conception of her Son, the visitation, the travel to Bethlehem, the birth of Jesus, the visit of the shepherds, the appearances in the temple at forty days and when Jesus was twelve years old—there would be no infancy narrative. Mary was simply doing what mothers do—remembering and reflecting on what has happened to her in the birth and childhood of Jesus—and now is telling others about these mighty acts of salvation.

In treasuring and pondering these things, Mary is sorting out the meaning of these events in the sweep of salvation history, from what she has heard from the sacred Scriptures and from the many messianic rumors that were rampant in the first century. She is certainly meditating on these events, but she is doing more than that. She is trying to make sense of them, interpret them from what she sees in the child who she knows is the Messiah but does not, perhaps, meet the messianic expectations of those around her. If Mary decreases after she gives birth to Jesus, as we suggested above, she becomes like any other Galilean mother and wife, with other children and a home where Jesus could experience a normal upbringing. But there must have been times when she discussed her pondering with others, telling the story of Jesus' remarkable conception and birth, like any mother would.[26]

26. Some will be disappointed that I don't have a section on the perpetual virginity of Mary. It is something I've struggled with since my seminary days. My doctoral father and I discussed it at length. Of all the extra-biblical Marian doctrines—the immaculate conception, co-redemptrix, and the assumption (the assumption is intriguing, as no church has ever claimed to have Mary's bones!)—the perpetual virginity is one that Lutherans could hold, following the early church, Luther, and the Confessions. But I am convinced of the argument "he will increase and I will decrease," namely, that Mary accepts her role as Israel, temple, ark at the conception, but when she gives birth to Jesus, she decreases and assumes a normal family life. That Jesus' brothers are cousins, although defensible, is not the marked meaning of ἀδδέλφος in most of the New Testament (some will argue that it always means "brother"—see my doctoral father for the best arguments here). The most persuasive argument for me is the continuing holiness of Mary's womb because of the temple/ark/holy of holies reality, e.g. Pitre, *Jesus and the Jewish Origins of Mary*, 115: "But if Joseph had even the slightest clue that Mary's body had been 'overshadowed' by the 'power of the Most High' (Luke 1:35)—that she was in some way like a new Ark—then you can understand why he would consider her consecrated to God. If the old Ark of the Covenant was so holy that a Levite could not even *touch* it and live (2 Samuel 6:6), then how much more the new Ark? If the early Temple in Jerusalem was so holy that even the priests were required to refrain from sexual relations before entering it (Exodus 19:15; 1 Samuel 21:4), then how much more Mary's body, the new dwelling place of God?" (My response would be: Mary is the ark as she carries the Christ child. At his birth, the ark becomes flesh in Jesus, and Mary's womb is empty, like the holy of holies after 587 BC, and therefore no longer holy in the same way). Pitre, *Jesus and the Jewish Roots of Mary*, 221n47, does offer the other point of view, from Anglican scholar J. H. Bernard, that to me is one of the most convincing of

Who knows what kind of family life Mary and Joseph had, but it must have been a loving home where parents and children live a Torah life of obedience. Luke gives us a glimpse of the dynamic between Jesus and his parents in an incident in the temple when Jesus is twelve years old—his bar mitzvah?—and Mary and Joseph seem confused about what is happening. What does Jesus mean when he says, "Did you not know that it is necessary (δεῖ) that I am among the things of my Father?" (my translation), or as some translations render it, "my Father's house" (Luke 2:49). Earlier, Mary referred to Joseph as Jesus' father, but now Jesus claims God as his Father. It is most significant that Jesus' first words refer to God as his Father; they are a statement that he is the Son of God (Cf. 10:22; 22:29; and 24:49 for Jesus calling God his Father).

Jesus must be present in the house of his Father, where the Father's business is transacted, among those to whom this business has been entrusted. And the business of his Father is sacrifice—the shedding of blood—and Jesus' first words are shot through with an understanding that his destiny is a sacrificial death in which there will be the shedding of his blood. Luke uses the passion language of necessity (δεῖ), and his words resonate as they are spoken during the Passover, when lambs are slain and eaten in a sacrificial meal of remembrance. Only two Passovers are mentioned in Luke: here at the beginning of Jesus' life in the infancy narrative and at the end of his life in the passion narrative (Luke 22). Only Luke describes the day of the Last Supper as "the day of Unleavened Bread, on which it was necessary (ἔδει) that the Passover lamb be sacrificed" (22:7—my translation). Jesus at a Passover in Jerusalem at twelve years old points to another Passover, where on the night in which he was betrayed he will preside over a meal that we now call Eucharist. Luke's infancy narrative anticipates Jesus' final days of passion and resurrection. But how do Mary and Joseph understand these words from the twelve-year-old Jesus?

The story ends on a note of misunderstanding by Jesus' parents concerning his words. Jesus is announcing to them that there will be a new family—the family of his heavenly Father. The amazement of Mary and Joseph when they find Jesus in the temple, and Mary's seemingly sharp words, pose questions. But Luke provides the solution when he

all the arguments against the perpetual virginity of Mary: "It is difficult to understand how the doctrine of the [perpetual] Virginity of Mary could have grown up early in the second century if her four acknowledged sons were prominent Christians, and one of them bishop of Jerusalem."

notes that "they did not understand the word (τὸ ῥῆμα) (2:50). This ῥῆμα word is a word about the passion. How ironic that Jesus' very first words are misunderstood *because they are words about his suffering and death*, a theme for his entire life. Since the necessity to be about the things of his Father has passion overtones, this misunderstanding fits well into the pattern of misunderstanding that accompanies the passion predictions (9:22; 9:44–45; 18:31–34). When Jesus' parents misunderstand his words which explain his need to be in the temple, it signals the reason for Luke's inclusion of this story at the close of the infancy narrative. Even though all things are clear for the hearer as to Jesus' identity and what he must do, Mary and Joseph, the ones who should know best, seem to be incapable of understanding Jesus' "word" (τὸ ῥῆμα). Simeon has already predicted that Jesus is destined for the fall and resurrection of many in Israel (see below), but little did we expect Mary and Joseph to be the first to stumble over the cross (see 20:17–18). "What Mary and Joseph did not understand was this: that in those first fateful words, 'I must be in my Father's home,' Jesus was darkly alluding to his future passion and Resurrection in the Holy City."[27]

Mary is sorting it out, trying to interpret what lies ahead for her Son and for her. Again, at the very end of his temple scene, Luke records that "his mother treasured up all these things in her heart" (Luke 2:51). Indeed!

During Paul's third missionary journey, Paul spent Pascha with Luke in Philippi, and then Luke accompanied him to Jerusalem to celebrate Pentecost. On the way to Jerusalem, Paul and Luke stop in Miletus for Paul to meet with the Ephesians elders, as Paul was wary of returning to Ephesus after what happened when he left. But Ephesus may not have known Luke. While Paul is meeting with the Ephesian elders in Miletus, could Luke have traveled to Ephesus to visit Mary, who was there with the apostle John, to hear from her all the details she had treasured and pondered in her heart, receiving what becomes his infancy narrative? Mary never wrote a Gospel, but by telling Luke what she had treasured and pondered in her heart, she contributed to the Gospel narrative. She is an evangelist, for she tells the story of Jesus, and it gets written down.

As Luke heard Mary's narrative about the conception, birth, and childhood of Jesus, he must have been struck how it is shot through with passion references, as we observed in the temple scene at twelve years old.

27. McHugh, *Mother of Jesus*, 124.

Much earlier, forty days after Jesus' birth, Mary finds herself with Joseph and Jesus for her purification and Jesus' presentation. It is here, in the place of sacrifice, that Mary hears those fateful words which must have set the trajectory of her life and been the source of much of her pondering: "Behold, this child is destined for the fall and resurrection of many in Israel, and for a sign spoken against, and of you yourself, through your soul a sword will go, in order that the thoughts out of many hearts may be revealed" (Luke 2:34–35; my translation). Here, Mary's hermeneutic of humility is given concrete substance as she learns the destiny of this forty-day-old child.

Simeon speaks only to Mary. In contrast to the *Nunc Dimittis*, which proclaimed peace, a somber note is sounded. There is a reason for the poverty of the child. His humble birth is a sign of foreboding. Many Jews will fall and rise as they meet Jesus; he is a stumbling block to everyone, including his own disciples and family—even Mary—because of the nature of his ministry and the nature of his kingdom. Again, the infancy narrative introduces a theme that finds a corresponding note at the end of Jesus' ministry, in his final parable about the workers in the vineyard (20:9–19), where Jesus sums up the parable by citing Ps 118:22: "The stone that the builders rejected, this has become the head of the corner" (Luke 20:17). His application of these words to the scribes and Pharisees echoes Simeon's words to Mary: "Everyone who falls on that stone will be dashed to pieces; on whomsoever it falls, it will crush him" (Luke 20:18). This child destined to be spoken against, a perfect image of the theology of the cross, Christ's rejection and atonement, and his resurrection and vindication.

There are three interpretations of the sword passing through Mary's soul. One interpretation accents Mary's sorrow at the crucifixion of her son. Another brings out the idea that she (like the other disciples) has misunderstood Jesus' destiny.[28] An additional possibility, corresponding with Luke's earlier portrayal of Mary as the personification of Israel, sees the sword as God's revelation in Jesus' words and deeds throughout his ministry:

> The meaning of Simeon's prophecy, therefore, is that the word of revelation brought by Jesus will pass through Israel like a sword and will compel men to reveal their secret thoughts. Thus, just as Jesus will fulfill the prophecy of Is 49:6 by being "light bringing

28.. Cf. Stein, *Luke*, 117, and Fitzmyer, *Luke I–IX*, 429–30, who state both interpretations but opt for the second.

> revelation to the Gentiles" (Luke 2:32), so he will fulfill the role assigned to the Servant of Yahweh in Is 49:2, for his message will be felt as a sharp sword.[29]

If the sword piercing Mary refers only to her own sufferings or misunderstandings, it is hard to see how this will reveal the thoughts of many hearts. However, if the sword is Jesus' preaching, which pierces Israel—represented here by one Israelite woman, Mary—then the statement makes perfect sense. Throughout the gospel, the thoughts of many continue to be revealed because of their reactions to Jesus and his proclamation. Mary the woman, as a part of Israel and as the mother of Jesus, will feel the pain of Jesus' words and his crucifixion. She herself will be pierced by Jesus' teaching, especially when he speaks about blood relationships giving way to the new family of the church (see below). All believers (including Mary) will belong to this family, consisting of "those who hear the Word of God and do it" (8:19–21). And the mother of Jesus will be pierced at the cross as she watches her son die the humiliating death of crucifixion. Like every other participant in Jesus' life, Mary, Israelite and mother, will experience sharp pain because of Jesus' teaching and death.

This sharp pain may have been hinted at in the annunciation by Luke, when he uses the word τὸ ῥῆμά in the exchange between Gabriel and Mary. To assure Mary that the conception has happened, he announces that her cousin is six months with child. Mary's astonishment at this must have been great, so the angel gives this further reassuring word: "Because with God nothing (πᾶν ῥῆμα) will be impossible" (Luke 1:37). "Nothing" should be translated as "every word." But ῥῆμα as *Word* is different from λόγος as *Word*, which Luke uses in his prologue (1:2).[30] ῥῆμα denotes both a word and the event(s) the word promises. The reference here in 1:37 is to the two miraculous conceptions of John and Jesus. Mary also uses the same word in the Marian fiat: "Behold, I am the servant of the Lord; let it be to me according to your word (τὸ ῥῆμά σου)."[31] But

29. McHugh, *Mother of Jesus*, 109. See his discussion on 106–12.

30 This expression betrays the liturgical and catechetical intent of Luke's Gospel in a prologue that many think is purely secular in its language. It is a technical expression that suggests the Christian message. Grammatically, it goes with both "eyewitnesses" and "ministers," suggesting that for Luke, the Word is living in the flesh of Jesus, who spoke to these eyewitnesses before he ascended and continues to speak through his ministers in the preaching of the Word.

31. Bauer, *Greek-English Lexicon*, 894: "τὰ ῥ. oft. takes a special significance fr. the context: *prophecy, prediction* . . . Luke 1:38; 2:29; 9:45ab; 18:34; 22:61 . . . 24:8; Ac 11:16."

could ῥῆμά refer to something more? Could ῥῆμά be a reference to the passion of Jesus?

Two of the four passion and resurrection predictions in Luke (9:43–45; 18:31–34) refer to the disciples' misunderstanding of what Jesus just told them. And in both cases, this word (τὸ ῥῆμα τοῦτο) refers to the passion and resurrection facts, something the disciples are finding difficult to grasp. Perhaps it is because the word of passion is described by a theological passive, which means that these things were hidden from them *by God*. No wonder it was difficult for them to understand!

Could τὸ ῥῆμα refer to the passion in the annunciation? When the angel says to Mary, "Every word is possible with God," could he be referring first to Elizabeth's miraculous conception and then Mary's but also, as Simeon will say, to the destiny of this child's sacrificial death? Gabriel declares to Mary that what is possible with God is both the creative Word of conception by the Holy Spirit and the Word that points to Jesus' passion and resurrection. So, when Mary declares, "Behold, I am the servant of the Lord; let it be to me according to your word," she consents to be the Mother of God and to be obedient to the way of suffering she must witness in her child.

There may be some support for this in the resurrection appearance of the angels to the women at the tomb. What the women are called to remember are the first passion predictions in Galilee (9:22; 43–45). And they remembered the angel's and Jesus' words—τῶν ῥημάτων αὐτοῦ! Luke uses here the technical word for the passion. Luke's phrase in 24:8, "and they remembered his words," contrasts with the comments in 9:45 and 18:34. There, the apostles "did not understand this word, and it was hidden from them . . . and they were afraid to ask him concerning this word" (9:45); "this word was hidden from them, and they did not know the things that were spoken" (18:34—my translation).

When the women return to the disciples to report what the angel said to the eleven, Luke describes the disciples' reaction this way: "But these words (τὰ ῥήματα ταῦτα) appeared before them as nonsense, and they were not believing them" (Luke 24:11—my translation). There is a growing recognition among the women that the passion is part of Jesus' messianic destiny. Although Mary is not mentioned by Luke at the crucifixion or resurrection, from John's Gospel we know that she was at the foot of the cross with John, the son of Zebedee, whose mother Salome was Mary's sister. Mary is given by Jesus to John: "Woman, behold your son! . . . Behold, your mother!" Mary witnessed her Son's death; she saw his blood which he received from her; there at the cross, she suffered alongside her son, uniting herself to his suffering. "Mary drank waters of sorrow more deeply than any other human mother ever has."[32] And in the moment she is given to John, she "cr[ies] out in birth pains and the agony of giving birth" (Rev 12:2) to the church.[33] David Flusser summarizes Mary's suffering in these poignant words:

> Mary can be understood as a symbol for the church and also for her own people. But one should never forget that this woman once walked on earth—this mother of sorrows. The Mater Dolorosa is not a theological concept or an overpowering experience of the archetypal but primarily a real person who was inspired by her joy and never defeated by her unspeakable pain.[34]

Brant Pitre draws this poignant conclusion:

> When it comes to suffering, sorrow, and death, *Mary knows what it is like* to endure excruciating pain—the kind of interior pain that can be described only as having one's 'soul' pierced 'by a sword' (Luke 2:35). Indeed, since Mary becomes our mother precisely through what she suffered at the foot of the cross, we can truly say that *we are the children of Mary's sorrow.*[35]

Mary as the New Eve and the Mother of the Family of God

Finally, as a reason for the church to show devotion to Mary, we might consider Mary to be the mother of the church by what she says in the Magnificat: "For behold, from now on all generations will call me blessed" (Luke 1:48). When we call her blessed, is it because she is the New Eve and the mother of the church?

32. Pitre, *Jesus and the Jewish Roots of Mary*, 152.

33. Pitre, *Jesus and the Jewish Roots of Mary*, 180: "[Mary] is the mother of the Church because she willingly consented to and shared in the sufferings of Christ on the cross, through which the redemption of the world is accomplished." He also cites John Paul II, 153: "The woman clothed with the sun is in a certain sense identified with Mary," for the imagery of "her pangs of birth" (Rev 12:2) "refers to the *Mother of Jesus on the Cross.*" Pitre, *Jesus and the Jewish Roots of Mary*, 178: "May the Christ from the height of the cross say also to each of you: 'There is your mother.' May he say also to the Church: 'There is your son.'" (Ambrose, On Luke 7.5 [4th century A.D.]

34. Flusser et al., *Images of the Mother of Jesus*, 7.

35. Pitre, *Jesus and the Jewish Roots of Mary*, 181.

Mary as the New Eve is nothing new in the church. Scott Hahn amasses the early church evidence for this. First, he interprets Justin Martyr's words about Mary as the New Eve in *Dialogue with Trypho*, written in Mary's town, Ephesus, in AD 135:

> In comparing and contrasting Eve with Mary, Justin follows Paul's discussion of Christ and Adam . . . Eve and Mary were both virgins; Eve conceived the "word of the serpent," while Mary conceived the Word of God. By God's providence, Justin concludes, Mary's obedience became a means of undoing Eve's disobedience and its most devastating effects."

Second, from Irenaeus himself, who wrote not much later than Justin Martyr:

> The knot of Eve's disobedience was loosed by the obedience of Mary. The knot which the virgin Eve tied by her unbelief, the Virgin Mary opened by her belief . . . and thus, as the human race fell into bondage to death by means of a virgin, so it is rescued by a virgin.

Finally, from Tertullian, another early father: "As Eve believed the serpent, so Mary believed the angel."[36]

Much of this discussion about Mary as the New Eve is appealing. We can see this unfold in John's Gospel as he lays out the new creation for us, which takes place in seven days (John 1–2), culminating on the seventh day at the wedding at Cana where, in calling his mother "woman," (John 2:4—the same thing he says of her in John 19:26), Jesus is not being rude or disrespectful but is addressing her at the New Eve. Again, Hahn: "'Woman' is the name Adam gives to Eve (Gen 2:23). Jesus, then, is addressing Mary as Eve to the New Adam—which heightens the significance of the wedding feast they're attending."[37] The typology is lovely, even ingenuous, especially Eve's disobedience that is reversed with Mary's obedience.[38]

36. Hahn, *Hail*, 12–13.

37. Hahn, *Hail*, 11.

38. McKnight, *Real Mary*, 63–64, 66, 67, 68, has an interesting observation about Mary at the wedding at Cana: "Mary, the mother, would learn to be obedient to her son . . . At the wedding in Cana the real Mary learned this kind of obedience . . . In the space of two sentences the word 'mother' and 'woman' are used synonymously. For Jesus to have used the word woman for his mother at the wedding of Cana was neither impolite nor rude . . . 'My hour has not yet come,' Jesus said to his mother . . . For Mary to know and do God's will, she would have to follow Jesus. Her honor would have to surrender

What becomes unsettling is when the New Eve typology is used to prove Mary's sinlessness. Brant Pitre makes this argument, even citing Augustine in support:

> Eventually, the understanding of Mary as the second Eve led to the realization that Mary—like Eve herself—was created without sin. The logic behind this belief is quite simple: If Mary is really the new Eve, then she must be greater than Eve . . .
>
> For Augustine, "Mary's freedom from sin is not the result of her own efforts. It is not something she earns but is a *pure gift* of God's grace."
>
> As the new Eve, Mary is created without sin to be a "living sign" of the righteous life of the new creation that is ushered in by Jesus' life, death, and resurrection from the dead. As Jesus himself says in the book of Revelation: 'Behold, I make all things new' (Revelation 2:1–15).[39]

This chapter is not intended to rehearse all the arguments against claims of Mary's sinlessness. As argued above, Mary's fear in the presence of the angel Gabriel marks her as a sinner. The immaculate conception was so troubling for many Roman Catholics that it did not become an official doctrine until 1854, by Pope Pius IX. It is unfortunate that the New Eve typology is used to support this. But with many of my Roman Catholic brothers and sisters, the New Eve typology does help us understand that as Eve was the mother of all the living, Mary—the mother of Jesus, the Mother of God, the *Theotokos*—is "the mother of the church" in the new creation.

Luke's Kinship Laws

Luke's kinship laws help us understand that kinship in the new creation is not by blood, as it was with the Jews with their need to hold to the genealogical bloodlines, but now the family of God is by faith and obedience to the Word of God. Who better to become the mother of the church than Mary, whose obedience to the Word of the angel marks her as the first believer (Luke 1:38). The "kinship laws" are part of the legal system of the Jews like the Sabbath laws, the table fellowship laws, and

---

to his honor. Jesus' words were subtle, and they pierced Mary's heart. She would have to allow her son to become her Lord . . . Honor of parents, in Jesus' case, was turned upside down: Mary could receive honor only when she honored her own son."

39. Pitre, *Jesus and the Jewish Roots of Mary*, 35, 37, 40.

most importantly, the purity laws. In his Gospel, Luke develops a careful understanding of how the nuclear family has now been superseded by the family of God.[40]

Acts 1:14—Pentecost

Where Mary occurs in the New Testament, particularly in Luke, is always significant. In those ten days between the Ascension and Pentecost, when the apostles gathered in the upper room to choose Matthias as Judas' replacement, Mary was with them: "All these with one accord were devoting themselves to prayer, together with the women and Mary the mother of Jesus, and his brothers" (Acts 1:14). By calling her the "mother of Jesus," Luke identifies her and tells us that she is present when the church began. Although she is not mentioned at Pentecost, it is likely she was there. Luke begins his two-volume work with Mary giving birth to Jesus by the power of the Spirit and now at the beginning of Acts, shows her present at the birth of the church by the coming of the Holy Spirit at Pentecost. The kinship laws have reached their end as the new family of God is born with the coming of the Holy Spirit.

Pentecost inspired Peter's *catechetical preaching*: "Repent and be baptized every one of you in the name of Jesus Christ for the forgiveness of your sins, and you will receive the gift of the Holy Spirit. (Acts 2:38); *water baptism*, "So those who received his word were baptized, and there were added that day about three thousand souls" (Acts 2:41); and *leitourgia*, "And they devoted themselves to the apostles' teaching and the fellowship, to the breaking of bread and the prayers" (Acts 2:42). The new family of God is constituted not by blood but by faith through Word, water, bread, and wine. Fifty days after the resurrection, Mary takes her place as the Mother of God and now at the birth of the church. "God is not like a family; God is a family."[41]

40. Neyrey and Malina, *Social World of Luke-Acts*. Feeley-Harnik, *Lord's Table*. The CPH Luke Commentary develops the kinship laws in the following passages: Luke 3:23–38—The Genealogy; Luke 8:19–21 and Luke 11:27–28—The New Kinship; Luke 12:49–53—The Baptism Jesus Must Undergo; Luke 14:25–35—Conditions for Discipleship.

41. Pope John Paul II, as cited by Hahn, *Hail*, 19. The entire citation is this: "God in His deepest mystery is not a solitude, but a family, since He has in Himself fatherhood, sonship, and the essence of the family, which is love . . . God is not like a family; God is a family."

Mary's Magnificat now takes concrete shape in the life of the church, flowing from *Leitourgia* and *Diakonia* for hearers and keepers of the Word of God: "And all who believed were together and had all things in common. And they were selling their possessions and belongings and distributing the proceeds to all, as any had need" (Acts 2:44–45). Scot McKnight has this astute observation on how the church embraced Mary's song at Pentecost:

> Even if Mary did not at first realize it, Pentecost brought all of God's promises to her together. The Magnificat's dream of a society governed by justice with peace streaming through its streets would come through the paradox of the Cross, the power of the Resurrection, and the life-giving creativity of the gift of the Spirit of God. The society of the Magnificat that Mary anticipated from the day Gabriel revealed it to her would come to pass in the Church. And in the middle of these church cells in Jerusalem was Mary.[42]

Concluding Thoughts

This chapter on a biblical (Lukan) theology of Mary began with my experiences in Latin America and Spain, where it is difficult to talk to Roman Catholics and former Roman Catholics without having a high view of Mary. What we can say to them, based primarily on Luke's writings, is that Mary was set apart by God, who made her womb holy, because she conceived the Holy One of God by Holy Spirit. But after giving birth, Mary decreased and her Son increased. From now on she would only point to Jesus and say, when asked, "Do whatever he tells you" (John 2:5). She became a normal wife and mother and struggled with Jesus' messianic identity, but from her Magnificat, gave him the hermeneutic of humility. And she showed us faithful obedience, "Let it be to me according to your Word,"[43] even when she herself was unsure about his destiny of suffering. She suffered alongside her Son and was present at the birth of the church. She knew that her home was no longer in Nazareth or in Ephesus but where her Son was, and that, of course, is at font, pulpit,

42. McKnight, *Real Mary*, 96–97.

43. Norris, *Blessed Mary*, x, offers these inspiring words: "When I am called to answer 'Yes' to God, not knowing where this commitment will lead me, Mary gives me hope that it is enough to trust in God's grace and promise of salvation."

and table.[44] She became an evangelist by telling her story to others, and finally telling it to Luke, who canonized it in his infancy narrative. But most of all, she was a mother, first to Jesus and then to his church. "For evangelization is all about building up a family, and no one can belong to a family without honoring the family's mother."[45]

So as Lutherans, we honor Mary, for her Son did. He had her blood, and it was her blood in him that washed away our sins. For this, we owe her our utmost devotion.

44. Hahn, *Hail*, 27: "In baptism . . . we are taken up into the very life of the Trinity, where we may live in love forever. If God is a family, heaven is home; and with Jesus, heaven has come to earth" . . . "Every family needs a mother; only Christ could choose His own . . . Now, everything He has He shares with us. His divine life is ours; His home is our home; His Father is our Father; His brothers are our brothers; and His mother is our mother, too."

45. Hahn, *Hail*, 145.

Liturgy, Catechesis, Diakonia, and Missions

8

Liturgy and the Catechumenate

What Is at Stake in the Worship Wars

On twenty-second of June, 1980, when I was ordained at St. Paul's Lutheran Church in Westport, Connecticut, and then a week later installed as pastor at Grace Evangelical Lutheran Church in Middletown, Connecticut, there were no worship wars as far as I knew. Liturgy was not an issue during my seminary years, and although I realized that I was brought up "high church," it was not a defining part of my theological identity. During the late 1970s at CTSFW, the hot-button issues were not liturgy but biblical inerrancy, objective justification, and the charismatic movement. I attended chapel regularly but chose not to join the chapel staff because I was more consumed with my studies. The music in the chapel was wonderful and much appreciated. We used *The Lutheran Hymnal* (*TLH*—1941), as did most congregations in the LCMS.

Little did I realize that a worship war was brewing that would explode a couple years later with the introduction of *Lutheran Worship* (*LW*—1982), which was an LCMS revision of the *Lutheran Book of Worship* (*LBW*—1978), a product of the Inter-Lutheran Commission of Worship (*ILCW*), which at one time was led by members of the LCMS (the LCMS chose not to approve *LBW* at the 1977 Dallas Convention).

There is a principle among liturgical scholars that liturgical texts are the most conservative texts in the church, next to the Holy Scriptures. This means that it is difficult to discern any meaningful change in a liturgical text over three generations. The liturgy of Justin Martyr in AD 150 could easily reflect what the apostle John might have experienced at the end of the apostolic era in AD 90–100. Changes in the liturgy could be perceived only over a long period of time, and the principle of *lex orandi, lex credendi* obtains—the way you worship shapes what you believe. The history of the church bears this out. The staying power of *TLH* is an excellent example of the conservative nature of liturgy. *TLH* lasted for forty-one years through World War II, the tumultuous cultural shifts in 1960s, the turmoil of the Vietnam War, right into the Reagan era. If there was one constant that held the LCMS together, especially during the 1960s and 1970s, it was *TLH*. For a hymnal to last that long in the twentieth century is somewhat of a miracle. But things were changing, especially with what happened throughout Christendom after Vatican II in the 1960s, especially among churches that embraced traditional liturgies.

La Iglesia Lutherana del Buen Pastor, our church in Mexico City, was founded by the LCMS in 1948 but became a joint mission with the American Lutheran Church (ALC) in 1959. When we were members there from 1966 to 1974, one of our pastors was the Reverend Thomas E. Herbranson of the ALC who confirmed me in 1967 and is the author of the baptism hymn "This is the Spirit's Entry Now" (*Lutheran Service Book*—*LSB*—591). He was an outgoing and gregarious pastor with a passion for music and liturgical innovation. He used his deep baritone voice to sing his sermons from the pulpit and enlisted me during my year of confirmation to participate with him in dialogical sermons where I stood up in the middle of his sermon and asked him questions. It was all very exciting. As a thirteen-year-old, I didn't realize that this sort of liturgical innovation was beginning to happen throughout the Lutheran Church, a movement towards "contemporary worship" that would explode in the 1980s after the introduction of the two Lutheran hymnals, *LBW* and *LW*, and the inception of the Church Growth Movement.

As pastor at Grace Lutheran in Middletown, Connecticut, I was untouched by the worship wars but not by the changes that were taking place in Lutheran liturgy. *LBW* was only two years old when I was ordained, and during my first years in the parish, I became aware of the controversies over what became known at "the green hymnal." A local congregation in Wallingford, Connecticut, adopted it as their hymnal, and in serving the vacancy there, I used *LBW* every week for over a year. During my parish years in Connecticut, I attended the roll-out of *LBW's* companion volume, entitled *Occasional Liturgies*, which I immediately used in my pastoral care at Grace, Middletown. After *LW* came out in

1982, it seemed a good thing to introduce it to my congregation. After careful teaching and many meetings, the congregation overwhelmingly voted to adopt *LW* as its hymnal, with only a few naysayers. The clinching argument was the age of the *TLH* hymnals in our pews and that both *LBW* and *LW* were taking the New England district by storm, in both the ELCA and LCMS. During all this liturgical change, there was still little controversy, and the worship wars that would rage in a few short years were not yet happening in New England.

As I mentioned earlier, the game-changer for me in terms of my liturgical formation happened during my studies at Yale Divinity School, in my classes with Aidan Kavanagh on liturgical texts. What captivated me in these classes was the liturgical theology of the ancient baptismal and eucharistic texts, particularly as they were reflected in the mystagogical catechesis of the fourth century church fathers, which were part of the ancient catechumenate. A whole new world opened for me. Later at CTSFW, in the class "Theologia: Baptism," I would give an opening lecture entitled "Organizing Your Church Around Baptism" as a way of introducing the catechumenate that reflected the ancient way of doing church.

My studies at YDS provided a theological foundation to address the issues that arose when the worship wars began in earnest in the late 1980s. As I often tell people, my vocation is teaching the New Testament, but liturgy is my hobby. During my entire seminary career, liturgy keeps pulling me into its orbit, and it all began with my studies at YDS with Aidan Kavanagh. Little did I realize then how significant those courses would become in the trajectory of my pastoral and academic life. The STM at Yale was my most significant academic experience, outside of the rigorous and foundational education I received at Phillips Academy in Andover. It provided the way forward for the rest of my career in the ministerium of the LCMS.

During the worship wars, congregations were making changes in the liturgy, not knowing the tradition and especially the theology of the historic liturgy. In the mid-1980s, David Scaer, the academic dean, began to receive inquiries about faculty speaking about liturgy and worship. Such a request was unheard of during my seminary days in the late 1970s, but five years later the call went out to address the liturgical changes that were being forced upon many congregations by their well-meaning pastors, who were unaware of the consequences of their actions, that is, they did not understand *lex orandi, lex credendi* (see below). Dr. Scaer looked over the *curriculum vitae* of his faculty and noted that I had studied liturgy at Yale, that I was one of the few who had any formal training in the liturgical traditions of the church, and that I was young, full of energy, and known for my diplomacy. He thought I would be the perfect person to address many of the issues facing congregations, pastors, and districts as the "worship wars" began.

What developed from my preparations for these events led to my teaching the Lutheran Worship course at CTSFW; my "dog and pony" excursions with Richard Resch that ended up becoming LCMS Worship Commission's "Real Life Worship"; my co-founding The Good Shepherd Institute with Richard in 2000; my participation in the development of materials for a Lutheran catechumenate with Augsburg-Fortress, through joint events with the ELCA and through a grant from Aid Association for Lutherans (AAL—now Thrivent); the infamous liturgy video *Liturgy: Yesterday, Today, and Forever*, filmed at Advent Lutheran Church in Zionsville, Indiana (1999); the enfleshment of the liturgy video in *Heaven on Earth: The Gifts of Christ in the Divine Service* (2008); the baptismal video *Baptism: Journey to Life in Christ*, filmed in New Mexico (2004); my participation in the formation of LSB as chairman of the lectionary committee; and in 2000, my becoming the dean of the chapel at CTSFW.

In the conclusion of *Heaven on Earth*, I discussed "Lutheran Liturgy in the Postmodern World" and lamented my own participation in the worship wars of the 1980s, relating the story of my five-year-old son, Nicholas, who asked me where I was going as I headed out to another conference on the liturgy. In essence, I said, I was going to defend the liturgy in the worship wars. It was then that I realized we needed a different strategy. Instead of being defensive about the historic Lutheran liturgy, we needed to go on the offensive—to show the great treasures in our liturgical tradition—to teach the church about the gifts of Christ in the Divine Service. Two of my conclusions in *Heaven on Earth* still obtain today: that our liturgy is biblical and that it is eschatological. These two issues are shaped by the main theological reality about what happens in our liturgy—that we gather around the bodily presence of Jesus Christ according to his divine and human natures. It was my contention in 1990, when I decided to proclaim the treasures of Lutheran liturgy instead of defending it, that if people understood that the liturgy is essentially biblical, they would not be speaking and acting the way they were in their "contemporary" liturgies *in the presence of Christ, the Pantocrator of the universe*. For in the liturgy, heaven is on earth in the fleshly presence of

Jesus Christ, that is, the infinite has broken into our finite world as we gather around the voice of Jesus and eat and drink his very body and blood.

This made me wonder what kind of church should be handed down to our children and our grandchildren, and it led to this question: How do we connect people in this postmodern world to the feast, to Christ, to his presence?

That's it, isn't it? Connecting people to Jesus Christ, to his flesh, to the whole Christ, divine and human natures, and by connecting them to Christ, to connect them to the church, which is his body. How do we help people today enter Christ's world, the biblical world, the world of faith and hope and love, the world of mystery and mercy, a world lived out every time we gather together at the feast?

This is what we are all about in the church—bringing people into communion with the flesh of Jesus Christ, whose bodily presence is at the heart of our life together as the people of God.

As a pastor and professor for over forty years, most of my professional life has been about the theological education of pastors and deaconesses, teaching them to go into church and world and bring people into communion with the flesh of Christ. So I've been thinking about how to teach the faith for many, many years—as professor; as a co-founder of the Good Shepherd Institute on Pastoral Theology and Sacred Music; as a member of the curriculum review committee of CTSFW; as a writer of curriculum for deaconess programs at CTSFW and in churches around the world; as the chief architect of the curriculum for the SMP program at CTSFW; and then, at the end of my career, overseeing global theological education for the LCMS in the Office of International Mission (OIM).

The Good Shepherd Institute of Pastoral Theology and Sacred Music

When Dean Wenthe became president of CTSFW in 1996, I was given tenure and made a full professor (twelve years is a long time to serve without tenure!). I was also appointed as dean of the graduate school and asked to develop an STM in Pastoral Theology. In my inaugural lecture on my appointment as professor in Easter of 1998, I reflected on what I hoped to accomplish in the next twenty years. I rehearsed the work I had done in liturgy as pastoral care, my work on Emmaus in *The Ongoing*

Feast and the publishing of a commentary on Luke, as well as the work I was doing on the Luke volume of the Ancient Christian Commentary on Scripture. This inaugural lecture also urged the seminary to establish an institute of pastoral theology to begin an ongoing conversation within a community of scholars, and among our colleagues in the ministerium, towards the development of an organic pastoral theology that sees the pastoral office holistically as the locus of Christ's work as preacher, liturgist, catechist, and caregiver. Jesus Christ is the chief pastor who speaks and acts through the pastoral office to create his church, which is both his kingdom and his new creation. The recovery of an organic pastoral theology from our patristic roots was one of my first goals towards an integrated pastoral theology that began with the church fathers.

This inaugural paper led to a proposal for an institute to develop some of these pastoral themes. A year later, in 1999, with Richard Resch as a co-director, the Good Shepherd Institute of Pastoral Theology and Sacred Music for the Church (GSI) was founded to serve as a place dedicated to the recovery of the classic care of souls, integrating theology into the pastoral life of our church, and engaging the church on issues related to liturgy and church music. Working alongside Richard in the GSI was one of the most satisfying experiences in my years of pastoral ministry. CTSFW, with Kramer Chapel as its focal point, is an ideal place for such an institute, with its rich exegetical, theological, homiletical, liturgical, and musical traditions. The institute was to provide a center dedicated to hearing and discerning the clear voice of Jesus Christ, the Good Shepherd, through preaching, historic liturgies, substantive catechesis, and hymns that communicate faith in Christ in the church's teaching and worship.

For fifteen years, Richard and I led the GSI through a series of conferences beginning in 2000 that explored topics such as "Christ's Gifts for Healing the Soul," "Christ's Gifts in Liturgy: The Theology and Music of the Divine Service," "The Psalms in the Life of Church," and so on. Richard and I chose the beginning of November for our conferences because it was close to All Saints Day, which captured best the theological soul of GSI. Each conference also included sublime music at a Choral Vespers, an organ recital, and later, a service of hymn singing with commentary to replace the banquet speech (this change was well received by all). After each conference, the papers and studies from the conference were published in a monograph. These GSI conferences offered an opportunity for pastors, church workers, musicians, and laypeople to retreat to the seminary for worship and study, reflection, and conversation with other church workers about the liturgical life of the church.

The original plan was to house GSI in a renovated and expanded Walther Library now known as "The Wayne and Barbara Kroemer Library." As such it was to become the theological center for pastoral retreats, as well as for scholarly research and writing dedicated to providing the facilities and resources required to carry on in-depth studies in pastoral theology and sacred music.[1] The impetus and working model behind the GSI came from Martin Chemnitz to show continuity with Lutheranism's confessional, orthodox, and Catholic traditions in catechesis and liturgy. Chemnitz's use of the fathers in his preaching, catechesis, and writing links him with the early church, and his catechetical book, *Ministry, Word, and Sacraments: An Enchiridion*, shows how he presented Luther's Small Catechism to his generation in a fresh and innovative way.

In founding the GSI, we believed that the time had arrived to tap the abundant resources God was providing for his church, proclaim without apology our rich heritage in pastoral theology, and present it afresh to a new generation that wanted to confess the biblical and Lutheran faith. Dean Paul Grime and Kantor Kevin Hildebrand now carry on our work after Richard retired and I stepped down. They have since been able to achieve one of our goals, that is, for the GSI to be a place for the ecclesiastical arts, displaying artwork, fabrics, designs for paraments, banners, paintings, and other ecclesiastical adornments.

Towards a "New" Curriculum

In our revision of the seminary's curriculum, we believed that postmodern people learn differently, process information differently, come to us with different expectations, even see the world in a different way than previous generations. A great challenge faces the church in how it hands down the faith to this next, postmodern generation. People today cannot listen to the twenty-minute sermons their grandparents or even their parents heard, and catechesis cannot be the old way of information download with a public examination.

1. The idea for "Doxology" came from a Lilly grant that Dr. Beverly Yanke and I wrote for CTSFW to be a retreat for pastors to provide for them pastoral care. It was not granted, but when Doxology was founded, I was on the constituting committee. The rest, as they say, is history.

From the moment I learned about the catechumenate during my STM studies at YDS, I was convinced that it could address many of the challenges facing the church today in connecting postmoderns to Christ and some of the theological considerations that must go into handing down the faith in a postmodern world. The genius of the catechumenate was that it was a *liturgical* way of making Christians, incorporating the entire church and her life into making Christians. It was the catechumenate more than anything else that taught me why the liturgy matters and what was at stake in the worship wars. The catechumenate also taught me that catechesis is *not* religious education but "an apprenticeship in the Christian faith,"[2] that is, a journey to life in Christ. And this also applies not only to the unchurched but to all people, both young and old, who are seeking baptism or reaffirmation of the faith.

In revising our curriculum, we determined that we were not "educating" pastors but forming them into servants of Jesus Christ, as we are now forming women as deaconesses who embody Christ's mercy. Thus, our mission statement begins with the words "forming servants in Jesus Christ." And what kind of servants are we forming? Servants who "teach the faithful, reach the lost, and care for all."[3] Catechizing postmodern people includes all three of these things—teaching, reaching, and caring—or in the words of our synodical mission statement, witness, mercy, and life together. The mission statement of OIM captures similar sentiments—our missionaries share the gospel, plant Lutheran churches (by forming Lutheran pastors), and show mercy (by forming Lutheran deaconesses).

The ancient catechumenate became the model for the new curriculum at CTSFW. Aidan Kavanagh called the catechesis of the early catechumenate "conversion therapy of a definite sacramental and ecclesial kind."[4] He lamented that the ancient catechumenate was lost in the medieval period to the larger church, "transferred into religious houses, becoming the novitiate and, later, a seminary education."[5] Although

2. This expression is from Hofstad, *Welcome to Christ*, 71. On the "apprenticeship in faith," see "How Does the Catechumenal Process Work?," 13–15.

3. Our mission statement was revised in the summer of 2025 to read, "Concordia Theological Seminary, Fort Wayne (CTSFW), is an institution of The Lutheran Church—Missouri Synod committed to the Holy Scriptures, the Lutheran Confessions, and the liturgical life of the Church, forming servants in Jesus Christ who teach the faithful, reach the lost, and care for all."

4. Kavanagh, "Christian Initiation in Post-Conciliar Roman Catholicism," 6.

5. Kavanagh, "Christian Initiation in Post-Conciliar Roman Catholicism," 4.

the catechumenate was meant for making Christians, not seminarians, today's students come to us as Lutheran Christians in need of "conversion" to a different way of thinking and doing theology that is "sacramental and ecclesial." In our seminary classrooms we teach *and convert*, especially in that first year, where seminary education is very much a kind of "conversion therapy." The catechumente not only teaches the essentials of the baptismal life but also prepares the catechumen to survive when the assaults of the devil become most fierce. Our students experience similar post-ordination, post-consecration assaults, both within and without the church. One survives them by understanding who they are in Christ—their christological identity—and that the life and community into which they are baptized is the body of Christ.

Like all the baptized, our students are pilgrims, "hearers of the Word" who commune at a feast with him and the whole company of heaven, where he is both host and victim. In the seminary chapel they learn the rhythms and the rituals of the feast, enter its mysteries. Teaching seminarians teaches truth embodied in a person who is the Way, the Truth, and the Life and whose body is the church. Seminarians must be stunned by our liturgical life—its beauty and its passion—and see it rooted in the truth of Christ's bodily presence, creating a hunger and thirst for righteousness. Casting all other "truths" aside, they will hear and see and touch holy things and so embrace the church's truth with a "passion" for Christ they see in a liturgical community captive to Christ's bodily presence.

This will happen if they experience what we are doing at the seminary as primary and real—that the story we tell is truly our story, the story of the world made new in Jesus Christ, and that they want to be part of that story, so that it becomes their story, a story that is told first in liturgy, then in hymns, and finally in preaching, culminating in a feast at a table of old friends who include Abraham, Isaac, Jacob, and all the saints, and they find delight in being invited to the party. The content of their seminary formation is lived out in faith and life—at font, at pulpit, at table, in acts of charity and mercy. This is not done primarily through propositional truths or a robust apologetic, even though they will always be part of the curriculum. For the way of the kingdom is not through the mind but through the heart, that is, through love, embodied love, love seen and experienced by people who are lovers of Christ—who sing to him, listen to him, feed upon him. As one postmodern author said, "The church doesn't have an apologetic; it is an apologetic."[6]

Matthew 28 as a Church Order

Tertullian, a church father from the second and third centuries, said it first and said it best—Christians are made, not born. That truth has been with the church ever since Paul visited gentile communities in Galatia, Western Asia, Macedonia, and Greece. Paul and Tertullian confronted a world where gentile adults were being catechized and then baptized, a practice that the church has continued ever since Paul's longer stays in Corinth and Ephesus, during his second and third missionary journeys. Paul understood that when the church moved into the gentile world and began baptizing gentiles, they needed to be taught for longer periods of time before being washed.

How, then, did Paul and Tertullian make Christians? By uniting them to the person of Jesus Christ so that their broken and sinful flesh may be made whole through their communion with his whole and holy flesh. How did they do this?

The rhythm of the early Christian communities was the rhythm of evangelization, catechesis, baptism, and Lord's Supper. This pattern was established by the earthly ministry of Christ himself in Matt 28, in fulfillment of the pattern of the Old Testament.

Paul and Tertullian listened carefully to Jesus' final words to his disciples in Matthew's Gospel, where he is instructing his eleven disciples how to do church (28:16–20). Church orders—how to plant a church—were a common genre in the early church. The *Didache*, or Teaching of the Twelve Apostles, was a highly Semitic church order used in the first century to plant churches among the Jews. Its structure follows the initiatory pattern of catechesis (chapters 1–6), baptism (chapter 7), and Lord's Supper (chapters 9–10). As a church order, it would be used by Jewish-Christian communities seeking to establish a Christian congregation through this pattern of initiation. Its very name, *Didache*, or "teaching," indicates that its purpose is instruction in the faith. It was written to assist leaders in the Christian community as they prepared catechumens for baptism and the Lord's Supper. Due to its Semitic character, it would

6. Smith, *Who's Afraid of Postmodernism?*, 28–29. The language of "lovers of Christ" also comes from Smith, in his book *Desiring the Kingdom*, 17–19, 32–33.

have served as a church order primarily during the early Jewish mission, where the pattern of making Christians is very clear: evangelization, catechesis, baptism, and Lord's Supper, a pattern that comes from Jesus' final words to his eleven disciples in Matt 28. The early church continued this pattern in the mission to both Jews and gentiles. They saw no alternative, no other way to make Christians, than to continue the New Testament pattern of Jesus.

In both the early church and now, adults were taught prior to baptism, except in the case of Jews who were already "catechized" by means of the Old Testament. Therefore, it seems strange that Jesus should put "baptizing" before "teaching." With the initiatory pattern of early Christians, one would expect Matt 28:19–20 to read "make disciples, teaching and baptizing." Baptism among early Christian adults, however, was always preceded by catechesis and then followed by a water bath in the name of the Triune God and eucharistic table fellowship. After baptism, the newly baptized continued to be taught by hearing the word of God in the context of the church's eucharistic liturgy, for the final words of Jesus in Matthew—"And lo, I am with you always, to the close of the age" (Matt 28:20)—are an expression of his ongoing presence in his church and are therefore eucharistic, for his abiding presence in his church is most clearly evident in the eucharistic banquet that he has given to church.

So, Paul and Tertullian went into the world making disciples who are learners. Learners—that's what a disciple is. Later the church called them catechumens, that is, "hearers of the Word." Paul and Tertullian made Christians by taking Jesus at his word, doing what the apostles did in those apostolic years—they made Christians by uniting disciples/catechumens with Christ, first by teaching them the Word, then baptizing them, then teaching them some more in the Liturgy of the Word, and finally leading them to a table where Christ fed them with body and blood as a way of being with them always, to the end of the ages.

In Matthew's final chapter Jesus offers the church the way to make Christians, even today—make them learners, then baptize them, teach them, and then feed them. "Lo, I am with you always, even to the end of the ages," and so he is, at Font, in Word, at Table. That's how simple adult catechesis is—catechesis through the pastoral acts. Some will ask about infants. The church's natural response was to make them learners right away by baptizing them as infants, then teaching and feeding them after their rebirth in the church's rich liturgical life for the rest of their lives until they entered full communion with Christ in death.

Catechizing adults in a postmodern world is not a lot different from catechizing adults in Paul's first-century world or the second-century world of Tertullian. At least, that's the claim of experts in postmodernism who see postmoderns desiring a return to premodern ways.[7] Catechizing adults today includes both the baptized and the unbaptized. It's increasingly common today to find that many of the people who come to our churches are unchurched and unbaptized.

How do we hand down the faith to those who know not Christ?

How do we make Christians of the unchurched in today's postmodern world?

A Word about Modernism, Postmodernism, and Theological Education

Each one of us is defined by the era in which we came of age, the time in which we were born and nurtured in the faith. Many today claim that we are in the postmodern age. Thomas Oden, in his *Requiem: A Lament in Three Movements*, writes that "by postmodern, I mean the course of actual history following the death of modernity. By modernity, I mean the period, the ideology, and the malaise of the time from 1789 to 1989, from the Bastille to the Berlin Wall."[8] Stanley Grenz, in *A Primer on Postmodernism*, offers this dating: "Many historians place the birth of the modern era at the dawn of the Enlightenment, which followed the Thirty Years' War. The stage, however, was set earlier—in the Renaissance, which elevated humankind to the center of reality."[9]

The consensus is that it's easier to define modernity than postmodernity. My one real exposure to postmodern literature occurred at Calvin College in 2003 with Bryan Spinks of Yale Divinity School, who served as mentor to fourteen post-doctoral students. We engaged in the topic "The Prospects of the Historic Liturgy in the Postmodern World." What we all agreed upon was that at the center of modernism stands the sovereign individual. Grenz puts it this way:

7. This is the impulse behind InterVarsity's *Ancient Christian Commentary on Scripture*, as well as its other offerings that seek the early church's understanding of doctrine and pastoral care.

8. Oden, *Requiem*, 110.

9. Grenz, *Primer on Postmodernism*, 2.

> The modern ideal champions the autonomous self, the self-determining subject who exists outside any tradition or community. This sovereign individual believes "that knowledge is not only certain (and hence rational) but also objective . . . the assumption of objectivity leads the modernist to claim access to dispassionate knowledge . . . that knowledge is certain and objective . . . it is inherently good . . . that progress is inevitable, that science, coupled with the power of education, will eventually free us from our vulnerability to nature, as well as from all social bondage."[10]

It should not be hard to see from these descriptions of modernity why postmodernism came of age. The experiences of our civilization in the twentieth century destroyed any hopes that our rational, humanistic capacities could provide the kind of progress where control over our world could be accomplished by our own efforts. Such things as two world wars, the Holocaust, the rise and fall of the Soviet Union, hurricanes, cyclones, tsunamis, and the martyrdom of more Christians in the twentieth century than in all previous nineteen centuries combined have thoroughly discredited any notions of "the Enlightenment optimistic outlook."[11]

Postmodernism, with its rejection of absolute truth and its relativism, gives us much to fear as well. Which is why James K. A. Smith wrote a book entitled *Who's Afraid of Postmodernism?* to offer a more optimistic assessment on postmodernism for the church. Smith claims that an authentic, confessional, orthodox Christianity is more possible in postmodernism than in modernity.

> I will argue that the postmodern church could do nothing better than be ancient, that the most powerful way to reach a postmodern world is by recovering tradition, and that the most effective means of discipleship is found in liturgy . . . Without being conservative or trying to recover a (mythical) pristine tradition in the name of "paleo-orthodoxy," postmodernism does stage a certain creative recovery of ancient themes and figures . . . The most persistent postmodernism should issue in a thickly confessional church that draws on the very particular (yet catholic) and ancient practices of the church's worship and discipleship. In other words, a "radical orthodoxy" is the

10. Grenz, *Primer on Postmodernism*, 4.

11. This is a variation of Grenz's words in *Primer of Postmodernism*, 4, where he says, "The assumption of the inherent goodness of knowledge renders the Enlightenment outlook optimistic."

> only proper outcome of the postmodern critique, and insofar as the emerging church shrinks from an unapologetic dogmatics (which isn't a rabid fundamentalism), it remains captive to the dreams, ambitions, and skepticism of modernity.[12]

Perhaps you cannot relate to Smith's assessment, but I sure can. I came of age through my formation in prep school and college by what many would describe as modernism's last gasp—born in the 1950s, a child of the 1960s, a thoroughgoing boomer (of which I repent every day). I am a cradle Missouri Synod Lutheran, trained in modernism's "Eastern" laboratories, where we were encouraged to discount the supernatural, mystery, and miracles as remnants of a superstitious, pre-scientific age.

Then I entered CTSFW in 1976, taking "Revelation and Scripture" from Kurt Marquart, reading Pieper, rebelling (by throwing Pieper across the room), and then submitting in obedience to a way of doing theology that resonated with the rigors of critical thinking I had learned in my Eastern schools, except for the embrace of mystery that somehow came easily to me. My seminary training was a sophisticated form of religious education that focused more on information than formation, where our liturgical life was detached from the classroom. Much of the curriculum then was what might be called "secondary theology" in that it was systematic, reflective, analytical, and critical—and I loved every minute of it. It did not proclaim but rather instructed with what we now call "information download." Its primary intention was information not formation, and it was identifiable with a person or with a school of thought. It was "Lutheran theology" with "Lutheran hermeneutical principles"; it studied "Walther's ecclesiology" and "Brunner's liturgiology." It was the theology of academe—a theology that produced curricula and assessment reports, conducted theological interviews and colloquiums, and evaluated case studies from counseling, evangelism calls, and catechesis.

This secondary theology of CTSFW that formed the core of my seminary education operated with theological language that included codewords known only to members of the guild. Exegesis was about learning rules of grammar so that we might know what the text said. But most exegetical classes never explored what the text meant, its theological significance, except in systematic classes, where there was more theological exegesis than in our biblical courses. We learned to preach sermons based on Aristotelian logic that tended toward propositional

12. Smith, *Who's Afraid of Postmodernism?*, 25.

structures, proof texts, and doctrinal content. Seminary education was centered in right concepts, and its passion was for precision, its nemesis ambiguity.[13] But this was all we knew to do, for it was the late 1970s when modernism reached its zenith. Seminaries were communities of secondary theologians with their discrete disciplines carefully kept in their own silos. Back then, seminaries handed down the faith to future generations of pastors through rigorous and analytical study of Scripture, theology, history, and pastoral practice.

That our curriculum in the twentieth century was deeply immersed in secondary theology was evident, although from the beginning we attempted to balance this heavy emphasis on secondary theology with "practical" experiences that were learned from field work in congregations, hospitals, and nursing homes and from a year-long vicarage, where students were immersed in congregational life and were able to put their theology into practice. And yet, despite efforts to integrate what went on in the classroom with the student's experiences in the field, a bifurcation existed between theology and practice, even in the department of pastoral ministry and missions, of which I was a member for my first twelve years of teaching at the seminary in homiletics and liturgy. Many of the theological problems we experience in the church today stem from this separation of theology and practice.[14]

But we are not in the 1970s or 1980s anymore. We are more than two decades into the twenty-first century. And no one writes their sermons on a typewriter, as I did during my years as a parish pastor. Students learn differently today, perceive reality differently, have moved from a modernist/noetic/disembodied world to one that is, shall we say, a desire for a kingdom that is real and embodied and fresh and living.

13. But compare Kavanagh, "Christian Initiation," in *Made, Not Born*, 4: "Learning to live with rich ambiguity is not a fault but a virtue. It is the poverty of precision that is killing us."

14. This was most evident in the 1980s with David Luecke's *Evangelical Style, Lutheran Substance.* He bristled when I told him I was going to write a book called *Roman Catholic Style, Lutheran Substance.* I wrote an essay for Bishop Roger Pittelko's English District entitled "The Contextualization of Worship: Cult and Culture in Conflict or Concord?" during the worship wars, addressing this gnostic understanding of separating substance and style, especially in the arts, where such a separation was unthinkable.

A New Curriculum for Postmodern Students

In the late 1990s, the faculty of CTSFW began a seven-year process of curriculum review that thoroughly endorsed James K. A. Smith's claim that "the primary responsibility of the church as witness, then, is not demonstration but rather proclamation—the kerygmatic vocation of proclaiming the Word made flesh."[15] We designed a curriculum for students today who, in the words of our former academic dean, William Weinrich, "are affected by habits of mind reflecting the postmodern emphasis on the individual and the division between truth and life" (or substance and style as it is sometimes called). This new curriculum is centered in the pastoral acts of the church, for we designed it around the reality that our students are sent to be shepherds of the sheep, representing Christ to church and world, embodying in their pastoral acts of baptizing, preaching, teaching, and celebrating the Lord's Supper, the very essence of the church's formation of them into Christ's representatives, who stand in his stead and by his command. Weinrich concludes his article on the new curriculum in *For the Life of the World* with this:

> Baptism-Preaching-Lord's Supper, these are the (primary) "disciplines" of theological education by which pastor and people in common drink of the cool waters of redemption and feed upon the pastures of the Spirit as they hear the voice of their Shepherd. To "learn"—that is, to be "educated"—is to participate in the gifts of God and to reflect on how best to "declare the mighty acts" of God.[16]

For our curriculum review committee, worship life at Kramer Chapel was the single most important part of the curriculum, for this is where Christ was present bodily in Word and Meal to shape and form men and women into his servants for the church. Theological "education" begins with the primary theology of the chapel that flows from Christ's bodily presence, and all theological discourse and reflection on what happens in chapel is secondary. *Lex orandi, lex credendi*. As more than one of us have observed over the years, it is no coincidence that Kramer Chapel governs the campus by size, height, and significance (see Pless below!).

So it is that the incarnation of Jesus Christ, God's embodied presence in the world, governed the way we would now both do and teach theology—what Dr. Weinrich called "the particularities, the concrete

15. Smith, *Who's Afraid of Postmodernism?*, 28–29.

16. Weinrich, *For the Life of the World*, April 2005, Volume 9, Number 2.

realities of our life together as the church." For postmoderns, such an approach is exactly what they are yearning for. James K. A. Smith describes it this way:

> "'Radical Orthodoxy'—a sensibility that seeks to articulate a robust confessional theology in postmodernity" that "begins from the scandalous reality that God became flesh, and became flesh in a particular person, at a particular time, and in a particular place . . . a more persistent postmodernism embraces the incarnational scandal of determinate confession and its institutions: dogmatic theology and a confessionally governed church."[17]

Two of the books we read for our revision of the curriculum were Edward Farley's *Theologia: The Fragmentation and Unity of Theological Education* and Reinhard Hütter's *Suffering Divine Things: Theology as Church Practice.*[18] In his article in *Concordia Theological Quarterly*, Professor John Pless describes our discussions as a committee and it's conclusions:

> Hütter develops the argument that doctrine is not a theoretical abstraction, but it is rather embodied in the concrete practices of the church: liturgy, preaching, pastoral care, catechesis, and mission. Hütter's insights, which were forged by his engagement with George Lindbeck, Oswald Bayer, and Erik Peterson were provocative in faculty discussion and formative for a curriculum centered in the practices of the church. Since the seminary's mission is "the preparation of pastors for the congregations and missions of the LCMS . . . Its programs and services offer an understanding of Christian faith which is Christ-centered and biblically-based, confessionally Lutheran and evangelically active," the new curriculum, too, is shaped by the realities that constitute the church, namely, the preaching of Christ crucified and the administration of the sacraments. A curriculum governed by the gifts of Christ in Word and Sacrament intentionally reflects both the life of the pastor and that of the congregation.
>
> Worship, therefore, is not a devotional addendum to the study of theology but the matrix for such study. Kramer Chapel dominates the campus of Concordia Theological Seminary not only architecturally but also thematically, as academic rigor is not separated from a life of faith nurtured by sermon and sacrament as well as doxologically expressed in the daily offices. The curriculum integrates exegetical and dogmatic studies, historical

17. Smith, *Who's Afraid of Postmodernism?*, 122.

18. Farley, *Theologia*; Hütter, *Suffering Divine Things.*

> investigation of the church's traditions, and the development of pastoral skills with the ongoing worship life of the church centered in font, pulpit, and altar. This is the key to the revised curriculum.
>
> This new curriculum seeks to catechize students into God's means of grace in a fundamental and holistic manner. It assumes regular participation in the Divine Service and the prayer offices of the church.[19]

All the members of our curriculum review committee were very excited about this radical new proposal. We believed that this model for pastoral formation fit our seminary, which was already committed to pastoral formation through the liturgical life of the seminary. Unfortunately, our faculty was not as enamored with our proposal as we had hoped. They rejected our proposal to shape the curriculum around one year of baptism, another of preaching, and a final one focused on the Lord's Supper. This was way too radical for them. Many of them still wanted to maintain the old Enlightenment model with the fourfold departments of Biblical Theology, Systematic Theology, Historical Theology, and Pastoral Theology.

So, we had to compromise. We did center the curriculum in the four Gospels and Greek readings that corresponded to the Gospel from the three-year lectionary, which was one of the foundations of our new curriculum. We also developed three courses entitled "Theologia: Baptism," "Theologia: Preaching," and "Theologia: Lord's Supper." The three "Theologia" courses intended to capture the essence of the original plan for the curriculum. Even now, our faculty speaks of the pastoral acts of baptizing, preaching, and celebrating the Lord's Supper as the heart of what it means to be a pastor. It was our hope and desire that these courses would be instrumental in the formation of our students into pastors for the church, providing the students an opportunity to reflect on the pastoral acts in a fundamental, holistic way.

Catechesis as Primary Theology

This fundamental idea of Hütter's "theology as church practice" or our curriculum committee's notion that the teaching of theology is through pastoral acts is nothing new. This "postmodern" idea is in fact premodern,

19. Pless, "Curriculum from and for the Church," 86. As I write this theological memoir, our faculty at CTSFW is revising "the new curriculum."

and for liturgical theologians like Alexander Schmemann and Aidan Kavanagh, this approach to teaching the faith is part of the great tradition. Schmemann describes this kind of formation through the pastoral acts in his book on the Eucharist, *For the Life of the World*, which is also the name of CTSFW's magazine.[20]

So, perhaps there is another theology that is primary because it is not systematic, reflective, analytical, and critical, but rather because it is uncritical, not analytic, active, foundational, and happens naturally. It is a theology not found in academe but among our people, in the worshiping congregations throughout our church. The people of God are theologians, not in an academic sense but in a primary way. And the most complete expression of their "primary theology" is in the liturgy, where theology is most real because it flows out of a presence that is real. Primary theology takes place when God speaks his word to his people; they are transformed by that speaking into christological beings, and then they respond back to God with words he has given them to speak. And what God speaks to us is his Word, revealed and inspired by his Spirit and enfleshed in his Son, and this speaking of God's Word takes place in the church. The church is the place where the source of God's self-revelation, his holy Scripture, is the source of God's people's identity as Christians.

This theology does not happen through scholarly papers about the Trinity but in the proclaimed word heard and inwardly digested by people who come with a vocabulary shaped not by an academic theology but by a theology that is biblical and liturgical, that is, given through preaching, and a catechesis intended to form catechumens into the life of Christ. This happens when people encounter Christ, who is enfleshed and revealed in preaching and sacraments. Theology at its highest level is done liturgically, that is, when God is present with his gifts as people gather around those gifts by gathering around Scripture read and proclaimed and around a table that is a foretaste of our eschatological banqueting with God. This theology is about participation in the divine life,

20. When Dean Wenthe became president, he called several of us together, including Bill Weinrich, the academic dean, to discuss what to name our new seminary magazine. In jest I said we should call it *For the Life of the World*, and everybody looked at each other and said, "That's it. That's what we'll call it." Little do people realize that it's named after what Jesus said in John 6:51: "I am the living bread that came down from heaven. If anyone eats of this bread, he will live forever. And the bread that I will give for the life of the world is my flesh," as well as from Alexander Schmemann's book on the Eucharist entitled *For the Life of the World*.

the embodiment of that divine life in a life of *diakonia* where Christians bear in their own bodies Christ's mercy and love.

David Fagerberg, in his book *What is Liturgical Theology? A Study of Methodology*, summarizes "primary theology" in this way:

> It is a truism to say encounter with God precedes reflection upon that encounter. Liturgy is encounter with God, but furthermore it is also a living adjustment, i.e., a theological response, to the Holy One . . . Because encounter with God precedes reflection upon that encounter, liturgy is the ontological condition for theology. This is what tradition means when it says that the law of prayer (*lex orandi*) establishes (*statuat*) the law of belief (*lex credendi*), and not vice-versa . . . The normative character of liturgical theology stems from the fact that it is in the liturgy, under God's judgment and in God's presence, that *theologia prima* is done . . . Whether the theologian be a monk in the cell, a believer in the pew, or an academic in the study, the subject matter being considered is the Church's corporate theological adjustment to encounter with the Father through Christ in the Holy Spirit.[21]

This maxim of Prosper of Aquitaine—"the law of worshiping founds the law of believing" (a lay monk and disciple of Augustine who was to have written this somewhere between 435 and 442 AD)—is at the heart of this distinction between primary and secondary theology. This maxim maintains that ever since the time of the apostles, liturgy and preaching have been the primary ways the church has handed down the faith to future generations. The liturgical rites, homilies, and hymns of a congregation shape the faith of the people more than anything else. A church's belief and confession may be observed from their liturgy, hymns, preaching, and catechesis. This maxim of Prosper of Aquitaine needs to be worked out in our church so that both scholars and the people of God come to understand the relationship between what we confess and believe and the way we worship. As Lutherans, we must at times reverse that maxim to read, "The law of believing founds the law of worshiping," for in fact the confessional nature of our church establishes our life in Christ and is foundational for the way we express that life in our primary theological life of worship.

Aidan Kavanagh illustrates the power and normality of primary theology in his description of our Lord's life and ministry:

21. Fagerberg, *What Is Liturgical Theology?*, 217–18.

> [Primary theology] is the same power which enabled a powerless young Jew to set the world of abnormality on its ear by seeming to dismiss all the heroes of Israel with the words, "Before Abraham was, I am"; to dismiss the pretensions of religion and politics with the words, "Render unto Caesar those things that are Caesar's, and to God those things that are God's." He then went about being so disconcertingly normal—healing the ill, telling the truth, feeding the hungry, raising the downcast, stampeding swine, withering fig trees—that systemic abnormality had him put away, as it thought, for keeps. It is the same power which enabled his at first paralyzed followers, clinging only to themselves around a simple table, to walk finally into the jaws of abnormality itself, pulling its teeth and getting themselves chewed up on the way.[22]

Primary theology, therefore, is the theology of the people of God as they enter God's presence, hear his word, receive his gifts, and respond to those gifts with words they have been given by him to speak back what has already been spoken. This primary liturgical language is the language of Scripture; it is handed down through catechesis, preaching, and the divine service; and it is the language of God's people as they journey from baptism to death or the parousia, whichever comes first.[23] This is the theology that Jesus gave to the Emmaus disciples, which opened the Scriptures to them and caused them to have burning hearts, the theology that opened their eyes in the breaking of the bread. This is the theology that postmodern adults are seeking and that our church needs to give them. This is the theology I hope my children and grandchildren come to embrace in their lives. It is at base a theology that is lived in community, embodied by community, a community that is Christ's body, the church. It is this primary theology that was the basis for this seminary's revision of the curriculum for the formation of pastors and deaconesses for a postmodern world.

A Lutheran Catechumenate for the Postmodern World

A few years ago, I was asked to teach a course for our DMin program that I entitled "A Lutheran Catechumenate for the Postmodern World." I was

22. Kavanagh, *On Liturgical Theology*, 164–65.

23. For a fuller discussion of primary theology, see Kavanagh, *On Liturgical Theology*, 151.

delighted to return to what had been a passion for me. For many years I had given up on the possibility of the catechumenate for our church. Whatever I had done in the 1990s towards promoting the catechumenate fell on deaf ears. This was the case even among our students as we began to roll out our new curriculum in 2005. We told them that our curriculum was based on the catechumenate, especially the "Theologia" courses on baptism, preaching, and the Eucharist, which were intended to capture the original thrust of the new curriculum, namely, that theology is done through these pastoral acts. The image we wanted the students to have in their mind was a pastor at the font, in the pulpit, at the table, and how all that he learned in exegesis, systematics, history, and pastoral theology led to this moment, when he was presiding over these pastoral acts of baptizing, preaching, and celebrating the Eucharist, that is, making Christ present for his people by bringing them into communion with Christ's flesh through the pastoral acts.

In teaching the DMin course on the catechumenate, I discovered that pastors are hungry for a new way of catechizing, baptizing, and confirming adults (although after teaching this course three or four times, I'm not sure any of them have fully grasped how to integrate this into their parish). Most of them were comfortable doing catechesis as they had been doing it for years—a "curriculum" based on Luther's Small Catechism that gathered people for four to twelve weeks to hand down the faith. The curriculum of my seminary years was not in any way postmodern, nor was the way I taught prospective members seeking to join our Lutheran communion on vicarage, and I'm sad to admit this was true during my first years in the parish, when we called our new member class "Pastor's Information Class"—about as modernist a title as you could possibly imagine. I have no memory of learning what to do for adult catechesis in my "Parish Education" class at CTSFW in the late 1970s, but my six week "Pastor's Information Class" seemed to be the norm among pastors at that time. Catechesis was education, not formation.

If the church was really interested in being the locale of Jesus' presence with all its earth-shattering mystery, it would do well to fully immerse itself in the ancient catechumenate and work hard to appropriate the catechumenate into its congregations. I still believe that if the church were to fully embrace the catechumenate and understand why the liturgy is the most important thing it does, then we might see the sort of "reformation" the church needs now as our society "slouches towards

Gomorrah."[24] The journey of the catechumens to life in Christ through baptism, the Lord's Supper, and an ongoing baptismal life also provides an opportunity for the entire congregational to be renewed in its own baptismal journey to the heavenly Jerusalem. The adult catechumenate offers the church a process of evangelization and catechesis that is biblical, historical, and thoroughly Lutheran in its form and substance.

It has been over forty years since I taught catechesis at Grace, Middletown. Christians are now living in the third millennium, a full-blown postmodern world much different than the modern world of their parents and grandparents, even the world of my parish years in the early 1980s. Today's world is more like the world early Christians confronted, where people are asking questions about God and church and life that are basic and foundational. Instruction in the faith in a classroom setting and format may not be the most appropriate way to form new converts into a life in Christ. The ancient pattern of making Christians through evangelization, catechesis, baptism, the Lord's Supper, and mystagogical catechesis seems particularly vital in our increasingly unchurched world. This is especially true when those seeking God are allowed time in their process of formation to ask basic questions and be formed gradually by Scripture, liturgy, and catechism, the three sources of catechesis for life in Christ.

24. There are many fine resources on the catechumenate, even the Lutheran Catechumenate, e.g. *Welcome to Christ* and the more modest LCMS, *Make Disciples Baptizing and Teaching: Resources and Ideas for Renewing the Lutheran Catechumenate.* Kent Burreson and Rhoda Schuler are reviving the catechumenate with an important resource: *Journey to Jesus: Faith Formation into Christ and Community.* I was honored to be asked to write a foreword for a book that I hope, once again, will capture the imagination of our churches to the genius of the adult catechumenate of the early church. They show how important liturgy and the catechumenate are for producing, nurturing, and preserving a Lutheran identity and ethos in four congregations, a rich and indispensable primer on what the catechumenate looks like in congregations that have been shaped by its ancient wisdom.

9

Diakonia

Matthew, Paul, and Luke on the Liturgy of Life

In the seminary brochure for our deaconess studies program, we claim that "One of the founders of our seminary, Pastor Wilhelm Loehe of Neuendettelsau, Germany, was committed to the training of deaconesses for service in the church through acts of mercy and charity. When the seminary began its deaconess program in the fall of 2003, it continued Pastor Loehe's longstanding tradition."

Cheryl Nauman, the esteemed historian of the Concordia Deaconess Conference and author of the CPH book *In the Footsteps of Phoebe: A Complete History of the Deaconess Movement in the Lutheran Church Missouri Synod*, could give you the real story behind all this. The truth is that ever since the presidency of Dr. Robert Preus in the mid-1970s, it has been the desire of CTSFW to train women to be deaconesses in the church. We came very close to doing this during the 1980s, but it took a synodical resolution from the 2001 convention to make possible what has been a dream for many of us. Little did we realize how such a program would affect our seminary and our church.

When President Dean Wenthe and Dean William Weinrich asked me to serve as director of the program in the fall of 2002, they did so for several reasons. All of us were enthusiastic supporters of deaconesses and understood the theological implications of *diakonia* as the embodiment of the gospel of Christ crucified, Christ raised from the dead. With our new seminary curriculum centered in the incarnational care of the pastor for his people, the presence of deaconess students on campus would be a concrete way of catechizing our community and the church on *diakonia* as Christ's mercy embodied in the world. Dean and Bill recognized that my work on Luke's Gospel accented *diakonia* in Jesus' teaching and miracles. But I was only one among many who could provide biblical and theological substance to the formation of deaconesses to serve the church as women of mercy. Deaconess formation was already happening at Concordia University in River Forest for almost twenty-five years, but now it would happen at our seminaries. The leadership at CTSFW wanted our deaconess program to receive a high profile, so they chose a seasoned faculty member, known in the church and with experience in starting new programs, to demonstrate to the seminary community, the community of deaconesses, and the larger church that the development of a program of deaconess studies on our campus would receive the full support of the seminary and her resources.

I shared the enthusiasm of Drs. Wenthe and Weinrich for bringing a deaconess program to our campus, but I was not as excited as they were about serving as director of the program. To start a new program demands a great deal of time and energy and immerses one in numerous bureaucratic details, and I was already deeply involved in teaching and leading the chapel life of our campus. But my greatest concern, however, was that I had never worked with women, except for a secretary in the parish in Connecticut and several administrative assistants at the seminary. Nor had I grown up around women: I have two brothers and one sister, my high school was an all-male boarding school, my college an all-male student body until my junior year, when a few token women began to take classes with us. My seminary training was all men, of course, and then returning to teach at the seminary, I spent nineteen years in all-male classrooms. And in our family, God blessed us with one daughter and two sons (as of this writing, however, we have nine granddaughters and only one grandson!). My life has, from the beginning, been among men, and here I was being asked to lead a program for women. The one advantage I had was that all the women in my life were strong, confident, bright, and feminine, including my wife and daughter, my mother and sister. So, I was comfortable around women who are forceful and articulate, not intimidated by them but thoroughly delighted in them, at least most of the time.

CTSFW has now been forming deaconess for over twenty years, and there has been a change on our campus that goes beyond the simple reality that there are women now in the classrooms studying theology alongside our pastoral students. In our "new" curriculum, we have intentionally affirmed that the full gospel is not taught unless our teaching includes a theology of *diakonia*. As dean of the chapel for seven years, a veteran of the worship wars, a member of the steering committee of the *Lutheran Service Book*, and a professor of exegetical theology, my primary theological interest remains matters exegetical and liturgical. Our life of *leitourgia* in Kramer Chapel hands down to our students the treasures of our Lutheran liturgical tradition by forming them around the presence of Christ. But Christ's presence in our *leitourgia* needs to be balanced by a healthy understanding of *diakonia* by which his presence goes out into the world.

This chapter on *diakonia* follows the one on liturgy and the catechumenate to show how becoming the director of deaconess studies joined together two aspects of our ecclesial life that are inseparable—*leitourgia* and *diakonia*. These two realities reflected my life at the seminary for about four years. As dean of the chapel at CTSFW, I oversaw the worship life of our campus, its *leitourgia*, where Christ serves us in the liturgy of the church. As director of deaconess studies, I oversaw the training of women in *diakonia*, where, in response to those gifts received in *leitourgia*, these women will go forth into the church as *diakonai*, deaconesses, into a life of *diakonia*, of service, as emissaries of his mercy. Deaconesses, like all the baptized, serve Christ by serving their neighbor through works of mercy and charity in the liturgy of life. The LCMS has a rich history of diakonic care that is deeply rooted in Scriptures and in our Lutheran Confessions. As so this chapter will explore what I call "the liturgy of life" through the teachings of Jesus and Paul, for it will demonstrate how important a theology of *diakonia* has been for my life and the life of CTSFW and how it has allowed me to integrate *diakonia* into my teaching of both the Gospels and Paul.

Out of Africa—Learning Mercy from the Deaconesses of Kenya

When we started the deaconess program in 2003, there was much to be learned to create a program for the formation of deaconesses. President Matthew Harrison, then the director of World Relief and Human Care, insisted that we visit Kenya to walk alongside the deaconesses there, for he knew we would learn from them what it meant to embody mercy. He pointed us to Pastor David Chuchu, director of Diakonia Compassionate Ministries: Bringing Hope to the Hopeless, a former student of mine in Luke class, who was the informal pastoral leader among the deaconesses in Kenya. Working with David was the inspiration I needed to lead a deaconess program at our seminary.

For nine summers we walked alongside the Kenyan deaconesses in their visitations to the sick and needy in both the country and in the slums of Nairobi. Even though they themselves were quite poor, we saw how they always brought a concrete expression of their mercy in a bag of maize and a jug of oil. They asked us to provide firmer theological foundations for the care and compassion that came naturally to them as women of mercy. On our first visit in 2005, the HIV/AIDS crisis was breaking out all through Africa, and we came to find that widows and orphans were a living reality. During those years we witnessed in these deaconesses what we wanted to teach our women at the seminary—how Christ is present in the suffering, the lonely, and the despairing—present by baptism and faith—present as they came alongside people in their sufferings, bringing them Christ's living voice, praying with them, sharing Scripture with them, offering them a cup of cold water. With them, we came to call this theology "taking care of body and soul," which led to their request for seminars on grief counseling and palliative care—and now the building of the first Lutheran hospice in Kenya.

The visitations with the Kenya deaconesses inspired me to finally do what I threatened in class many years before—write a book that could be used by pastors, deaconesses, and laity in visiting the sick and the homebound. Scot Kinnamon, an editor at Concordia Publishing House, remembered what I said in class and together we edited a book entitled *Visitation* with the help of CTSFW pastoral and deaconess students. *Visitation* addresses many of the human care needs we see in our parishes and what we saw and heard from the deaconesses in Kenya. It was gratifying to see how they used this book in their visitations. Seeing these women of mercy in action, led me to deeper reflection in the New Testament about a theology of diakonia and mercy, especially in Matthew, Luke, and Paul.

"Blessed are those who hear the Word of God and keep it"—Luke 11:28

Those words from Luke's Gospel are written over the arc of the chancel of St. Paul's Evangelical Lutheran Church, my home church in Fort Wayne. Every Sunday I read those words as I also see in my mind's eye John Hrehov's painting of the chancel of St. Paul's for her 175th anniversary, which joins heaven and earth at the eucharistic table. In his painting the saints kneel below to receive the body and blood of the Lord, the angels hover over them, and above the angels is another arc of the heads of all the saints who have gone before us and are now with Christ. These two things—Hrehov's painting of heaven on earth and the citation from Luke 11:28—sum up my theology and the focus of this theological memoir. To be united with Christ and all the saints as we hear the Word of God, receive it in our mouths at the altar, and then keep that Word heard and consumed in our daily lives is how the liturgy of heaven and earth becomes the liturgy of life. *Leitourgia* and *Diakonia*—two of the themes of my life at CTSFW as dean of the chapel and the founder and director of deaconess studies.

The beatitude from Luke 11 is a Lukan theme and the focus of my work in both liturgy and diakonia—hearing the Word unites you to Christ and gives you your "being," then in this new christological identity, you are now able to keep that Word by your "doing." Being gives way to doing. This movement from "being" to "doing" is how I believe we should understand "sanctification" in both the teaching of Jesus and Paul. What I've always told the deaconess students is that *diakonia* is just another way of speaking about sanctification, and both are best embodied in our life of stewardship. For the supreme act of sanctification/*diakonia*/stewardship in our lives is when we are merciful as our Father in heaven is merciful (Luke 6:36—one of the theme verses of our deaconess program at its inception). The teaching of Jesus in the Sermon on the Mount shapes Paul's matrix of love in Galatians and both Matthew and Paul give structure to Luke's Sermon on the Plain. Through these two evangelists and Paul, we see how *diakonia* is a source of courage and encouragement through the law fulfilled in Christ in love.

The Sermon on the Mount

Even for those who hold to Markan priority, Matthew's Sermon on the Mount preceded Luke's Sermon on the Plain and served as its model. There is no doubt that they are similar sermons but shaped for the purpose and context of each evangelist and the period of evangelization in which their Gospels were written—Matthew for the Jewish/Petrine mission (AD 30 to 46) and Luke for the gentile/Pauline one (AD 46 to 58).[1] One might think of Luke's thirty verses in the Sermon on the Plain as a short, ten-minute homily for a Kramer Chapel Eucharist and of Matthew's 109 verses in the Sermon on the Mount for the good old days of twenty-to-thirty-minute sermons. The difference between the two sermons is summed up nicely by Luke T. Johnson:

> The major difference in the two discourses is that Luke lacks entirely the distinctively Matthean material dealing with the "Law and the Prophets" and their interpretation, a concern that clearly reflects the situation in Matthew's Church vis-à-vis the developing rabbinic tradition. As a result, Luke's sermon is notably more spare and focused, with an ethical emphasis entirely intelligible to Gentile readers.[2]

One of my interests in teaching sanctification in the New Testament is how Paul incorporates the teaching of Jesus in his development of paraenesis, especially in Galatians. This is significant, for if Matthew's Gospel was written at the end of the Jewish/Petrine mission, in the mid-late 40s, and Galatians was Paul's first letter written before the Apostolic Council in AD 48/49, Paul would know the Sermon on the Mount, especially these difficult words:

> You have heard that it was said, "You shall love your neighbor and hate your enemy." But I say to you, Love your enemies and pray for those who persecute you, so that you may be sons of your Father who is in heaven. For he makes his sun rise on the evil and on the good and sends rain on the just and on the unjust. For if you love those who love you, what reward do you have? Do not even the tax collectors do the same? And if you greet only your brothers, what more are you doing than others? Do not even the Gentiles do the same? You therefore must be perfect, as your heavenly Father is perfect. (Matt 5:43–48)

1. Just, *Concordia Commentary: Luke I–IX*, 16.
2. Johnson, *Gospel of Luke*, 110.

Paul wrote to the Galatians because of the mischief of Jewish-Christian opponents, his enemies, who wanted to undermine his teaching. As he wrote Galatians, Paul did not know the outcome of his relationship with Peter after the Antioch incident (Gal 2:11–14), nor did he know whether the bishop of Jerusalem, James the brother of our Lord, was with Paul on his mission to the gentiles, in particular whether gentiles needed to be circumcised before baptism and then keep the law of Moses as newly formed Christians. This is what the Pharisaical-Christian party insisted on, which led to the Apostolic Council: "It is necessary to circumcise them and to order them to keep the law of Moses" (Acts 15:5). Paul was unsure whether Peter and James would fully affirm what he said to Peter in Gal 2:15–16, Paul's first statement on justification: "A person is not justified by works of the law but through the faith of Jesus Christ . . ." (my translation). Paul's uncertainty about Peter and James led to his "matrix of love" that he develops in Gal 5–6, his paraenetic chapters, specifically in response to the way his opponents portrayed his understanding of the law.

Although many may disagree with Richard Hays's thesis about the genitive in his book *The Faith of Jesus Christ: The Narrative Substructure of Galatians 3:1–4:11*, his subtitle is exactly right—Paul's theology in Galatians is centered in the Gospel narrative, namely, "A story about Jesus Christ is presupposed by Paul's argument in Galatians, and his theological reflection attempts to articulate the meaning of that story."[3] As Hays himself notes, his study is not simply a matter of the subjective versus objective genitive but has more to do with the narrative substructure of the Gospels in Galatians. Why this seems so right is that it states the obvious but often overlooked foundation for Paul's theology, namely, that everything changes in the cosmos with the incarnation, death, resurrection, and ascension of Jesus Christ. Paul's theology is fundamentally centered in this cosmic change, that Paul died "to the law through the law." The Gospel narrative of Jesus' life—his teaching and miracles, his journey to Jerusalem, his passion, resurrection and ascension—is the foundation for every theological reflection Paul has about Jesus, the Father, and the Spirit. Every Gospel theme is related to this fundamental reality of Jesus' incarnation and ongoing presence in his creation. As I am more a student of the Gospels than of Paul, Hays's thesis about the Gospel narrative substructure of Paul resonated with me when *The Faith of Christ* was finally

3. Hays, *Faith of Jesus Christ*, xxiv (emphasis Hays).

published in 2002. As he was my advisor at Yale Divinity School from 1982 to 1984, his thesis about the subjective genitive and the foundation of Paul's theology was already being discussed among the New Testament faculty. Arguing for the subjective genitive is not a popular stance in the LCMS, although I am always gratified when my colleague, friend, and provost, Charles Gieschen, supports such a reading.

That Gospel narrative that is the substructure of Paul's theology is Matthew's Gospel, if one accepts my first-century dating of the Gospels, so the substructure of Paul's paraenesis is Jesus' Sermon on the Mount, what my esteemed colleague David Scaer calls "The Church's First Statement of the Gospel."[4] It is Jesus who gave Paul the Pharisee the proper christological understanding of the law, and Gal 5–6 is Paul's attempt to unravel what Jesus meant when he said:

> "Do not think that I have come to abolish the Law or the Prophets; I have not come to abolish them but to fulfill them. For truly, I say to you, until heaven and earth pass away, not an iota, not a dot, will pass from the Law until all is accomplished." (Matt 5:17–18)

The Law and the Prophets are now fulfilled in Christ and only comprehended in his sacrificial death, where he loved his neighbor as himself by giving up his life for them. The Law and the Prophets can only now be understood in Christ.

This radical christological understanding of the Law and the Prophets comes only if one understands the Beatitudes as christological. Who might Matthew's first hearers have in mind when they hear the beatitudes? Who are blessed because of their poverty, their hunger, their crying? Who are blessed for the hate, insults, and exclusion they receive on account of the Son of Man? Would these hearers in the first century not recall the martyrs who went before them, the saints who preceded them and now stand with them in the church? Would they not see themselves? For when one enters the Christian community by baptism, these beatitudes describe the character of those who belong to this community.[5]

Matthew's hearers, then and now, should also see beyond themselves to the One who was poor for them, who hungered in the wilderness for

4. Scaer, *Sermon on the Mount*. David was persecuted for making the bold, but most certainly true claim, that Jesus' teaching in the Sermon on the Mount was Gospel and not Law, the common interpretation at that time. The powers that be at CPH first kept him from publishing his book on Jesus' teaching until more enlightened editors saw the genius in what he was saying.

5. See Just, *Concordia Commentary: Luke 1:1–9:50*, 287, for a fuller discussion.

them, who wept for them as he entered Jerusalem, who received hate, insults, and exclusion for them, who was cast out and crucified outside Jerusalem as evil—the Son of Man. The christological character of the beatitudes would not be lost on the first-century hearers, who see themselves only in terms of how they see Jesus, who understand their baptismal incorporation into his body and into all that he brings. The hearer of the Word, who enters the christological life through baptism, is taught about the stage of this life by being told in the Gospel how Jesus lived his life in a hostile world that put him to death. Those who join his community will live this same life in this same world. This christological reading applies not only to the beatitudes but also to the rest of the Sermon on the Mount, especially Jesus' words about his fulfillment of the law.

So, Matthew's hearers would understand the beatitudes as describing who Jesus is and then who they are by their union *in Christ* by baptism and faith. Jesus' beatitudes in the Sermon on the Mount are ontological, that is, they describe *Being*—who the believer is in Christ, and therefore, his or her identity as a baptized Christian. This will become crucial when we return, at the end of this chapter, to Luke's Sermon on the Plain.[6]

The Atonement and Baptism are the Foundations of Paul's Matrix of Love[7]

The basis for Paul's matrix of love is the atonement. It has been a defining part of my teaching, again, through the influence of David Scaer.[8] When Paul preached the Gospel to the Galatians it was based on the narrative of Christ's passion and resurrection from the Gospel of Matthew. He describes his preaching this way: "It was before your eyes that Jesus Christ was publicly portrayed as crucified" (Gal 3:1). This must have been powerful stuff, a vivid and detailed picture of what happened to Jesus' body on the cross and how it was the death of the one who "gave himself for our sins to deliver us from this present evil age, according to the will of our God and Father" (Gal 1:5), the theme of Paul's homily to the Galatians. This prescript not only places the death of Christ and the atonement at the

6. For the inspiration behind these final three paragraphs, see Just, *Concordia Commentary: Luke 1:1–9:50*, 287.

7. Part of the following section was published as Just, "Paul's Matrix of Love in Galatians," 30–39.

8. See Just, "Cross, the Atonement, and the Eucharist in Luke," 227–44.

center of Galatians, but it also suggests the language of new creation, and points to the Eucharist.

1:3 *Grace* to you and *peace* from God our Father
and the Lord Jesus Christ,
1:4 *who gave himself for our sins*
to deliver us from the present evil age,
according to the will of our God and Father,
1:5 to whom be the *glory* forever and ever. *Amen*.

Grace and peace are to be understood in a liturgical context. Grace defines the space, the cosmos in which we now live, and that space is the new creation where Christ is present in his flesh, liberating his people from this present evil age. For sacramental communities, that space is also at a table where fellowship with God and other believers, both Jew and gentile, takes place in Christ, who is present with his gifts of grace, or in the words of one theologian, "What one witnesses in the liturgy is the world being done as the world's Creator and Redeemer will the world to be done."[9] The Galatians are constituted in this space of grace because of the greater reality that "our Lord Jesus Christ . . . gave himself for our sins to deliver us from the present evil age."[10] Grace embraces Christ's substitutionary atonement and the new creation—Christ's death liberates us from an evil age in which we were enslaved *to deliver* us into a new age where "the world has been crucified to me, and I to the world" (Gal 6:14). By asserting that we are rescued from this present evil age, Paul introduces the language of the new creation.[11] The one who gave himself for our sins now says, in the words of Luke's institution narrative, "This is my body which is being given *on behalf of you*" (Luke 22:19—my translation). The body Christ gave on the cross *on our behalf* is now given to the Galatians in a eucharistic feast of body broken and blood poured out.

The occasion for Paul's first preaching of justification by grace through faith is the historical event of Peter's retreat from a Gospel that is

9. Kavanagh, *Elements of Rite*, 46.

10. See Martyn, *Galatians*, 98: "In Paul's vocabulary the expression that stands opposite "the present evil age" is "the new creation" (Gal 6:15), yet another indication of apocalyptic thought . . ."

11. Seifrid, *Christ, Our Righteousness*, 81, also sees the connection between 1:4 and 6:15 and expresses the significance of Paul's eschatology in a stirring manner: "Underlying Paul's theology of promise and fulfillment is the stark contrast between 'the present evil age' and the 'new creation' (1:4; 6:15). The promise has come to fulfillment apart from and in opposition to fallen humanity (4:21–31). *That fulfillment represents the entrance of the eschaton into this world in Jesus Christ* (3:27–29)." (emphasis mine)

for all people, Jews and gentiles, embodied in the intimate act of Christ's table fellowship among them. Peter, living like a gentile, withdraws from table fellowship with the Galatians when "some from James" come to Antioch. In effect, Peter is compelling gentiles to live like Jews *by his actions*. For Paul in Galatians, justification by grace through faith is a doctrine both he and Peter know as the heart of the gospel, a doctrine one could not expect "gentile sinners" to understand. It is through this doctrine that Paul constructs his matrix of love, which enables him to "love his enemies" even though he is distressed by what his "enemies" have done to his beloved mission to the gentiles in Galatia.

2:15 We ourselves are Jews by birth and not Gentile sinners;
2:16 yet we know that
a a person is not justified *by works of the law*
b but *through faith in Jesus Christ*,
c *so we also have believed in Christ Jesus*,
b[1] in order *to be justified by faith in Christ*
and not *by works of the law*,
a1 because *by works of the law* no one will be justified.

If we understand "to justify" or "declare righteous" as "God's *making right what has gone wrong*,"[12] it ties justification to the new creation, for the image here is not a courtroom but a world infected by sin and in need of being made right by being made new. Justification and new creation are two different ways of speaking about the impact of the presence of Christ in the cosmos. What has gone wrong is very clear to Paul as he writes the Galatians. Humanity is enslaved in "the present evil age" to the forces of sin (1:4), the flesh (5:13), and the elemental spirits of the universe (5:25; 6:16). Luther's triad of sin, death, and the devil captures Paul's view of what has gone wrong in the cosmos.

12. Martyn, *Galatians*, 250. He is the first to recommend to me this way of looking at justification. He translates it "rectify" and righteousness as "rectification." Hays, "Letter to the Galatians," 238, has a brief excursus on "the Language of Righteousness" that supports Martyn's perspective. This also could be seen as covenantal language. See Hahn, *Hail*, 130–31: "But the deeper I went into Romans and Galatians, the more I realized that the ancient authors were *Hebrew* before anything else. Their categories, language, and assumptions were steeped in covenants, not in the juridical structures of the Roman Empire . . . In a covenant, *I* am yours and *you* are mine. Thus, the covenants God makes always say the same thing: I will be your God and you will be My people—My family, My kinfolk—because covenant creates kinship . . . Covenant creates family bonds that are even stronger than biological family bonds . . . [When Paul and John and James] heard that God was making a covenant with them, they know that He was no longer merely a lawgiver or judge. He was a Father foremost, and forever."

The question facing Paul, the Galatians, and his opponents is this: How does God make things right? Thus far, Christ's incarnation, his liberating death and resurrection, are the center of his theological reflection about the gospel. There has been no mention in Galatians about an individual's faith in Christ or works of the law. Christ's faithful death, where he "gave himself for our sins to deliver us from the present evil age," is how God is making things right in a world where things have gone very wrong. Here, "objective justification" takes center stage, and Paul's Gospel of Christ's liberating death and resurrection is placed at the center of his theology. The accent, then, is on God's objective act in Christ on the cross and in his resurrection for the life of the world.

Justification by grace through faith provides the foundation for Paul's first developed statement about our "incorporation into Christ." So, in the very next verses, Paul connects this sacrificial death on our behalf to the law in that lyrical statement that follows his statement on justification and faith:

> 2:19 For *through the law* I died *to the law*,
> so that I might live to God.
> I have been crucified with Christ.
> 2:20 It is no longer I who live,
> but Christ who lives in me.
> And the life I now live in the flesh
> I live by faith in the Son of God,
> who loved me and gave himself for me.

The first phrase should make us pause. Paul uses two prepositional phrases with respect to the law—that he died *to the law through the law*. The prepositional phrase *to the law* is easier to understand, for Paul is speaking about his death to his nomistic life as a Pharisee because of Christ's death and resurrection and his baptism into that saving reality. He now lives to God, or in Jesus' words from the Sermon on the Mount, he lives to the One who fulfilled the Law and the Prophets. So, Paul dies to the law by moving from his nomistic life under the power of the law to a christological life under the power of the Gospel.

It is the other prepositional phrase that is difficult. How does Paul die to the law *through the law*? Here, Paul is referring to the cosmic collision of Christ and the law on the cross. The law condemns sin, and Jesus is a sinner at the cross, not because he himself committed sins but because he has absorbed all sin, sickness, and death into his own body. What now must the law do to him as it sees him on the cross? It must condemn him as a sinner, the greatest of all sinners, as the one who is "cursed," and it must kill him. It is fair to say, from this prepositional phrase, that what kills Jesus is the law. The condemning and cursing power of the law reaches its goal and is fulfilled as Jesus hangs on the cross and is cursed by the law. This prepositional phrase anticipates Paul's most profound statement of the Gospel in the next pericope in Galatians.

Galatians 3:10–14 is where Paul proclaims how Christ and the law, as well as the blessing of God and the curse of the law, meet at the cross.[13] This is the only place in the Pauline corpus where Paul uses the language of the "curse of the law." He describes those who observe the law to be "under the power of a curse."[14]

For us, Christ's faithfulness to his Father is so radical that he is not only the faithful one but embodies his faithfulness as he is lifted up on the tree of the cross so that he might now also embody the curse of the Law, becoming a curse for us.[15] For Luther, Jesus becomes the greatest sinner at the cross:

> And all the prophets saw this, that Christ was to become the greatest thief, murderer, adulterer, robber, desecrator, blasphemer, etc., there has ever been anywhere in the world. He is not acting in His own Person now. Now he is not the Son of God, born of the Virgin. But he is a sinner, who has and bears the sin of Paul, the former blasphemer, persecutor, and assaulter; of Peter, who denied Christ; of David, who was an adulterer and a murderer, and who caused the Gentiles to blaspheme the name of the Lord (Rom 2:24). In short, He has and bears all the sins of all men in His body—not in the sense that He has committed them but in the sense that He took these sins, committed by us, upon His own body, in order to make satisfaction for them with his own blood.[16]

13. Martyn, *Galatians*, 307.

14. Martyn, *Galatians*, 308: "Reaching back to his apocalyptic interpretation of the Jewish-Christian atonement formula of 1:4a, Paul strikes a note that subsequently permeates the whole of the exegetical section of 3:6–4:7: the human dilemma consists at its base, not of guilt, but of enslavement to powers lying beyond the human being's control. As the quotation from Deut 27:26 will show, the first such power specified by Paul is a curse pronounced by the Law."

15. See the quotation from Martyn below.

16. Luther, *Lectures on Galatians*, 277. Cited from Mannermaa, "Justification and Theosis in Lutheran-Orthodox Perspective," 29–30 who introduces Luther with these words: "The second person of the Trinity did not take upon himself merely human nature as such, in a 'neutral' form, but precisely *sinful* human nature. This means that Christ has and bears the sins of all human beings *in a real manner* in the human nature

The sacrificial overtones here are unmistakable. Paul states that Christ redeemed us "having become a curse for us," using the formula that links this passage with the self-sacrificial language of Paul's opening greeting—"who gave himself for our sins" (1:4)—and his programmatic statement on the death of Jesus—"who loved me, that is, he gave himself for me" (2:20).[17]

What is most remarkable is Paul's claim that this Christ—embodied faith and embodied curse—now lives in him *because he is co-crucified with Christ.* Christ is embodied in him because Christ was apocalyptically revealed *in him* (Gal 1:16), and Christ's crucifixion becomes his when he is crucified with Christ in baptism (Rom 6). This is why Paul proclaims, "I have been crucified with Christ. It is no longer I who live, but Christ who lives *in me*" (2:20).[18] Incorporation into Christ flows from justification and is framed by references to justification (2:16) and the atonement (2:20) where Christ gives himself on behalf of Paul.

Now that Christ has invaded our cosmos, he will never leave us, *for he is still here in the flesh*, embodied in Word, Sacrament, and in the communion of saints by baptism and faith. As important as it is to proclaim that objective justification finds its source in the atonement, it is equally important to affirm that this atonement is now ours in the waters of holy baptism and at the eucharistic table.

At the climax of Galatians, in 4:4–6, the death of Christ and our incorporation into him are linked (as they were in Gal 2:16–20).[19] Paul

---

he has assumed. The sins of humankind are not only imputed to Christ; he '*has*' the sins in his human nature. Therefore, Christ is the greatest sinner (*maximus peccator, peccator peccatorum*)" (emphasis Mannermaa.)

17. Martyn, *Galatians*, 318, describes the theological significance of this sacrificial language: "[2nd Corinthians] clearly reflects sacrificial language that was employed in ancient Israel. By laying his hands on an animal that was to be sacrificed a man transmitted his sin to it, the result being that the animal, having become sin, was itself called "sin" (*het'*, often translated as "sin-offering") . . . Sin is something that can be transferred from one person to another . . . God transferred our sin to Christ, thus freeing us from its effect. By analogy it seems that in Gal 3:13 Paul does not intend to say that Christ fell under the Law's curse because he committed discrete transgressions. On the contrary, just as Christ embodied (and elicited) the faith spoken of by Habakkuk (Gal 3:11), so he embodied the Law's curse. When one looked at him, as he was being crucified (3:1), one saw the only juncture at which that embodied faith met that embodied curse in all its power."

18. For an astounding account what it means to have "Christ in you," see the entire "Christ in You" issue of *Good News*: Schulz, "Christ in You." In the introductory essay, Schulz cites Gal 2:20, which he describes as a great mystery and miracle.

19. The climax of Galatians occurs in 4:4–5. Longenecker, *Galatians*, cxiii, in his

introduces this climactic section (3:26–4:7) with "in Christ" language that highlights our incorporation into Christ by baptism and faith. Our incorporation into Christ through "in Christ" language and its derivatives are shot through this passage:[20]

3:26 for *in Christ Jesus you are* all sons of God, through faith.
3:27 For as many of you as were baptized *into Christ*
have put on Christ.
3:28 There is neither Jew nor Greek,
there is neither slave nor free,
there is neither male and female,
for you are all one *in Christ Jesus.*
3:29 And if *you are Christ's,*
then you are Abraham's offspring,
heirs according to promise.

The Matrix of Love

When I first started teaching Galatians, the final two chapters of Galatians were unsettling—they were paraenesis and exhortation. Lutherans may believe in paraenesis and exhortation, but they are hesitant to preach them! During my first twelve years of teaching homiletics at CTSFW, we struggled with how to preach sanctification, that is, how to exhort and encourage the saints who listened to our preaching. This was, of course, tied up with our notion that exhortation must always be law and the

introduction under "Diachronic Rhetorical Analysis" notes that J. B. Lightfoot first posited a chiasm in 4:4–5 that Bligh, *Galatians: A Discussion of St. Paul's Epistle*, expanded into a chiasm for the whole epistle with Gal 4:1–10 as the central, climactic chiasm. Martyn, *Galatians*, 388 would affirm that Gal 4:3–5 "is nothing less than the theological center of the entire letter."

20. Cf. Longenecker, *Galatians*, 153–54, notes the mystical possibilities with the ἐν χριστῷ formula and its relationship to forensic justification: "Of course, in positing a local or personal flavor for the phrase 'in Christ' one is acknowledging a mystical mode of thought in Paul . . . It is not a mysticism of absorption, for the 'I' and the 'Thou' of the relationship retain their own identities. Nor is it something separate from forensic righteousness before God, as though open to and experienced by only those who have been initiated into the more developed stages of the Christian life. 'In Paul,' as A. Oepke points out, 'there is no suggestion of cleavage between a forensic and a mystical mode of thought. Forensic justification leads to pneumatic fellowship with Christ' (*TDNT* 1:541). Being 'in Christ' is, for Paul, communion with Christ in the most intimate relationship imaginable, without ever destroying or minimizing—rather, only enhancing—the distinctive personalities of either the Christian or Christ. It is 'I-Thou' communion at its highest."

confusion Lutherans have with the third use of the law. In the 1980s, in *CTQ*, David Scaer clearly affirmed that sanctification is always christological, especially his articles "Sanctification in Lutheran Theology" (1985)[21] and "Sanctification in the Lutheran Confessions" (1989).[22] Sixteen years later he would publish "The Third Use of the Law: Resolving the Tension" (2005)[23] in a *CTQ* dedicated to this theme. But now, after almost thirty years of teaching Galatians, and after starting a deaconess program and thinking about how mercy is part of the Gospel, these chapters in Galatians are my favorite to teach.

In class I set the stage for Gal 5–6 by doing a mirror reading of what Paul's opponents/enemies might be saying about him. These opponents are likely former Pharisees, now Christians, who knew Paul well, perhaps classmates in the school of Gamaliel. As the smartest guy in the room, they may have characterized Paul as a little out of touch with reality, kind of like a seminary professor, and who, because of his difficult personality, may have been hard to like. That is why, when coming to the Galatians after Paul and Barnabas's first missionary journey, they might have said that Paul didn't tell them the whole truth—he only spoke to them about the gospel and not about the law. He didn't tell them how to live in this world, and that you can't really live in the world if all you have is the gospel. You must also have the law, so "the truth" is more than just the gospel—the truth must be the gospel plus the law. Since most of the Galatians were military folks, some of the best mercenaries in the Roman Empire, they should understand that to live in this world, you had to have laws to give life order and meaning. That's why these men from Jerusalem, seen by Paul as his opponents (his enemies), came to Galatia: for the same reason they came to Antioch—to give the Galatians the whole truth, namely, that in order to live in this world they must have laws—starting with the Jewish ceremonial laws—and what better way to show their commitment to the law than to submit to circumcision. What the opponents of Paul were giving the Galatians was a map on how to live in this world through the gospel *and the law*.

As Paul knew them well, he was aware of their plan. So, in this final, pastoral section of Paul's homily to the Galatians in chapters five and six, Paul tells the Galatians that he is the one who is truly in touch with reality because he preaches *a real presence* of the one came in the flesh

21. Scaer, "Sanctification in Lutheran Theology," 181–95.

22. Scaer, "Sanctification in the Lutheran Confessions," 165–81.

23. Scaer, "Third Use of the Law," 237–57.

to fulfill the law in love by his faithful death on their behalf. Paul now shows the Galatians in these final chapters that since Christ has made the world right through his death, those who are justified by the faith, who are "in Christ," now embody Christ in their lives by demonstrating Christ's presence in the world through their love, showing the world how God is now making things right through them, through his love in them. What Paul is providing them is a map for this world *in which they now actually live*—the map of what "justification looks like in the daily life of the church"[24]—a map of the new creation (Gal 6:14).[25]

This map is a map of love. Paul begins this matrix of love by first calling them to the freedom they live in because of Christ's liberating death and resurrection:

> 5:1 *For freedom* Christ has set us free;
> stand firm therefore,
> and do not submit again to a yoke of slavery.

This freedom is a space, a liturgical space, where Christ is making right what has gone wrong by joining them to himself through Paul's preaching and the celebration of the Eucharist. But his exhortation to stand firm and not submit to the yoke of slavery is a warning not to follow his opponents with their nomistic map of the world. Rather, constituted by this freedom in the church's liturgy, they now take this freedom out into the world in a liturgy of life by following Paul's map of love. Paul will now string together several passages that form for the Galatians a map for embodying Christ's life in the world:

Galatians 5:6—Faith working through love

Galatians 5:13–14—Love your neighbor as yourself

Galatians 5:22—Love as the first fruit of the Spirit

Galatians 6:2—Bear one another's burdens and so fulfill the law of Christ

Galatians 6:15—New creation

24. Martyn, *Galatians*, 482.

25. Martyn, *Galatians*, 482n41.

Galatians 5:6 and 6:15

As is often the case, there is an inclusio, a frame or bookend, in Paul's matrix of love that governs the entire matrix (Gal 5:6 and 6:15). Circumcision has been a major theme in Paul's homily so far, a thorn in his side, but now he indicates that, at the end of the day, circumcision is not the issue:

> 5:6 For in Christ Jesus neither circumcision nor
> uncircumcision counts for anything,
> *but only faith working through love.*

The voice of the participle is important. Is it passive, thus translated "faith that is activated by love," or middle, which translates "faith that is actively expressing itself through love"?"Here is the essence of our understanding between faith and love, between justification that is received in faith and sanctification, that is actively expressing itself through love—between "being" and "doing." Lutherans embrace the middle voice, for faith does not come from love, but love comes from faith. Paul is showing his annoyance with his opponents. He doesn't really care if they are circumcised or not—in fact, he's tired of talking about circumcision. What he wants to talk about is faith and love.

Paul clarifies what he means by this phrase by echoing it in the postscript of his homily—but not before he returns to the death of Jesus. Paul claims that instead of boasting in circumcision, he will boast in something outside himself, in the cross of Jesus Christ, "the cosmic event in which God stepped on the scene, in order to make things right . . . the watershed event for the whole of the cosmos."[26] Curiously, here at the very end of this epistle, he does not return to justification language but introduces a new saying that reflects what justification looks like in real life:

> 6:14 But far be it from me to boast
> except in the cross of our Lord Jesus Christ,
> by which the world has been crucified to me,
> and I to the world.
> 6:15 For neither circumcision counts for anything,
> nor uncircumcision,
> *but a new creation.*

Here, at the very end of his impassioned plea to the Galatians, Paul returns to the issue of circumcision, yet he states again that neither

26. Martyn, *Galatians*, 564.

circumcision nor uncircumcision matters, but what matters is new creation. Christ's crucifixion inaugurates the new creation because on the cross Jesus made right what had gone wrong. And what is the new creation? Faith working through love. No mention of justification here, for God is not in a courtroom declaring people righteous, but he is in his creation making right what has gone wrong through Jesus by casting out demons, healing the sick, forgiving sins, and raising the dead (the Gospel narrative!). Christ the incarnate one is now present in his creation sacramentally, where he continues to make all things new. The new creation—Christ's bodily presence in his creation—is the "rule" or "canon" by which we must walk (Gal 6:16), and for those who walk according to this rule, they receive the blessing of "peace," the apocalyptic peace that formed the apostle's liturgical greeting in the prescript of this homily (1:3) and which, along with mercy, now rests on the "Israel of God" that consists of both Jews and gentiles, a benediction of peace and mercy Paul now confers upon the Galatians (Gal 6:16).

So conflating Gal 5:6 and 6:15, we have:

For those who are "in Christ Jesus," neither circumcision nor uncircumcision has any power—what has power is *faith working through love—new creation.*

Galatians 5:13–14; 5:22; and 6:2

In the center of Paul's matrix of love are three passages that define how faith working through love is the new creation. In the first passage in 5:13–14, Paul returns to the two tables of the law in the Old Testament and the Gospel of Matthew (22:36–40), for "on these commandments hang all the law and the prophets" (22:40). In Matt 22, Jesus expands on how he is the fulfillment of the Law and the Prophets—he is the embodiment of the one who loves the Lord his God with all his heart, soul, and mind, and the one who loves perfectly his neighbor as himself. In Galatians, Paul cites only the second table of the law:

5:13 For you were called to freedom, brothers.
Only do not use your freedom as an opportunity
for the flesh,
but through love serve one another.
5:14 For the whole law is fulfilled in one word:
"You shall love your neighbor as yourself."

The call to live in the liturgical space of freedom that began this paraentic section is now explicitly connected with love. Freedom could be used as "a military base of operations"[27] for the flesh, an expression the military men of Galatia would understand. Instead, Paul is calling these Galatian mercenaries to serve one another in love, and his prooftext is the second table of the law: "love your neighbor as yourself." It might be asked, "How is the whole law brought to perfect fulfillment in one word: 'loving one's neighbor as oneself'"? Paul does not use "command" here but "word," and his verb is in the indicative passive, not the imperative, and it is a theological passive, so it speaks first of Christ—the whole law is brought to perfect fulfillment (by Christ)—and only then by the Christian.[28] As in the beatitudes in the Sermon on the Mount, Paul sees the Christian following in the steps of Christ, and like Jesus, the Christian is *fulfilling* the law, not *doing* the law.

The Christian is able to fulfill the whole Law in loving his neighbor as himself because Jesus first did this in his sacrificial death on the cross, where he loved his neighbor as himself *by giving up his life for his neighbor*. Jesus looked at himself during his passion, starting in the garden, where he sweat drops of blood, and what he saw as the God-man was someone infected with our sins, our diseases, and our death. Loving us all the way to the cross, he submitted himself to the Father's wrath and the Law's curse, becoming a curse for us, his neighbors, loving himself by loving his Father (first table of the law) and all those who were created in his image. Embodying his neighbor's sin, he became the greatest sinner on behalf of all sinners so that the Law could do to him what it had to do—curse him and kill him—and in killing him, Christ fulfilled the Law and brought it to its perfect completion. This is how Christ dies to the law *through the law* (2:19)—that in the collision between Christ and the law on the cross, the law curses him and kills him as he loves his neighbor as himself.

Love is the first fruit of the Spirit and governs all the other fruits (5:22–23). The fruits of the Spirit are the fruits of a community, not an individual, even though individuals within the community embody these

27. Martyn, *Galatians*, 485.

28. Martyn, *Galatians*, 489–90: "A strong case can be made, then, for the thesis that in 5:14 Paul thinks of an act of Christ . . . To be sure, at first glance, this reading may seem rather wild. Neither in 5:13 nor in 5:14 does Paul speak of Christ directly. The freedom to which Paul refers at the outset of 5:13, however, is the freedom Christ has won for the Galatians, and this freedom is precisely liberation from the tyranny of the Law: Christ has done something that has affected the Law (5:1)."

fruits. In speaking of love here, "Paul does not speak of a romantic emotion between two persons, but rather the kind of love that was defined by Christ when he gave his life 'for us.'"[29] Thus, this love is cruciform, or in Paul's words in his final chapter of Galatians (the other theme verse for the deaconess program at its inception):

> 6:2 Bear one another's burdens,
> and so *fulfill the law of Christ.*

What surprises us, and must have surprised the Galatians, is to hear Paul speak of *the law of Christ.* Thus far in Galatians, the law is not something we would associate with Christ. In fact, what we might think Paul should have said was "bear one another's burdens and so fulfill the *love* of Christ." But in a way, that is exactly what he is saying here. *The law of Christ is love.* He has been developing this from his first call to freedom at the beginning of chapter five: *The law of Christ* is faith working through love, serving one another in love, the fulfillment of the law in loving your neighbor as yourself. Love is, after all, the first and most important fruit of the Spirit and governs all the other fruits of the Spirit. In other words, something happened to the Law when Christ bore our burdens in his self-sacrificial love on the cross.[30] The Law changed at the cross when Christ brought it to its perfect completion through his death, *where he loved his neighbor as himself.* Now, like Paul, we have died to the law through the law, and we can no longer look at the law except through the cross of Christ, "by which the world has been crucified to me, and I to the world" (6:14). Perhaps, if John's Gospel was written as early as my colleague William Weinrich claims it was, Paul understood "the law of Christ" as John records it in his farewell discourse:

> A new commandment I give to you, that you love one another: just as I have loved you, you also are to love one another. By this all people will know that you are my disciples, if you have love for one another." (John 13:34–35)

29. Martyn, *Galatians*, 458.

30. Das, *Concordia Commentary on Scripture*, 611, also sees this connected to Christ's sacrifice on the cross: "In Gal. 6:2 Christ is the one whose power is at work as the Law is understood through the lens of Christ self-sacrifice (1:4; 2:20). Christians therefore fulfill Moses' Law in a Christlike love in 5:13–14. Jesus often summarized the Law through the command to love (Lev 19:18; see Mt 19:19; Mt 22:39/Mk 12:31; cf. Mt 7:12; Lk 10:27) [I would add Jn 13:34–35!] . . . As Christians bear one another's burdens, they more than sufficiently satisfy the Law as understood through the lens of Christ's self-sacrifice."

To bear one another's burdens is to follow the one who bore our sins, to assume the same self-sacrificial love that Christ showed on the cross. Perhaps Paul is thinking of Matthew's citation of Isaiah after Jesus' healing of Peter's mother-in-law: "This was to fulfill what was spoken by the prophet Isaiah: 'He took our illnesses and bore our diseases'" (Matt 8:17). But how do we do show self-sacrificial love today? How do we "fulfill the Law of Christ"? Perhaps Luther gives us a glimpse of how we love our neighbor as ourselves at the Lord's Supper as we participate in Christ's suffering through the sufferings of the whole company of saints:

> Whoever is in despair, distressed by a sin-stricken conscience or terrified by death or carrying some other burden upon his heart, if he would be rid of them all, let him go joyfully to the sacrament of the altar and lay down his woe in the midst of the community [of saints] and seek help from the entire company of the spiritual body . . . The immeasurable grace and mercy of God are given us in this sacrament to the end that we might put from us all misery and tribulation [*anfechtung*] and lay it upon the community [of saints], and especially on Christ. Then we may with joy find strength and comfort, and say, "Though I am a sinner and have fallen, though this or that misfortune has befallen me, nevertheless I will go to the sacrament to receive a sign from God that I have on my side Christ's righteousness, life, and sufferings, with all holy angels and the blessed in heaven and all pious men on earth. If I die, I am not alone in death; if I suffer, they suffer with me. [I know that] all my misfortune is shared with Christ and the saints, because I have a sure sign of their love toward me" . . . Be certain that Christ and all his saints are coming to you with all their virtues, sufferings, and mercies, to live, work, suffer, and die with you, and that they desire to be wholly yours, having all things in common with you . . . You must take to heart the infirmities and needs of others, as if they were your own. Then offer to others your strength, as if it were your own, just as Christ does for you in the sacrament. This is what it means to be changed into one another through love, out of many particles to become one bread and drink, to lose one's own form and take on that which is common to all.[31]

31. Luther, *Blessed Sacrament*, 10, 15–16. This conforms with the context of Gal 6:1–2, where "bear one another's burdens" follows Paul's exquisite pastoral advice in the previous verse: "Brothers, if anyone is caught in any transgression, you who are spiritual should restore him in a spirit of gentleness. Keep watch on yourself, lest you too be tempted." Martyn, *Galatians*, 547, interprets 6:1–2 in a way that conforms to Luther's eucharistic application: "In its context this injunction [bear one another's burdens] may

The Sermon on the Plain—Love Your Enemies

In light of Paul's matrix of love, Luke's Sermon on the Plain seems anticlimactic. Written over ten years after Paul's letter to the Galatians, Luke would not only know Matthew's Sermon on the Mount, having preached on Matthew for years in Philippi, but would have discussed these things with Paul from the time of their first meeting in Troas in A.D. 51 (or even earlier if Luke was from Antioch—see chapter 7).[32] So Luke's Sermon on the Plain is a carefully crafted homily on how our "being" in Christ is embodied in our "doing." Luke continues the Old Testament catechetical tradition of the two ways with his beatitudes and woes: the way of life (blessings) and the way of death (woes—cf. Deut 30:15–20; Ps 1:6; Prov 4:18–19; Jer 21:8; Didache 1:1). Luke's Sermon on the Plain portrays this classic Old Testament and Christian antinomy between life and death more starkly than Matthew's Sermon on the Mount. The catechumen is to see that life is filled with these two alternatives and that in himself and his teaching, Jesus is offering the way of light and life.

The Old Testament background illuminates many of the concepts here. In Deuteronomy "to hear" God's Word really meant "to hear and believe, and so to put into practice." Jesus emphasizes that point when he states that it is not enough to "hear" his Word; one must hear it and also "do" it (Luke 6:47,49). A particularly close parallel to the Sermon on the Plain, with its beatitudes and woes and its theme of the two ways, is Deuteronomy 11:26–28: "See, I am placing before you this day blessing and curse; the blessing as you *listen to* [believe and practice] the commands of Yahweh your God . . . and the curse if you do not listen." In the language of the Torah and of Jesus, "to listen" to God's Word is to hear in faith—faith that is created by the Word itself, faith that shows itself in works of love (Luke 6:27–30), and faith that receives the blessings promised in the Word.[33]

---

imply the transgressing brother or sister is a burdened person, a person who carries, for example, the load of some kind of addiction. In that case Paul seems to say in effect: 'I know that, in his addiction, brother Dionysius has wronged several of you. Together with other members of the church, you are to restore him to his former condition in the community, doing so in full knowledge of the fact that you are as subject to missteps as he is. In this way all of you are to bear the burden of Dionysius *as though it were your own, for, in the solidarity of the community, it is*'" (emphasis mine). This is done best at the eucharistic table.

32. Just, "Luke's Canonical Criterion," 245–60.

33. See Just, *Concordia Commentary: Luke 1:1–9:50*, 284.

The second section of the Sermon on the Plain Luke offers us "The Imperatives of Catechesis" because of the sixteen imperatives that occur in 6:27–38. There is a natural connection between this section and the previous one. If the beatitudes describe the characteristics of disciples or catechumens, who are incorporated into Christ in baptism, this imperatival section describes the shape of the catechumen's life as he shares in the life of Christ. The beatitudes describe "being" and this series of catechetical imperatives describe "doing." Thus, even though I. H. Marshall calls this the "heart of the discourse"[34] and J. Fitzmyer "the most important part, for which the exordium [beatitudes and woes] has been preparing,"[35] these imperatives are only an extension of the beatitudes and the logical application of what hearers become through baptism. This section is divided into three parts: eight imperatives in 6:27–34; four imperatives in 6:35–36; and four imperatives in 6:37–38. This breakdown is meant to accent the three important summary imperatives at the end of each of these sections:

> 6:31 "Just as you wish that men do to you, do to them likewise" (the golden rule).
> 6:36 "Become merciful, just as your Father is merciful."
> 6:38 "Give and it will be given to you."

In writing the commentary, the imperative "love your enemies" was one of the most challenging verses to exegete, especially as I was writing the commentary during those difficult years in the early 1990s when I was not allowed to teach Luke's Gospel. I remember calling Linda into my study and showing her these words and asking her how to offer commentary on them when "enemies" within our own seminary were persecuting us and trying to get rid of us. Her wise words were simple: "Pray for them."

The radical command "love your enemies" is a call to action, not just emotion, for to love one's enemies requires an unnatural act of the will.[36] Your enemies are those who hate and persecute you, and the final beatitude (6:22–23) describes hateful persecution in detail (cf. 1:71

34. Marshall, *Gospel of Luke*, 257.

35. Fitzmyer, *Gospel According to Luke I–IX*, 637.

36. Johnson, *Gospel of Luke*, 108, says, "Like the other evangelists, Luke prefers to think of this characteristic Christian attitude in terms of a verb (the noun *agape* is used only in 11:42). In the NT, it appears as an attitude and mode of action rather than an emotion." There is consensus on this among these commentators: Marshall, *Gospel of Luke*, 259; Stein, *Luke*, 206; Nolland, *Luke 1–9:20*, 294.

in the Benedictus: "salvation from our enemies and from the hand of all who hate us"). The context here is religious persecution, which Jesus pictures as an inevitable consequence of being part of the baptized community. The general attitude that Christians must have is love for all who persecute them "on account of the Son of Man" (6:22).

Like many believers, some of the worst "persecution" they might receive comes within the church, not outside of it (although this is soon to change, I'm afraid). The highest form of love is to love one's enemies by forgiving them and praying for them, as Jesus did from the cross—"Father, forgive them for they know not what they do" (Luke 23:43). Paul's "for the whole law is fulfilled in one word, 'You shall love your neighbor as yourself'" may have been his midrash on these words of Jesus from the cross. This exhortation to love your enemies by forgiving them and praying for them is all gospel. It's how we embody Christ's self-sacrifice love in absolving and loving our enemies. Here is the golden rule, how we may be merciful as our Father in heaven is merciful.

Love expresses itself in concrete actions of doing good, through works of mercy, even to those who hate you. This is what the baptized do. In the assembly of the baptized, this will take place liturgically as the persecuted Christians bless those who curse them and offer petitions for those who insult them. Liturgies from the fourth and fifth centuries (likely preserving earlier practice) included prayers of blessing and petitions offered for heretics, schismatics, Jews, pagans, for all in tribulation, and for the needs of the whole world.[37] Such prayers show how the church loves all, even her enemies, as she stands in the presence of God and petitions the Father.

Leitourgia and *diakonia* taken together are the whole gospel—receiving the gifts and then embodying those gifts in the world through the liturgy of life where we love our neighbor as ourselves just as Christ loved us, his neighbors and his enemies, all the way to the cross.[38]

37. Dix, *Shape of the Liturgy*, 43.

38. For the inspiration behind this section on the Sermon on the Plain, see Just, *Concordia Commentary: Luke 1:1—9:50*, 291–96.

10

"I Will Leave for Spain by Way of You"

A Lutheran Mission in Spain

St. Paul desired to carry the Gospel to Spain, as he indicates in Romans, after delivering the collection from Macedonia and Achaia to Jerusalem and his subsequent visit to Rome. His goal was to reach the ends of the earth:

> I hope to see you in passing as I go to Spain, and to be helped on my journey there by you, once I have enjoyed your company for a while . . . When therefore I have completed this and have delivered to them what has been collected, *I will leave for Spain by way of you*" (Rom 15:24, 28).

Did Paul ever visit Spain as part of his missionary journeys? There is a period between those two visits to Rome for him to make his way to Spain, returning to Rome during the persecutions of Nero, where he was martyred along with Peter in AD 64 to 65. The saints in Tarragona, Spain, believe that Paul visited there. So did Jerome. There is evidence in the fourth century of a very well-organized church in Spain, with a pre-Constantinian church council in Elvira, outside Granada, that included nineteen bishops and twenty-four presbyters. Such a church could have come from the evangelization of Spain by Paul, and maybe even by James. In the late first century, Clement of Rome wrote of Paul's visit to Spain, calling Spain the "extreme limit of the West":

> Because of jealousy and strife Paul pointed the way to the prize for endurance. Seven times he bore chains; he was sent into exile and stoned; he served as a herald in both the East and the West; and he received the noble reputation for his faith. He taught righteousness to the whole world, and came to the limits of the West, bearing his witness before the rulers. And so he was set free from this world and transported up to the holy place, having become the greatest example of endurance.[1]

Spain was an apostolic destination. Tradition tells us that St. James the elder, the son of Zebedee, the first martyred apostle, is buried in the cathedral in Santiago de Compostela, a legend that is worthy of our consideration, for legends have consequences. Sorting out this legend means unraveling the mysteries of what is known as "the Santiago Creed," that is, what the saints in Spain believe and confess about their patron saint. Consider these two parts of the creed, as formulated by T. D. Kendrick in his erudite study *Saint James in Spain*:

> Firstly, that he preached Christianity in the country . . . thirdly, that after his execution in Jerusalem the apostle's body was taken to Galicia in north-west Spain and buried at the place where now stands the cathedral of Santiago de Compostela.[2]

1. Clement, "1 Clement 5:5–7," 45.

2. Kendrick, *Saint James in Spain*, 13. Remarkably, of all the books on the camino to Santiago de Compostela, most give a narrative of the legend of St. James mission to Spain but none of the sources. Only T. Kendrick has provided them, so thus our dependence on him. The other parts of the Santiago Creed stretch the capacities of most Lutherans but need to be included in a footnote because they are intimately tied to the two parts cited above by Spaniards who wholeheartedly affirm this creed:

> Secondly, that during his mission there the Virgin Mary, while still a living woman, was miraculously transported, accompanied by angels bearing a marble pillar, to the banks of the River Ebro; that she talked with St James and told him to build a church dedicated to herself on the site where the pillar had been placed, a church that is now the Basilica of Nuestra Senora del Pilar in Zaragoza . . .
> Fourthly, that in the ninth century St James appeared on earth and helped a Spanish army to win a decisive victory over the Moors.

The Roman Martyrology, 62–63, affirms the Santiago Creed:

> St. James the Apostle, brother of the blessed evangelist John, who was beheaded by Herod Agrippa at about the feast of Easter. He was the first of the apostles to receive the crown of martyrdom. His sacred bones were on this day carried from Jerusalem to Spain, and placed in the remote province of Galicia, where they are devoutly honored by

The details of the Santiago Creed, concerning James's preaching the Gospel in Spain and his burial in Santiago de Compostela, are quite simple. Working with the date of his martyrdom in Jerusalem, during the reign of Herod Agrippa I, between AD 41 to 44, James had about eleven to fourteen years after the ascension of Jesus to travel to Spain and back, so there is certainly no reason to believe that such a trip would have been impossible because of time. The Spaniards certainly believe that these two apostles—James and Paul—evangelized Spain: one a member of the inner circle of Jesus who witnessed the raising of Jairus's daughter and the transfiguration, fell asleep in the garden of Gethsemane, and provided leadership for the Jerusalem church in the first twelve chapters of Acts; the other, the great apostle to the gentiles.[3]

As Spain has been part of my family's life and my pastoral life working with the Lutheran church of Spain from its inception, this chapter will relate our personal family history, my many overtures to the LCMS to serve as a missionary to Spain, and my service to the Spanish Lutheran mission since 2002, showing how deeply embedded I became in the life of a country and in the life of a partner church.

The Just Family in Algorta, Vizcaya, Spain—1974 to 1978

Our family moved to Spain from Mexico in spring of 1974, when Franco was still dictator, when I was unaware of St. Paul's words to the Roman saints (15:8) or any of the Santiago legends, or that James the Son of Zebedee was the patron saint of Spain. Two years later, in the spring of 1976, I decided to attend the seminary. By then our family had all fallen in love with Spain and one of my first thoughts as a seminarian was to return to Spain as a missionary, especially after the death of Franco, when Spain was now open to Lutheran missionaries.

How we ended up in Spain in the 1970s was a surprise to all of us. We were convinced that we would spend the rest of our lives in Mexico. Although Spain was in Europe, which had its own appeal, we had been so Mexicanized that we couldn't imagine leaving the comfort and joy of our life in Mexico City. Our father's instincts were always right, and somehow

---

the far-famed piety of the inhabitants, and the frequent concourse of Christians, who visit them through piety and in fulfillment of vows . . .

3. See my essay in the festschrift for Dean Wenthe entitled "The Eyewitness of the Other Son of Zebedee: A Pilgrimage with James through Scripture and Tradition."

he knew that the family needed a change. Our mother, however, was not convinced. Yet in the end, she always deferred to my father's wisdom.

At first the move was an utter disaster for my mother, who went into a deep depression during her first few months in Bilbao. Who could blame her. We left a party house and a party life in Mexico, lots of great weather, a world of light, color, music and fiesta all the time and especially, great friends, most of whom came from *La Iglesia Luterana del Buen Pastor*, our church in Mexico City. Bilbao, on the other hand, was dismal and dark, described by many in 1974 as the Pittsburgh of Spain—a dirty industrial town on the brown Nervión River, a gray city with lots of rain and with somber and serious people—in every way the opposite of Mexico. Since then, Bilbao has not only cleaned up its act (as has Pittsburgh), but it has also become one of the premier destinations of Spain, especially after the Guggenheim Museum was dedicated on the now-blue Nervión River on October 18, 1997 (St. Luke's Day!). But for our first year in Spain, we all thought my father had made a very bad decision. Then my sister Karen, my mother's alter ego and her greatest companion, left for Aiglon, a high school in Switzerland, and dear, sweet Christopher, our fourteen-year-old littlest brother, was left to console my mother. In a year he would be off to Connecticut and the Kent School.

As a carpenter's son, my father knew that place and space mattered. He always seemed to find the right home for our family. In Scotia, New York, it was a new split-level home in a suburb full of kids; in Pelham Manor in Westchester County, an early twentieth-century colonial, a stone's throw from the Bronx but an easy commute to New York City where he worked, with great schools and great neighbors; in Mexico City, "the pink house" in the tony suburb of Lomas de Chapultepec, near our Lutheran church, with a huge central room surrounded by all the other rooms in the house. As I said, it was a great party house, especially on New Year's Eve, which coincided with my sister's birthday. My father's magic touch with homes extended to Spain, where he lucked into a grand old house overlooking the Bay of Biscay in Algorta, a suburb of Bilbao that removed us from the ugliness of the city and its environs. As we looked out at the Bay of Biscay, we could see the clear demarcation between the brown of the Nervión River and the blue of the bay. The house even had a tower that extended over its three floors where, during Christmas break from CTSFW in 1976, I read Hans Lietzmann's *History of the Early Church* for Dr. Weinrich's early church class to prepare for his first, brutal test. Today the house stands as majestic as ever but now houses several roomy condominiums.

This house was on the walking street of Algorta, which led to bars and cafés. My mother soon became enchanted with the rhythm of Spanish life, with its late breakfasts, the even later substantial lunches that were the main meal of the day, and the dinners at 10 p.m. (along with the other small moments of formal snacking—*almuerzo*, a light lunch before noon, and *merienda*, tea or coffee and a sweet in the early evening). She also discovered how wonderful and rich the food was in the Basque Country, and it was during these years that our family discovered the wonderful wines of Spain and France, since we lived very near the French border and my mother would frequently travel to Biarritz with Noël, her dear French friend who had married a Basque from Algorta. We lived near the Rioja province of Spain—their wines were rich, plentiful, and inexpensive, and we became partial to them. I can still smell its earthy aroma. My father was a moderate man in everything, yet he loved the taste of good alcohol, whether it be beer, scotch, or wine. His palate was superb, even though he had never studied wines. He knew what he liked. Spain became his special playground. He was partial to Jerez (sherry), which he always had when he came home from work at 8 or 9 p.m.—and there were so many sherries to choose from—the Osbornes, Gonzalez Byass—but he always returned to his favorite—Williams and Humbert's Dry Sack.

During school holidays from Union or CTSFW, one of my cherished adventures was to accompany my mother to the bodegas, dark warehouses where they sold wine in large quantities. You had to know where they were, and she did, even though she was notorious for her bad sense of direction. Somehow, she always found that nondescript door along a narrow street that would open up to a dark, damp room lined with huge oak barrels. She seldom lacked confidence with her kitchen Spanish, and dressed in her unique, eclectic style, she would glide into these dark caverns and charm the Basque men, the keepers of the wine. They would, in a completely unceremonious but loving gesture, hand her a stubby water glass, and she would go from barrel to barrel testing the wines. She had almost as fine a palate as my father, and she would want me to try each one with her, asking me what I thought and why. She was teaching me about wine! By the end of the tasting, she would put in her order with a tipsy giggle and coquettish smile, which melted the Basque bodega men. These wines were delivered in small glass barrels on a swivel, and we would enjoy them for every lunch and dinner. Within a year my mother had conquered the town, knew the best stores for all the great Spanish foods, and through her joyous manner and fashionable style, made many great friends among the French, Swedish, and British expatriates, visiting with them in the cafes and bars along the walking street. She soon forgot how miserable she was leaving Mexico, and when we finally had to leave Spain, she mourned leaving as much as she did Mexico City.

One aspect of life in Algorta was that we had no Lutheran church, even though there was a rich tradition of Lutheranism in Spain during the Reformation, especially in Seville and Valladolid. After such a rich church life in Mexico, this was a huge hole in what had become central to our family's life. It was another reason we questioned my father's decision, as he was a devout and pious Lutheran and had loved his church life in Mexico City. But as we were now away at college or prep school, our social life was not as dependent on a church as we were in Mexico. Our family was our social life, along with the friends my mother had made and the classmates of my brother Christopher.

When we moved to Spain at the very end of Franco's reign, it was illegal to be a Protestant. But in the Basque Country, one of the provinces along with Catalonia, Valencia, and Galicia that were traditionally anti-Franco, we were encouraged, even protected, by the Basque nationalists. One of the most virulent terrorist groups in the world at that time was the separatist group *Euskadi Ta Askatasuna* (ETA), part of the Basque National Liberation Movement (from the 1970s until a ceasefire was called in 2010). But the Basques allowed our Anglican friends to worship in safety in a small chapel within the grounds of the British cemetery, about eight miles from our home. We always felt like we were hiding from the authorities when we gathered for worship. For decades, even before the Spanish Civil War, there had always been a strong relationship between Britain and the Basques, with regular flights from London to Bilbao. The Anglican bishop would fly into Spain once a month for catechesis, Eucharist, and pastoral care. This clandestine worship in a British cemetery with devout Anglicans was a memory I carried with me throughout my seminary studies and during my years in the parish, even while teaching at the seminary. It was one of the reasons why I wanted to start a Lutheran mission in Spain, which only happened in 2000 by our sister church in Argentina and which I have been serving since the spring of 2002, a little over a year after its founding (see below).

Generalissimo Francisco Franco Bahamonde died on the twentieth of November 1975, a year and a half after we moved to Spain. Two days later, Juan Carlos I was declared the King of Spain. Franco's death and Juan Carlos's assumption to the throne changed Spain forever, and it certainly changed our lives. Franco named Juan Carlos his successor, thinking he would continue his legacy. It turned out that Juan Carlos was more interested in establishing a true democracy in Spain. During those years he was our hero, although now his image has been tarnished by personal and financial scandals, and even more, by his rabid support for abortion rights. Things were happening fast in Spain as our family watched with great interest the events swirling around them as Spain emerged from the darkness of a Fascist regime to a legitimate democracy that was liberal in the true sense of the word.

For better and for worse, Spain was opening up, which affected our lives in two significant ways. First, terrorist groups like ETA were emboldened, so American companies like General Electric became targets of violent protests, which led to our family leaving Spain in the spring of 1978. Secondly, it was now legal to be a Protestant, and Pentecostal ministries started popping up here and there. Now was the perfect time to start a Lutheran mission in Spain, especially to rediscover the history of Lutheranism during the time of the Reformation, led by Casiodoro de Reina, who was one of the two Spanish reformers behind the Spanish translation of the Bible called the *Reina-Valera* (also called *Biblia del Oso*—Bear Bible—because of the illustration on the cover of a bear seeking honey from a jar—the *oso* is a symbol of Madrid that appears on a statue on the Plaza del Sol where we have our photo taken during every visit to Madrid). The other Protestant reformer from whom the Bible gets its name was Cipriano de Valera. To this day, the *Reina-Valera* is the Bible most used by Protestants who speak Spanish.[4]

As this was happening, I was studying at the seminary (1976 to 1980). At that time my hopes were threefold: take a parish in New England near a university where I could continue by theological education; apply to graduate schools in a PhD program; or encourage the Board for Mission Services (BMS) to send me to Spain as a missionary. I was most interested in the third option. Spain was fresh in our experience, as we had left in the middle of my seminary studies (1978). The timing was perfect, my Spanish was as good as it had ever been, and we would have been on the ground floor of Spain's opening to other Christian denominations. I met the head of BMS during vicarage, and he was interested in

4. See Rosales, *Casiodoro de Reina.*

my experience in Mexico and Spain and asked that I contact him about serving as a missionary. I was hopeful. But for whatever reason, I could not persuade anybody in the BMS that this was the right time to start a mission in Spain.

There were two other occasions when I made overtures to the BMS to serve as a missionary in Spain. In 1983, Linda and I took a three-week vacation to Spain so that she could see what all the excitement was about when my family talked about our time there. We traveled hard for two weeks, hitting all the great sights in Madrid and its surroundings—El Escorial, Segovia, Avila, and Toledo—then headed south to Cordoba, Seville, and Granada. Iberia Airlines had this incredible deal that if you flew with them, they'd give you a free week on the beach in Malaga, hotel and meals included. So, we spent our last week on the beach in a kind of cruise experience on land. But instead of this lovely vacation, both Linda and I were willing to give it up to devote those three weeks to surveying the situation in Spain to discover what the Protestant churches in the larger cities of Madrid and Seville were doing and the possibility of a Lutheran mission. I contacted the BMS again with my proposal, but this time there was literally no response, so we enjoyed our Spanish holiday.

Eight years later, in 1991 during my first sabbatical at CTSFW, I arranged through my doctoral father to study the Targums with his colleague from the Pontifical Biblical Commission at a university in Madrid. This would be a new venture for me. All I needed was funding for housing and transportation for our family. I petitioned the BMS for the third time about starting a mission in Spain. I was willing to commit half of my sabbatical to doing the groundwork of establishing a Lutheran presence in Madrid. The cost to them was minimal (at that time, it would have been about $12,000 for housing and transportation for a year). If there was a clear sign that we could create a Lutheran foothold in Spain, I was willing to serve as the first missionary. At least this time they answered my request, but again, they indicated that Spain was not a part of their mission strategy at that time.

Missionary in Pola de Siero, Asturias, Spain—2002

In 1999, with Douglas Rutt, Robert Roethemeyer, and Lawrence Rast, I visited the seminary and church in Buenos Aires, Argentina, at the end of an International Lutheran Council (ILC) conference in Porto Alegre,

Brazil (the only ILC conference I've even attended). Larry and I slept on the floor in the church offices in Buenos Aires. As we drove from the airport, I realized that this was the first Spanish-speaking country I had visited since our trip to Spain in 1983. What struck me about Argentina, even though I had never been there before, was how much at home I felt in the Latin America environment (Brazil did not give me the same vibe). I missed it more than I realized. We met with the President of the Lutheran Church in Argentina, Waldomiro Mailli, who informed us the Argentinian Lutherans had decided to start a mission in Spain. Finally, something was going to happen in the country I loved and had been trying to serve as a missionary for twenty years.

The Argentinian mission to Spain that started in the fall of 2000 suffered difficulties from the beginning, not uncommon to new missions. The source of the problem was a triangulation between the church in Argentina, which had all the power, the LCMS, which provided all the funding, and the fledging group of Spaniards and Latinos who were struggling to identify as Lutherans in a Roman Catholic country. Spaniards and Argentinians are very different—one European, the other Latino. As one Spaniard said, "We don't really speak the same language." The Spaniards always felt more in common with the LCMS North Americans than with the Argentinians (as well as other Latin Americans). Unlike the Spaniards, because my first love was Latin America, I felt very comfortable with both Latinos and Spaniards.

The triangulation between Argentina, the LCMS, and Spain did not make for a successful mission. Pastor Marcos Berndt from Argentina started the Spanish Lutheran mission in 2000 with the help of two Spaniards, Javier Sanchez from Toledo, who worked as an English teacher in Llanes, Asturias, and Virginia, a Spaniard who moved to Venezuela, married a Venezuelan, became a Lutheran, then moved back to Spain with her two children to her hometown in El Berrón, Asturias, just east of Oviedo and south of Gijón. Virginia's home in El Berrón was where we held services. Both Javier Sanchez and Virginia were fiercely committed to confessional Lutheranism, so Marcos chose Pola de Siero near El Berrón as his home base, as the only two members of the church in Spain lived in Asturias. Marcos was a natural-born missionary who could talk easily about confessional Lutheranism with Spaniards in a way that was not threatening yet captured the depth of our dogmatic tradition. In a little over a year, he did a remarkable job of starting the mission, gathering people from all over Spain in Madrid, Seville, Granada, Malaga, and

Barcelona. To this day, the Lutheran church in Spain has members all over the country. The great challenge of the mission is to bring the gifts of Christ's bodily presence to these people who have joined the church in these many different places. It was one of the ways the Argentinian and LCMS missionaries to Spain used me during my visits, helping them keep up with these members who were not part of one of our more established congregations in Madrid, Seville, Cartagena, and Valencia. I was essentially a visitation pastor throughout much of my service to Spain.

After a year, Marcos needed to return to Argentina. At that time, Dr. Douglas Rutt was both on the CTSFW faculty as a professor of missions and the regional director of Latin America and Spain. Spain was considered part of the region of Latin America because it was a mission of Argentina. The church in Argentina sent a new graduate from their seminary, Pastor Walter Ralli, to relieve Marcos and take over the mission. CTSFW had granted my second sabbatical in the spring of 2002 to finish the final draft of the Ancient Christian Commentary (ACCS) on Luke. Dr. Rutt knew of my desire to start a mission in Spain, so he asked if I could work on the commentary in Spain while mentoring this new, young seminary graduate. Finally, I would go to Spain to help a Lutheran mission there, albeit as an advisor and counselor.

This all developed very quickly in February of 2002. After leading our first seminary tour to Greece and Turkey, Linda went back to Fort Wayne, and I flew to Madrid. Marcos met me at the Barajas Airport in his tiny Seat that, by government decree, was not allowed to travel faster than eighty/ninety kilometers an hour (about fifty miles per hour). It had now been almost twenty years since I had spoken Spanish, and even though Marcos spoke some English, we decided that what I needed was full immersion in the language. For two weeks we took a *gira* (tour) around Spain through Andalusia, visiting Seville and Granada, then to Malaga on the coast, up north to Barcelona, and then west to Madrid, visiting members and prospective members along the way. We ended up in Asturias, at his apartment in Pola de Siero. That Sunday Marcos celebrated Eucharist at the home of Virginia for the last time. Even though we had known each other only a few weeks, our *despedida* (goodbye) was a sad one, and even sadder for Virginia and Javier Sanchez.

Marcos left me with a visual and written record of everyone he had contacted during his time as a missionary to Spain to hand over to Pastor Walter Ralli. The expectation was that Walter would come soon, but visa issues delayed his arrival, so I ended up running the mission from Pola de

Siero (on my credit card) for two months, making two more *giras* around Spain visiting the members, one alone, and then later on with Walter Ralli after he arrived, along with my daughter Abigail, who was transitioning back to the United States through Spain after her term abroad from Valparaiso University at Westfield House in Cambridge, England.

For ten weeks I did what Marcos taught me—to be a pastor to people, to invite them to hear the gospel, to present confessional Lutheranism in a winsome way, and to keep meticulous records of every visit, every prospective, every member, every Eucharist, every catechesis. Life as missionary in Pola de Siero was extremely lonely. I only saw Virginia on Sundays, and the rest of the church only during the *giras* around Spain. Like the Basques, Asturianos are very reserved people, so when I'd venture out for lunch or shopping, it was difficult to engage them in conversation. I made friends with the lady who ran the fruit stand outside our apartment, "Pili," whose daughter took Abigail shopping and for tapas and vino. It was during this time that I became a Real Madrid fan, watching them late at night while having a small supper of cheese, chorizo, and *tinto* (red wine). How I looked forward to those games! Linda and the boys came for Semana Santa, and we celebrated the holy days all around Spain, ending up in Pola de Siero for Easter with Virginia. When they left, the loneliness was even more acute. But I soldiered on, working on the ACCS commentary every day, a very productive sabbatical that brought this rewarding project to a close.

The most memorable visit in that first *gira* with Marcos was our visit with Juan Carlos and Ana in Seville and their young family. In many ways, it changed my life and gave me a sense of both the joys and challenges of missionary service. This was the beginning of a warm and lively lifelong friendship with Juan Carlos, a pious and erudite man who would become the first Spaniard ordained into the holy ministry, as well as his beautiful and hospitable wife, Ana, and their three children. In my first visit with Marcos, I dropped the pretense of Spanish because Juan Carlos's English was so good and his theology was at the level of a PhD student at CTSFW. He had studied for a MA in theology, served his Roman Catholic church as a deacon, and found himself teaching Luther's Small Catechism in his classes, which did not go over well with the local priest. Many years later he received an invitation from that same priest, Padre Alberto, for me to present an hour lecture on "Mercy in Luke's Gospel" to the laity at *La Parroquia de Nuestra Señora de la Antigua y Beato Marcelo Spinoza*. It was a remarkable experience in every way, over fifty in attendance, mostly women, and they received my presentation with enthusiasm (at that time PowerPoints with lots of images were appealing to people).

There was, however, one thing that shocked them, especially the women in the parish. They struggled to fully grasp my interpretation of the beatitude in Luke 7:23: "Blessed is the one who is not scandalized in me," namely, the scandal was that the vengeance and wrath of God was not on the enemies of God but on Jesus, who absorbed in his flesh all our sicknesses and sin. Jesus was God's enemy and the object of his Father's anger against sin as the sin-bearer, dying on the cross in our place as the greatest sinner. To his credit, Padre Alberto came to my defense. "This is what the atonement means," he said. "This was the sacrifice Jesus made on our behalf; this is the great mystery of the incarnation and the atonement." I could not have said it better.

Juan Carlos found the Lutheran Confessions to be compelling. The propositional truths of the confessions resonate with Spanish men and why they are drawn to Lutheranism. It is more difficult for Spanish women to leave the Roman Catholicism of their mothers, even though they may resonate with what Lutherans confess and teach, especially the evangelical character of our sermons. But what many Spaniards miss most in Lutheranism, especially under the low-church Argentinians in their Geneva gowns, is the majesty and richness of the ancient liturgy and some of the traditions of their church (see chapter eight on "A Lukan [and Lutheran] Theology of Mary").

Juan Carlos and Ana understood Lutheranism and its differences with Roman Catholicism. Their joy and comfort from the Lutheran Gospel were palpable. Marcos and I were encouraged by their enthusiasm, knowing in our hearts that they would become the foundation of the Lutheran Church in Spain. When I returned alone to Seville a month later, we did not meet in their home but at a cafe in the Plaza de la Incarnación near where they would build *Las Setas* (The Mushrooms). Juan Carlos and Ana chose to meet away from their home because they were going to tell me some bad news—that they decided to stay in the Roman Catholic Church and try to reform it from within. Lutheranism appealed to them because the Christian life was embodied in daily life, unlike many Catholics in Spain who were nominal at best, attending baptisms, confirmations, weddings, and funerals, and of course, the feasts (not unlike some LCMS Lutherans).

When they told me their news, I supported their decision, rejoiced that we share a common Savior and that we are always united at the

Eucharist. We bid each other a sad farewell. I was staying in Seville for a few more days as I was going to visit some prospective members in Cadiz. To my surprise, when I returned to Seville, I received a note that they would like to meet with me again at their home. They were shocked by my reaction about their decision to stay with the Roman Catholic Church. They expected me to argue and cajole them into remaining on track for catechesis and confirmation into Lutheranism. Taken aback by my gentle and loving acceptance of their decision, they reconsidered their decision to stay with the Roman Catholic Church, and they wanted to continue with their catechesis, and looked forward to becoming members of the fledgling Lutheran Church in Spain. I was as surprised by this turn of events, as I was their decision not to pursue Lutheranism. Seville would become the center of the Lutheran church in Spain for the next decade.

Valencia, Spain—2012

Ten years later, in 2012, I returned to Spain for another spring sabbatical. The circumstances for this sabbatical were another "divine intervention," not unlike what happened in 2002.

There was to be a dedication of the new seminary in Haiti in middle of January that year. Timothy Quill asked me to represent him. It was my first visit to Haiti. I would return later with Timothy after the earthquake to write curriculum for this new seminary. The missionaries from the Dominican Republic (DR) were also at the dedication: Walter Ríes Jr., a recent graduate from the seminary in Brazil, and Ted Krey, the regional director who had assumed his position in 2010. Ted had been my sexton in 2000, my first year as dean of the chapel. I had not seen him in the ten years since he became a missionary in Venezuela.

I was seated next to Ted in the backseat on our way to the dedication. He was telling me about the challenges in his region. One of them was Spain, where he was dealing with an immature mission, an Argentinian missionary who had recently arrived and was not sure what he was doing, and real tensions between the Spaniards and the Argentinians. Ted was looking for a mature and seasoned pastor who spoke Spanish to help them in the short term. He was completely unaware of my ten-week sabbatical in Spain at the beginning of the mission in 2002. When I told him about it, he turned to me and said, "Can you go to Spain?" My immediate response was, "Yes. I have another sabbatical in the spring. I can do this."

It was only later that I recalled Paul's words: "I will leave for Spain by way of you." That car ride in Haiti changed the trajectory of the rest of my life.

A little over six weeks later, at the end of February, I left for Spain. My desire was to be in Seville or Madrid, where we had established congregations, but the Argentinian missionary and Juan Carlos insisted that I spend the ten weeks in Valencia mentoring the now sainted bishop José Luis de Miguel as he was preparing for the holy ministry. Valencia!? I was not happy. I had never been to Valencia, I didn't know José Luis, and I wanted to be in the center of things, in either Madrid or Seville. What I really wanted was to work alongside Juan Carlos in Seville. After spending a few days with the Argentinian missionary in Madrid, where I experienced real concerns about his capacity to lead the church, I visited Juan Carlos in Seville, who encouraged me to go to Valencia to mentor José Luis, a fine fellow and a Spaniard who needed more Lutheran catechesis and whom the church needed as a pastor. Being a good soldier, I flew to Valencia from Seville, arriving during Las Fallas, a festival for the feast of Saint Joseph (March 19th). I had never heard of this festival before. José Luis picked me at the airport and whisked me directly to the Plaza del Ayuntamiento (town hall) for the 2 p.m. *mascleta*, a unique firework display that is more sound than light. His wife Elena worked nearby so she joined us for this spectacle in a street that leads to the Plaza del Ayuntamiento, which was packed with thousands of people. It's hard to describe how percussive these fireworks are. You feel them more than you can see them. It's why everyone comes for them—people just love *the feel* of the fireworks—they make you smile, laugh out loud, especially as they build towards the end. It's a joy that's hard to explain. When it's over, everyone claps and heads to lunch. Quintessential Spain—and my introduction to Valencia and José Luis and Elena, right off the plane from Seville.

The sabbatical in Valencia was completely different from the one in Asturias. There was little loneliness in Valencia. I was welcomed into a family of *Valencianos* and a town that embraced me with an affection I reciprocated. As I was not a missionary with the Office of International Mission (OIM) and Ted was supporting me out of his budget, we did everything on the cheap. All it cost Ted was airfare and some funds for traveling around Spain, mostly for gas for José Luis who drove me around to preach and celebrate Eucharist on what the Spaniards call "El Levante," the eastern coast of Spain (one of the football clubs in Valencia goes by this name). José Luis had arranged for me to stay for free in the apartment (piso) of his mother, Pepita, on Calle Sagunt near Santa Monica church on the old road to Sagunto. This is the home where José Luis grew up. It was a very old apartment, and I had a front room overlooking the street, with the bed on the outside wall next to an empty lot, while Pepita was in the back of the piso. We shared a bathroom and kitchen, which dated to the 1950s.

March in Valencia is cold and damp, and I'd never been so cold in all my life. Pepita heated the apartment with a gas stove in her living room, and the heat never reached my bedroom, although the noxious smells of the old gas stove did. I tried not to complain, but it was practically unlivable. After a couple of days of negotiation with Pepita, I moved to an interior room and bought some warm jogging clothes to sleep in and a really nice blanket. Hot water was a luxury, and so I adopted the European style of showering less frequently. I discovered this in our house in Algorta in the 1970s, where the water was tepid and the bathrooms cold. Linda stayed with me here when she visited, as well as my son Nicholas, who came at the end of the sabbatical. After the first night I forgot to tell Linda that Pepita would often burst into my room without knocking to go stand on the balcony for *aire.* She did this everyday, so I tried to be gone by the time she needed air. José Luis said she liked to check out what was happening in the neighborhood. She and many other Spanish women were precursors of the Ring doorbell.

I met with José Luis almost every day. We talked theology incessantly, and I was able to teach him two courses, one on liturgy and one on pastoral theology in Luke–Acts. We had regular services in Valencia, normally in a hotel room, where I was preacher and celebrant, and José Luis served as my deacon, the way we did it in Kramer Chapel. Later in the spring, José Luis started preaching. We also traveled along the Levante, which included trips to the saints in Cartagena, Alicante, Benidorm, and to members and prospective members around Valencia, always bringing "heaven on earth—the gifts of Christ in the Divine Service." It was an exhilarating time. And we attended meetings, one in Madrid with the Argentines that was as tense a meeting as I have ever attended. You could see the division in the room, and I was proud of the Spaniards, especially Juan Carlos, José Luis, and Antonio Suarez from Cartagena, who held their ground and advocated for their vision of what the Lutheran church in Spain should look like.

It was during this sabbatical that I came to understand better the Spanish way of doing church. José Luis and Juan Carlos were faithful

Roman Catholics before becoming Lutherans. Unlike Juan Carlos, José Luis had tried other expressions of Christianity, even other non-Christian religions (he flirted with the Eastern religions). But what converted both to Lutheranism was the clarity of the gospel, and they never wavered from the joy this gave them. As a result, they both understood that for Lutheranism to appeal to Spaniards, they had to be "Catholic," that is, liturgical with a biblical Marian piety. They believed that Lutheranism needed a healthy "Catholic" identity to appeal to most Spaniards.

This I learned slowly with José Luis as we discussed at length how to bring Spaniards to Lutheranism. In Valencia, with its deep Catholic culture, I discovered that Spain was not as secular as I thought. What I observed was that many *Valencianos* are religious, at least on the public holidays. José Luis encouraged me to attend Mass when I could, to see how Spaniards worshiped, and I had my favorites—*Santa Catalina*, just off *la Plaza de la Reina*, and *San Juan Hospital*, a church that goes back to 1238 and is now the home for *Opus Dei* in Valencia. But the most distinctive place of all was *La Basilica de la Virgen de los Desamparados. Desamparados* is one of my favorite Spanish words, describing the forsaken, the poor, the needy—a word that sums up why the church needs *diakonia.* I would visit the *Basílica* frequently and listen to Mass there.[5] It was fascinating to watch all kinds of people come and go, some staying for a long time, others paying their respects and then on to the rest of their day, always with such reverence. In all these churches there is such peace when you enter and let the beauty of the space and the familiar words of the liturgy pass over you. I loved watching as the faithful *Valencianos* went forward to receive the soul-nourishing food from the simple eucharistic liturgy of the Spaniards that is so flat-footed and clean. There's none of the fussiness you find among some of our LCMS churches that strive to be high church. It's because the liturgy is so much a part of their identity that it is impossible to imagine life without it. It's who they are—no hurry, no time constraints, no wasted movement or action, nothing extra, everything in order—a confident liturgy. And almost always a Eucharist in no more than a half an hour on weekdays and an hour on Sundays. Listening to the Mass and the sermon helped my Spanish. I would usually attend after a morning of reading and writing in *Carlos Res*, a library off the *Plaza de la Virgen* alongside the cathedral and the *Basilica of la Virgen de los Desamparados*, filled with students studying

5. See chapter eight: "A Lukan (and Lutheran) Theology of Mary."

for their classes. I was working on that novel that will never be published, enjoying the experience more than I should have.

But it was the cathedral that came to be my home, especially on Sundays before our Lutheran Divine Service and always during the feast days with José Luis and Elena. Everyone is at home at the altar. This is not a foreign space for Spanish clergy. It is where they belong, and they know what to do, when, and how. It has flow. The verger, a layman, would be the master of ceremonies at the festival liturgies. He would direct traffic, making sure everything and everyone were in the proper place, like a faculty marshal. It was a pleasure to watch him work. He would often eat at a place I frequented, *Los Oberos* , where students, many of them disabled in some way, would cook excellent meals, serving a *menu del día* for 5 euros. The verger was a simple, unassuming man, and he watched over the bishop and priests and the liturgy in like manner. I sometimes wish our liturgical pastors would come and learn from these Spaniards. I think the overwhelming presence of Protestant evangelicalism in the States influences the way we do liturgy. How could it not?

Churches are better attended on Sunday than I expected, and even during weekday masses there is a decent crowd. But on festivals the churches are packed. In Valencia most of the festivals are in the spring—*San Vicente, Mártir y Diacono, Las Fallas for St. Joseph*, and *Semana Santa.* On the second Sunday of May in 2012, on the feast day of the *Traslado de la Virgen*, from the *Basilica de la Virgen de los Desamparados* to the cathedral, my son Nicholas and I, along with many *Valencianos*, attended Mass in *Plaza de la Virgen*, right next to her *Basilica*. Chairs filled the plaza and an outdoor altar was set up outside the *Basilica's* walls. Clergy were decked out in their finest, along with a huge choir and orchestra. We were wondering how they would distribute the sacrament and commune so many, but they followed the pattern of the ancient church by using stations, which here were identified by yellow umbrellas. There must have been thousands, yet they communed all of them in no time—about fifteen minutes. After the liturgy, a full baritone voice began singing the hymn of Valencia, with orchestra and choir and thousands of *Valencianos* joining in. People were completely engaged for the entire Mass, tears streaming down the faces of many in the congregation gathered for the feast day of Virgin. After the Mass was over, they took all the chairs out of the plaza in a matter of minutes for the "translation" of the Virgin (*traslado*) from the *Basilica* to the cathedral, passing her above the crowds in the jam-packed plaza, bearing her to the cathedral as they offered her passionate poems, passing children, even infants, over the top of the crowd on hands so that they might touch her. Everyone was trying to touch her. By the time she arrived to where we were, the crowd almost crushed us. But we went with the flow, joining them in following the Virgin and the archbishop into the cathedral. For both of us it was one of those once-in-a-lifetime experiences.

The Spanish Catholic Church uses their saints to great advantage by taking holidays for their feast days. *San Vicente*, from the late third century, is buried in the cathedral in the back of the church, where you can see his arm at the place of his tomb. The cathedral in Valencia is known for housing what many people believe is the holy grail in the *Capilla del Santo Cáliz*. Many scholars swear by it—a simple agate cup nestled in a stand of gold and jewels. These legends have been around a long time, and people believe them and shape their lives around them. Like the legend of Santiago coming to Spain—who knows if there's any truth to it? The spring I spent in Valencia, there was a conference of reputable scholars who gave much support for this claim. I sat in on some of the lectures, and these historians take the legend seriously. I could be persuaded. But even it it's not the holy grail, it is housed in one of the most magnificent chapels I have ever seen. It is so worshipful to just sit there and pray and meditate, even read. I love reading in the cathedral and the other churches, especially when it was hot, for the churches are always cool.

In Spain there is a coexistence between secularism and Catholicism. Some of the pious Spaniards complain about the bifurcation between the church, her cult, and everyday life, but how are we that much different? One could say that throughout the Western world, the church is a separate event from everyday living. In Spain they call them "liturgical" Catholics, "feast-day" Catholics—Catholics who show up for the big events but are not practicing Catholics the rest of the week or the rest of the year. We call them Christmas and Easter Lutherans. Spaniards order their life around the feast days, and Holy Week is central to their lives—the churches are packed and the processions well attended. But the rest of the time most Spaniards seem detached from the church. At least in Spain the Holy Week processions are about the biblical events and in this way witness to the essence of the faith as the narrative of Christ's passion and resurrection is embodied and acted out in real life—in the streets of the city.

One of the problems in Spain is that life is too good, family is generally strong, and people have rich social lives, spending time in the bars talking, eating great food, and drinking great wines.[6] The need for church, or a church piety, is not as acute, like it might be in other places that don't have the advantages Spaniards have, where church becomes for the people a refuge amid suffering or persecution or both. You hear a lot about the rise of secularism and modernity in Spain after Franco's death. Spaniards rejected the church when democracy finally came because the church had been so wedded to Franco's totalitarianism. But now, fifty years later, there seems to be less hostility to the church yet also less interest.

Franco's death led to the rise of some Protestant denominations after their persecution during the Franco years. But evangelical Protestants have a rough go in Spain. Their missionaries are very frustrated by the slow advance of their teaching among the Spaniards. They seem so opposed to everything that Spaniards love—especially good wine and going to bars and drinking in general—and they are so anti-Catholic. One Spaniard told me that if you want to be with Spaniards you must go to the bars—it is the way they socialize, and they love to socialize. They don't entertain in their homes, except their families. So, if you're a Protestant pastor evangelizing Spaniards, you better like to visit bars. You can drink coffee or soda or sparkling water, but Spaniards were often judged by evangelical pastors for drinking their *tintos* or vermouths or *cervezas.* Sadly, some of these missionaries were dismissive of Spaniards, especially their lifestyle, for as evangelicals and Pentecostals, they were more pietistic and were offended by the Spanish way of life and the Roman Catholic church, with its high liturgical traditions, its saints and devotion to Mary, its excessive feasts and gaudy processions. You couldn't help but feel that they didn't like Spain or Spaniards or the religious culture of Spain, with its thick Roman Catholicism.

During my sabbatical in 2002, when the mission was just over a year old, Marcos Berndt and I consulted with the *Federación de Entidades Religiosas Evangélicas de España* (FEDERE), a loose organization of Protestants in Spain, mostly evangelicals, that dates from 1986. We were seeking their advice on how to register the Lutheran Church in Spain as a religious organization, something Marcos accomplished before he left me alone in Asturias. We also met with the *Fundación Federico Fliedner,*

6. Bars in Spain are more like cafes or restaurants that serve as gathering places for family and friends.

which celebrated its 150th anniversary in 2020. Federico Fliedner was the son of Theodor Fliedner, a prominent nineteenth-century German Lutheran pastor from Kaiserswerth, Düsseldorf, known for his establishment of Lutheran deaconess training in 1836. One of his students was Florence Nightingale. Although his son identified more as a Reformed pastor than a Lutheran one, he was an iconic Protestant pastor in Spain who began his work in 1870. Most Protestants in 2002 had started their missions back in the 1970s after Franco's death, but we listened to their frustration over how little success they had among Spaniards since the 1970s. Their churches were made up mostly of Latinos who tended, in their words, to be more interested in church than the Spaniards. As someone whose parents lived in Spain in the 1970s and in Mexico before that, we loved the culture of Spain and Latin America, had many friends during those years who we cherished, and we even admired parts of the Roman Catholic culture of both countries. What struck us in the 1970s, and then again for Linda and me and our three children when I returned on sabbatical in 2002, was that all those feasts and procession were, by and large, very biblical, and attending the Semana Santa processions, you could not help but be moved by the portrayal of the events of Holy Week by real people, especially Jesus carrying the cross.

As one Spaniard put it: to be a Spaniard is to be a Catholic, and to reach out to Spaniards you must appropriate as much of their Catholicism as you can, highlighting what is biblical and what is not. That meant being liturgical and sacramental, for not only is this the way Spaniards do church—this is the way they do life. To be sacramental is to be in love with the world. As George Weigel, a Roman Catholic theologian, said, "Stuff counts."[7] But how can you reach Spaniards when you're constituted against the "stuff" of creation? Spaniards cannot embrace Christians who reject that God comes to us through "stuff," through water and oil, through bread and wine, through the person of the priest. The worship services of the Assemblies of God—I attended one—are remarkably detached from Spanish reality. As the Spaniards say, "They're not very serious." It seems absurd to be in Catholic Spain and preaching against Mary and the saints, against dead ritual and fiestas. No wonder these Protestant churches are empty, except for immigrants from Latin and South America, many of whom were co-opted by the Pentecostals, who are very appealing to many Latinos. What I tried to tell my Protestant

7. See chapter seven, "Returning to Emmaus," fn 7.

friends was that Spaniards are not like these immigrants from Latin America. Spaniards are European; Spanish identity is completely tied up with their liturgical style. There are moments of great passion from the ritual action, but it's controlled, and they return to that sophisticated manner that characterizes most Spaniards.

There were two events that shaped my understanding of Spain, both the religious and secular side of the festivals, both of which occurred within weeks of one another in the spring of 2012—*Las Fallas* and *Semana Santa*. What you're seeing during the festivals in Valencia and the rest of Spain is the church's faith motion. The biblical narrative of St. Joseph and events of Holy Week are lived out in these festivals that have the capacity to move people both spiritually and emotionally, as well as through all the senses. The story of Jesus' passion, death, and resurrection was displayed for all to see, and there were thousands who participated in this story, both by enacting it and by seeing it lived out before their eyes. These festivals reflect on the biblical narrative, comment on it, analyze it, even meditate on it. The processions are embodying the biblical stories, getting it out into the streets, living and enacting the faith. That's primary theology—as primary as it gets.

Madrid in the Barrio of Salamanca—2015

In 2012 Pastor Ted Krey unofficially appointed me the liaison for the LCMS with the church in Spain. Since then, I have made twenty-eight trips to support, teach, preach, and visit members scattered throughout Spain. In 2014 the church experienced the departure of the last Argentinian missionary under sad and troubling circumstances. This was a trying moment for the church. It led to the Lutheran church in Spain ending its relationship with Argentina—no more triangulation. As there was no missionary in Spain from the winter of 2014 to the spring of 2015, I served as the de facto missionary, traveling to Spain four times a year, usually during the CTSFW quarter breaks, to bring preaching and the Eucharist to the membership scattered across the country, catechizing the children and adults seeking to be members in the church.

The hospitality shown to me by the Spanish Lutherans reflected the kind of welcome the apostles received in the first century, as I stayed in people's homes and celebrated the Eucharist at their kitchen tables. In some ways, I have the longest memory of the history of the Lutheran

Church of Spain since its beginning in 2000, even more than the key players from Spain. I came to know everyone in the church. Although these were difficult days, they were also very fulfilling for me, as I was able to assume a pastoral role, bringing the gifts to the saints throughout the country. Since working closely with Pastor Ted Krey in Latin America, I have learned that missionaries plant churches. But my role in Spain was to water the churches that were planted by the Argentinian missionaries, especially those who were not members of any established congregation. I will never know whether I would be a good church planter like my dear friend John Fiene. But taking care of people as a pastor is what I know and love.

In the spring of 2015, I took Pastor David Warner, a new missionary from the LCMS, on a *gira* through Spain to mark a new era in the mission of the Lutheran church in Spain. David was a perfect candidate for Spain, with excellent Spanish from his years of service at the military base in Rota in southern Spain, near Jerez de la Frontera. Later that year, Pastor Adam Lehman from the LCMS would arrive (another Marine). He grew up in Fort Wayne, and his wife was a classmate of our daughter, Abigail. Both were placed in Seville, following the practice of OIM to place two missionaries in one place so they could support one another. They were to prop up the ministry there, encourage Juan Carlos, the Spanish pastor, and return Seville to its place as the preeminent congregation in Spain.

In the fall of 2015, after Pastor Warner was now in place in Seville, I entered an unofficial arrangement with OIM and CTSFW to spend fall quarters serving in Spain. Later, my responsibilities would shift to providing leadership in the Dominican Republic in the formation of the seminary in Santiago de los Caballeros (2017) and in teaching (2018). I lived in the Salamanca barrio of Madrid with the Blake family from Houston. Salamanca is an upscale suburb where we worshiped at St. George's Anglican Church, the place of worship for the Madrid congregation to this day and where the Alliance missionary from Venezuela, Isaac Machado, lives in the apartment above the church offices. Some of my best memories were getting to know Bruce and his wife, Missouri-Synod Lutherans from Texas, and the remarkable hospitality they afforded Linda and me. From Madrid, I was able to help Pastor Warner transition to Spain, first by serving as pastor of the congregation in Madrid and then by doing some teaching, catechizing, and visiting folks throughout Spain, as I had been doing for years.

The LCMS missionaries provided stability and continuity to the church in Spain. Like me, they were caretakers rather than church planters, and the way they took care was by normalizing the liturgy with booklets that provided continuity among all the congregations, making sure that the Eucharist was celebrated every Sunday somewhere in Spain, and bringing administrative and financial stability. Their missionary service was well received by the saints in *Iglesia Evangélica Luterana de España* (IELE). *Asambleas* (the Lutheran Church of Spain's annual "Synodical conventions" around October 12th—the *Día de la Hispanidad*—Columbus Day) were well organized, and the missionaries provided continuing education through Luther Academy. They always welcomed me to participate in the life of the church in Spain and used me for both theological education and pastoral visitations. It was a sad day when they took calls and left Spain at the beginning of Covid. At the time they were departing, Pastor Isaac Machado from Venezuela, one of my students at the seminary in the DR, was called to Madrid as an Alliance missionary. He has been a huge blessing to the church in Spain, especially in bringing Latinos into the church in Madrid, many of them Venezuelans. The departure of the LCMS missionaries now offered the Lutheran Church in Spain an opportunity to take leadership in every aspect of the ministry in Spain. One of the great blessings is the development of a deaconess program I helped launch, the first consecration of deaconesses occurring at the Asamblea in 2025.

It was at this time that, at the encouragement of the executive committee of OIM, the Lutheran Church in Spain decided to pursue a longstanding desire to move from the Latin American Region of OIM to Eurasia. As long as I can remember, this move was a goal for the church in Spain, especially Juan Carlos and José Luis, for Spaniards considered themselves Europeans and not Latinos. Although I was supportive, even encouraged, this move to Eurasia, in retrospect, it may have been wiser to stay with LAC. But it does give Spain access and easy proximity to conferences and meetings in Europe, and in the end, it was what the Spaniards wanted.

Some Final Thoughts

The climax of my work came with the ordination of José Luis de Miguel in 2017 and then his consecration as bishop in 2021. Sadly, José Luis had to resign as bishop in 2022 because of his health, which was more severe than even he thought, leading to his untimely death in February of 2023. This was one of the saddest moments in our lives, for José Luis, his wife, Elena, and his two children, had become part of our family.

The Lutheran Church in Spain is now in transition, led by a new bishop who is a Spaniard, another Spanish pastor from the Canary Islands and Venezuela, and two Alliance missionaries, one from Venezuela and the other from Brazil. There is a growing Latino census in the church. I hope to continue to support this maturing mission in my retirement from OIM, for it is hard not to consider them as much my church family as the saints in my home congregation at St. Paul's in downtown Fort Wayne. These Lutheran saints have embraced me (and Linda!) in my halting Spanish as the Galatians embraced Paul when he was left half-dead alongside of the road—as an angel of God, as Christ Jesus himself.

In Spain I learned about missions, how to reach across cultures as a missionary from a foreign country. I say this sheepishly, as my work in Spain was nothing like all the missionaries and their families who leave home and live full-time in countries much more foreign and stranger to our American way of life than Spain. Ten-week sabbaticals or two-week stints a couple of times a year doesn't qualify me as a bona fide missionary. So much of what I say about missions should be taken with some skepticism. But having lived overseas as a youth, through my many international travels for CTSFW and OIM in theological education, my ability to preach and teach in Spanish, as well as the long and deep relationships with many people in the church in Spain and around the world, I do have some sense of what it means to advise a mission.

Although I sometimes had my own opinions about what was best for Spain, I always deferred to the Spaniards, to their sensibilities, after long conversations over tapas and wine, offering my thoughts when asked but letting their *consejo*, their *cuerpo pastoral* (council and pastoral body), make the final decision. What I have learned in serving the Lutheran Church is Spain is that one must gently guide and lead but always defer and let the local church decide. When we started the Russian project with the seminary in Novosibirsk, we learned quickly that even though we might have other ideas, the Siberians knew their situation better than we did, and we always tried to honor their decisions. Perhaps we acted as we did at CTSFW in the Russian project because we saw the paternalistic attitude of the Board for Mission Services (BMS) in 1990s reflected in what they were doing around the world and what they wanted us to do in

Siberia. We resisted this paternalistic impulse in our dealings with other church bodies and tried to trust those who had spent decades building relationships. We need to listen to our partner churches and those LCMS folks who have some experience and knowledge of the mission.

From the beginning, the Lutheran church in Spain has been made up of converts from Spain and Lutherans from Latin America (and some converts from there as well). From 2002, I encouraged the leadership of the church in Spain to develop a strategy to reach more Spaniards, something that is still a work in progress. Lutheran liturgy and the Lutheran Confessions are two things that appeal to Spaniards. They love discussing philosophy and theology, love abstract thinking, and they are ritual people, as is witnessed by the whole span of the Roman Catholic liturgy and festivals that define Spain. Although our liturgical life in Spain has come a long way since the pietistic, low-church, black-robed Argentinians, especially now with Isaac Machado's strong liturgical leadership, there is always more that we could do. The challenges of a mission like Spain continue—how to appeal to Roman Catholic Spaniards with a Lutheran confessional and liturgical ethos. Lots of conversations, much teaching and catechesis—this is the way of a fledgling mission like Spain—and always over a tapa and glass of *tinto*.

But one thing everyone agrees upon—Word and Sacrament are the means for mission, following the tradition of Jesus in Luke 24, the apostles in the first century, and the apostolic church through the ages, which is the topic for the next chapter.

11

Word and Sacrament

The Means for Mission

AS THIS MEMOIR PROGRESSED, I had decided not to include this chapter on theological education for several reasons. Although international theological education has been a huge part of my life since 1996, I did want to write a chapter that came across as a travelogue, and the most important aspect of my international work was described in detail in the previous chapter on the mission to Spain.

Then the most extraordinary thing happened. Out of the blue, a complete surprise, I received notice from Concordia University Irvine (CUI) that the faculty and board of regents had voted to grant me the "Great Commission Award." At first I thought it was a joke—me, the liturgy guy, the one who was persecuted early in his career by his own department for claiming that the mission of the church proceeds from the liturgy—who claimed that the liturgy was the essence of the church alongside the Great Commission—who wrote an essay for the Festschrift of David Scaer claiming that Matt 28 was more a "church order" than the Great Commission[1]—*I was receiving the Great Commission award?* I could think of other colleagues who were more deserving, but they had chosen me and I happily accepted it. At this moment in my life, after retiring (with some sadness) from the Office of International Mission

1. Just, "Why Luke Is Indebted to Matthew as the First Gospel," 19–33.

(OIM), this recognition came as a welcome balm. Maybe I did need to include a chapter on my work in global theological education.

Linda and I went to Concordia University Irvine (CUI) for the weekend of their graduation at the beginning of May 2024. As we arrived on campus we immediately ran into a former student and colleague, Dr. Scott Stiegemeyer, who made us feel right at home. I couldn't help but ask Scott to help us solve the mystery of why I was nominated. He told us it came from a most unexpected source, Dr. Bret Taylor, the dean of the arts and sciences, a professor of mathematics who became acquainted with my writings and presentations. When the president and some of the faculty who knew me heard of his nomination, they all agreed I was a good choice. I was able to meet Bret and thank him (he even sent me a wonderful CUI bow tie and Linda a scarf). Bret embodies everything we hope for in the professors at our Lutheran universities.

From that first moment of meeting Scott, Linda, and I were blown away by the kindness and hospitality with which we were greeted and how many friends and colleagues we had on the faculty and staff. We were so impressed by all that is happening at CUI under the leadership of President Michael Thomas and my former student and colleague Dr. Steven Mueller, whose gracious words accompanied the presentation of my award. The graduation ceremony itself was a walking train of students with their families through the beautiful CUI campus, greeting the faculty gathered at their schools in academic garb for conversations and photos, with the granting of each degree in the chapel individually (this "new" system was implemented during Covid and was so well received that they have continued it). I was invited to stand with the Christ College faculty, and for over two hours it was pure delight to be part of the joy of faculty, students, and families at this happy occasion. As we left the campus, Linda said, "I don't want to leave this wonderful place," and I couldn't have agreed more.

They asked me to respond to this Great Commission Award, and my remarks also serve as a fitting introduction to this final chapter of my memoir:

> What a gift to be honored for one's passion and one's joy. Many thanks to the faculty and board of regents for this Great Commission Award. In the Great Commission, Jesus gives his disciples a church order, which was used by them to plant churches. They made disciples by teaching people about Jesus through Matthew's Gospel, then baptizing them, then teaching

them more about Jesus through the Gospels so that Jesus might be with them always through the Lord's Supper.

The evangelist St. Luke echoes Matthew's Great Commission in the Emmaus story, a narrative that has shaped my entire life. In Jesus' teaching on the road he creates burning hearts in the Emmaus disciples and then opens their eyes in the breaking of the bread. Word and Meal—the means for mission—like Matthew's Great Commission—planting churches through making disciples, baptizing, teaching, and celebrating the Lord's Supper.

Through global theological education these great truths have been shared throughout the world in our partner churches and missions. Through global theological education we share the gospel, plant Lutheran churches by forming pastors, and show mercy by forming servants of mercy.

The Jerusalem cross has been my guide throughout my life [I was wearing one in my lapel]. The cross in the middle is Jesus' cross, where he laid down his life for us. The four other crosses represent the four Gospels that teach us about Jesus and his suffering, death, resurrection, and ascension. And they also represent the four corners of the world where these Gospels are to be taught. That is at the heart of the Great Commission and why the church is ever to Emmaus. This has been the essence of my life as a pastor and professor. Thank you for this great honor.

In My End Is My Beginning

If my beginning was through the liturgy, that beginning has brought me to a missiological end, and in that end, I also found my beginning. Emmaus was not simply the foundation of my teaching and scholarly reflections on Scripture and liturgy; it also became foundational for the way I understood my contributions to the remarkable work our seminary has done in theological education since I joined the faculty in 1984.

Just as I am always returning to Emmaus, so am I returning to Grant Osbourne's felicitous phrase "the word and the bread . . . the means for/to mission."[2] Although I cited Osbourne in both *The Ongoing Feast* and

2. Osborne, *Resurrection Narratives*, 124. I have changed the preposition from "to" to "for" to suggest that Word and Sacraments are the means *for the sake of mission*, that is, mission is done through them, and not that Word and Sacrament are simply the means to the goal that is mission. If our mission does not see the liturgical structures of Word and Meal as the essence of what the church is in her mission, then it misses the eschatological character of liturgy. Heaven will be an ongoing, eternal liturgy. Mission

the CPH commentary on Luke, this was not something I developed in my work on Emmaus. But little did I realize that thirty-two years after completing my doctorate I would be serving OIM in global theological education, something I had informally been involved in since 1996.

Global theological education has always been a vital part of the mission of CTSFW, going back to 1976 under the presidency of Robert D. Preus, when the Springfield seminary moved back to Fort Wayne, the city of its origin, the year that I began my seminary studies. During the fifty-year sojourn of CTSFW in Fort Wayne, there were only four years—from 1980 to 1984—when I was not associated with CTSFW, either as a student or a faculty member. It was clear when I was a student in the late 1970s that a confessional and missiological revival was taking place on this new campus. No one could question Robert Preus's academic pedigree, with his two doctoral degrees and his legendary teaching at the St. Louis Seminary, nor the academic credentials of the new professors he was bringing to the campus from places such as St. Andrews, Princeton, Basel, Notre Dame, and Cambridge. The inception of the Symposium on the Lutheran Confessions in 1977 demonstrated his commitment to restoring the Lutheran Confessions to its proper place in the theological conversation. But Dr. Preus was also a man committed to the mission of the church, and the development of the Doctor of Missiology program in the 1980s was the culmination of his vision to train pastors at the doctoral level who could provide theological education in seminaries and schools around the world. Perhaps Dr. Preus would have resonated with Grant Osborne's pithy summary of Luke 24 and what has happened at CTSFW in global theological education since his untimely death in 1995.

It was under the presidency of Dean Wenthe that CTSFW really stepped on the world stage, with the initiation of the Russian Project in 1996. It was our Macedonian call to help start a seminary in Siberia, but soon other partner church seminaries were asking us to teach courses, help in curriculum development, and train men and woman at our seminary to serve as leaders in theological education around the world.

In our curriculum revisions, described in chapter nine, we were intentional in placing the mission of the church in the center of our vision of theological education. As Dr. Weinrich put it in an article on the new curriculum in *For the Life of the World*:

---

will be over. Matthew 28 will have reached its goal.

> The more the faculty of CTS reflected on this Biblical image [of the pastor as shepherd], the more it became evident that the old four-fold structure of the curriculum was *theologically* inadequate . . . What was missing in the old curriculum—and this is worth thinking about!—what was missing was Christ and his Church! . . . We were teaching "about" Christian truth. In a strange but real way, theological education *as* a four-fold discipline dislocated the true object of theological education . . . But the Scriptures speak of "education" in the language of participation and formation . . . "Do not be conformed to this world, but be transformed by the renewing of your mind" (Rom 12:2) . . . If we think of "education" as "formation," then we must think of a spiritual "discipline" by which we are formed . . . *Theological education is fundamentally the forming of the mind according to the life of Christ in the context of the Church in Mission.* This is what "From the Church, for the Church—In Mission" provides . . . Baptism–Preaching–Lord's Supper, these are the (primary) "disciplines" of theological education by which the pastor and people in common drink of the cool waters of redemption and feed upon the pastures of the Spirit as they hear the voice of their Shepherd. To "learn"—that is, to be "educated"—is to participate in the gifts of God and to reflect on how best to "declare the mighty acts" of God.[3]

Theological education is fundamentally the forming of the mind according to the life of Christ in the context of the Church in Mission. This guiding principle in our curriculum review perfectly reflected the essence of what Luke teaches us from the Emmaus story. On the road to Emmaus, Jesus formed the mind of the two Emmaus disciples to the meaning of the life of Christ by burning their hearts in breaking open the scriptures to them and then opening their eyes in the breaking of the bread to feed them his holy flesh. And then he sent them off to mission armed with the means for mission—Word and Sacrament.

When the faculty of CTSFW revised the curriculum, it was based on the biblical foundation that Word and Sacrament are the means for mission and on the ancient catechumenate that formed Christians by immersion in the Scriptures and the liturgy of the church. Earlier in this memoir, I related how the early church catechumenate, the ancient way of evangelizing and catechizing adults towards baptism, was a template for our reflections on what might go into a postmodern seminary

3. Weinrich, "From the Church, for the Church," 20–21 (emphasis Weinrich).

curriculum. Since our faculty believed that theology is done through the pastoral acts of baptism, preaching, and the Lord's Supper, we designed a curriculum that formed pastors to carry out these means for mission. Integration, interdisciplinary courses, and team teaching would be required to accomplish this.

Rising over one hundred feet above the Upper Plaza at CTSFW, Kramer Chapel is the physical and spiritual center of the campus—our Jerusalem, where Christ is present with his gifts in Word and Sacrament. The classroom is our Athens, where we engage in lively discussions about the theological significance of Christ's presence. Theological formation begins in the chapel and is centered there. Every weekday the seminary community gathers in the chapel to receive the gifts of forgiveness, life, and salvation, to pray, sing, and make music to the Lord. It is in the chapel that the seminarian is shaped as a child of God, and it is where future pastors learn to worship, lead the liturgy, sing and preach and become formed into pastors by Christ through the Scriptures read and proclaimed, and through the regular celebration of the Lord's Supper.[4] This is one of the ways we prepare our students at CTSFW to make known the deeds of Jesus—our 175th anniversary theme—hearing his Word and then reflecting on that Word in our classes. Shot through every course at the seminary was how the liturgy, embodied in the life of the seminary at the daily Kramer Chapel services, formed our students to be Lutheran pastors and was also, at the same time, teaching them how Word and Sacrament are the means for evangelizing the world.

Our curriculum review committee was determined not to pit liturgy against mission, as so many tried to do during the worship wars. Rather, we wanted to show how the mission of the church flows from the presence of Christ in the liturgy in love for our neighbors who know not Christ. There is no greater act of love to our unbelieving neighbors than to bring them into the liturgical assembly to receive the gifts of salvation.

4. During my years as student, faculty member, and dean of the chapel, the Eucharist was celebrated each week, alternating between Tuesday and Wednesday, as some students had M/W/F classes and others Tues/Thurs classes. When Paul Grime took over for me as dean, he convened the chapel staff (Richard Resch and Kevin Hildebrand), inviting me to the meeting as the former dean. He asked what changes we might consider making. I suggested that the one thing that would be very helpful would be to have Eucharist every Wednesday (not alternating week to week between Wednesday and Tuesday), and to also offer it whenever there was a feast or festival. In this way, students could count on Wednesday as the day of Eucharist every week and look forward to more opportunities to receive the body and blood of Christ on Feast days. It has been this way now since Paul Grime has been the dean (2007).

The Great Commission is an act of love, inspired by faith that receives the gifts in the liturgy to go out to the highways and byways and bring our lost neighbors into the liturgy so they may behold the presence of Jesus Christ and receive the gifts of the Gospel proclaimed in the liturgy of the Word. In the prayers of the church, we pray for the world and its needs, that all people may join us in faith and eventually in the reception of the supper.

As a Lutheran, pastoral identity is centered in preaching, teaching, and administering the sacraments: what better foundation for this pastoral identity than a curriculum that forms pastors through the four canonical Gospels—books of the church, written for the church, to be used by the church in its proclamation of the gospel to the unbaptized and the baptized—written for the purpose of evangelization of Jews and gentiles? The Gospels became the basis for forming the minds of seminarians according to the life of Christ. Pastors for a postmodern world value narratives over propositional truths, for those they will catechize will be incorporated into a person, Jesus Christ, not a body of doctrines. So, in the new curriculum Jesus' story takes precedence. The world is evangelized through the story the Bible tells about Jesus in the Gospels, and this story must become the world's story for indeed, as Robert Jenson said, "the world has lost its story."

The three-year lectionary was developed to reflect the way the early church used the Gospels in the liturgy and catechesis, namely, a continuous reading of the Gospel to hear the story of Jesus as the evangelist intended it to be heard. What formed early Christians into the life of Christ was hearing that life as Matthew, Mark, Luke, and John narrated that life in the Gospels. The ancient catechumenate was three years, following the pattern of Christ's catechesis of the twelve and the seventy during his three-year ministry. This conformed to our three years of theological education at the seminary, with a fourth year of vicarage.

As valuable as the historic lectionary is for its catechetical repetitiveness, the three-year lectionary reflects both an ancient and postmodern emphasis on formation through narrative, in this case, the narrative of the life of Christ. More could be said about the postmodern proclivities towards narrative, in both its positive and negative aspects, but we believed that students today, and their parishioners, hear and learn differently than most of us who were nurtured during the height of modernism and its climax in the Enlightenment in the mid-twentieth century. We believed that the narrative based three-year lectionary reflected the postmodern emphasis that one is formed as a Christian, and pastor, through incorporation into a life—the life of Christ—by immersion in that life by hearing it unfold every Sunday as the evangelists intended it to unfold.

As Luke says in his prologue—his Gospel is an orderly kerygmatic account meant to catechize his hearers about the certainty of his narrative about Jesus. Early Christians read the Gospel as a continuous narrative—a *lectio continua*. This continuous reading of the Gospel in the liturgy proved the perfect way for early Christians to evangelize the world and catechize catechumens, and now in the twenty-first century to form pastors for the postmodern world into which these students will be sent, a world closer to the early Christian world than that of our Lutheran fathers.

CTSFW as an International Seminary

Our experience in helping establish a seminary in Siberia in 1996 confirmed for us that the means for mission were the pastoral acts of baptizing, preaching, and Lord's Supper. As theological educators, our calling was to help international seminaries form students to plant Lutheran churches through the pastoral acts. We believed that theological education was foundational for our partner churches to spread the Gospel. The success of the Russian project showed us that, for Lutherans, the biblical mandate of Jesus to the Emmaus disciples of Word and Sacrament as the means for mission is also central to our mission as a seminary to assist in international theological education. For many, CTSFW has now become the "Wittenberg of the Twenty-First Century," a confessional and missional seminary committed to academic excellence with a passion for global theological education. This title as the new Wittenberg comes honestly, for in many ways CTSFW followed in the spirit of reform in theological education by Luther and Melanchthon in the sixteenth century.

Our mission statement reflects this connection between theology, mission, and mercy: "CTSFW exists to form servants in Jesus Christ who teach the faithful, reach the lost, and care for all." Sharing the gospel begins with pastors who are formed to plant Lutheran churches *through the pastoral acts of baptism, preaching, and the Lord's Supper* and deaconesses who show compassion *as women of mercy*. This happens best through theological education. This is why CTSFW is committed to develop, nurture, and sustain theological education around the world. As a seminary we are not called to plant churches, but we are called to form pastors through rigorous theological education who then plant Lutheran churches and to form deaconesses who show mercy even as they work alongside LCMS missionaries and pastors in our partner churches. The last part of that mission statement acknowledges the huge move CTSFW made in training over 150 deaconesses for our church since 2003. Forming pastors and deaconesses is integrally related to reaching the lost and caring for all.

At CTSFW we believe that residential pastoral and diakonal formation is the gold standard, and our assistance in establishing the Siberian seminary affirmed this. Since 1996, CTSFW faculty have been instrumental in providing our expertise in theological education in other parts of the world as well.

Theological Education in Russian and Spanish, English, Romanian, Mandarin, Farsi, Urdu, and Arabic

At the tower of Babel, Moses writes, "And the Lord said, 'Behold, they are one people, and they have all one language, and this is only the beginning of what they will do. And nothing that they propose to do will now be impossible for them. Come, let us go down and there confuse their language, so that they may not understand one another's speech'" (Gen 11:6–8).

Fifty days after the resurrection of Jesus, on the day of Pentecost, the Holy Spirit came upon the apostles with tongues of fire, and they began to speak in other languages. And when the people gathered there in Jerusalem heard the apostles, "they were amazed and astonished, saying, 'Are not all these who are speaking Galileans? And how is it that we hear, each of us in his own native language?'" (Acts 2:1–8).

God reversed the confusion of languages at Babel in the coming of the Holy Spirit at Pentecost. In his letter to the Romans, Paul writes, "How then will they call on him in whom they have not believed? And how are they to believe in him of whom they have never heard? And how are they to hear without someone preaching? And how are they to preach unless they are sent? As it is written, 'How beautiful are the feet of those who preach the good news!' . . . So, faith comes from hearing, and hearing through the word of Christ" (Rom 10:14–5, 17). Fundamental to forming pastors, missionaries, and deaconesses to send them into the world to reach the lost is equipping them to teach the good news of Jesus Christ *in their own language*. This is the lesson of the tower of Babel and Pentecost.[5]

In my end is my beginning. Since 2017, when I was called by the Office of International Mission to serve in global theological education, I have walked alongside pastors and missionaries of the LCMS, some of them former students, who are reaching out in theological education to people who speak Russian, Spanish, Romanian, English, Mandarin, Farsi, Urdu, and Arabic. A church and seminary that reaches the lost through theological education, especially in English, Spanish, and Mandarin, is covering most of the world. Here are a few examples of my experience in global theological education.

"Come Over to Novosibirsk and Help Us"—A Lutheran Seminary in Siberia

When Dean Wenthe took over the presidency of CTSFW in the spring of 1996, the future of our seminary looked bleak. The previous administration had intended to close the seminary, beginning with a sabotage of our accreditation that sent us reeling from a poor report by our accreditors. Our faculty needed new blood, and one of the first people President Wenthe and Dean Weinrich called to the seminary was Dr. Timothy Quill, a PhD in Liturgical Studies from Drew University, to help us fulfill what we called the Macedonian call from the Lutherans in Siberia to start a new seminary. Timothy was a natural-born missionary who grew up on the mission field and who had an uncanny way of opening doors in places where no one thought we had a chance to start a mission. Timothy and I were close friends from our days when we were called out of the seminary to serve in New England District (1980—Timothy from Concordia Seminary, St. Louis). We were installed a week apart in our congregations, Timothy at St. Paul's in New Hartford, Connecticut (June 22—the day of my ordination at St. Paul Lutheran in Westport, Connecticut, by David Scaer) and me at Grace in Middletown, Connecticut (June 29), where Timothy attended my installation.

5. These three paragraphs are from Just, "Servants Formed to Reach," 7–8.

Timothy and I became fast friends during my four years in Connecticut, as did our wives. Timothy and Annette became godparents for our daughter Abigail, born in 1981. We were mentored by Pastor George Kraus and his wife, Helen, who were in New Britain, Connecticut, equidistant between our two parishes, which were sixty miles apart. We were the "Confessional pastors" in Connecticut and developed our own little Winkel. George was a special blessing to both Timothy and me, and we would talk theology and casuistry over a good scotch many a night. I know that both Timothy and I would call George when a tough situation arose in our church, and he always gave us the best pastoral advice. George left us after two short years to teach at the CTSFW in 1982. Timothy and I soldiered on without him and continued our reputation as the Confessional pastors in New England. We both remember the time at a district convention when we overheard some of the longer-tenured pastors in the district calling us "dangerous." We laugh at those comments to this day.

The inspiration behind the Russian Project came from Dr. Wallace Schulz, former Lutheran Hour speaker and second vice president of the LCMS, who was one of the first to travel to the former Soviet Union, especially Siberia. While in Siberia he discovered many former Lutherans who had been deported there after the Bolshevik Revolution, most of them from Saint Petersburg and the Volga River Valley. He saw hymnals and catechisms that had been written by hand from memory by faithful Lutherans while they were on the trains to Siberia. This was the only thing they had to form and keep them in the faith. Even in Siberia, Lutherans in Communist Russia lived in fear, many grandmothers secretly baptizing their grandchildren. We met many who were told they were baptized but couldn't be sure. We wrestled over this pastoral problem, and after much debate, decided to ease their anxious consciences and uncertainty by baptizing them.

During the early 1990s, after the fall of the Soviet Union, Wallace organized a series of theological seminars on the campuses of Fort Wayne and St. Louis seminaries. Among the more than two hundred visitors from the nations of the former Soviet Union were Pastor Vsevolod Lytkin and several young members of what became the Siberian Evangelical Lutheran Church, including Rev. Alexey Streltsov, who is currently the Rector (President) of Lutheran Theological Seminary in Novosibirsk, as well as other young men who have become pastors and church leaders throughout Russia and other former Soviet countries. Alexey and his wife, Elena, would become the first students in our Russia project. In 1995, because of Wallace's effort, Pastor Lytkin asked Dr. Schulz for help in training pastors and deacons in Siberia, the first part of our Macedonian call. In April 1996, the month Dean Wenthe was inaugurated as president of CTSFW, he and Bill Weinrich received the second part of the Macedonian call in St. Louis from Rev. Larry Burgdorf and Dr. Schulz, who offered CTSFW a life-saving donation from the Marvin M. Schwann Charitable Foundation to develop the Russian Project. Timothy would oversee the project. It is not an overstatement to say that this donation and project "saved" our seminary.[6]

> The original charter for the project had three simple goals: (1) Preparation of men for the pastoral ministry on the Fort Wayne campus to replace the hundreds of pastors killed by the communists; (2) Assist Lutherans in Siberia to establish a seminary in Russia for the training of pastors and lay leaders; (3) Work with Russian speakers in the former Soviet Union to organize evangelism/catechetical summer seminars.[7]

The third goal was the means for accomplishing the other two goals. Dean asked Bill and me to join Timothy in July 1996, in summer seminars in Kazakhstan and Novosibirsk, Russia. In those days, Frankfurt was our hub, and we flew first to Almaty to start the seminars and recruit pastoral students. Each of us was carrying $10,000 for the summer seminars, and for all the years we flew back and forth to Siberia, we always carried as much cash as we could. In those days we were told that there was more American currency circulating in Russia than in the United States. On one of the early trips, I met Timothy in Frankfurt, and from under a stall in the airport bathroom, I slipped him $10,000 from the $20,000 I was carrying from the United States. It felt like a bad Peter Sellers movie. During those early years we could not use a credit card, and we never stayed in a hotel and seldom ate in a restaurant. The roads were horrific, the plumbing lousy, and we soon realized that Russia was not a lot different from many third-world countries. In many ways, it was shocking to see how far behind they were in the very basic things of life.

As we flew over the vastness of Kazakhstan in an empty plane, we looked out the window wondering what adventures lay ahead of us. We were nervous and anxious but also hopeful that this would rejuvenate

6. See Denzler, "Missionary and Catechist to Siberia."

7. Quill, "Novosibirsk," 2–3.

our seminary and make a substantial contribution to the mission of the church. As we stepped down exit ramp of the plane into the darkness of a Kazakh night, we could smell the sweetness of the wood fires, something you don't often smell getting off a plane. I turned to Quill and said, "You're on." He looked back with a nervous grin and said, "I guess I am." We stood outside in the cool evening, nervously waiting while someone took our passports to a building high above us. Pleading our case was the inimitable Gennadij Khonin, who somehow convinced the authorities to let us in, for we should have flown through Moscow to Almaty and not directly from Frankfurt. This muscular former KGB agent embraced us with such a bear hug that it took our breath away. He would become one of the stalwarts of the Russian Project. He hustled us off to bed for a short night and then the next day gave us a tour of Almaty and the surrounding countryside that offered spectacular views of snow-covered mountains surrounding the city.

We had one day to adjust from jet lag. On our second night, as we were about to flop down from exhaustion, Gennadij wished us a good night with our first bottle of Russian vodka. We couldn't not sample it. We quickly discovered that it was stronger than what we drink in the States. I never understood why people drank vodka, as it is relatively tasteless, but I came to learn its virtues after our many trips to Russia. The next day was a tough one for all of us, but we soldiered on through jet lag and a night of Russian vodka. This was one of my first teaching experiences in translation, and I discovered how much I enjoyed the time between sentences to think through what I would say next. It was an energizing three days of teaching and recruiting, and then we were on to the main show in Siberia.

Almaty is about 1,100 miles directly south of Novosibirsk, but there were no flights in those days between the two cities, so we had to fly back to Moscow, 2,400 miles northwest of Almaty. When we arrived in Moscow, we immediately discovered we had a problem. Our visas were no good, and our trip to Almaty was illegal and they didn't think we could continue to Novosibirsk. We were abruptly whisked off to a room by very officious and stern-looking guards, where we sat for hours waiting to hear our fate. Fortunately, we had a long layover between flights. Miraculously, they came back with our passports and permission to continue our travels with no explanation and no apologies.

The summer seminars were in a "resort" on the Orb River outside of Novosibirsk, one of the great academic centers in Russia, next to Moscow and St. Petersburg. It is a scientific center, and we soon learned that on the American strategic plans for nuclear war, Novosibirsk was the second target after Moscow. Over a hundred people, mostly young Siberian university students, gathered in this resort to listen to us lecture all day for two hot and humid weeks in a cramped room full of people who did not shower as often as we do in the United States (when my boys were teenagers and waited too long to shower, I would tell them they smelled like a Russian). This was when we first met many of the Siberian Lutherans who would become such a huge part of our lives in the next decade and beyond.

In all my forty years of teaching, there has never been a more exciting and exhilarating moment than that first summer seminar with students who were ravenous for Lutheran theology and had high hopes for what we were bringing them. Bill lectured first on the history of the early church. We had asked at what level we should lecture, and we were told to teach like it was an adult Bible study. Bill, of course, just launched into full seminary mode, and you could tell that they were hanging on his every word. When he received his first question, something about the Manichean heresy and the theology of the Pentecostal church, he turned to me and said, "Have you ever received as sophisticated and erudite a question as this in your seminary classes?" We knew then and there that we could teach as we did in our seminary classes. As many of the students were Baptist or Pentecostal, our teaching was new to their ears, but this is what the Siberian Lutherans like the future Bishop Vsevolod Lytkin and Rector Alexey Streltsov wanted us to teach. At the center of our teaching and fundamental to the mission of the Siberian Lutheran church was that Word and Sacraments are the means for mission.

As the *Concordia Commentary on Luke* had just been published that year, my focus was Luke and liturgy. The Siberians became immediately interested in creating liturgies we could use for Matins and Vespers. Every evening, while we were relaxing, many of the future leaders of the church were creating translations of our *Lutheran Worship* versions of Matins and Vespers, including the music. The joy between us and the students was as palpable as any teaching experience I had ever had in my first twelve years of teaching at the seminary. It was intoxicating and formed in me a love for teaching international students that continues even now. Many of my colleagues would agree on how satisfying and enriching it is to teach in our partner churches.

But not everyone in the LCMS agreed with our intentional move to engage in global theological education that formed pastors to plant Lutheran churches. The Board for Mission Services (BFMS) sent their director of theological education to observe what we were doing. At that time, the BFMS did not privilege theological education as we do now and focused more on lay volunteers who shared the gospel but did not necessarily connect people to churches that celebrated Word and Sacrament. The battles Dean and Bill had with the BFMS during the entire Russian Project were legendary, and we were always confident we would prevail because, with Dean and Bill in charge, we always had the smartest guys in the room. What the BFMS wanted was total control, and they could not abide that we were doing missions through theological education. But we always maintained we were doing what we were called to do at CTSFW: forming pastors, and later deaconesses, through what we do best—teaching the faith. In Timothy Quill's article "Novosibirsk: A Lutheran Seminary Model for Theological Education in Russia" in the *Journal of Lutheran Mission*, there is a footnote by the editor that tells the story of our struggles with the BFMS. Sadly, even though things are much better between the seminaries and the current OIM, many of the same impulses exist for control and fear of seminary involvement in missions.[8]

The Spirit blows where it wills, and although our church needs to maintain some sense of control on how it follows the Spirit's leading, to hinder that Spirit does not reflect the way the apostles or the early church spread the gospel throughout the world. Through our participation in the Russian Project, we discovered that the BFMS had lost its Lutheran roots and did not see how the goal of mission was to bring people into churches, where they could have communion with the flesh of Jesus through preaching and the sacraments. What delighted us about our Siberian brothers and sisters is that they not only understood this but that this is what they were asking of us with their Macedonian call. The BFMS were threatened by our approach through theological education, but we ultimately prevailed and then demonstrated that this is the way to do missions. This is now the current approach to missions we now have in OIM that led to the appointment of Timothy Quill as director of global

8. Quill, "Novosibirsk," 2n1: "EDITORS' NOTE: 'A seminary has the freedom to send faculty anywhere upon invitation; A seminary has the freedom to receive students from anywhere for any degree program; A seminary has the freedom to give advice and consent to anyone who seeks help; A seminary has the freedom to invite faculty from elsewhere to teach on seminary campus.'"

theological education, a position I later held at the end of my tenure with OIM by the gracious invitation of Pastor Daniel McMiller, the Executive Director of OIM. There will always be others who will try to do Lutheran missions in a different way, and although we cannot control them, we can share with them what we believe about how the Spirit works through means and that the best long-term approach to missions is to have solid theological education with well-trained pastors and vital congregations where people can receive the gifts. I believe this is what the Russian project taught us at CTSFW.

In September, after that first summer seminar in 1996, Dean received a letter from Rev. Vsevolod Lytkin, written on behalf of the West Siberian Christian Mission that gave us our purpose for the next decade:

> For many years we think and dream about the foundation of a Confessional Training Center (Seminary) in Siberia. After years of official atheism, the people are mostly unbelieving . . . As Lutherans we know that only Confessional Lutheran teaching can give people the pure understanding of the Christian faith so that they could find real comfort in the true Gospel . . . Also, our Christians need to know how to resist the liberal theological influence that is growing in Russia at present time. According to our experience of studying on the Fort Wayne campus in the summer of 1995, and after our experience this past summer of having professors in Novosibirsk, I can say that only the Lutheran Church—Missouri Synod can help us in Siberia to fulfill our dream and only your Seminary can help Russian Lutherans to establish a training center in Siberia . . . So, we ask you to assist us in setting up this training center in Siberia. We don't know how long this religious freedom will last in our country. So, we need to start education project here as soon as possible.[9]

So many stories could be told about those early years of summer seminars—about the midnight suns smoking Cuban cigars, or sneaking little bottles of vodka or scotch, as alcohol at that time was a stigma among the young Siberian Lutherans, or deciding not to swim in the Orb River as the fish floated on top of the water because of the tumors resulting from the pollution from the university and its scientific experiments, yet how this didn't prevent our Russian friends from enjoying bathing in those waters.

9. Quill, "Novosibirsk," 3.

During those first years, we were aware of the reality that the fall of the Soviet Union had just happened, that this was a young country and a young church. In college I took several Russian history courses, so being part of living history was a real thrill. One final story illustrates how the Russian Project shaped me during 1990s. In the third summer seminar in 1998, Dr. Ronald Feuerhahn and his wife, Carol, as well as Dr. Scott Murray, joined Timothy and me in Siberia. We stopped first in Ekaterinburg in the Ural Mountains, named after Catherine the Great, the city where the Czar and his family were assassinated. Timothy had arranged a visit to the religion officer in the city offices to clarify our invitation from our sponsors about holding summer seminars. Olga Suhinna, our finest translator, was frustrated by the bureaucracy, the back and forth between their own officials, and their lack of understanding of what we were asking. At one point when we were left alone in the meeting room, this normally serious Russian woman said of the leader of the Russian delegation, "Lights on, but nobody's home." At first, we weren't sure we heard her right but then burst out laughing because not only did she nail the obtuseness of our Russian host, but she also used this American colloquialism to perfection. In the end, because of our discussions, the religion office of Ekaterinburg agreed to sponsor our seminars the next year, and they made arrangements for Dr. Feuerhahn to lecture in the State University on ecumenism and Lutheran theology. This all led to the formation of Lutheran congregations in Ekaterinburg.

On July 3rd we boarded the Trans-Siberian railroad to travel to Novosibirsk. As July 4th dawned on the train in that famous midnight sun, the waiter delivered to our table a bottle of vodka and poured each of us a half a glass. We looked puzzlingly at our Russian translators, Alexei Strelsov and Olga Suhinna, who lifted their glasses and said, "To the American Revolution," and we laughed and rejoiced that nine years earlier, it would have been inconceivable for such a toast to take place on the Trans-Siberian railroad, or that as a result of our efforts Lutheranism was growing in the former Soviet Union. Traveling by train, we were struck by the vastness of Russia and the challenge such spaces present in the spread of Christianity. The greeting we received by the saints in Novosibirsk was warm and affectionate, for many of them remembered our presence among them, particularly, as one of them said, our "passionate confession of faith." Once again, our seminars revolved around the rhythm of Matins and Vespers, where we joined our Russian brothers and sisters in prayer and thanksgiving for the gifts that come to us through the presence of Jesus Christ, gifts they felt they received from our teaching among them.

Formación Pastoral para Hispanoamérica and Seminario Concordia "El Reformador"

In July of 2015, President Lawrence Rast and I traveled to Buenos Aires, Argentina, to consult with the faculty of *Seminario Concordia* about their seminary curriculum. Regional Director Ted Krey had arranged for us to visit the seminary to offer advice and counsel to them on their curriculum and offer some suggestions and possible changes. Pastor Krey was so completely committed to theological education that he was hoping this might be an opportunity for CTSFW to partner with the only Spanish-speaking seminary in the Southern Hemisphere. The surprising result of that meeting was the online program *Formación Pastoral para Hispanoamerica* (FPH).

As our meeting began in 2015, Pastor Sergio Fritzler, the director of *Seminario Concordia* in Buenos Aires, asked President Rast to tell his faculty about the curriculum review at Concordia Theological Seminary in Fort Wayne, Indiana (CTSFW), that began in 1999 and ended in "the new curriculum" instituted in 2005. President Rast related how our curriculum review was founded on this very simple premise: that theology is done through the pastoral acts of baptizing, preaching, and celebrating the Lord's Supper. The structure of that curriculum was simple: the first year focuses on teaching baptism, the second-year preaching, and, after a vicarage, a third year on the Lord's Supper. In each year all the biblical, systematic, historical, and pastoral aspects of baptism, preaching, and the Lord's Supper would be brought to bear on the meaning of each pastoral act, teaching the students the full meaning of what it meant to stand at the font, in the pulpit, or at the altar and the pastoral realities that attended them in each of these pastoral acts.

The faculty at *Seminario Concordia* in Buenos Aires, especially Professors Fritzler and Bustamante, understood what we were proposing and were enthusiastic about this vision of theological education. We were surprised when they asked us if we could help them develop a distance learning curriculum that revolved around forming pastors through the pastoral acts. On that cold night in July, in the upstairs bedroom of the home of Professor Antonio Schimpf, I developed a rough outline of the four-year program of *Formación Pastoral para Hispanoamérica*. The next day, and in a subsequent meeting in Buenos Aires, we developed the entire curriculum, which included an introductory year of preparation and then a year devoted to baptism, one to preaching, and the final one to the Lord's Supper. It was never my intention to take the lead on this curriculum, but along with Professors Fritzler and Bustamante, we oversaw the development of courses, the choosing of the professors, and the formation of these courses on the Moodle of CTSFW that now form the basis of the FPH program of studies.

This was intended to be an asynchronous online program for students from small congregations, who could not afford to travel to Buenos Aires or later, to the seminary in the Dominican Republic. In many ways it was the Spanish equivalent to our SMP program, and we used FPH as the foundation for our CTSFW Español/English (SMP Es/E) program, eventually uniting FPH in the DR and the SMP Es/E in Fort Wayne on the same Moodle platform. The FPH program started with many students and lots of enthusiastic energy but found that real-life issues like availability of internet and decent computers became an issue, as well the reality that these students, many with growing families, worked all day and had little time at night to study. Some of our courses were too demanding, and I worked with our professors to make the expectations more reasonable. But even with technology issues and the rigorous curriculum, the FPH became foundational for the future of theological education by OIM in the Latin America, the Caribbean, and Spain (LAC).

As we only saw the students "online," I was gratified to meet some of them in my travels in overseeing LAC. I was honored to be invited to the *Conferencia Presencial FPH 2023* (eight years after that fateful meeting in Buenos Aires) to meet many of the students whom I knew only from their online presence. At this conference I could now see and talk to these wonderful men, and they could observe firsthand how feeble my Spanish really is. Unfortunately, President Rast was unable to attend this conference, for he feels like a father to this program and rejoices in the formation of pastors through the FPH program. No one understands better than him how profound it is to form pastors through the pastoral acts.

For many years, Pastor Ted Krey knew that we needed a seminary in the northern part of Latin America, for during his tenure as a missionary, many seminaries and theological colleges were either closed or moved away from a confessional Lutheran focus. In the fall of 2017, Pastor Krey convened pastors from Latin America and the United States to form a confessional Lutheran seminary in *Santiago de los Cabelleros* in the Dominican Republic, on the same location of a mercy center. The constituting committee included Pastors Ted Krey, Sergio Fritzler and Dr. Roberto Bustamante from the seminary in Argentina, Pastor Joel Fritsche from OIM, and Pastor Sergio Maita from Venezuela. I represented CTSFW. After Joel was appointed director, they asked me to be a co-director and faculty member for the first year. It now has a full-time faculty, with Joel serving as director until 2023, when Sergio Fritzler took over. Sergio was a member of the faculty from the beginning, having served many years as the director of the Lutheran seminary in Buenos Aires. He was called by CTSFW to assist in the coordination of FPH and CTSFW's SMP Es/E program. Since 2017, *Centro de Misericordia y Seminario Concordia "El Reformador"* has prepared many pastors and deaconesses, as well as organizing theological conferences for church workers from all over Latin America and the Caribbean which all the LCMS partner churches are invited to attend. In May 2023 they held a conference in which they introduced a new hymnbook in Spanish for all of Latin America, including the Hispanic ministries in the United States and the church in Spain. Being part of this seminary's formation and development has been one of the most gratifying experiences in theological education, as significant as our work with the seminary in Siberia.

Transylvanian Lutheran Saxons—Why I Am a Lutheran

Growing up in Massachusetts and New York for my first thirteen years, my parents inculcated in us how special it was that they were born and raised in Rhode Island. As a kid, I would have rather been born in Providence than in Salem, Massachusetts, especially because my birthplace immediately prompted remarks about the famous Salem Witch Trials of 1692. But after visiting Jerusalem three times and falling in love with this holy city, and from my teaching about Jerusalem as instrumental to Luke's journey motif and my STM thesis on Cyril of Jerusalem, I have come to cherish Salem because it comes from the Hebrew word for "peace" (Jeru*salem*). Salem was founded in 1626, six years after the pilgrims arrived at Plymouth Rock, which makes it even older than Boston (1630). We visited it a few years back, my first time returning since my birth, and both Linda and I were enchanted by what a beautiful town it is.

Both my paternal and maternal grandparents came to Rhode Island as Lutherans but in completely different ways. My paternal grandmother's family (Schaeffer) were LCMS Lutherans going back to the very beginning—to C. F. W. Walther and Martin Stephan through Martha Erck, my great-grandmother. There were many pastors in our family, but it was my great grandfather, the Reverend Henry A. E. Schaefer, who brought his family to Providence, Rhode Island, from Missouri in 1910 to serve as pastor of St. Paul Lutheran Church after serving parishes in Michigan and Missouri.

The Just family came to Providence in the late nineteenth century and joined St. Paul's as Lutherans from Cottbus, Germany, in the part of lower Lusatia, located in the state of Saxony, seventy-five miles southeast of Berlin. The people from Cottbus are considered Sorbs, also called Wends. It may be an overstatement to say the people of Cottbus were Saxons, but they hailed from the state of Saxony. It was only a few years ago, after visiting the birthplace of both my grandfathers, that I realized that both had Saxon roots, so that I could say that I am 100 percent Saxon.

My grandmother Concordia would tell the story that as a young teenager recently moved to Providence, she saw my grandfather, Arthur Gustav Albert Just, sitting in a windowsill in the church basement near the bowling alley, in the first meeting of the church with the pastor's family. She knew right then she would marry that man, even though he was a carpenter and not a pastor. Thus, the union of the Schaeffers and the Justs. My father was Arthur Albert Just, and so I am a junior. Both my father and I regretted that they dropped the Gustav.

My maternal grandparents arrived in Rhode Island at the beginning of the twentieth century as Transylvanian Lutheran Saxons. They were from two small towns seven kilometers apart from one another, outside of the larger city of Mediaş (Mediasch) in Sibui County, Transylvania, Romania—Metiš (Martinsdorf) for my grandmother and Motiš (Mortesdorf) for my grandfather. Between Salem, Massachusetts, and her witches and Transylvania's Dracula, my personal history locates me in two of the major horror capitals of the world. My grandfather, Michael Stamp, is named after Michael the Brave (1558–1601), one of Romania's greatest national heroes and considered the symbol of national unity. As a young man, my grandfather shepherded Transylvanian Lutheran Saxons to immigrate to the United States. My grandmother Hermina Anna Mueller wanted to escape a failed engagement (the oral tradition is that she left her fiancée at the altar), so he invited her to join a group of immigrants to Rhode Island. They were married on the voyage to America and never left the United States again. This was her second trip to the United States, as her parents immigrated to Pennsylvania where she was born but returned to Transylvania when she was an infant, so she grew up in Metiš (Martinsdorf).

My grandfather bought a farm in Johnston, Rhode Island, and joined St. Paul's Lutheran Church, along with other good Transylvanian Lutheran Saxons. The Stamp farm became a place for Walther League get-togethers in both summer and winter, as there was a pond on the property and a lovely little cottage we called "the farm house," where family and friends could picnic and eat outside, play games, and swim in the pond.[10] Some of my earliest memories were meals outside the farmhouse with fresh corn and Romanian food. My parents were in the same confirmation class at St. Paul's, and my mother says she fell in love with my father while learning Luther's Small Catechism. She said he was the smartest one in the class and she was a close second. But they didn't reconnect until my father was a junior at Yale University, after the war. His father was very outgoing and a great athlete, and everyone trusted him to test out the ice at the pond at the Stamp farm in Johnston during a Thanksgiving break in 1947 to see if it was fit for skating. That Thanksgiving my parents skated together, joined all the Walter Leaguers for dinner at the great Stamp table, noted for its lavish hospitality, and were married the following fourth of September, 1948. They honeymooned at Watch Hill, Rhode Island, and their first year of marriage was my father's final year at Yale University.

From the moment I was conscious of my Romanian and Transylvanian roots, I was fascinated by this place in the world. We heard many stories of Romania from my mother and the "Rhode Island cousins," all of whom were Stamps or Mueller's from Transylvania. My whole life I wanted to go to this exotic land, never thinking it would ever happen. But at the 2016 Good Shepherd Institute (GSI), I was introduced to Sorin Trifa from Bucharest, Romania, who was preparing to be a Lutheran pastor in Romania through the support of the Eurasia region of OIM. Like me, he had Transylvanian roots, but he grew up Romanian Orthodox and became a Lutheran later in life. We had a lively conversation, and he was

10. Later I will describe entering the garden of Johanna Hartmann, where there was an outdoor eating area that immediately reminded me of my grandparents' farm in Johnston. The same impression happened when we had an ordination of the second Romanian pastor and the first Pakistani pastor in Prod, Romania, near where my grandparents grew up.

very moved that my grandparents were Transylvanian Lutheran Saxons and considered me the first Confessional Lutheran from Transylvania.

On the fifth of June 2017, after visiting Spain for OIM, Linda flew home from Madrid and I flew to Bucharest. Sorin thought it best to go immediately to Transylvania, so on the next day, June 6, my sixty-fourth birthday, we drove north from Bucharest through the fields of Wallachia, until we came to the majestic Carpathian Mountains. We stopped in the charming ski resort Sinaia to visit Peleş Castle, built by King Carol I of Romania and dedicated in 1883. It became a haven for him and other rulers of Europe in the late nineteenth and twentieth centuries, visited by both Richard Nixon and Gerald Ford.

Soon after Sinaia, one enters the province of Braşov in Transylvania, where Pastor Sorin Trifa's family now lives, as he started a mission there among the Transylvanian people. Transylvania is commonly known as *Siebenbuergen* (seven citadels). During my grandparents' lifetime in Transylvania, they spoke German at home but were also fluent in Romanian and Hungarian. Braşov is where Lutheranism came to Transylvania through Johannes Honterus in 1542, during the lifetime of Martin Luther (the Synod of Mediasch, where my grandparents are from, was the first to accept the Augsburg Confession in 1572). Outside the Black Church in Braşov, named for a fire that stained its roof and walls in 1689, stands a noble statue of Honterus, a photo op for Lutherans visiting Braşov to discover their Lutheran roots. Lutheranism flourished in Romania until the twentieth century and the Communist regime of Nicolae Ceauşescu, when more than one hundred thousand Germans from Transylvania fled the Soviet Army because they had supported Nazi Germany. Seventy thousand were sent to labor camps, most of them Lutherans. The rest of the Transylvania Saxons left Romania for Germany after the fall of Communism in 1989, as they were considered "Germans from abroad," including most of my Romanian cousins. One of the Transylvanian Lutheran pastors commented that his family was one of the few that continued to stay in their beloved Romania. Ironically, after surviving two world wars, what led many Transylvanian Lutheran Saxons to leave Romania was Communism. When given the chance to immigrate in 1989 by the German government, they left Transylvania. We witnessed the same thing when we were in Siberia in the mid-1990s, when German peasants from Siberia were on Lufthansa flights from Novosibirsk to Frankfurt that were created for a few years for the repatriation of thousands of Siberian Germans to Germany.

From Braşov we headed through what Sorin called "savage" country, reaching the town of Metiš (Martinsdorf), where my grandmother grew up. He had received from a friend the name of the church lady who would be able to open the church. Johanna Hartmann's home was just across the road from the church, a beautiful example of a Transylvania Lutheran Church but clearly in need of some serious attention. Johanna's home, like many in Translyvania, is behind a high wall. When she opened the door, I almost fell over—she looked just like my grandmother. She invited us into her beautiful garden where she was having lunch with visitors on an outside table under a canopy. They were from Germany, visiting the towns of their relatives, part of that migration of families from Transylvania to Germany after the end of Communism. She offered us some crepes with bean soup, and it tasted just like my grandmothers, a powerful memory like all memories from taste and smell. We told her our story, why we were in Metiš, and she knew my grandmother's family and told us we would see the Mueller name in the church, the cemetery, and on a home that overlooked the town, even though it was now occupied by gypsies. When all the Transylvania Saxons repatriated to Germany, they left everything behind in their homes except what they could carry on their backs. The Romanian government gave these fully furnished homes to the gypsies if they wanted to settle in one place. Such was the situation with the Mueller home in Metiš.

As our conversation continued, with the help of Sorin as translator, we told them we would be heading to Motiš (Mortesdorf) to see the place where my grandfather was born. These German visitors were also from Motiş and asked what his name was. I told them Michael Stamp. For a moment there was silence. Then Johanna introduced us to Daniel Ruhland, who came from the Stamp family. He asked me, "Did your grandfather Michael own a chicken farm in the United States?" That was one of the businesses my grandfather had on his farm in Rhode Island. "Is it somewhere on the East Coast?" That confirmed that these were my cousins. A little later we drove on a rough road between Metiš and Motiš, stopping for sheep along the way. In a beautiful spot between the two towns the Stamp family was gathered for lunch. Standing on a dirt road, surrounded by Stamp cousins with glasses of white wine, they toasted their American cousin's sixty-fourth birthday. Sorin put these photos on Facebook later than evening, and the next morning Linda woke up in Fort Wayne, after traveling from Madrid the previous day, to see me in the "savage" country of my grandparents with my Transylvanian Saxon cousins, toasting my birthday. She would go on to tell everyone that only I could blunder into the wilds of Transylvania and meet a bunch of relatives.

We would venture on to Motiš to visit Stamp graves. A few years later with Linda, we found the home where my grandfather was born, even found someone to let us into the house. It had not been occupied in over a decade, as the owners had moved to Italy. We were told we could buy it for under 5,000 euros. The church was not accessible, but we saw the hall where the Stamps held their reunions every three years, when over one hundred of my relatives gather from Germany. Sorin had at one time encouraged me to get a Romanian passport, as I was eligible since my grandfather was born in Romania, and we were able to gather all the documents I needed from the town offices in Valea Viilor. But when we applied for the passport, we realized I needed to speak more Romanian than I could possibly learn to qualify. It would have been great to have a passport where I could have traveled, and worked, in the European Union.

Our final stop that eventful day was in Mediaş, the major town of that area, where my grandparents would have attended St. Margaret's, the magnificent Gothic-style fortified church that dominates the skyline. There are over 150 of them in Transylvania that were built as both places of worship and to defend against their enemies (*Siebenbuergen*). I was very moved by the beauty of this church, with its Persian carpets hanging from the walls and on all the floors, an acknowledgment of its history as a place once occupied by the Mongols, some of them going back to the sixteenth century. I could imagine my grandparents coming here to the big city from their small villages for festivals and other religious holidays. In speaking to the docents, whose English was quite passable, we told them about our Lutheran history and how we were trying to revive a Confessional Lutheran Church in Romania. Sadly, the two official Lutheran churches in Romania—the Evangelical Lutheran Church, which is Hungarian-speaking, and the German-speaking Evangelical Church of the Augsburg Confession—have completely succumbed to the liberalism of the Word Council of Churches and are in full fellowship with the Calvinist Reformed Church of Romania. To maintain their beautiful churches, they agreed with the Romanian Orthodox Church not to evangelize in the Romanian language but to hold services only in Hungarian and German. What distinguishes Sorin's efforts is that not only is it a Confessional Lutheran Church in partnership with the LCMS, but he holds all his services in the Romanian language. No one presides at an altar as well as Sorin, with confidence and dignity. He has incorporated into our Lutheran liturgy a Romanian Orthodox flair that is both lively and solemn, a perfect example of how one might reflect the culture while preserving a Lutheran ethos. He has tried to find a way to work alongside these other Lutherans, offering to rent their facilities for his services, but they have completely shunned him because of his Confessional stance.[11]

Those docents listened carefully to what we were telling them and seemed to resonate with the idea of liturgies in the Romanian language, but as I looked up at the beautiful altar that my grandparents would have gazed on over a century ago, I felt both sadness and joy—sadness that Lutheranism had essentially died in Transylvania after the years of Communism and the retreat to Germany of all those Transylvanian Lutheran Saxons but joy that someone like Sorin Trifa was now trying to bring true, authentic Lutheranism back to the country of my grandparents. Like all our missions in Europe, it's a daunting task, and there seems little we can do to help revive Confessional Lutheranism in such secular cultures, where even the Lutheran Church has jettisoned its biblical and Confessional roots. But like the miracles of Jesus, small and humble examples of the new creation that would burst forth with his death and resurrection, our small and humble missions are a light in the darkness of secular humanism. Our support, outside of financial and moral help, is to hold up these brave and lonely prophets and offer in our preaching and teaching examples of why Confessional Lutheranism is still vital for our world.

In both Spain and Romania, my deeply personal connections to these two countries and their fledging Lutheran missions are an example of how foreign missions are all about relationships. With Sorin in Romania and José Luis and Juan Carlos in Spain, what encourages them is our travel to their countries, our service to them as preacher and celebrant in their services and teaching them the depths of our Lutheran faith. For me, this could not have happened without Emmaus. I began with the liturgical structures of Word and Meal and now end with these same structures as the means for mission. It was a privilege to participate in global theological education with International Mission and now to continue to serve our partner churches as a professor at CTSFW as we prepare pastors in the ministry of Word and Sacrament—the Means for Mission.

11. I had a unique opportunity to advise Sorin on his STM at CTSFW but also to serve as a member of the committee for his PhD thesis at the University of Bucharest as an adjunct faculty member of that university.

Epilogue

In My Beginning Is My End—Time with Eternity

In my beginning is my end. So, if Emmaus is my beginning, how to bring this memoir to a close?

Although I did not understand this when I was ordained on the twenty-second of June in 1980, the beginning and end of my pastoral ministry was to give the Eucharist to as many people as I could, or as a professor, to teach men preparing for the ministry that this is why they are seeking this high office. As my students will tell you, in almost every class I say, "Your goal as pastor is to bring people into communion with the flesh of Christ." For this is our final destiny, to sit at the marriage feast of the Lamb in his kingdom which has no end because we have already now—even now in the liturgy—here—in time—participated in eternity. In the Word in our ears and the body and blood in our mouths, we have communion with the flesh of Jesus.

On the eleventh of September 1980, less than three months from my ordination, Linda's sister Barbara was murdered in Dallas, Texas. 9/11 has always been a difficult day for our family. Even though it was forty-five years ago, the pain and sorrow of that day is still palpable, and it certainly shaped the rest of our lives, our marriage, even my identity as a pastor and professor in my teaching, preaching, and pastoral care. It taught me how to address the suffering of the saints at Grace Lutheran in Middletown, Connecticut, and perhaps the suffering of my family.

But not right away. I was ill-equipped at first to give meaning to people's suffering. I did not have the language. I did not understand that the language to comfort those who are suffering comes from the narrative of Christ's passion, from his suffering body, and that to give meaning to the suffering of my members, *to my family*, I had to connect them to

Christ's suffering, to help them in their suffering "to hide in the wounds of Christ." This is when I realized what it means to take care of the body of Christ, his church.

Perhaps it's unsettling to end this memoir with a memory of great sorrow for our family, but it is difficult to take a measure of my life and my ministry as pastor and professor without reflecting on Barbara's suffering and death. On occasion, I do refer to it in my teaching as this great suffering was my great teacher, and I want others to learn what I learned through a very painful experience. I have written about what it taught me concerning the comfort of the Eucharist in suffering, how through Barbara and the suffering of the saints at Grace, I was finally able to understand the meaning of the proper preface in the eucharistic liturgy, "therefore with angels and archangels and the whole company of heaven." This is what earlier in this memoir I called the *blick*—that in the fleshly presence of Christ in Word and Sacrament heaven is on earth—that time is now with eternity.

At every Eucharist, I think of Barbara as I wait to receive the body and blood of Christ. How, during her last moments, her body, tortured and violated, in pain and great suffering, yearning for death, yearning for peace, she cried out the Lord's Prayer—the prayer we pray right before the Words of Institution—right before the simple bread and wine become also the very body and blood of the crucified and risen Christ. That now she is in heaven in communion with the flesh of Christ—as we here on earth are in communion with Christ in his body and blood—that in our liturgy, heaven and earth are joined together in the flesh of Jesus. I also think about how in the resurrection of the body, Barbara and all the saints will rise with a new body and that our bodies "will show gloriously all the pain [we] suffered and all the love [we] received. It will not be just *a* body. It will be [our] body, a new body, a body that can be touched but is no longer subject to torture and destruction," a body that has overcome the world in Jesus—a body, like Jesus, that will show forth the glorious wounds we suffered that are now marks of our triumph. Our suffering will be over.[1]

When our family finally came to understand the reality of the angels and archangels and all the company of heaven—of heaven on earth in the person of Jesus—there was joy inside our tears at every celebration of the Lord's Supper. For at the Eucharist, we knew Barbara was present in Jesus,

1. This last paragraph is both a citation and a paraphrase of Nouwen, *Show Me the Way*, 176–79.

who was now here on earth in Christ. Our hearts rejoiced, our joy was full, and even in our sorrow, no one could take this joy from us.

For much of my career at CTSFW, I have talked about the Eucharist and suffering. In *Heaven on Earth: The Gifts of Christ in the Divine Service*, I wrote about this from my experience as a pastor at Grace, Middletown, and through this memoir you saw hints of it—even from Ernest Hemingway! I threatened to write a biblical theology of suffering (like I threatened to write a biblical theology of Mary), and I finally wrote a brief essay for the Exegetical Symposium in 2022, right after Covid, when our theme was the "Male and Female He Created Them: Recovering a Theology of the Body." I chose to go in a little different direction, entitling my paper "Taking Care of the Body of Jesus: Towards a Biblical Theology of Suffering."[2] I was struck by Christopher West's *Our Bodies Tell God's Story*,[3] a book our exegetical department read in preparation for this symposium. West claims that our bodies are more than biological—they are also theological. By our creation in the image of God as male and female, our bodies are storytellers, and that in suffering our bodies tell the story of Christ's suffering. I had never really thought of Barbara's final day of life in that way, that the narrative of Christ's passion was written all over her body at the very end of her life, that she proclaimed the gospel as she cried out the Lord's Prayer in her intense suffering before her tragic death. Even though I taught that Paul's body preached the gospel to the Galatians, I hadn't made the connection to Barbara's suffering and death. Now I do.

Even now Barbara's body tells us the story of the gospel—the story of Christ's sufferings. For the same hostile powers that attacked her are the ones that caused Jesus to suffer during his passion—the same powers that caused the darkness and killed Jesus—those same powers attacked her body and killed her. Her Jesus scars are God's angel, a messenger of the Gospel, because in her suffering we see Christ Jesus, the one we now receive in his body broken, his blood poured out. Perhaps now we might understand the meaning of Jesus' suffering through the suffering body of Barbara and all the saints who suffered and died in the faith. All of us need to be prepared to imitate Christ in his sufferings, for this will give meaning to our own suffering.

2. This essay was published by the same title in *CTQ*, 251–63.

3. Cf. West, *Our Bodies Tell God's Story*, 4–5.

That essay on how our suffering bodies tell the story of Christ's suffering was the first step in writing about suffering. It said what I wanted to say about how to understand what Jesus and Paul say about suffering. I left that essay open-ended, about how Linda and I only began to understand the meaning of suffering after that great loss. That full understanding of what it meant to participate in the sufferings of Christ only came when we began to understand the mystery of these words of St. Paul:

> The cup of blessing that we bless is it not a participation in the blood of Christ? The bread that we break, is it not a participation in the body of Christ? (1 Cor 10:16)

There is much more that could be said about this. Perhaps I'm still not yet prepared to say more. Perhaps in my end is my beginning.

Let me close this memoir as I do in my lecture on "Eucharist and Eschatology" in the "Theologia: Lord's Supper" course. For forty-five years my life has been shaped by CTSFW, so it's fitting to offer these words from a hymn by Wilhelm Löhe, one of the founders of our beloved seminary:

> The cherubim, their faces veiled from light,
> While saints in wonder kneel,
> Sing praise to Him whose face with glory bright
> No earthly masks conceal.
> This sacrament God gives us
> Binds us in unity,
> Joins earth with heav'n beyond us,
> Time with eternity![4]

4. Löhe, "Wide Open Stand the Gates," in Grime and Vieker, *Lutheran Service Book*, 639.

Bibliography

All Things Considered. "Saint Luke." NPR, October 16, 2001. https://www.npr.org/2001/10/16/1131534/saint-luke.

Augustine. *Confessions.* Book 13, chapters 35–37. Translated by R. S. Pine-Coffin. New York: Penguin, 1961.

Bailey, Kenneth. *Poet and Peasant.* Grand Rapids: Eerdmans, 1976.

Bauer, Walter A. *Greek-English Lexicon of the New Testament and Other Early Christian Literature.* 2nd ed. Translated, revised, and augmented by W. Arndt, F. W. Gingrich, and F. Danker. Chicago: University of Chicago Press, 1979.

Bellow, Saul. *Humboldt's Gift.* London. Penguin Modern Classics, 2015.

Bligh, John. *Galatians: A Discussion of St. Paul's Epistle.* London: St. Paul, 1969.

Boers, Arthur Paul. *The Way Is Made By Walking: A Pilgrimage Along the Camino de Santiago.* Downers Grove, IL: InterVarsity, 2007.

Braaten, Carl E., and Robert W. Jensen, eds. *Reclaiming the Bible for the Church.* Grand Rapids: Eerdmans, 1995.

Brown, Peter. *Augustine of Hippo.* Berkeley; Los Angeles: University of California Press, 1967.

Bruccoli, Matthew J., and Judith S. Baughman, eds. *F. Scott Fitzgerald: A Life in Letters.* New York: Charles Scribner's Sons, 1994.

Burreson, Kent, and Rhoda Schuler. *Journey to Jesus: Faith Formation into Christ and Community.* Eugene, OR: Wipf and Stock, 2025.

Cameron, Ron. *The Other Gospels: Non-Canonical Gospel Literature.* Louisville: Westminster John Knox, 1982.

Clement of Rome, "I Clement 5:5–7." *Apostolic Fathers Volume I.* Edited and translated by Bart D. Ehrman. Loeb Classical Library. Cambridge, MA: Harvard University Press, 2003.

Contino, Paul. "This Writer's Life: Irony and Faith in the Work of Tobias Wolff." *Commonweal* (Oct. 21, 2005) 52–72.

Court, John. *Reading the New Testament.* London: Routledge, 1997.

———., and Kathleen Court. *The New Testament World.* Cambridge University, 1990.

Cyril. *Mystagogical Catechesis III.* In *St. Cyril of Jerusalem's Lectures on the Christian Sacraments*, edited by F. L. Cross. Crestwood, 63–67. New York: St. Vladimir's Seminary Press, 1986. First published 1951 by SPCK (London).

Danielou, Jean. *The Bible and the Liturgy.* Notre Dame: University of Notre Dame, 1956.

Das, Andrew. *Concordia Commentary on Scripture: Galatians*. St. Louis: Concordia, 2014.

Denzler, Douglas. "A Missionary and Catechist to Siberia." *Steadfast Lutherans*. Feb. 24, 2013.

Dillon, Richard D. *From Eye-Witnesses to Ministers of the Word: Tradition and Composition in Luke 24*. Rome: Biblical Institute, 1978.

Dix, Gregory. *The Shape of the Liturgy*. Westminster, UK: Dacre, 1945.

"Do Whatever He Tells You: The Blessed Virgin Mary in the Christian Faith and Life." *First Things* 197 (November 2009) 109–30.

Dunn, James D. G. *The Baptism in the Holy Spirit*. Philadelphia: Westminister, 1970.

Fagerberg, David. *What Is Liturgical Theology? A Study in Methodology*. Collegeville, MN: Pueblo, 1992.

Farley, Edward. *Theologia: The Fragmentation and Unity of Theological Education*. Eugene, OR: Wipf and Stock, 2001.

Feeley-Harnik, Gillian. *The Lord's Table: Eucharist and Passover in Early Christianity*. Philadelphia: University of Pennsylvania, 1981.

Fitzgerald, F. Scott. "Absolution." In *The Short Stories of F. Scott Fitzgerald*, edited by Matthew J. Bruccoli, 259–72. New York: Charles Scribner's, 1989.

———. *The Great Gatsby*. New York: Simon and Schuster, 2003.

Fitzgerald, Penelope. *The Blue Flower*. Boston; New York: Houghton Mifflin, 1995.

Fitzmyer, Joseph. *The Gospel According to Luke I–IX*. Anchor Bible. New York: Doubleday, 1981.

Flusser, D., et. al. *Mary: Images of the Mother of Jesus in Jewish and Christian Perspective*. Minneapolis: Fortress, 1986.

Franzmann, Martin. *Ha! Ha! Among the Trumpets*. St. Louis: Concordia, 1966.

Geertz, Clifford. *The Interpretation of Culture*. London: Hutchinson, 1975.

Gioia, Dana. *The Catholic Writer Today*. Menomonee Falls, WI: Wiseblood, 2014.

Goodrich, Richard, and Albert Lukaszewski. *A Reader's Greek New Testament: Third Edition*. Grand Rapids: Zondervan, 2015.

Gregory XII (Pope). *The Roman Martyrology*. Rome: Aeterna, 2014.

Grenz, Stanley. *A Primer on Postmodernism*. Grand Rapids: Eerdmans, 1996.

Grime, Paul, and Jon Vieker, eds. *Lutheran Service Book*. St. Louis: Concordia, 2006.

Guillaume, J. *Luc interprète des anciennes traditions sur la résurrection de Jésus*. Paris: Gabalda, 1979.

Hahn, Scott. *Hail, Holy Queen: The Mother of God in the Word of God*. New York: Image, 2001.

Hansen, Ron. "John Irving, The Art of Fiction No. 93." *Paris Review* 100 (1986). https://www.theparisreview.org/interviews/2757/the-art-of-fiction-no-93-john-irving.

Hays, Richard B. *The Faith of Jesus Christ: The Narrative Substructure of Galatians 3:1—4:11*. Grand Rapids: Eerdmans, 2002.

———. "The Letter to the Galatians: Introduction, Commentary, and Reflections." In *The New Interpreter's Bible: Second Corinthians—Philemon*. Vol. XI. Nashville: Abingdon, 2000.

Hemingway, Ernest. "American League of Authors in New York City. Carnegie Hall, (4 June 1937)." In *For Whom the Bell Tolls: The Hemingway Library Edition*, app. 1. New York: Scribner's, 2019.

———. *For Whom the Bell Tolls*. New York: Charles Scribner's Sons, 1968.

Hofstad, Robert. *Welcome to Christ: A Lutheran Introduction to the Catechumenate*. Minneapolis: Fortress, 1997.

Hütter, Reinhard. *Suffering Divine Things: Theology as Church Practice.* Grand Rapids: Eerdmans, 1999.

Irving, John. *A Prayer for Owen Meany.* New York: William Morrow and Company, Inc., 1989.

Jenson, Robert. "How the World Lost Its Story." *First Things* 36 (October 1993) 19–24.

Jeremias, Joachim. *Jerusalem in the Time of Jesus.* Philadelphia: Fortress, 1969.

Johnson, Luke T. *The Gospel of Luke.* Sacra Pagina. Collegeville, MN: Liturgical, 1991.

Just, Arthur. "An Analysis of Cyril of Jerusalem's Use of Scripture in the Third Mystagogical Catechesis on the Holy Chrism." Unpublished STM thesis. Yale Divinity School, 1984.

———. *Ancient Christian Commentary on Scripture: Luke* (ACCS).Volume 3. Edited by Thomas C. Oden. Downers Grove, IL: InterVarsity, 2003.

———. *Concordia Commentary: Luke 1:1–9:50.* St. Louis: Concordia, 1996.

———. *Concordia Commentary: Luke 9:51–24:53.* St. Louis: Concordia, 1997.

———. "The Cross, the Atonement, and the Eucharist in Luke." *Concordia Theological Quarterly* 84 (2020) 227–44.

———. "The Eyewitness of the Other Son of Zebedee: A Pilgrimage with James Through Scripture and Tradition." In *The Restoration of Creation in Christ: Essays in Honor of Dean O. Wenthe,* edited by Arthur Just and Paul Grime, 141–58. St. Louis: Concordia, 2014.

———. *Heaven on Earth: The Gifts of Christ in the Divine Service.* St. Louis: Concordia, 2008.

———. "Luke's Canonical Criterion." *Concordia Theological Quarterly* 79 (2015) 245–60.

———. "My Soul Magnifies the Lord: Luther's Hermeneutic of Humility." *Concordia Theological Quarterly* 81 (2017) 37–53.

———. *The Ongoing Feast: Table Fellowship and Eschatology at Emmaus.* Collegeville, MN: Pueblo, 1993.

———. "Paul's Matrix of Love in Galatians: Paraenesis for Lutheran Preachers." In *Shepherding the Flock of God: A Festschrift in Honour of Andrew K. Pfeiffer,* edited by Joshua Pfeiffer and Thomas Pietsch, 30–39. Tarrington, Australia: Kairos, 2024.

———. "Servants Formed to Reach: Confessional Theological Education." *For the Life of the World* (Spring 2023).

———. "Taking Care of the Body of Jesus: Towards a Biblical Theology of Suffering." *Concordia Theological Quarterly* 87 (2023) 251–63.

———. "T. S. Eliot: A Pilgrim in the Wasteland." *Concordia Theological Quarterly* 88 (2024) 254–70.

———. "Why Luke Is Indebted to Matthew as the First Gospel." In *All Theology Is Christology: Essays in Honor of David P. Scaer,* edited by Dean O. Wenthe, William C. Weinrich, Arthur A. Just Jr., Daniel Gard, and Thomas L. Olson, 19–33. Fort Wayne, IN: CIS, 2000.

Justin Martyr. *First Apology, The Second Apology, Dialogue with Trypho, Exhortation to the Greeks, Discourse to the Greeks, The Monarchy of the Rule of God.* Fathers of the Church Patristic Series. Washington, DC: Catholic University Press of America, 2008.

Karr, Mary. *The Art of Memoir.* New York: Harper Collins, 2015.

Kavanagh, Aidan. "Christian Initiation in Post-Conciliar Roman Catholicism." *Living Water, Sealing Spirit: Readings on Christian Initiation.* Edited by Maxwell E. Johnson. Collegeville, MN: Pueblo, 1995.

———. "Christian Initiation: Tactics and Strategy." *Made, Not Born: New Perspectives on Christian Initiation and the Catechumenate.* Notre Dame: University of Notre Dame Press, 1976.

———. *Elements of Rite.* Collegeville, MN: Pueblo, 1982.

———. *On Liturgical Theology.* New York: Pueblo, 1981.

———. *The Shape of Baptism.* Collegeville, MN: Pueblo, 1978.

Kendrick, Thomas Downing. *Saint James in Spain.* London: Methuen and Company, 1960.

Kuehl, John, and Jackson R. Bryer, *Dear Scott/Dear Max: The Fitzgerald-Perkins Correspondence.* New York: Charles Scribner's Sons, 1971.

Lenski, Richard C. H. *The Interpretation of Luke's Gospel.* Minneapolis: Augsburg, 1961.

Leon Dufour, Xavier. *Sharing the Eucharistic Bread.* New York: Paulist, 1987.

Leupold, Ulrich S. and Helmut T. Lehman, eds. *Luther's Works.* Vol. 53: "Liturgy and Hymns." St. Louis: Concordia, 1965.

Longenecker, Richard. *Galatians.* Vol. 41. Word Bible Commentary. Grand Rapids: Zondervan, 1990.

Luecke, David. *Evangelical Style, Lutheran Substance: Facing America's Mission Challenge.* St. Louis: Concordia, 1988.

Luther, Martin. *The Blessed Sacrament of the Holy and True Body of Christ, and the Brotherhoods.* LCMS World Relief and Human Care. St. Louis, MO: The Lutheran Church–Missouri Synod, 2004.

———. *Lectures on Galatians.* 1535. *Luther's Works.* Vol. 25:277. Cited from T. Mannermaa, "Justification and Theosis in Lutheran-Orthodox Perspective." *Union with Christ: The New Finnish Interpretation of Luther.* Edited by Carl Braaten and Robert Jenson. Grand Rapids: Eerdmans, 1998.

———. "The Magnificat." Translated by A. T. W. Steinhauser. *Luther's Works.* Vol. 21. Edited by Jaroslav Pelikan. St. Louis: Concordia, 1956.

———. "The Sacrament of the Body and Blood of Christ—Against the Fanatics." *Luther's Works.* 36:341. Philadelphia: Fortress, 1959.

———. *Sermons of Martin Luther.* Edited and translated by John Nicholas Lenker. Vol. 4. St. Louis, MO: Concordia, 2000.

Machado, Antonio. *Border of a Dream: Selected Poems of Antonio Machado.* Translated by Willis Barnstone. Port Townsend, WA: Copper Canyon, 2003.

Marshall, I. Howard. *The Gospel of Luke.* New International Greek Testament Commentary. Grand Rapids: Eerdmans, 1978.

Martin, Regis. *The Last Things: Death, Judgment, Hell, Heaven.* San Francisco: Ignatius, 1998.

Martyn, J. Louis. *Galatians.* New York: Doubleday, 1997.

McCain, Paul Timothy. *Concordia: The Lutheran Confessions.* 2nd ed. St. Louis: Concordia, 2005–2006.

McEwan, Ian. *Saturday.* New York: Vintage, 2006.

McHugh, John. *The Mother of Jesus in the New Testament.* New York: Doubleday, 1975.

———. "The Sacrifice of the Mass at the Council of Trent." *Sacrifice and Redemption: Durham Essays in Theology*, edited by S. W. Sykes, 157–81. Cambridge University Press, 1991.

McKnight, Scot. *The Real Mary: Why Protestant Christians Can Embrace the Mother of Jesus.* Brewster, MA: Paraclete, 2007.

Nauman, Cheryl. *In the Footsteps of Phoebe: A Complete History of the Deaconess Movement in the Lutheran Church Missouri Synod.* St. Louis: Concordia, 2009.

Neyrey, Jerome, and Bruce Malina. *The Social World of Luke-Acts.* Peabody, MA: Hendrickson, 1991.

Nolland, John. *Luke 1–9:20.* Word Biblical Commentary. Dallas: Word, 1989.

Norris, Kathleen. *Blessed Mary: Protestant Perspectives on Mary.* Edited by Beverly R. Gaventa and Cynthia L. Rigby. Louisville: Westminster John Knox, 2002.

Nouwen, Henri. *The Return of the Prodigal Son: A Story of Homecoming.* New York: Image Book by Doubleday, 1992.

———. *Show Me the Way.* New York: Crossroad, 1992.

O'Connor, Flannery. *The Habit of Being.* Edited by Sally Fitzgerald. New York: Vintage, 1979.

Oden, Thomas. *Requiem: A Lament in Three Movements.* Nashville: Abingdon, 1995.

O'Donnell, Brennan. "A Conversation with Mary Karr." *Image* 56 (2007) 55–71. https://imagejournal.org/article/conversation-mary-karr/.

Osborne, Grant R. *The Resurrection Narratives: A Redactional Study.* Grand Rapids: Baker, 1984.

Pearce, Joseph. *Literary Converts: Spiritual Inspiration in an Age of Unbelief.* San Francisco: Ignatius, 1999.

Pitre, Brant. *Jesus and the Jewish Roots of Mary: Unveiling the Mother of the Messiah.* New York: Image, 2018.

Pless, John. "A Curriculum from and for the Church." *Concordia Theological Quarterly* 70 (2006) 86.

Plimpton, George, editor. *Writers at Work: The Paris Review Interviews.* Eighth Series. New York: Penguin Books, 1988.

Quill, Timothy. "Novosibirsk: A Lutheran Seminary Model for Theological Education in Russia." *Journal of Lutheran Mission* 1 (April 2016) 2–9.

Raabe, Paul. *The End Times: A Study on Eschatology and Millennialism.* A document prepared by the Commission on Theology and Church Relations of the Lutheran Church—Missouri Synod, Sept. 1989, 17–19.

Rieff, Philip. *The Triumph of the Therapeutic: Uses of Faith After Freud.* 40th anniversary ed. 1966. Wilmington: Intercollegiate Studies Institute, 2006.

Riley, Hugh M. *Christian Initiation: A Comparative Study of the Interpretation of the Baptismal Liturgy in the Mystagogical Writings of Cyril of Jerusalem, John Chrysostom, Theodore of Mopsuestia, and Ambrose of Milan.* Washington: Catholic University of America Press, 1974.

Rosales, Raymond. *Casiodoro de Reina: Patriarca del Protestantismo Hispano.* Concordia Seminary Publications Monograph Series, Number 5. St. Louis: Concordia, 2002.

Scaer, David P. "Sanctification in Lutheran Theology," *Concordia Theological Quarterly* 2–3 (Apr.–Jul. 1985) 181–95.

———. "Sanctification in the Lutheran Confessions," *Concordia Theological Quarterly* 3 (Jul. 1989) 165–81.

———. *The Sermon on the Mount: The Church's First Statement of the Gospel.* St. Louis: Concordia, 2000.

———. The Third Use of the Law: Resolving the Tension." *Concordia Theological Quarterly* 3–4 (Jul.–Oct. 2005) 237–57.

Schneemelcher, Wilhelm, ed. "Acts of Paul and Thecla 3:2." *New Testament Apocrypha.* Vol. 2: *Writings Relating to the Apostles; Apocalypses and Related Subjects.* Translated By R. McL. Wilson. Louisville: Westminster John Knox, 1992.

Schulz, Wallace, ed. "Christ in You." *Good News* 22 (2005).

Scott, Anthony Oliver "Famous Writers School," *New York Times*, Nov. 23, 2003.

Scott, David. "God, the Hound of Heaven." Ch. 2 in *The Catholic Passion: Rediscovering the Power and Beauty of the Faith*. Chicago: Loyola, 2005.

Seifrid, Mark. *Christ, Our Righteousness: Paul's Theology of Justification*. Vol 9. New Studies in Biblical Theology. Downers Grove, IL: InterVarsity, 2016.

Smith, James K. A. *Desiring the Kingdom: Worship, Worldview, and Cultural Formation*. Grand Rapids: Baker, 2009.

———. *Who's Afraid of Postmodernism? Taking Derrida, Lyotard, and Foucault to Church*. Grand Rapids: Baker, 2006.

Stein, Robert. *Luke*. New American Commentary. Nashville: Broadman, 1992.

Stevens, Wallace. *The Necessary Angel: Essays on Reality and the Imagination*. New York: Vintage, 1965.

Stoker, Bram. *Dracula*. Ignatius Critical Edition. Edited by Joseph Pearce. San Francisco: Ignatius, 2012.

Strelan, Rick. *Luke the Priest: The Authority of the Author of the Third Gospel*. Burlington, VT: Ashgate, 2013.

Sumption, Jonathan. *The Age of Pilgrimage: The Medieval Journey to God*. Mahwah, NJ: Hidden Spring, 2003.

Tannehill, Robert. *The Narrative Unity of Luke–Acts*. Vol. 1: *The Gospel According to Luke*. Philadelphia: Fortress, 1986.

Taylor, Charles. *A Secular Age*. Cambridge, MA: Belknap of Harvard University Press, 2007.

Thompson, Francis. *The Hound of Heaven*. Morehouse, 1988.

Trueman, Carl R. *The Rise and Triumph of the Modern Self: Cultural Amnesia, Expressive Individualism, and the Road to Sexual Revolution*. Wheaton, IL: Crossway, 2020.

Wade, Nicholas. "'Body of St. Luke' Gains Credibility." *The New York Times*, October 15, 2001. https://www.nytimes.com/2001/10/16/world/body-of-st-luke-gains-credibility.html.

Wanke, Joachim. *Die Emmauserzählung. Eine redaktionsgeschichtliche Untersuchung zu Lk 24,13–35*. Leipzig: St. Benno-Verlag, 1973.

Waugh, Evelyn. *Brideshead Revisited*. Everyman's Library. New York: Knopf, 1993.

Weigel, George. *Letters to a Young Catholic*. New York: Basic, 2015.

Weinrich, William. "Concordia Theological Seminary 1985–2010: A Story of Decline and Revival." *Concordia Theological Quarterly* 85 (2021) 279–96.

———. "From the Church, for the Church—in Mission." *For the Life of the World* 2 (April 2005) 19–21.

West, Christopher. *Our Bodies Tell God's Story*. Grand Rapids: Brazos, 2020.

Wilcken, Robert L. *The Spirit of Early Christian Thought: Seeking the Face of God*. New Haven: Yale University Press, 2003.

Wilkinson, John. *Egeria's Travels to the Holy Land*. Warminster, England: Aris and Phillips, 1981.

Wojcik, Jan. *The Road to Emmaus: Reading Luke's Gospel*. West Lafayette, IN: Purdue University Press, 1989.

Wolff, Tobias. *Old School*. New York: Knopf, 2003.

Wright, N. T. *Paul: A Biography*. New York: HarperCollins, 2018.

www.ingramcontent.com/pod-product-compliance
Lightning Source LLC
LaVergne TN
LVHW020536100826
845148LV00010B/1491

* 9 7 9 8 3 8 5 2 7 1 4 4 3 *